5th International Workshop on Computational Approaches to Historical Language Change (LChange 2024)

Bangkok, Thailand
15 August 2024

ISBN: 979-8-3313-0168-2

Printed from e-media with permission by:

Curran Associates, Inc.
57 Morehouse Lane
Red Hook, NY 12571

Some format issues inherent in the e-media version may also appear in this print version.

Printed with permission by Curran Associates, Inc. (2025)

Association for Computational Linguistics
209 N. Eighth Street
Stroudsburg, Pennsylvania 18360

Phone: 1-570-476-8006
Fax: 1-570-476-0860

acl@aclweb.org

Additional copies of this publication are available from:

Curran Associates, Inc.
57 Morehouse Lane
Red Hook, NY 12571 USA
Phone: 845-758-0400
Fax: 845-758-2633
Email: curran@proceedings.com
Web: www.proceedings.com

LChange 2024

5th International Workshop on Computational Approaches to Historical Language Change 2024

Proceedings of the Workshop

August 15, 2024

Association for Computational Linguistics (ACL)
209 N. Eighth Street
Stroudsburg, PA 18360
USA
Tel: +1-570-476-8006
Fax: +1-570-476-0860
acl@aclweb.org

Preface by the General Chair

Welcome to the 5th International Workshop on Computational Approaches to Historical Language Change (LChange'24) co-located with ACL 2024. LChange is held on August 15th, 2024, as a hybrid event with participation possible both virtually and on-site in Thailand.

Characterizing the time-varying nature of language will have broad implications and applications in multiple fields including linguistics, artificial intelligence, digital humanities, computational cognitive and social sciences. In this workshop, we bring together the world's pioneers and experts in **computational approaches to historical language change with a focus on digital text corpora**. In doing so, this workshop carries out the triple goals of disseminating state-of-the-art research on diachronic modeling of language change, fostering cross-disciplinary collaborations, and exploring the fundamental theoretical and methodological challenges in this growing niche of computational linguistic research.

In response to the call, we received 24 submissions. Each of them was carefully evaluated by at least two members of the Program Committee, whom we believed to be most appropriate for each paper. Based on the reviewers' feedback we accepted 17 full and short papers as oral or poster presentations. We had two distinguished keynote presentations: the first by Antske Fokkens (Professor at the Computational Linguistics and Text Mining Lab at the Vrije Universiteit Amsterdam, Netherlands) who presented a talk entitled "What Changes in Language Modeling mean for Modeling Language Change", and the second by Johann-Mattis List (Professor and Chair of Multilingual Computational Linguistics at the University of Passau, Germany) with the talk "New Approaches in Computer-Assisted Language Comparison". Finally, we invited two ACL'24 Findings papers to be presented at the workshop, which are not included in the workshop proceedings.

We hope that you will find the workshop papers insightful and inspiring. We would like to thank the keynote speakers for their stimulating talks, the authors of all papers for their interesting contributions, and the members of the Program Committee for their insightful reviews. Our special thanks go to the emergency reviewers who stepped in to provide their expertise. We also express our gratitude to the ACL 2024 workshop chairs for their kind assistance during the organization process. Finally, our thanks go to our sponsors, the research program "Change is Key!" (Riksbankens Jubileumsfond, contract M21-0021).

Nina Tahmasebi, chair, University of Gothenburg (Sweden)
Syrielle Montariol, EPFL (Switzerland)
Andrey Kutuzov, University of Oslo (Norway)
David Alfter, University of Gothenburg (Sweden)
Francesco Periti, University of Milan (Italy)
Pierluigi Cassotti, University of Gothenburg (Sweden)
Netta Huebscher, University of Gothenburg (Sweden)
LChange'24 Workshop Chairs

Organizing Committee

General Chair

Nina Tahmasebi, University of Gothenburg, Sweden

Program Chairs

Syrielle Montariol, École polytechnique fédérale de Lausanne, Switzerland
Andrey Kutuzov, University of Oslo, Norway
David Alfter, University of Gothenburg, Sweden
Francesco Periti, University of Milan, Italy
Pierluigi Cassotti, University of Gothenburg, Sweden
Netta Huebscher, University of Gothenburg, Sweden

Program Committee

Program Chairs

David Alfter, University of Gothenburg
Pierluigi Cassotti, University of Gothenburg
Netta Huebscher, University of Gothenburg
Andrey Kutuzov, University of Oslo
Syrielle Montariol, Ecole Polytechnique Fédérale de Lausanne
Francesco Periti, University of Milan
Nina Tahmasebi, University of Gothenburg

Reviewers

Pierpaolo Basile, University of Bari
Pierluigi Cassotti, University of Gothenburg
Jing Chen, Hong Kong Polytechnic University
Stefano De Pascale, Vrije Universiteit Brussel and KU Leuven
Haim Dubossarsky, Queen Mary University of London and University of Cambridge
Mariia Fedorova, University of Oslo
Karlien Franco, QLVL | KU Leuven & FWO Vlaanderen
Mario Giulianelli, University of Amsterdam
Mauricio Gruppi, Villanova University
Vaibhav Jain, Delhi Technological University
Andres Karjus, Tallinn University
Andrey Kutuzov, University of Oslo
Barbara McGillivray, King's College London, University of London
Timothee Mickus, University of Helsinki
Filip Miletić, University of Stuttgart
Syrielle Montariol, Ecole Polytechnique Fédérale de Lausanne
Pablo Mosteiro, Utrecht University
Krzysztof Nowak, Polish Academic of Science
Lidia Pivovarova, University of Helsinki
Martin Pömsl, School of Computer Science, McGill University
Ella Rabinovich, International Business Machines
Martin Ruskov, University of Milan
Dominik Schlechtweg, Institute for Natural Language Processing, University of Stuttgart
Taichi Aida, Tokyo Metropolitan University
Ludovic Tanguy, University of Toulouse
Stephen Eugene Taylor, University of West Bohemia

Keynote Talk: What Changes in Language Modeling mean for Modeling Language Change

Antske Fokkens
Vrije Universiteit Amsterdam

Abstract: Language change detection has emerged as a subdomain that has caught the interest (computational) linguistics, historians, social scientists and computer scientists. Despite this enthusiasm and stable attention from the NLP community over multiple years, our methods keep on having difficulties in distinguishing valid signals of change from noise. This holds both for methods using static word embeddings as well as for more recent explorations with methods that make use of contextual embeddings. The question of how to distinguish true signal from noise has received substantial attention from the field, with the design of benchmarks, control tests and artificially created samples and data. An aspect that has, to my knowledge, received less attention is the fundamental differences between most methods using static on the one hand, and most methods using contextualized embeddings on the other hand. Mainly, methods that make use of static embeddings involve creating new embeddings for the full vocabular creating general shifts in space.
Methods using contextualized embeddings on the other hand mostly make use of pretrained language models, either as is or with some continual training on the target corpus. Change is then studied by comparing instances including target terms from different corpora. In this talk, I will explore what these fundamental differences mean when carrying out methodological checks and balances for studying language change with the aim of answering the question: how can we find meaningful change and know that is meaningful.

Bio: Antske Fokkens is a researcher at the Computational Lexicology and Terminology Lab and a visiting researcher at the Web and Media group at VU University Amsterdam, where she is also part of the Network Institute. Her main interest lies in the methodological aspects of Computational Linguistics, particularly how computational models of language work and which methods are suitable for modeling or analyzing linguistic phenomena. Her recent work focuses on applying NLP to digital humanities, enhancing historical research through the BiographyNet project. Additionally, she addresses methodological issues in system architecture and large-scale news processing through projects like NewsReader and Can we Handle the News. Her PhD thesis proposed a methodology for developing linguistic precision grammars, applicable across various theories.

Keynote Talk: New Approaches in Computer-Assisted Language Comparison

Johan-Mattis List
University of Passau

Abstract: The field of computer-assisted language comparison seeks to develop interactive computational workflows that facilitate those tasks that linguists working in the field of historical or typological language comparison usually carry out manually. While the field has substantially grown over the past decade, with new tools and new workflows that support computer-assisted analyses, there remain many challenges that have so far not yet been addressed in computer-assisted approaches. In this study, three new approaches that facilitate detailed comparative analysis will be presented. The first approach allows for an efficient manual labeling of correspondence patterns in comparative wordlists, the second approach allows to group sounds in phonetically transcribed wordlists and to segment words into morphemes. The third approach allows to correct individual word forms in comparative wordlists, by contrasting the reflexes of a proto-form that one would expect under the assumption of regular sound change with the reflexes that are attested in the data. All approaches are implemented in an interactive web-based tool that is freely available and integrated with previous computer-assisted tools and workflows.

Bio: Johan-Mattis List is a comparative linguist and Chair for Multilingual Computational Linguistics since January 2023, leading the ERC-funded ProduSemyresearch group. Previously, he was a stand-in professor at Bielefeld University and a senior researcher at the Max Planck Institutes in Leipzig and Jena. He earned his doctorate at Heinrich Heine University in Düsseldorf and completed his habilitation at Friedrich Schiller University in Jena. His research focuses on the evolution of human language lexicons and language change, with particular interest in Southeast Asian and South American languages. He advocates for open research and draws inspiration from bioinformatics to improve language comparison methods.

Table of Contents

Program

Wednesday, December 6, 2023

09:15 - 09:30 *Introduction*

09:30 - 10:30 *Keynote Antske Fokkens*

10:30 - 11:00 *Coffee Break*

11:00 - 12:00 *Session 1*

***Findings paper**: A Semantic Distance Metric Learning approach for Lexical Semantic Change Detection*
Taichi Aida and Danushka Bollegala

Towards a GoldenHymns Dataset for Studying Diachronic Trends in 19th Century Danish Religious Hymns
Ea Lindhardt Overgaard, Pascale Feldkamp and Yuri Bizzoni

***Findings paper**: Definition generation for lexical semantic change detection*
Mariia Fedorova, Andrey Kutuzov and Yves Scherrer

12:00 - 13:00 *Lunch Break*

13:00 - 13:45 *Keynote Johann-Mattis List*

13:45 - 14:45 *Session 2*

Towards an Onomasiological Study of Lexical Semantic Change Through the Induction of Concepts
Bastien Liétard, Mikaela Keller and Pascal Denis

Towards a Complete Solution to Lexical Semantic Change: an Extension to Multiple Time Periods and Diachronic Word Sense Induction
Francesco Periti and Nina Tahmasebi

AXOLOTL'24 Shared Task on Multilingual Explainable Semantic Change Modeling
Mariia Fedorova, Timothee Mickus, Niko Partanen, Janine Siewert, Elena Spaziani and Andrey Kutuzov

Wednesday, December 6, 2023 (continued)

14:45 - 15:30 *Session Poster Pitch*

15:30 - 16:30 *Poster Session*

TartuNLP @ AXOLOTL-24: Leveraging Classifier Output for New Sense Detection in Lexical Semantics
Aleksei Dorkin and Kairit Sirts

Deep-change at AXOLOTL-24: Orchestrating WSD and WSI Models for Semantic Change Modeling
Denis Kokosinskii, Mikhail Kuklin and Nikolay Arefyev

Can political dogwhistles be predicted by distributional methods for analysis of lexical semantic change?
Max Boholm, Björn Rönnerstrand, Ellen Breitholtz, Robin Cooper, Elina Lindgren, Gregor Rettenegger and Asad Sayeed

EtymoLink: A Structured English Etymology Dataset
Yuan Gao and Weiwei Sun

Similarity-Based Cluster Merging for Semantic Change Modeling
Christopher Brückner, Leixin Zhang and Pavel Pecina

Historical Ink: Semantic Shift Detection for 19th Century Spanish
Tony Montes, Laura Manrique-Gómez and Rubén Manrique

Complexity and Indecision: A Proof-of-Concept Exploration of Lexical Complexity and Lexical Semantic Change
David Alfter

Exploring Sound Change Over Time: A Review of Computational and Human Perception
Siqi He and Wei Zhao

A Few-shot Learning Approach for Lexical Semantic Change Detection Using GPT-4
Zhengfei Ren, Annalina Caputo and Gareth J. F. Jones

A Feature-Based Approach to Annotate the Syntax of Ancient Chinese
Chenrong Zhao

Exploring Diachronic and Diatopic Changes in Dialect Continua: Tasks, Datasets and Challenges
Melis Çelikkol, Lydia Körber and Wei Zhao

Improving Word Usage Graphs with Edge Induction
Bill Noble, Francesco Periti and Nina Tahmasebi

Presence or Absence: Are Unknown Word Usages in Dictionaries?
Xianghe Ma, Dominik Schlechtweg and Wei Zhao

16:30 - 17:30 *Round Table*

17:30 - 17:45 *Closing Remarks*

Computer-Assisted Language Comparison with EDICTOR 3

Johann-Mattis List and **Kellen Parker van Dam**
Chair for Multilingual Computational Linguistics
University of Passau
Passau, Germany

Abstract

Computer-assisted approaches to historical and typological language comparison have made great progress over the past two decades. Specifically for the classical tasks of historical language comparison, many computational methods have been published that mimic certain steps of the traditional workflow of the comparative method. In contrast to the diversity of new computational methods, there is only a limited number of interactive tools and interfaces that help scholars to curate and refine their data both before and after the application of computational methods. One of the few publicly available interfaces is EDICTOR (https://edictor.org), an interactive tool for computer-assisted language comparison. EDICTOR has been around for some time, and allows scholars to annotate and align cognate sets in various ways. With EDICTOR 3, the original tool has been enhanced, offering not only new features for data annotation, but also providing the possibility to use purely automatic methods for initial cognate detection, phonetic alignment, and correspondence pattern inference in an integrated workflow.

1 Introduction

The traditional comparative method in historical linguistics relies on a multitude of techniques for historical language comparison that have been established to compare languages systematically in order to shed light on their internal and external history (Ross and Durie, 1996). While having been traditionally carried out manually for more than 200 years (see Atkinson 1875 for an early and detailed description of the method), the last two decades have seen many attempts to provide automatic approaches for various individual steps of the comparative method and beyond (List, forthcoming(a)), reflecting some kind of a *quantitative turn* in historical linguistics (Geisler and List, 2022). Among the automated approaches most directly addressing the individual steps underlying the traditional workflow of the comparative method, we find methods for the detection of cognate words (List, 2012a; Jäger et al., 2017; Dellert, 2018), methods for pairwise and multiple phonetic alignment (Prokić et al., 2009; List, 2012b; Kilani, 2020), and methods for the identification of regular sound correspondence patterns (List, 2019).

While these methods have been shown to work rather well for language families with a shallow time depth (List et al., 2017), with phylogenetic trees inferred from automatically annotated cognate sets showing only minor differences to phylogenetic trees inferred from manually annotated cognate sets (Rama et al., 2018), the black box character by which these automatic methods arrive at their results, along with their failure to find deep etymological relations (Greenhill et al., 2023), has prevented scholars from switching to completely automated workflows. At the same time, however, the manual compilation of etymological datasets, where scholars compare thousands of words across dozens and at times even hundreds of languages, has reached its practical limits.

In a situation where computational methods cannot be used to replace humans and humans cannot cope with increasing amounts of digital data, computer-*assisted* solutions – as opposed to fully computer-*based* or fully manual – may offer an alternative in combining the best of both worlds by uniting the efficiency of computers with the accuracy of human annotation. In 2017, it was tried to put this idea into praxis by proposing a new framework for *Computer-Assisted Language Comparison* (CALC) that would not only try to enhance existing methods for computational historical language comparison, but also seek to develop web-based tools that could serve as an interface between computational and manual approaches, allowing for an interactive workflow in which data – which must be provided in human- and machine-

Proceedings of the 5th Workshop on Computational Approaches to Historical Language Change, pages 1–11
August 15, 2024

readable form – would be constantly passed back and forth between computers and machines (List, 2017b). Instead of identifying cognate sets from scratch in larger datasets, the idea was to employ automated methods for the pre-processing of linguistic data and then have human experts correct these initial analyses. Given that the correction of pre-processed data would be done in a dedicated web-based tool, it would also be possible to test the consistency of human annotation and offer annotators additional possibilities to explore cross-linguistic data in order to improve their analysis.

With the introduction of the EDICTOR tool (see Version 1.0, https://one.edictor.org, List 2017a), a first step in this direction was carried out. EDICTOR offered a web-based interface to annotated cognates in multilingual wordlists and align them at the same time. Via its simplified data structure (using a single TSV file to represent words, cognates, and alignments in multilingual wordlists), EDICTOR was also integrated with the LingPy library (List and Moran, 2013) that provided access to automatic methods for cognate detection and phonetic alignments. Later enhancements of EDICTOR (see Version 2.0 at https://two.edictor.org, Version 2.1 at https://two-1.edictor.org) have offered more features for annotation, but the basic character of the tool as a purely web-based application that could be used for annotation but not for the conduction of automatic methods has not changed since then.

With EDICTOR 3, not only new features, but also some substantial modifications are introduced to the tool. As of Version 3, EDICTOR will not only be distributed as a web-based tool that can be accessed via its URL (https://edictor.org), but also in the form of a software package written in Python that can be locally installed and does not require internet access to run. The advantage of this new architecture is that EDICTOR can also integrate with external software packages and thus allow for a true exchange with external software packages that provide enhanced methods for basic steps of the comparative method.

2 Background

Although tools and interfaces that would assist linguists in the annotation of etymological data have been around for several decades now, the number of linguists who would make active use of these tools is rather small. One of the first software packages that offered full support for various important tasks in historical language comparison is the STARLING database program, originally designed and created by Sergey Starostin (1953-2005). The origins of the software go back to the early 1990s (Starostin, 2000b). In its core, STARLING is a database system that offers users the possibility to create small databases consisting of multiple tables linked with each other. The software offers dedicated functionality to annotate cognates, to check for the individual sounds in a given wordlist, and to carry out distance-based phylogenetic reconstruction analyses based on the implementation of several ideas proposed by Starostin (Starostin, 2000a).

A second interactive tool for computer-assisted language comparison that is important to mention in this context is RefLex (Segerer and Flavier, 2015). Unlike STARLING, which comes as a software package that has to be installed on the users computers, RefLex is entirely web-based, written mostly in PHP, and accessed by connecting to the server maintained by the RefLex authors. Using RefLex requires a user account, and data must be imported and exported from the internal database. Originally designed to analyze data from African languages, RefLex offers many general functionalities that are very useful for etymological analysis in historical linguistics, including an alignment editor by which cognate sets can be aligned manually, methods to match elicitation glosses for concepts across different sources, and the possibility to annotate cognates in multilingual wordlists.

As impressive and useful as STARLING and RefLex are on their own, both tools have major drawbacks that prompted the development of an alternative interface for computer-assisted language comparison, taking nevertheless a lot of inspiration from the other tools. A major drawback of STARLING is that it does not work well on Unix systems, given that it is based on the now outdated *dBase* database management system that only runs on Windows operation systems. The major disadvantage of RefLex is that it requires a server with users having to log into the system when using it. This means that the tool can only be used with an active internet connection. In addition, import and export options have always been limited in RefLex and it was – for example – never clear how alignments could be exported to text files in order to use them in combination with other software tools.

As a result of these drawbacks, work began already in 2014 to work on my own interactive tool for computer-assisted language comparison. The goal was to design a tool that would offer functionality similar to those features that were considered most useful in STARLING and ReFLex, while at the same time offering a closer integration with automatic methods, most importantly those offered by the LingPy software package for quantitative tasks in historical linguistics (`https://lingpy.org`, List and Moran 2013).

The first version of this tool (that would later become the core of the CALC framework) was published in 2017 under the title *EDICTOR* (short for *Etymological Dictionary Editor*, List 2017a) and successfully employed to annotate the data underlying a larger phylogenetic analysis of Sino-Tibetan languages (Sagart et al., 2019). The first version of EDICTOR was written in JavaScript and was made accessible in the form of a website that users could access by opening the URL. Since the tool was entirely client-based, users could independently load their files to the JavaScript sandbox and later save them after editing. Data was never sent to any server, but was only edited inside the users browsers on their client systems. EDICTOR offered basic modules to annotate cognate sets (both full and partial cognates, see List et al. 2016), these cognate sets could be aligned with the help of a specific alignment editor, and rudimentary methods were available in order to check sound correspondences for language pairs. With EDICTOR 2 (List, 2021a), this functionality was further expanded by adding methods for the exploration and annotation of *morpheme glosses* (Hill and List, 2017; Schweikhard and List, 2020), extended exploration and export options for cognate sets (including direct export to the NEXUS format used in many phylogenetic applications, see Maddison et al. 1997 and Forkel 2023 for details on the format), and an initial interactive correspondence pattern browser that would display correspondence patterns inferred with the help of the method by List (2019).

EDICTOR has played a crucial role in the further development of computer-assisted techniques on historical language comparison. The tool proved not only important in the creation of reliable datasets (of which quite a few were later included in the Lexibank repository, List et al. 2022). It turned out that the tool was also crucial for the development of new computer-based methods, where it was used to visualize findings in order to check preliminary results and to create high-quality data for testing of new methods for which test and training data were usually lacking. Thus, in the retrospective, it would not have been possible to develop the method for partial cognate detection presented in List et al. (2016) without EDICTOR, since it would not have been possible to create the data that was later used to test the method. Similarly, the algorithm for the inference of sound correspondence patterns presented in List (2019) would not have been possible without the interactive sound correspondence pattern browser, which was crucial for the development of the new method, allowing to inspect findings immediately.

However, with time, EDICTOR also accumulated a considerable number of bugs and strange behaviors. Certain design problems that were not identified as such in the beginning later turned out to be problematic, and users' design suggestions or bug reports could often not be addressed immediately.

There were different reasons for the slow process with respect to the development of the tool. On the one hand, for scientists who develop tools and software packages, there is always a tension between the time they spend on development and the time they spend on proper research, since development is not necessarily seen as truly scientific work. On the other hand, many problems that the tool was supposed to handle turned out to be much harder than expected. As a result, solutions often were not available, and it was instead necessary to enter very detailed discussions on the proper modeling of particular problems before any changes to the tool could be made.

Not all of these problems can be solved with EDICTOR 3, but in contrast to previous releases of EDICTOR, EDICTOR 3 tries to set several new standards for the future development of the tool. As a result, the list of features was for the first time not only expanded, but certain features that had never proven to be useful for historical language comparison, were also discarded.

3 A New EDICTOR Version

3.1 Overview

EDICTOR 3 is a web-based tool that allows its users to carry out several steps of the comparative method interactively, producing data that can be digested by computer programs. EDICTOR 3 comes in two forms. Users can access the tool via its URL at https://edictor.org or download the source code and create another instance of the tool on a local or public server. Additionally, users can also install a local version of EDICTOR 3 on their own computer and access EDICTOR 3 locally, with no active internet connection being required. Both the public and the local version of EDICTOR 3 basically support the same functionalities, but the local version allows to save and access files stored locally (as pure files or with the help of an SQLite database) without having to go through the upload procedure that passes local data to the JavaScript sandbox. In addition, only the local version allows to obtain high quality cognate judgments, phonetic alignments, and sound correspondence patterns from dedicated Python packages (see § 3.3).

Like previous versions of the EDICTOR, EDICTOR 3 is organized in panels that allow to initiate actions or provide additional views on the data. The core is a multilingual wordlist that stores data in tabular form in a TSV file (see List et al. 2018 for an overview on the basic format). Panels are currently grouped into three basic modules. The *Edit* module offers basic functionality to edit data in various forms (see § 3.2), the *Compute* module offers methods for cognate detection, phonetic alignments, and correspondence pattern inference (see § 3.3), and the *Analyze* module offers additional tools by which the data can be analyzed and inspected (see 3.4).

3.2 Editing Data

In EDICTOR 3, data can be edited in five different ways. The most basic way to edit the data is to use the *Wordlist* panel that allows to edit data in a way similar to a spreadsheet editor but with some additional functionalities that facilitate the annotation of cognates and phonetic transcriptions. New functionality has been added that allows users to group segment data morphologically and to modify the representation of sounds by grouping distinct sounds into evolutionary units (List et al., 2024). The *Cognate Sets* and *Partial Cognate Sets* panels allow to edit cognate sets in a principled way. he *Morpheme Glosses* panel, introduced with EDICTOR 2 (see List 2021b), offers enhanced functionality for the annotation of morphological data with the help of morpheme glosses (Hill and List, 2017; Schweikhard and List, 2020). Finally, the *Correspondence Patterns* panel, which had been introduced earlier, now offers the possibility to edit correspondence patterns *actively* and to identify and mark exceptions in the reflexes of individual cognate sets (List, forthcoming(b)).

3.3 Computing Data

So far EDICTOR has not allowed users to compute data. The only exception was the alignment of individual of cognate sets, where EDICTOR offered the possibility to align words in the interactive window prior to carrying out manual refinements. With EDICTOR 3, basic methods for *cognate detection*, *phonetic alignment* (multiple sequence alignment), and *correspondence pattern detection* are now available as part of the newly introduced *Computing* module of the tool.

For each of the three tasks, two basic solutions are offered to the users. When running with Python internally and having installed the required software packages, the data is passed to Python and the dedicated methods are used to carry out the task. If EDICTOR 3 is accessed via the website, simplified implementations of the three methods in JavaScript are being used.

The basic approach for cognate detection is the LexStat method for full cognates (List, 2012a) or its counterpart for partial cognates (List et al., 2016). Implementations for both methods are available from LingPy (https://pypi.org/project/lingpy, List and Forkel 2023a, Version 2.6.13). The fallback function is based on matching consonant classes, as originally introduced by Dolgopolsky (1964) and then popularly employed in the STARLING package (see Turchin et al. 2010 for a detailed description and List 2014 for details on the implementation). For partial cognates, the approach is adjusted in order to be applied to individual morphemes rather than full words.

The basic approach for phonetic alignments of multiple sound sequences is based on the *Sound-Class based Alignment* method (List, 2012b). The method itself breaks down the complexity in linguistic sequences by converting phonetic transcriptions to sound classes and then conducts traditional multiple sequence alignment analyses using an adjusted version of the T-Coffee algorithm (Notredame et al., 2000). The method is also implemented in LingPy. As a fallback method, EDICTOR 3 employs a very simple and very fast method for multiple alignments that runs in linear time. This method first selects the longest sequence among the candidate sound sequences and then aligns all remaining sequences one by one with this longest sequence. The individual alignments are stored and later combined in such a way that all individual gaps introduced in the longest sequence are preserved. Despite the simplicity of the approach, it yields useful results in the majority of cases. When being confronted with complex alignment tasks, it clearly lags behind the SCA approach. However, since the method was created to speed up manual alignments, it is always easier to align sound sequences automatically in a first step and then refine them in a second step manually than starting the alignment manually from scratch.

The basic approach for correspondence pattern detection follows the method proposed in List (2019), which makes use of a greedy approach to solve the *minimum clique cover problem* in undirected networks (Bhasker and Samad, 1991) to group alignment sites (individual columns of a multiple alignment) into clusters from which correspondence patterns can be inferred. This method is implemented in the LingRex package (https://pypi.org/project/lingrex, List and Forkel 2023b, Version 1.4.2). The fallback method offered by EDICTOR 3 is based on a much simpler strategy that uses the sorting method QuickSort (Hoare, 1962) to arrange compatible alignment sites next to each other in a table and then groups those alignment sites that are compatible to each other into correspondence patterns. In contrast to the method by List (2019), this approach does not guarantee to find an exhaustive clique cover of the alignment site network. For the practical purpose of getting a first grouping of alignment sites into correspondence patterns, however, it has turned out to be very useful to speed up the process of manually annotating correspondence patterns.

The three methods in combination equip users with a workflow that starts from a raw wordlist in phonetic transcription, then identifies cognates, aligns them, and finally infers correspondence patterns from the data. In this form, the workflow accounts for the majority of the individual steps of the classical comparative method (Ross and Durie, 1996). What it leaves out are methods for phonological reconstruction and phylogenetic reconstruction. Since classical phonological reconstruction, however, builds on previously identified correspondence patterns (Anttila, 1972), EDICTOR 3 offers a very solid basis to build phonological reconstructions on top of explicitly annotated sound correspondence patterns. For phylogenetic reconstruction, the aforementioned option to export data to the NEXUS format comes in handy.

3.4 Analyzing Data

EDICTOR 3 not only supports editing and computing of multilingual wordlist data but also allows to inspect the data in different ways through the *Analyze* module of the tool. With the help of the *Sounds* panel, users can inspect the individual sounds in individual language varieties, by comparing how frequently and in which words they occur and how they fit into classical phoneme inventory tables. The *Colexifications* panel allows for a quick investigation of full and partial colexifications, the former referring to cases of polysemy or homophony, in which a word form expresses two or more concepts in a wordlist (François, 2008), and the latter referring to those cases where morphemes with identical forms recur across different words (List, 2023). The panel offers additional functionality to visualize full and partial colexifications with the help of bipartite networks (Hill and List, 2017). The *Correspondences* panel allows users to compare the sound correspondences inferred from the pairwise alignments of two language varieties. While this functionality may seem much less useful and important, it may prove useful in those cases where one the focus lies on specific relations between two language varieties, such as – for example – in the case of two alternative proposals for phonological reconstruction (Pulini and List, 2024). The *Cognates* panel allows for a detailed inspection o the distribution of cognate sets across a multilingual wordlist, providing a tabular view in which each column is reserved for one language and each row represents one cognate set. Through this specific panel, users can also export their cognate sets to the above-mentioned NEXUS format, which can then be fed to dedicated software packages for phylogenetic reconstruction.

3.5 Implementation

EDICTOR 3 is implemented as a web-based application written in JavaScript. The newly introduced local server functionality that allows users to employ the tool locally is implemented in Python. The code base is curated on GitHub (https://github.com/digling/edictor, and archived as part of the Python Package Index (https://pypi.org/project/edictor). For users who prefer to use the tool without installing it, the most recent version of EDICTOR can be accessed from https://edictor.org, a development version is usually accessible from https://dev.edictor.org, and earlier

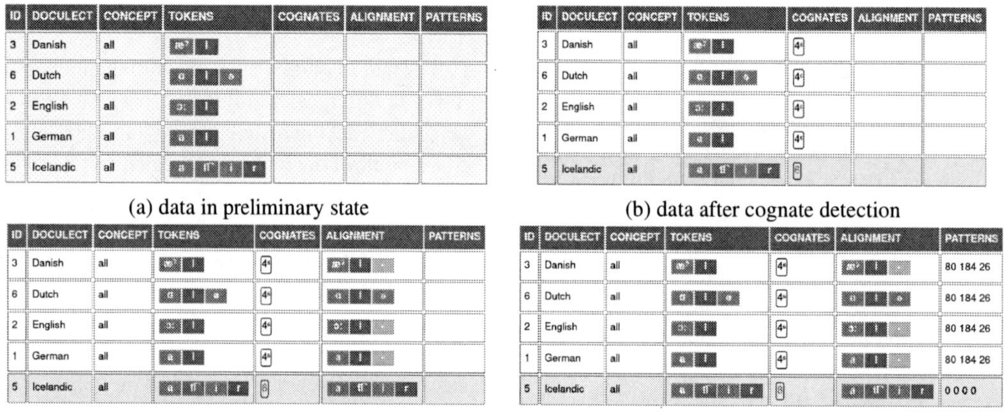

(a) data in preliminary state

(b) data after cognate detection

(c) data in aligned form

(d) data with inferred patterns

Figure 1: Integrated computer-assisted workflow in EDICTOR 3. The screenshots represent the different stages by which analyses with LingPy and LingRex applied to the Germanic wordlist data are carried out in the interactive mode.

versions are accessible from https://one.edictor.org (Version 1.0), https://two.edictor.org (Version 2.0), and https://two-1.edictor.org (Version 2.1). Issues in the code as well as discussions about particular features are typically handled via GitHub's issue tracker (https://github.com/digling/edictor/issues).

4 Examples

In the following, we will try to illustrate the new features and ideas that made it into EDICTOR 3 with the help of three examples. These consist of (1) an integrated computer-assisted workflow that can be used to compute cognates, alignment, and correspondence patterns from scratch, (2) an illustration of the new functionalities for the annotation of correspondence patterns, and (3) a discussion of the new approaches that allow to speed up the process of manipulating data provided in phonetic transcription.

4.1 Integrated Computer-Assisted Workflow

To illustrate how an integrated computer-assisted workflow can be carried out with the help of EDICTOR 3, we make use of a small dataset of 110 basic concepts translated into seven Germanic languages. This dataset was originally compiled by Starostin (2005) and later adjusted later adjusted to the format required by EDICTOR and LingPy for testing purposes (List, 2014). The dataset itself can be accessed directly from EDICTOR 3, by opening the landing page (https://edictor.org) and then navigating to the tab *Examples*, where it can be selected under the title `Germanic Wordlist (List 2014)`. Screenshots that illustrate the different stages of the workflow are shown in Figure 1 (a-d).

The analysis itself shown in this example fails to identify the Icelandic wordform as being cognate with the forms in the other languages, which is most likely due to the specific phonetic transcriptions chosen. For computer-assisted purposes, however, the ultimate accuracy of any algorithm is much less important than the general reliability and – as neatly illustrated in this example – the integration with interactive tools that allow scholars to quickly preprocess a given dataset automatically in order to refine the individual findings in a second stage.

4.2 Inspecting and Editing Correspondences

Correspondence patterns inferred by the automatic workflow shown in the previous section can be further edited and modified by the user. Patterns are reflected in the form commonly employed by EDICTOR and LingRex. Patterns are defined with respect to the phonetic alignment. Sites in an alignment are grouped into patterns by assigning them common integers that serve as identifiers and must be greater than zero. The value 0 itself is reserved for those cases in which an alignment site is not assigned to *any* pattern in the data. This holds for cases of singletons (words that are not cognate with any other words in a given dataset) or where the method for correspondence pattern detection cannot find enough evidence to group the data further (e.g. for cognate sets that do not have enough reflexes in the data).

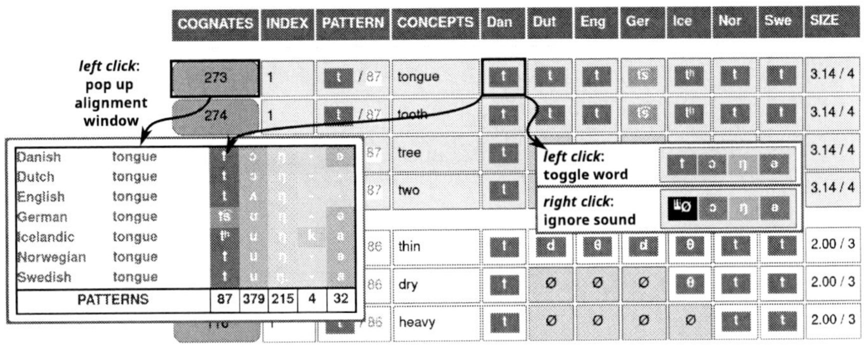

Figure 2: Correspondence patterns inferred by the computational workflow. Additional editing of corresponcence patterns is possible by clicking into the pattern identifiers in the column *PATTERN* and editing values there directly.

Figure 2 shows how correspondence patterns are visualized in EDICTOR 3. Each alignmen site is listed in one row of a table, preceded by the cognate set identifiers, followed by the position of the site in the alignment, followed by the pattern identifier and the concepts reflected by the cognate sets. For each language, the alignment site value is then listed in fixed order. This order itself can be edited by the user in order to put related language varieties together or to put proto-languages in front. Clicking on a particular sound will show the full word, allowing users to toggle between different views, highlighting particular sounds or individual words in which the sounds occur. With the help of a right mouse click, the pattern can be toggled in such a way that the particular sound is ignored when assembling the pattern, using *inline alignments* for the representation (List, forthcoming(b)). This allows users to explicitly ignore certain reflex sounds from correspondence patterns that might show unexpected results. Ultimately, this comes close to a formal version of Grimm's handling of Germanic data, when he noted exceptions from the consonant shift that he had observed (Grimm, 1822). By putting exceptions at the side, one can collect them to try and resolve them later.

As can be seen from the example illustration, the automated workflow has no problem in detecting the classical correspondence of the affricate initials in German corresponding to alveolar stops in the other Germanic languages. This proves again the usefulness of computer-assisted approaches in increasing the efficiency of linguistic annotation.

4.3 Segmenting and Grouping

The wordlist panel in EDICTOR 3 comes with a new feature that allows for an improved editing of sound sequences. Already in the first version, it was possible to insert phonetic transcriptions in SAMPA / X-Sampa (see Gibbon et al. 1997, 60-108 for a specification of SAMPA), which would then automatically be converted to the International Phonetic Alphabet in plain Unicode (IPA, 1999) and automatically *segmented* into individual sounds, following the standards proposed by the Cross-Linguistic Data Formats initiative for the handling of phonetic transcriptions (Forkel et al., 2018). In EDICTOR 3, these editing functionalities were streamlined and extended by adding additional possibilities to segment words into morphemes and to group individual sounds into evolving units.

The extended sequence editing features are illustrated in Figure 3, where some German words are provided as sample sequences along with their morpheme structure, annotated with the help of morpheme glosses. While the conversion from input in SAMPA/X-SAMPA is automatically triggered when selected by the user (conversion can also be turned of if phonetic transcriptions are provided from the original data or if users prefer to user their own IPA keyboard), the segmentation of individual characters into speech sounds in phonetic transcription is carried out when inserting a sequence with a preceding space. Since trailing spaces are disallowed in the standard format of the column storing sound sequence data in EDICTOR (typically called *TOKENS*), this does not conflict with alternative annotations or other forms of user input. Once sound sequences are inserted into the text fields, EDICTOR automatically colors them, using a color schema that distinguishes 10 different sound classes, as originally proposed by Dolgopolsky (1964). These sequences can then be edited in consecutive steps. First, by right-mouseclicking

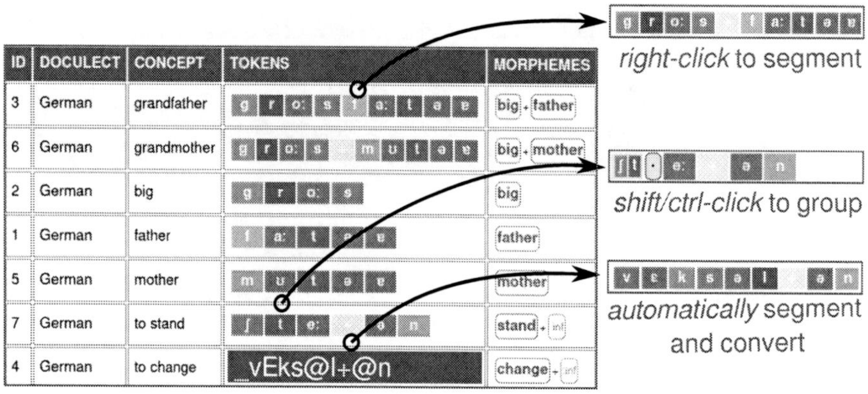

Figure 3: Sequence editing in EDICTOR 3. In addition to the conversion from SAMPA to IPA, EDICTOR 3 also supports the convenient segmentation of sound sequences into morphemes and the grouping of sounds into evolving units.

on individual sound segments, a morpheme boundary marker (the +) is inserted *before* the segment that was clicked, thus allowing users to quickly segment their words into morphemes. Second, by pressing the SHIFT or the CTRL button *and* right-mouse-clicking a segment, it will be grouped with the segment *following* it, using the specific annotation for grouped sounds developed in List et al. (2024).

In combination with additional panels, such as the dedicated panel for the handling of *Morpheme Glosses* that was introduced with an earlier version of EDICTOR, the tool now equips users with multiple possibilities to efficiently annotate language-internal cognates by segmenting words into morphemes and handling co-evolving sounds as single units. Our hope is that these additional methods will soon allow us to create a larger collection of morpheme-segmented wordlists that could later be used to test automatic approaches to the task of morpheme segmentation in computational historical linguistics, for which by now no satisfying solution exists (List, 2024).

5 Outlook

With EDICTOR 3, we hope to enter a new stage of computer-assisted language comparison, by providing a tool that is increasingly robust, allowing for multiple ways of access, and offering sophisticated methods for data annotation and analysis that are more and more fine-grained and adapted to the complex task of etymological analysis in historical linguistics. For the future, we plan not only to improve the integration with existing tools (for example by providing enhanced export functionalities to major phylogenetic software packages), but also to consolidate the current code base. While unit tests for the Python code running the local server application have now been set up, with the tool being tested on all major operation systems, the JavaScript code base was written over a long time frame, containing numerous lines of code that should be refactored. In order to improve the accessibility of the tool further, we also plan to conduct more explicit trainings by offering webinars and by sharing tutorials in video form where we run users through major annotation stages and workflows.

Although not perfect yet, however, we think that EDICTOR 3 already now provides a greatly improved user experience with new functionalities, and we hope that the tool will prove useful for those who want to work with computer-assisted workflows instead of conducting purely quantitative or purely qualitative analyses. The tool is intended to help linguists in their etymological work, not to replace them by switching to exclusively automatic approaches that discard 200 years of scholarship. This general spirit of computer-assisted language comparison has not changed with EDICTOR 3, and we hope that the tool will prove *actually* useful for comparative work in historical linguistics.

Supplementary Material

EDICTOR 3 has been archived with PyPi at https://pypi.org/project/edictor (Version 3.0), is curated on GitHub at https://github.com/digling/edictor, and can be accessed online from https://edictor.org.

Limitations

Computer-assisted approaches to historical language comparison still face many limitations that cannot be overcome by one single tool. The majority of the limitations we face in building tools that assist linguists conducting computer-assisted as opposed to purely classical studies consist in the modeling of etymological relations between words (both when comparing words inside one and the same language and across multiple languages). Regarding EDICTOR 3, three very urgent limitations can be found in the lack of a principled handling of complex paradigms in multilingual wordlists (1), the limitation of the models used to handle partial cognates to account for non-concatenative morphology (2), and the absence of general procedures to check or annotate conditioning context that would explain multiple sound reflexes in individual languages for the same proto sound (3). We do not have any concrete ideas to solve any of these three problems at the moment, but we discuss them often and hope to be able to improve our work on these open problems at some point in the future.

Acknowledgments

This project was supported by the ERC Consolidator Grant ProduSemy (PI Johann-Mattis List, Grant No. 101044282, see https://doi.org/10.3030/101044282). Views and opinions expressed are however those of the author(s) only and do not necessarily reflect those of the European Union or the European Research Council Executive Agency (nor any other funding agencies involved). Neither the European Union nor the granting authority can be held responsible for them.

We thank all those who have been supporting the development of EDICTOR in the past by testing the tool, suggesting modifications, and discussing new features and annotations. Special thanks in this context go to Carlos Barrientos, Frederic Blum, Nicolás Brid, Fabrício Gerardi, Abbie Hantgan, Nathan W. Hill, Guillaume Jacques, John Miller, Laurent Sagart, and Roberto Zariquiey. We also thank the doctoral students in the ProduSemy project – Katja Bocklage, Alʒbęta Kuçerová, Arne Rubehn, and David Snee – for testing and discussing development versions of EDICTOR 3.

References

Raimo Anttila. 1972. *An introduction to historical and comparative linguistics*. Macmillan, New York.

Robert Atkinson. 1875. Comparative grammar of the Dravidian languages. *Hermathena*, 2(3):60–106.

J. Bhasker and Tariq Samad. 1991. The clique-partitioning problem. *Computers & Mathematics with Applications*, 22(6):1–11.

Johannes Dellert. 2018. Combining information-weighted sequence alignment and sound correspondence models for improved cognate detection. In *Proceedings of the 27th International Conference on Computational Linguistics*, pages 3123–3133.

Aron B. Dolgopolsky. 1964. Gipoteza drevnejšego rodstva jazykovych semej Severnoj Evrazii s verojatnostej točky zrenija [A probabilistic hypothesis concering the oldest relationships among the language families of Northern Eurasia]. *Voprosy Jazykoznanija*, 2:53–63.

Robert Forkel. 2023. *CommonNexus. A nexus (phylogenetics) file reader and writer [Software, Version 1.9.1]*. Max Planck Institute for Evolutionary Anthropology, Leipzig.

Robert Forkel, Johann-Mattis List, Simon J. Greenhill, Christoph Rzymski, Sebastian Bank, Michael Cysouw, Harald Hammarström, Martin Haspelmath, Gereon A. Kaiping, and Russell D. Gray. 2018. Cross-Linguistic Data Formats, advancing data sharing and re-use in comparative linguistics. *Scientific Data*, 5(180205):1–10.

Alexandre François. 2008. Semantic maps and the typology of colexification: intertwining polysemous networks across languages. In Martine Vanhove, editor, *From polysemy to semantic change*, pages 163–215. Benjamins, Amsterdam.

Hans J. Geisler and Johann-Mattis List. 2022. Of word families and language trees: New and old metaphors in studies on language history. *Moderna*, 24(1-2):134–148.

Dafydd Gibbon, Roger Moore, and Richard Winski, editors. 1997. *Spoken Language Reference Materials*. De Gruyter Mouton, Berlin and Boston.

Simon J. Greenhill, Hannah J. Haynie, Robert M. Ross, Angela Chira, Johann-Mattis List, Lyle Campbell, Carlos A. Botero, and Russell D. Gray. 2023. A recent northern origin for the uto-aztecan family. *Language*, 0(0).

Jacob Grimm. 1822. *Deutsche Grammatik*, 2 edition, volume 1. Dieterichsche Buchhandlung, Göttingen.

Nathan W. Hill and Johann-Mattis List. 2017. Challenges of annotation and analysis in computer-assisted language comparison: A case study on Burmish languages. *Yearbook of the Poznań Linguistic Meeting*, 3(1):47–76.

Charles A. R. Hoare. 1962. Quicksort. *The Computer Journal*, 5(1):10–16.

IPA. 1999. *Handbook of the International Phonetic Association.* Cambridge University Press, Cambridge.

Gerhard Jäger, Johann-Mattis List, and Pavel Sofroniev. 2017. Using support vector machines and state-of-the-art algorithms for phonetic alignment to identify cognates in multi-lingual wordlists. In *Proceedings of the 15th Conference of the European Chapter of the Association for Computational Linguistics. Long Papers*, pages 1204–1215, Valencia. Association for Computational Linguistics.

Marwan Kilani. 2020. FAAL: a feature-based aligning ALgorithm. *Language Dynamics and Change*, 11(1):30–76.

Johann-Mattis List. 2012a. LexStat. Automatic detection of cognates in multilingual wordlists. In *Proceedings of the EACL 2012 Joint Workshop of Visualization of Linguistic Patterns and Uncovering Language History from Multilingual Resources*, pages 117–125, Stroudsburg.

Johann-Mattis List. 2012b. SCA: Phonetic alignment based on sound classes. In Marija Slavkovik and Dan Lassiter, editors, *New directions in logic, language, and computation*, pages 32–51. Springer, Berlin and Heidelberg.

Johann-Mattis List. 2014. *Sequence comparison in historical linguistics.* Düsseldorf University Press, Düsseldorf.

Johann-Mattis List. 2017a. A web-based interactive tool for creating, inspecting, editing, and publishing etymological datasets. In *Proceedings of the 15th Conference of the European Chapter of the Association for Computational Linguistics. System Demonstrations*, pages 9–12, Valencia. Association for Computational Linguistics.

Johann-Mattis List. 2017b. *Computer-Assisted Language Comparison. Reconciling computational and classical approaches in historical linguistics [Research Project, 2017–2022].* Max Planck Institute for Evolutionary Anthropology, Leipzig.

Johann-Mattis List. 2019. Automatic inference of sound correspondence patterns across multiple languages. *Computational Linguistics*, 45(1):137–161.

Johann-Mattis List. 2021a. *EDICTOR. A web-based tool for creating, editing, and publishing etymological datasets.* Max Planck Institute for Evolutionary Anthropology, Leipzig.

Johann-Mattis List. 2021b. Using EDICTOR 2.0 to annotate language-internal cognates in a German wordlist. *Computer-Assisted Language Comparison in Practice*, 4(4).

Johann-Mattis List. 2023. Inference of partial colexifications from multilingual wordlists. *Frontiers in Psychology*, 14(1156540):1–10.

Johann-Mattis List. 2024. Open problems in computational historical linguistics [version 2; peer review: 3 approved, 1 approved with reservations]. *Open Research Europe*, 3(201):1–27.

Johann-Mattis List. forthcoming(a). Computational approaches to historical language comparison. In Claire Bowern and Bethwyn Evans, editors, *Routledge Handbook of Historical Linguistics*, 2 edition, pages 1–20. Routledge, London and New York.

Johann-Mattis List. forthcoming(b). Productive Signs: A computer-assisted analysis of evolutionary, typological, and cognitive dimensions of word families. In *International Conference of Linguists*, 0, pages 1–12. De Gruyter.

Johann-Mattis List and Robert Forkel. 2023a. *LingPy. A Python library for quantitative tasks in historical linguistics [Software Library, Version 2.6.13].* MCL Chair at the University of Passau, Passau.

Johann-Mattis List and Robert Forkel. 2023b. *LingRex: Linguistic reconstruction with LingPy.* Max Planck Institute for Evolutionary Anthropology, Leipzig.

Johann-Mattis List, Robert Forkel, Simon J. Greenhill, Christoph Rzymski, Johannes Englisch, and Russell D. Gray. 2022. Lexibank, a public repository of standardized wordlists with computed phonological and lexical features. *Scientific Data*, 9(316):1–31.

Johann-Mattis List, Simon J. Greenhill, and Russell D. Gray. 2017. The potential of automatic word comparison for historical linguistics. *PLOS ONE*, 12(1):1–18.

Johann-Mattis List, Nathan W. Hill, Frederic Blum, and Cristian Juárez. 2024. Grouping sounds into evolving units for the purpose of historical language comparison [version 1; peer review: 2 approved]. *Open Research Europe*, 4(34):1–8.

Johann-Mattis List, Philippe Lopez, and Eric Bapteste. 2016. Using sequence similarity networks to identify partial cognates in multilingual wordlists. In *Proceedings of the Association of Computational Linguistics 2016 (Volume 2: Short Papers)*, pages 599–605, Berlin. Association of Computational Linguistics.

Johann-Mattis List and Steven Moran. 2013. An open source toolkit for quantitative historical linguistics. In *Proceedings of the ACL 2013 System Demonstrations*, pages 13–18, Stroudsburg. Association for Computational Linguistics.

Johann-Mattis List, Mary Walworth, Simon J. Greenhill, Tiago Tresoldi, and Robert Forkel. 2018. Sequence comparison in computational historical linguistics. *Journal of Language Evolution*, 3(2):130–144.

David R. Maddison, David L. Swofford, and Wayne P. Maddison. 1997. NEXUS: an extensible file format for systematic information. *Syst. Biol.*, 46(4):590–621.

Cédric Notredame, Desmond G. Higgins, and Jaap Heringa. 2000. T-Coffee. *Journal of Molecular Biology*, 302:205–217.

Jelena Prokić, Martijn Wieling, and John Nerbonne. 2009. Multiple sequence alignments in linguistics. In *Proceedings of the EACL 2009 Workshop on Language Technology and Resources for Cultural Heritage, Social Sciences, Humanities, and Education*, pages 18–25.

Michele Pulini and Johann-Mattis List. 2024. First steps towards the integration of resources on historical glossing traditions in the history of Chinese: A collection of standardized fǎnqiè spellings from the Guǎngyùn. In *Proceedings of the 2024 Joint International Conference on Computational Linguistics, Language Resources and Evaluation (LREC-COLING 2024)*, pages 7343–7348, Torino, Italy. ELRA and ICCL.

Taraka Rama, Johann-Mattis List, Johannes Wahle, and Gerhard Jäger. 2018. Are automatic methods for cognate detection good enough for phylogenetic reconstruction in historical linguistics? In *Proceedings of the North American Chapter of the Association of Computational Linguistics*, pages 393–400.

Malcom Ross and Mark Durie. 1996. Introduction. In Mark Durie, editor, *The comparative method reviewed. Regularity and irregularity in language change*, pages 3–38. Oxford University Press, New York.

Laurent Sagart, Guillaume Jacques, Yunfan Lai, Robin Ryder, Valentin Thouzeau, Simon J. Greenhill, and Johann-Mattis List. 2019. Dated language phylogenies shed light on the ancestry of Sino-Tibetan. *Proceedings of the National Academy of Science of the United States of America*, 116:10317–10322.

Nathanael E. Schweikhard and Johann-Mattis List. 2020. Developing an annotation framework for word formation processes in comparative linguistics. *SKASE Journal of Theoretical Linguistics*, 17(1):2–26.

Guillaume Segerer and S. Flavier. 2015. *RefLex: Reference Lexicon of Africa*. CNRS, Paris and Lyon.

Sergej A. Starostin. 2005. *Germanic 100 wordlists*. The Tower of Babel, Moscow.

Sergej Anatolévič Starostin. 2000a. Comparative-historical linguistics and lexicostatistics. In *Time depth in historical linguistics*, volume 1 of *Papers in the prehistory of languages*, pages 223–265. McDonald Institute for Archaeological Research, Cambridge.

Sergej Anatolévič Starostin. 2000b. *The STARLING database program*. RGGU, Moscow.

Peter Turchin, Ilja Peiros, and Murray Gell-Mann. 2010. Analyzing genetic connections between languages by matching consonant classes. *Journal of Language Relationship*, 3:117–126.

Exploring Diachronic and Diatopic Changes in Dialect Continua: Tasks, Datasets and Challenges

Melis Çelikkol[*1] **Lydia Körber**[*1] **Wei Zhao**[2]
[1]University of Heidelberg [2]University of Aberdeen
{firstname.lastname}@stud.uni-heidelberg.de
wei.zhao@abdn.ac.uk

Abstract

Everlasting contact between language communities leads to constant changes in languages over time, and gives rise to language varieties and dialects. However, the communities speaking non-standard language are often overlooked by non-inclusive NLP technologies. Recently, there has been a surge of interest in studying diatopic and diachronic changes in dialect NLP, but there is currently no research exploring the intersection of both. Our work aims to fill this gap by systematically reviewing diachronic and diatopic papers from a unified perspective. In this work, we critically assess nine tasks and datasets across five dialects from three language families (Slavic, Romance, and Germanic) in both spoken and written modalities. The tasks covered are diverse, including corpus construction, dialect distance estimation, and dialect geolocation prediction, among others. Moreover, we outline five open challenges regarding changes in dialect use over time, the reliability of dialect datasets, the importance of speaker characteristics, limited coverage of dialects, and ethical considerations in data collection. We hope that our work sheds light on future research towards inclusive computational methods and datasets for language varieties and dialects.

1 Introduction

Language continuously changes, varies and transforms on all levels of linguistics. Research in sociolinguistics assumes five dimensions of language variation, the so-called diasystem, that are mutually influential: diaphasic (situation), diamesic (medium), diastratic (social group), diachronic (time), and diatopic (space), as shown in Figure 1 (Zampieri et al., 2020).

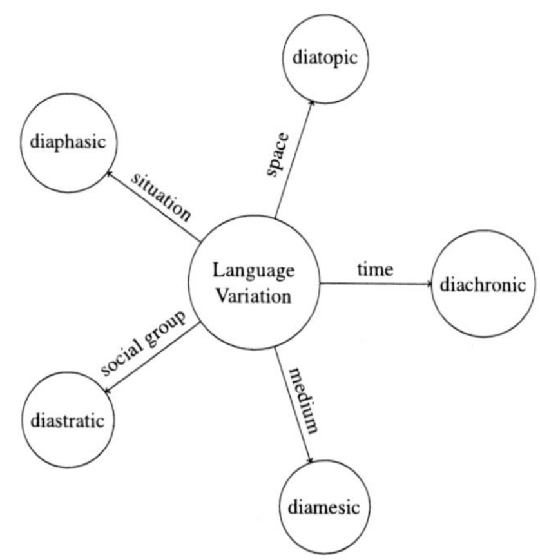

Figure 1: Language variation and the diasystem.[1]

Diaphasic, diamesic, diastratic and diatopic variation can be grouped to synchronic variation, as opposed to diachronic variation which spans several points in time. Diachronic variation is not limited to decades and centuries, but may already be observed within years, months, and even weeks or days. Especially with computer-mediated communication and social media platforms, language change appears to spread at a faster pace (Eisenstein et al., 2014). This exposes a challenge in NLP applications, as models remain static after training and struggle to understand the evolving nature of language[2]. As a result, model performance decreases over time. For instance, headline generation models decrease in performance after a few years, while emoji prediction models do so even within a month (Søgaard et al., 2021). As shown in the (socio-)linguistic work (Beeching, 2006), diachronic and synchronic variation are closely linked in the sense that language change often manifests first in synchronic variation

*These authors contributed equally to this work.

[1]Inspired by: http://phylonetworks.blogspot.com/2015/06/the-diasystematic-structure-of.html, accessed on 11.03.2024.

[2]Although there are methods to keep models up-to-date, such as re-training, fine-tuning, and RAG (Retrieval-Augmented Generation) leveraging up-to-date information sources at inference, the process is time-consuming and costly.

Proceedings of the 5th Workshop on Computational Approaches to Historical Language Change, pages 12–22
August 15, 2024 ©2024 Association for Computational Linguistics

before entering a diachronic level. Additionally, there is a strong spatial component in language change, as language change is caused by contact between people and speech communities (lately by online interactions too), which gives rise to dialects (Jeszenszky et al., 2018). While *isoglosses* separate dialects by drawing the geographic boundaries, the consensus among dialectologists and sociolinguists today is to speak of *dialect continua*, which assume gradual transitions between central areas of different dialects over time (Jeszenszky et al., 2018). In these continua, as proposed by the *wave model* (Wolfram and Schilling-Estes, 2017), language change is propagated from a certain locus at a certain point in time and spread layer-wise, radiating from the central point of contact. This is indeed a result of both spatial (diatopic) and temporal (diachronic) interactions within dialect continua.

An example of diatopic variation over time can be seen in Figure 2: the usage of the German dialect word *bissel* (a bit). A query in the ZDL-Regionalkorpus (Nolda et al., 2021, 2023), a collection of regional newspaper texts from Germany, Austria, and Switzerland, reveals its constant usage in Austria (A), and an increased usage in other, more northern regions over time, first in Bavaria (D-Südost) possibly due to geographic proximity, and a more recent rise in Central Eastern Germany (D-Mittelost).

In this work, we explore the intersection of diachronic and diatopic changes in language variants and dialects within the NLP community. To do so, we investigate nine tasks and datasets across five dialects from three language families to address the following research questions:

- What are the characteristics of dialect datasets across different time periods and geographic areas, and what NLP tasks have been established based on these datasets (§3)?
- What is the current state of computational methods and their results in these dialect-related NLP tasks (§4)?
- What are the challenges in dialect NLP research that have not been addressed in previous works (§5.1)?

[3]Usage graph for *bissel*, created with Digitales Wörterbuch der deutschen Sprache (DWDS, Digital Dictionary of the German Language), `https://shorturl.at/9XVwt`, accessed on 04.07.2024.

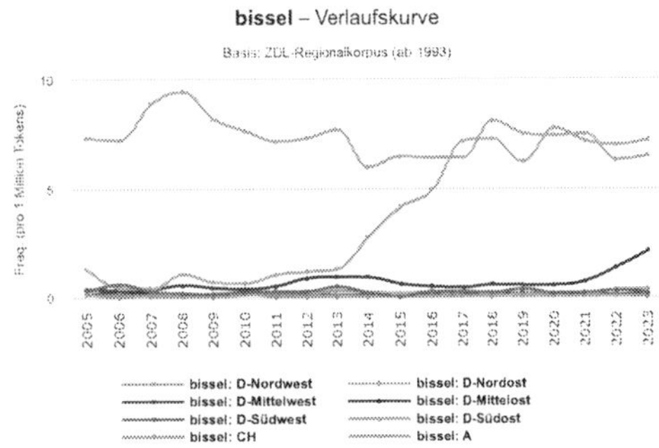

Figure 2: Diachronic usage of *bissel* in the years 2005-2023 in a regional newspaper corpus of German across dialect areas in frequency per 1M tokens.[3]

In this work, we aim at exploring the intersection of diachronic and diatopic variation in dialect NLP research. Research questions on this topic include (a) how to detect and quantify language change in dialect continua over time, and (b) how to build and process diachronic-diatopic datasets. Previous approaches leveraged machine learning methods to compute the distance and similarity of different varieties on various linguistic levels such as graphemics (Waldenberger et al., 2021), syntax (Jeszenszky et al., 2018; Chen et al., 2024), phonetics (Boldsen and Paggio, 2022; He and Zhao, 2024), semantics (Montanelli and Periti, 2023; Ma et al., 2024b,a), and built diachronic-diatopic datasets in both written and spoken modalities (Kopřivová et al., 2014; Komrskova et al., 2017).

Here, we critically review nine tasks and datasets, highlighting their strengths and limitations, as well as identifying challenges that have not been previously addressed. We discuss seminal works in Indo-European languages and their varieties, as well as recent works on this topic. The dialect continua covered here include the Slavic family with the Czech dialect landscape (Kopřivová et al., 2014; Komrskova et al., 2017), the Romance language family with Italian (Ramponi and Casula, 2023) and Portuguese (Pichel Campos et al., 2018; Zampieri et al., 2016), as well as the Germanic language family with Swiss German (Jeszenszky et al., 2018, 2019) and historical German varieties (Dipper and Waldenberger, 2017; Waldenberger et al., 2021).

2 Related work

To our knowledge, there is no survey examining the intersection of diachronic and diatopic variation in dialect NLP so far. However, there are survey papers examining the diachronic and diatopic components separately, which will be briefly presented here. Diachronic language modeling has been surveyed with regard to embeddings (Kutuzov et al., 2018) and semantic shift detection (Montanelli and Periti, 2023).

The comprehensive survey on diatopic language modelling by Zampieri et al. (2020) evaluates computational methods for processing similar languages, language varieties, and dialects, with a focus on diatopic language variation and integration in NLP applications. The work identifies the availability of suitable data as a key challenge, as the classical NLP data sources like newspaper text and Wikipedia do not cover dialectal data. Instead, social media posts and speech transcripts can be used. More recently, an evaluation benchmark for different NLP tasks in dialects, varieties and closely-related languages, DIALECTBENCH, was published (Faisal et al., 2024), proving that variation is of current interest in the research community. Joshi et al. (2024) survey Natural Language Understanding and Generation in dialects, without taking other axes of the variation diasystem into account. There exists a designated series of workshops on NLP for Similar Languages, Language Varieties, and Dialects (VarDial)[4], which also proposes several NLP shared tasks in dialects and other varieties, such as dialect classification and identification itself. Even though the workshop has featured a number of publications and talks dealing with the intersection of diachronic and diatopic variation over the years (Sukhareva and Chiarcos, 2014; Baldwin, 2018; Vidal-Gorène et al., 2020), this has not been a separate workshop or shared task topic up until now.

3 Tasks and Datasets

In this section, we review the dialect-related tasks and datasets from a unified perspective considering both diachronic and diatopic aspects, and organize them by languages (See Table 1 for tasks and datasets, and Table 2 for data statistics).

3.1 Czech

A very interesting albeit not very recent paper by Kopřivová et al. (2014) explains the building process of their later released ORTOFON and DIALEKT corpora (Komrskova et al., 2017). Although both papers are mention-worthy, we focus on Kopřivová et al. (2014) due to the presentation and depth of explanation for the data collection processes.

The ORTOFON corpus relies on spontaneous conversations recorded between 2012-2017, where nobody was aware that the conversations were recorded except for the person who made the recording. The non-scripted interactions recorded this way are then separated into the closest one of 12 situation categories which were created with the topics of Czech daily-life in mind. What makes this corpus really strong is that Kopřivová et al. (2014) consider several missing elements in other corpora all at once: relationship between speakers is noted alongside the total number of generations present in each conversation, as well as the speaker characteristics, such as education, occupation, region of residence (with subtypes such as longest, childhood and current residence) and speech defects. After factoring these elements into the data collection process, the corpus is balanced according to the speaker's gender, education (binary as tertiary/non-tertiary), age (binary as >35 or <35), and childhood region of residence. As promising as Kopřivová et al. (2014)'s collection methods are to provide natural results, the approach is not discussed in terms of ethics in their presentation.

DIALEKT on the other hand presents a collection of regional dialects from the 1960s-1980s. The DIALEKT corpus includes dialects, some of which are even extinct now. The DIALEKT monologues are all by people who have always lived in rural areas and are all natives to their regions. One can argue that DIALEKT also considers generational difference, as the birth years of speakers range from the end of 19th century to the start of 20th century, although may not be to the extent of ORTOFON in some cases. Another feature of DIALEKT worth mentioning is that it allows users to search for dialect features captured with regards to all levels of linguistic analysis.

Both corpora utilize ELAN linguistic transcription software (Sloetjes and Wittenburg, 2008), going through annotation in two tiers. For ORTOFON, the first layer is close to Czech orthography while the second adapts phonetic transcription. The latter enables collecting features such as stress groups, vowel reductions and cliticization which might have been lost otherwise. For DIALEKT, the first layer is dialectological, and the second

[4] cf. 2024 edition https://sites.google.com/view/vardial-2024/home, accessed on 11.03.2024.

Languages	Tasks	Datasets
Czech	Corpus Construction (Kopřivová et al., 2014; Komrskova et al., 2017)	ORTOFON, DIALEKT
Italian	Geolocation Prediction (Ramponi and Casula, 2023)	DIATOPIT
Portuguese	Language Distance Estimation (Pichel Campos et al., 2018)	DiaPT
Portuguese	Century Classification (Zampieri et al., 2016)	Colonia
Swiss German	Modeling of Dialectal Variant Transition (Jeszenszky et al., 2018)	SADS
Swiss German	Predicting Which Regions Use Which Dialectal Variants (Jeszenszky et al., 2019)	SADS
German	Investigating Diachronic Changes in Dialects (Dipper and Waldenberger, 2017)	Anselm
German	Investigating Graphemic Variation in Dialects (Waldenberger et al., 2021)	ReM
English, French	Semantic Change Detection (Montariol and Allauzen, 2021)	Le Monde, NY Times[5]

Table 1: An overview of the presented papers in Section 3.

is the ortographic one same as ORTOFON. In this case, the dialectological layer allows distinguishing speech sounds which are special to non-standard varieties of Czech via the use of a set of symbols. These qualities make the corpora later presented by Komrskova et al. (2017) worth of note.

3.2 Italian

Recently, Ramponi and Casula (2023) present DIATOPIT, a corpus built by analyzing Twitter posts of non-Standard Italian use. They use Twitter APIs to locate non-standard use of language across Italian borders. Moreover, they collect data that comes from accurate coordinates throughout two years to ensure no occasional visitors will disturb the data. They also consider a variety of "out of vocabulary" (OOV) tokens that they use to deduct which of the Twitter posts collected may be from a regional language user. OOV tokens contain tokens which may not be special tokens (i.e. hashtag) and also may not exist in the Aspel dictionary for Italian, but do not include common interjections, elongated words, slangs, wrong diacritics or foreign language tokens, as well as named entity tokens. In doing so, the coordinates from Twitter API and the OOV tokens can be matched to create a map of data by the administrative region.

They also include experiments for evaluating the DIATOPIT's representativeness of real varieties of Italian, which is shown to yield satisfying results in their metrics. While they list a variety of goals for their corpus, what we can say truthfully is that the main contribution is to enable a starting point for those interested in applying NLP methods to research varieties of dialects spoken within Italy. It also serves as first example focusing Italian diatopic variation.

3.3 Portuguese

A different approach works with historical Portuguese to identify different time periods within the historical evolution of a language. Pichel Campos et al. (2018) use a perplexity based measure for this task. Perplexity is a metric indicating how well a system fits a text sample, with a lower score being the better score. It is commonly used as a measure to evaluate the quality of a system, Pichel Campos et al. (2018) note that this is the first attempt utilizing perplexity to calculate diachronic language distance between different periods of historical Portuguese. Their corpus includes six time periods of European Portuguese ranging from the 12th century to the 20th century. They collect their data from various open historical text repositories and historical corpora, and keep the original spelling whenever possible. The perplexity-based approach is noted to successfully identify three main periods for European Portuguese, and should be applicable with other languages as well.

There is another study that works with Portuguese: Zampieri et al. (2016) build upon the Colonia corpus that is an already existing historical Portuguese corpus with texts from the 16th century to the early 20th century. Additionally, they include Part-of-Speech tags for the corpus.

3.4 Swiss German

An interesting approach of modeling transition areas between different dialectal variants using logistic functions is proposed by Jeszenszky et al. (2018): The idea is to model geographic areas,

[5]These corpora are not listed in Table 2, as they are not described in detail.

where one dialectal variant transitions into another, i.e. where language change is taking place. They base their analyses on the SADS dataset (Glaser and Bart, 2015), a linguistic survey with questions on different dialectal phenomena in Swiss German which provides detailed geolocations. Even though the method is very elaborate on a geo-linguistic level, a major drawback is that it can only model the transition of two variants, whereas in real-world scenarios, variation patterns are much more complex and numerous variants are assumed to coexist and influence one another. In a subsequent study on the same dataset, the authors focused further on the temporal aspect (Jeszenszky et al., 2019), and also took the age of respondents into account, an approach similar to Kopřivová et al. (2014). With the sociolinguistic diasystem of language variation, these studies model not only two, but three dimensions: diachronic, diatopic, and diastratic by taking the social variable of age into account.

3.5 German

There are two noteworthy diachronic-diatopic studies on historical corpora of German: Dipper and Waldenberger (2017) examine language change across dialects on a graphemic level. They use aligned equivalent word forms (i.e. word forms that have the same normalization to Standard German) from different German regions to derive rewrite rules with insertions, replacements and identity and create mappings based on weighted Levenshtein Distances. The results show differences across linguistic levels including morphology, phonology and graphemics. The results align with findings from historical linguistics on specific phenomena, such as the High German consonant shift. A follow-up work by (Waldenberger et al., 2021) uses a different dataset, Reference Corpus of Middle High German (Referenzkorpus Mittelhochdeutsch, ReM) (Petran et al., 2016), and generate difference profiles based on weighted Levenshtein distance. The work includes word boundaries as well which allows for capturing further linguistic phenomena. The created mappings from one historical and dialectal variety to another are then compared on a graphemic and graphophonemic level. On a broader level, they conduct further statistical analyses by comparing the intersection of shared mappings between texts in a diatopic subcorpus, and find that this measure indeed reflects the similarity of neighboring dialects.

3.6 English and French

An example of using diachronic word embeddings to model semantic change in the English and French languages is the work by Montariol and Allauzen (2021). Although this work does not work with dialectal data, we still decided to include it, as the approach is interesting and could be applied to (non-continuous) dialect data, e.g. Standard German and Swiss German. Since the datasets are not described in detail, we decided to not include them in Table 2. Overall, the work proposes learning word embeddings from a synthetic corpus with the CBOW (continuous bag-of-words) approach and M-BERT (Devlin et al., 2019), and experiments with different training and aggregation techniques. Computing the divergence of word senses in the two languages, they analyze different language change patterns such as stability in both languages, drift in the same direction, and divergence in word senses with culture-specific contexts. Cathcart and Wandl (2020) propose a related approach experimenting with word embeddings to model phonological change in related varieties of historical Slavic languages in a continuous and discrete way. These approaches are quite interesting and could be applicable to dialect data as well, given the availability of a large amount of training data for dialect embeddings and an evaluation corpus that includes sense and phonetic information.

3.7 Data Characteristics

Data Sources. Different text sources have been used for collecting diatopic datasets: While some approaches work with social media data from Twitter (Dunn and Wong, 2022; Ramponi and Casula, 2023), historical corpora mainly contain religious text or official documents (Dipper and Waldenberger, 2017; Waldenberger et al., 2021) and are usually not suited for a geographical analysis on a fine-grained level. The approaches working on Swiss German (Jeszenszky et al., 2018, 2019) do not base their analyses on natural language data, but on a linguistic multiple-choice survey, the Syntactic Atlas of German-speaking Switzerland (SADS). This kind of data can still be very useful, as it provides direct information about specific language phenomena paired with a very fine-grained, reliable geolocation.

Modality. Most of the corpora rely on written language, only Kopřivová et al. (2014) create two spoken language corpora. From a linguistic point

Languages	Datasets	Tokens	Source/Register	Time Span	Modality
Czech	ORTOFON (Komrskova et al., 2017)	1.24 M	dialogue	2012-2017	spoken
Czech	DIALEKT (Komrskova et al., 2017)	126,131	monologue	1960s-1980s	spoken
Italian	DIATOPIT (Ramponi and Casula, 2023)	388,069	Twitter	2020-2022	written
Portuguese	DiaPT (Pichel Campos et al., 2018)	-	historical text	1100-2000	written
Portuguese	Colonia (Zampieri and Becker, 2013)	5.1 M	media, historical text	1500-2000	written
Swiss German	SADS (Glaser and Bart, 2015)	-	linguistic survey	2000-2002	written
German	Anselm (Dipper and Schultz-Balluff, 2013)	30,000	religious text	1350-1600	written
German	ReM (Petran et al., 2016)	2.5 M	historical text	1050-1350	written
German	ZDL-Reg. (Nolda et al., 2021)	11.78 B	regional newspaper	1993-2024	written

Table 2: An overview of the dialect-related datasets discussed in Section 3. ZDL-Reg. is dynamically enlarged; the number of tokens is taken from `https://www.dwds.de/d/korpora/regional`, accessed on 05.03.2024. SADS does not contain natural language data, but 118 multiple-choice questions about 54 (morpho-)syntactic phenomena. Additionally, we include another corpus of regional newspaper data in German, the ZDL-Regionalkorpus (Nolda et al., 2021, 2023)—which has not been explored for diachronic-diatopic studies yet.

of view, this is very effective, since variation usually is much stronger in spoken compared to written language, as most dialects do not deviate markedly from Standard languages in the written modality.

Time Span. The diachronic spans of the datasets also vary strongly: While some historical corpora cover very long periods of time, e.g. the Diachronic Portuguese Corpus (DiaPT) (Pichel Campos et al., 2018) spans almost one millennium, social media-based corpora like DIATOPIT or linguistic survey data like SADS only span two years.

Data Imbalance. It must be noted that the Colonia corpus used by Zampieri et al. (2016) does not contain the same amount of text from each period it covers. For instance, there are 38 documents available from the 19th century, while there are only 13 available from the 16th century. Due to this, Zampieri et al. (2016) generate artificial texts with around 330 tokens for their train and test sets in order to conduct their main experiments.

4 Experiments

Experimental setups and results of the presented studies are difficult to compare, as the tasks and datasets presented in Section 3 are very different. Some of the papers focus on corpus construction (Kopřivová et al., 2014) or qualitative analysis (Dipper and Waldenberger, 2017), while some present quantitative results in the tasks of measuring language distance, predicting geolocation or dialect variant usage, will briefly be compared here.

Czech. Since Kopřivová et al. (2014) aims to build/present corpora, there are no experiments to mention. But one can argue that when ORTOFON and DIALEKT are used interconnectedly, they will present a good outlook on diachronic and diatopic variation in Czech. The work by Kopřivová et al. (2014) is to set apart with their detailed annotation system separated with several parallel layers to accommodate speakers individually. In the follow-up work by Komrskova et al. (2017), the advantages are evident thanks to the use of this multi-tier transcription.

Italian. Ramponi and Casula (2023) evaluate geolocation predictions on two levels: coarse-grained geolocation (CG, i.e. region classification), and fine-grained geolocation (FG, double-regression i.e. for latitude/longitude coordinates). They measure the accuracy of the prediction results in the macro-averaged Precision, Recall, and F1 score. Baseline models are mostly built upon BERT (Devlin et al., 2019). Both monolingual (Italian-only) and multilingual models are investigated, including AlBERTo (Polignano et al., 2019), UmBERTo (Parisi et al., 2020) and mBERT (Devlin et al., 2019), XLM-R (Conneau et al., 2020). Additionally, for CG they use Logistic Regression (LR) and SVM classifiers, and for FG they use a centroid baseline and a regression model based on k-nearest neighbors alongside a decision tree regressor. Results averaged across five runs with random seeds for shuffling the data and initializing model parameters are presented. For CG, AlBERTo achieves best results, and LR performs the worst. SVM proves to be competitive for the task. In FG's case, AlBERTo achieves the best scores again. Interestingly, the decision tree performs competitively despite being a much more cost-efficient system.

Portuguese. Pichel Campos et al. (2018) aims to compare six time periods of historical European Portuguese. They implement a perplexity-based language distance (PLD) measure with 7-gram models alongside a linear interpolation based smoothing technique. They conduct experiments on two levels: PLD with original spelling, and PLD with transcribed spelling. For the first instance, they compute PLD for each possible train-test pair. For the latter instance, they adjust the Diachronic Portuguese Corpus to have all periods share the same spelling. This is achieved by transliterating all historical periods into Latin scripts and then normalizing it with a generic orthography similar to phonological style. The resulting encoding of spelling normalization consists of 34 symbols, including 10 vowels and 24 consonants.

Overall, the results in both experiments observe a similar pattern. It is shown that language distances between different time periods are correlated with chronology. Moreover, there is not a huge divergence within the different periods investigated. The longest difference between periods scores roughly 6.19 with original spelling and 5.92 with transcribed spelling, which is still lower than the distance between closely related languages, such as Spanish-Portuguese's score of 7.74. The results suggest that, at least for the case of Brasilian-Portuguese, the language has remained similar over time.

For the other study that works with Portuguese, Zampieri et al. (2016) conduct experiments in three steps. They first have a preliminary session where they test a small sample with 87 documents from their corpus. They train SVM alongside Multinominal Naive Bayes (MNB) to predict which century a text belongs to, using both words and Part-of-Speech (POS) tags.

Secondly, they start their main experiments where they use 1500 artificially generated documents, and use the SVM classifier to execute predictions. They observe a performance increase due to the implementation of POS tags or words represented as uni-, bi-, and trigrams. Results show that POS trigrams yield the 90.7% accuracy when tested with century classification of the presented documents. Zampieri et al. (2016) note that this emphasises the existence of difference in structural properties in each time span by an important level; this means changes in structural properties take place at both the word level and beyond, and these changes can be captured through uni-, bi-, and trigrams.

Lastly, they conduct experiments across a smaller time span of 50 years. Their findings show that many time periods exhibit high similarity in grammatical structure. This presents a challenge for century classification of documents. It is noted that POS tags perform the best with trigrams.

Swiss German. Jeszenszky et al. (2018) conceptionalize transitions between dialectal variant areas via logistic regression and intensity maps in an attempt to present spatial distribution of syntactic variants in Swiss. The results show gradual and sharp transitions between variants alongside distinct spatial patterns. Subdivision analyses further elucidated the characteristics of dominance zones and transition areas. Overall, the findings shed light on the spatial distribution and dynamics of linguistic features. A drawback of the methodology is that only 40% of the variables in the SADS dataset (Glaser and Bart, 2015) can be modeled. An important take-away is that the transition of dialectal variants is a highly complex phenomenon, which cannot be fully modeled by only taking the spatial dimension into account.

Jeszenszky et al. (2019) use logistic regression on a global level to model the association of linguistic variation and age with 10-fold cross-validation. The AUC scores (area under the curve) reveal that for more than half of the variants considered, age is not a significant predictor. On a local level, they classify whether a specific linguistic variant is used at a survey site given the respondent age. The survey site is chosen from the k-nearest neighbors based on Euclidean distance, k ranging from 5 to 50. They conclude that the significance of age as predictor variable is correlated with space: When a specific age group within a region is significant, the prediction of which dialect that region speaks is more accurate. However, the prediction becomes less accurate when a region associates with multiple age groups. They attribute this finding to a sociolinguistic fact that lexicon in dialects is more prone to change with respect to speaker age than syntax.

German. Dipper and Waldenberger (2017) and Waldenberger et al. (2021) combine quantitative with an in-depth qualitative analysis. Both do not experiment with complex methods, but conduct a simple frequency-based, statistical analysis. Dipper and Waldenberger (2017) find quantitative proof for morphological, phonological, and graphemic phenomena by deriving replacement rules. They show insightful results into nuances of linguistic change across different regions and periods from a historical linguistic perspective: finding quantitative prove for theories like the High German consonant shift. The second study by Waldenberger et al. (2021) employs slightly more elaborate statistical measures to quantify differences between texts and subcorpora. The results confirm the diatopic and diachronic variation: By analyzing Levenshtein mappings and computing similarity scores, the study demonstrated that texts from closely related dialects exhibited higher similarity scores compared to those from more distant regions. Overall, Upper German texts are found to be more similar to each other than Middle German texts.

English and French. Montariol and Allauzen (2021) experiment with two kinds of embeddings, continuous bag-of-words (CBOW) and BERT (Devlin et al., 2019), to detect whether meaning changes of a word and its translation in English and French are consistent or divergent over time. They show a trade-off between performance and efficiency: While BERT with k-means clustering achieves the best performance, the CBOW model with incremental training is computationally the most efficient and offers very competitive results.

Their findings are summarized as follows: Semantic meanings drifting in the same direction across languages mainly occurs with words related to technology and society. On the other hand, meanings diverging in different directions implies that the meaning of a word might remain unchanged over time in one language, but drift in the other. This is mostly seen for words related to culture-specific concepts or controversial topics. It would be interesting to apply this approach not only to related languages, but to an actual dialect continuum to investigate whether these findings are confirmed in closer related language varieties as well.

5 Discussion

Almost all languages in the world have distinct dialects varying by location that change quickly due to complex factors related to contact. Taking these two dimensions of language variation, diachronic and diatopic, into account can improve the diversity and representativeness of languages covered in this field , and benefit the communities of non-standard language users. Our research shows that the intersection of diachronic and diatopic variation is an under-studied topic in dialect NLP. Although there are some approaches experimenting with diachronic word embeddings on a multilingual level (Montariol and Allauzen, 2021), there is currently a lack of state-of-the-art machine learning and NLP approaches.

This is a challenging topic to work with, considering its interdisciplinary nature combining historical linguistics, dialectology, machine learning and NLP. Perhaps this is a factor contributing to the status of deep learning based NLP methods having not yet been applied to studying language change in dialect continua.

5.1 Open Challenges

Do language variants and dialects change over time? While Pichel Campos et al. (2018) show that the difference in perplexity-based language distances between different time periods of European Portuguese is not substantial, Zampieri et al. (2016) suggest that grammatical structure can be substantially different in some time periods of Portuguese; however, their study was conducted on artificial documents. This means that either perplexity-based language distance fails to capture the differences in grammatical structures of different time periods, or such differences are not present in the real-world historical Portuguese documents investigated. We leave this question to future work.

Is the construction of dialect-related datasets reliable? The reliability of Ramponi and Casula (2023) is also worth mentioning: They rely on the belief that the locals may write things that deviate from Standard Italian just because they speak it so, but they also rely on Twitter language identifiers to deduct whether a tweet is in Italian or not. This, of course, is a double-edged sword and may cut back on data reliability. If their assumption is correct, in extreme cases some societies whose language use deviate from the standard may remain completely under-represented and their twitters might be misclassified as Standard Italian. However, if it is incorrect (i.e., the language use of the locals follows the standard), the tweets written by the locals and those in standard Italian become indistinguishable. Considering their access to speakers of regional Italian varieties (curators), Kopřivová et al. (2014) set a good example they could follow to ensure more varieties are correctly represented. However, one can argue that if someone was to use VPN for any reason, the coordinates would also be set for the entire time of use. Thus, Twitter APIs may not provide completely accurate data either, though this may be minimal to consider in most cases.

Are speaker characteristics important? Additionally, although Kopřivová et al. (2014) show that tracking the number of generations present in a conversation is beneficial for building speaker-characters, Jeszenszky et al. (2019) suggest that age is not a definitive for prediction. This means the usefulness of age information is quite task-dependent. An interesting follow-up work would be to incorporate other speaker characteristics, such as gender and education, into the analysis.

Limited coverage of dialects. There are numerous dialects spoken in the world. For instance, English alone has approximately 160 dialects (Aeni et al., 2021). However, only a small number of dialects have been researched in the NLP and machine learning communities. Future work could establish a data center to manage and update world-existing dialect corpora. Indeed, many corpora are publicly available but are little explored. For instance, the German regional newspaper corpus ZDL-Regionalkorpus (Nolda et al., 2021) has not been used for diachronic analysis so far, despite its size of more than 11 B tokens covering a time span 1993-2024 with regular updates which could enable use for data-intensive machine learning and word embedding approaches.

Ethical considerations in the collection of dialectal data. Although the data collection methods of Kopřivová et al. (2014) promise to provide near authentic results, no ethical issues are mentioned. As the conversations are recorded without the knowledge of the participants to ensure natural quality, it would not have been possible to get individual consent from the participants, although the person recording may have agreed otherwise. This, therefore, shows risk of privacy breach, and may not be an acceptable approach in a lot of data collection cases. Whether this would be acceptable if the speakers are informed after the data is collected may still be questionable to some people's discretion, however, this doesn't change the fact that despite being a breach, Kopřivová et al. (2014)'s approach does provide data as close to real-life situations as possible. This is of value in itself.

6 Conclusion

While there is a rising interest in modeling diachronic and diatopic variation in the NLP community, the intersection of both, i.e. language change in dialect continua, remains an under-studied topic. Even though findings from linguistics and sociolinguistics stress the importance of the diatopic dimension when modeling language change, the topic has not yet received as much attention in computational linguistics and not many methodological advancements have been made. Our work has been a first step in closing this research gap, and we hope to give inspiration to future research.

Acknowledgements

We thank the anonymous reviewers for their thoughtful feedback that greatly improved the texts.

References

Nur Aeni, Like Raskova Octaberlina, Nenni Dwi Aprianti Lubis, et al. 2021. A literature review of english language variation on sociolinguistics.

Timothy Baldwin. 2018. Language and the shifting sands of domain, space and time (invited talk). In *Proceedings of the Fifth Workshop on NLP for Similar Languages, Varieties and Dialects (VarDial 2018)*, page 76, Santa Fe, New Mexico, USA. Association for Computational Linguistics.

Kate Beeching. 2006. Synchronic and diachronic variation: the how and why of sociolinguistic corpora. In *Corpus linguistics around the world*, pages 49–61. Brill.

Sidsel Boldsen and Patrizia Paggio. 2022. Letters from the past: Modeling historical sound change through diachronic character embeddings. In *Proceedings of the 60th Annual Meeting of the Association for Computational Linguistics (Volume 1: Long Papers)*, pages 6713–6722, Dublin, Ireland. Association for Computational Linguistics.

Chundra Cathcart and Florian Wandl. 2020. In search of isoglosses: continuous and discrete language embeddings in Slavic historical phonology. In *Proceedings of the 17th SIGMORPHON Workshop on Computational Research in Phonetics, Phonology, and Morphology*, pages 233–244, Online. Association for Computational Linguistics.

Yanran Chen, Wei Zhao, Anne Breitbarth, Manuel Stoeckel, Alexander Mehler, and Steffen Eger. 2024. Syntactic language change in english and german: Metrics, parsers, and convergences. *arXiv preprint arXiv:2402.11549*.

Alexis Conneau, Kartikay Khandelwal, Naman Goyal, Vishrav Chaudhary, Guillaume Wenzek, Francisco Guzmán, Edouard Grave, Myle Ott, Luke Zettlemoyer, and Veselin Stoyanov. 2020. Unsupervised cross-lingual representation learning at scale. In *Proceedings of the 58th Annual Meeting of the Association for Computational Linguistics*, pages 8440–8451, Online. Association for Computational Linguistics.

Jacob Devlin, Ming-Wei Chang, Kenton Lee, and Kristina Toutanova. 2019. BERT: Pre-training of deep bidirectional transformers for language understanding. In *Proceedings of the 2019 Conference of the North American Chapter of the Association for Computational Linguistics: Human Language Technologies, Volume 1 (Long and Short Papers)*, pages 4171–4186, Minneapolis, Minnesota. Association for Computational Linguistics.

Stefanie Dipper and Simone Schultz-Balluff. 2013. The anselm corpus: Methods and perspectives of a parallel aligned corpus. In *Proceedings of the workshop on computational historical linguistics at NODALIDA*, pages 27–42.

Stefanie Dipper and Sandra Waldenberger. 2017. Investigating diatopic variation in a historical corpus. In *Proceedings of the Fourth Workshop on NLP for Similar Languages, Varieties and Dialects (VarDial)*, pages 36–45, Valencia, Spain. Association for Computational Linguistics.

Jonathan Dunn and Sidney Wong. 2022. Stability of syntactic dialect classification over space and time. In *Proceedings of the 29th International Conference on Computational Linguistics*, pages 26–36, Gyeongju, Republic of Korea. International Committee on Computational Linguistics.

Jacob Eisenstein, Brendan O'Connor, Noah A. Smith, and Eric P. Xing. 2014. Diffusion of lexical change in social media. *PLOS ONE*, 9(11):1–13.

Fahim Faisal, Orevaoghene Ahia, Aarohi Srivastava, Kabir Ahuja, David Chiang, Yulia Tsvetkov, and Antonios Anastasopoulos. 2024. Dialectbench: A nlp benchmark for dialects, varieties, and closely-related languages. *Preprint*, arXiv:2403.11009.

Elvira Glaser and Gabriela Bart. 2015. *4. Dialektsyntax des Schweizerdeutschen*, pages 81–108. De Gruyter, Berlin, München, Boston.

Siqi He and Wei Zhao. 2024. Exploring sound change over time: A review of computational and human perception. In *Proceedings of the 5th Workshop on Computational Approaches to Historical Language Change*, Bangkok. Association for Computational Linguistics.

Péter Jeszenszky, Panote Siriaraya, Philipp Stoeckle, and Adam Jatowt. 2019. Spatio-temporal prediction of dialectal variant usage. In *Proceedings of the 1st International Workshop on Computational Approaches to Historical Language Change*, pages 186–195, Florence, Italy. Association for Computational Linguistics.

Péter Jeszenszky, Philipp Stoeckle, Elvira Glaser, and Robert Weibel. 2018. A gradient perspective on modeling interdialectal transitions. *Journal of Linguistic Geography*, 6(2):78–99.

Aditya Joshi, Raj Dabre, Diptesh Kanojia, Zhuang Li, Haolan Zhan, Gholamreza Haffari, and Doris Dippold. 2024. Natural language processing for dialects of a language: A survey. *Preprint*, arXiv:2401.05632.

Zuzana Komrskova, Marie Kopřivova, David Lukeš, Petra Poukarová, and Hana Goláňová. 2017. New spoken corpora of czech: Ortofon and dialekt. *Journal of Linguistics/Jazykovedný casopis*, 68.

Marie Kopřivová, Hana Goláňová, Petra Klimešová, and David Lukeš. 2014. Mapping diatopic and diachronic variation in spoken Czech: The ORTOFON and DIALEKT corpora. In *Proceedings of the Ninth International Conference on Language Resources and Evaluation (LREC'14)*, pages 376–382, Reykjavik, Iceland. European Language Resources Association (ELRA).

Andrey Kutuzov, Lilja Øvrelid, Terrence Szymanski, and Erik Velldal. 2018. Diachronic word embeddings and semantic shifts: a survey. In *Proceedings of the 27th International Conference on Computational Linguistics*, pages 1384–1397, Santa Fe, New Mexico, USA. Association for Computational Linguistics.

Xianghe Ma, Dominik Schlechtweg, and Wei Zhao. 2024a. Presence or absence: Are unknown word usages in dictionaries? In *Proceedings of the 5th Workshop on Computational Approaches to Historical Language Change*, Bangkok. Association for Computational Linguistics.

Xianghe Ma, Michael Strube, and Wei Zhao. 2024b. Graph-based clustering for detecting semantic change across time and languages. In *Proceedings of the 18th Conference of the European Chapter of the Association for Computational Linguistics (Volume 1: Long Papers)*, pages 1542–1561, St. Julian's, Malta. Association for Computational Linguistics.

Stefano Montanelli and Francesco Periti. 2023. A survey on contextualised semantic shift detection. *Preprint*, arXiv:2304.01666.

Syrielle Montariol and Alexandre Allauzen. 2021. Measure and evaluation of semantic divergence across two languages. In *Proceedings of the 59th Annual Meeting of the Association for Computational Linguistics and the 11th International Joint Conference on Natural Language Processing (Volume 1: Long Papers)*, pages 1247–1258, Online. Association for Computational Linguistics.

Andreas Nolda, Adrien Barbaresi, and Alexander Geyken. 2021. Das ZDL-Regionalkorpus: Ein Korpus für die lexikografische Beschreibung der diatopischen Variation im Standarddeutschen. Deutsch in Europa. Sprachpolitisch, grammatisch, methodisch, pages 317 – 321. de Gruyter, Berlin [u.a.].

Andreas Nolda, Adrien Barbaresi, and Alexander Geyken. 2023. Korpora für die lexikographische Beschreibung diatopischer Variation in der deutschen Standardsprache. Das ZDL-Regionalkorpus und das Webmonitor-Korpus. Korpora in der germanistischen Sprachwissenschaft. Mündlich, schriftlich, multimedial, pages 29 – 52. de Gruyter, Berlin/Boston.

Loreto Parisi, Simone Francia, and Paolo Magnani. 2020. Umberto: an italian language model trained with whole word masking. https://github.com/musixmatchresearch/umberto.

Florian Petran, Marcel Bollmann, Stefanie Dipper, and Thomas Klein. 2016. Rem: A reference corpus of middle high german – corpus compilation, annotation, and access. *Journal for Language Technology and Computational Linguistics*, 31(2):1–15.

Jose Ramom Pichel Campos, Pablo Gamallo, and Iñaki Alegria. 2018. Measuring language distance among historical varieties using perplexity. application to European Portuguese. In *Proceedings of the Fifth Workshop on NLP for Similar Languages, Varieties and Dialects (VarDial 2018)*, pages 145–155, Santa Fe, New Mexico, USA. Association for Computational Linguistics.

Marco Polignano, Pierpaolo Basile, Marco De Gemmis, Giovanni Semeraro, Valerio Basile, et al. 2019. Alberto: Italian bert language understanding model for nlp challenging tasks based on tweets. In *CEUR workshop proceedings*, volume 2481, pages 1–6. CEUR.

Alan Ramponi and Camilla Casula. 2023. DiatopIt: A corpus of social media posts for the study of diatopic language variation in Italy. In *Tenth Workshop on NLP for Similar Languages, Varieties and Dialects (VarDial 2023)*, pages 187–199, Dubrovnik, Croatia. Association for Computational Linguistics.

Han Sloetjes and Peter Wittenburg. 2008. Annotation by category-elan and iso dcr. In *6th international Conference on Language Resources and Evaluation (LREC 2008)*.

Anders Søgaard, Sebastian Ebert, Jasmijn Bastings, and Katja Filippova. 2021. We need to talk about random splits. In *Proceedings of the 16th Conference of the European Chapter of the Association for Computational Linguistics: Main Volume*, pages 1823–1832, Online. Association for Computational Linguistics.

Maria Sukhareva and Christian Chiarcos. 2014. Diachronic proximity vs. data sparsity in cross-lingual parser projection. a case study on Germanic. In *Proceedings of the First Workshop on Applying NLP Tools to Similar Languages, Varieties and Dialects*, pages 11–20, Dublin, Ireland. Association for Computational Linguistics and Dublin City University.

Chahan Vidal-Gorène, Victoria Khurshudyan, and Anaïd Donabédian-Demopoulos. 2020. Recycling and comparing morphological annotation models for Armenian diachronic-variational corpus processing. In *Proceedings of the 7th Workshop on NLP for Similar Languages, Varieties and Dialects*, pages 90–101, Barcelona, Spain (Online). International Committee on Computational Linguistics (ICCL).

Sandra Waldenberger, Stefanie Dipper, and Ilka Lemke. 2021. Towards a broad-coverage graphemic analysis of large historical corpora. *Zeitschrift für Sprachwissenschaft*, 40(3):401–420.

Walt Wolfram and Natalie Schilling-Estes. 2017. *Dialectology and Linguistic Diffusion*, chapter 24. John Wiley & Sons, Ltd.

Marcos Zampieri and Martin Becker. 2013. Colonia: Corpus of historical portuguese. *ZSM Studien*, 5:69–76.

Marcos Zampieri, Shervin Malmasi, and Mark Dras. 2016. Modeling language change in historical corpora: The case of Portuguese. In *Proceedings of the Tenth International Conference on Language Resources and Evaluation (LREC'16)*, pages 4098–4104, Portorož, Slovenia. European Language Resources Association (ELRA).

Marcos Zampieri, Preslav Nakov, and Yves Scherrer. 2020. Natural language processing for similar languages, varieties, and dialects: A survey. *Natural Language Engineering*, 26(6):595–612.

Similarity-Based Cluster Merging for Semantic Change Modeling

Christopher Brückner[1] and **Leixin Zhang**[2] and **Pavel Pecina**[1]
[1]Charles University, Faculty of Mathematics and Physics
{bruckner,pecina}@ufal.mff.cuni.cz
[2]University of Twente
l.zhang-5@utwente.nl

Abstract

This paper describes our contribution to Subtask 1 of the AXOLOTL-24 Shared Task on unsupervised lexical semantic change modeling. In a joint task of word sense disambiguation and word sense induction on diachronic corpora, we significantly outperform the baseline by merging clusters of modern usage examples based on their similarities with the same historical word sense as well as their mutual similarities. We observe that multilingual sentence embeddings outperform language-specific ones in this task.

1 Introduction

Semantic change modeling is the task of computationally determining how the meanings of words change over time. This semantic shift can be observed in the change of contexts in which the words appear (Kutuzov et al., 2018).

Given a diachronic corpus of old and new word usage examples and an inventory of old word senses with their dictionary definitions, the modeling task can be split further into the disambiguation and the induction of word senses: New usage examples are aligned with old usage examples and sense definitions. If an appropriate old sense does not exist in the sense inventory and an alignment is thus impossible, a novel word sense is induced instead, indicating that the word gained a new meaning.

This joint task has been defined by Subtask 1 of the AXOLOTL-24 Shared Task (Fedorova et al., 2024), our contribution to which we describe in the following sections. Like the baseline proposed by the shared task organizers, we approach the challenge by measuring the similarity of modern usage example clusters and old sense definitions. We further explore impacts on the performance by merging clusters based on a similarity criterion and by ensembling different embedding models and different clusterings.

Our implementation is available on GitHub.[1]

2 Related Work

The idea of unsupervised clustering to discriminate word senses goes back at least to using Gaussian Mixture models on a synchronic corpus (Schütze, 1998). More recently, neural approaches have been applied to diachronic corpora to detect and quantify semantic change (Kutuzov et al., 2018).

SemEval-2020 Task 1 produced several approaches for lexical semantic change detection between two time-specific corpora (Schlechtweg et al., 2020). The task was split into the binary classification of whether words lost or gained senses, and the ranking of words according to their degree of change. These sub-tasks were solved, e.g., by clustering contextual word embeddings and comparing their cluster assignments (Karnysheva and Schwarz, 2020), or by measuring the average cosine distances between contextual embeddings of the same word (Kutuzov and Giulianelli, 2020). In contrast with AXOLOTL-24, this task considers whether an old word sense is still present in the new time period.

Another task more similar to AXOLOTL-24 was defined by the *Reverse Dictonary* track of SemEval-2022 Task 1 (Mickus et al., 2022): Given a dictionary consisting of words, their definitions, and definition embeddings, user-written definitions are to be mapped to the correct word by reconstructing the reference embedding. As these embeddings were pre-computed, submitted systems were limited to three specific models. While participating teams achieved reasonable average cosine similarities using token-level transformers, this was not evaluated as a classification task.

The Sentence-BERT architecture promises better performance than token-level transformers on sentence-level downstream tasks such as paraphras-

[1]https://github.com/chbridges/axolotl24

Proceedings of the 5th Workshop on Computational Approaches to Historical Language Change, pages 23–28
August 15, 2024 ©2024 Association for Computational Linguistics

ing and the measurement of sentence similarities (Reimers and Gurevych, 2019). While the original publication proposes a model for paraphrasing in over 50 languages based on MPNet (Song et al., 2020), the general-purpose LaBSE doubles the size of the language inventory and suggests current state-of-the-art performance in cross-lingual settings (Feng et al., 2022).

3 Datasets and Task Definition

The AXOLOTL-24 Shared Task provides training corpora in Finnish and Russian. The Finnish corpus covers the years 1543 to 1650 in its old time period and the years 1700 to 1750 in its new period, whereas the Russian corpus covers approximately the 19th century and the years after 1950. Both datasets consist of different target words with multiple word senses, and each sense comprises a sense ID, a definition, and a usage example. In the case of Russian, usage examples of old words are often noisy or missing.

The goal of Subtask 1 is to determine the correct sense IDs of word usage examples in the new period. Thus, the corresponding test datasets only contain sense IDs and definitions in the old period. Subtask 2, the generation of novel sense definitions, is out of the scope of this paper. In addition to the Finnish and Russian test datasets, a third, German test set based on the DWUG dataset (Schlechtweg, 2023) is provided to quantify the developed systems' multilingual performance.

Systems are evaluated with respect to word sense disambiguation and the joint task including the induction of novel word senses. System performance on the disambiguation task is measured with the macro F1 score of sense classifications only of sense IDs present in the old sense inventory. Additionally, the overall performance is measured with the adjusted Rand index, thus ignoring specific sense assignments but validating whether modern usage examples of old and novel word senses are correctly grouped together.

4 Methodology

In this section, we briefly summarize the baseline algorithm before describing our improvements.

4.1 Baseline

The general approach can be divided into two steps: the embedding of old word sense definitions and modern usage examples, and the alignment of the respective embeddings to assign word senses to the examples. These steps are computed target word by target word, i.e., no defined sense of a different word can leak into the assignment.

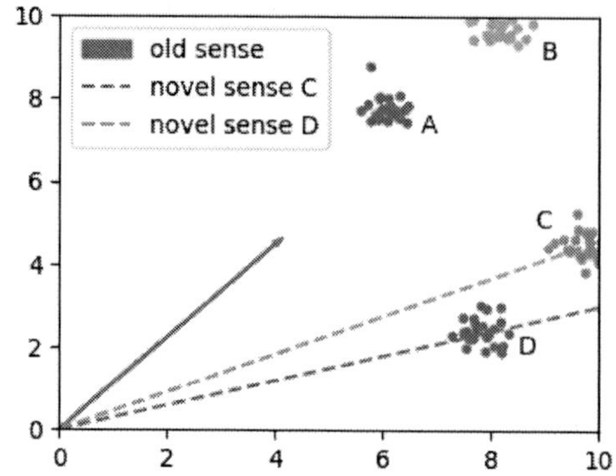

Figure 1: A conceptual cluster merging. Clusters A and B get merged, as the angles of their centers with the old sense vector are small. Novel senses are generated for clusters C and D. In the second pass, novel sense vectors are fitted through C and D, merging them if the angle between these vectors is sufficiently small.

In the first step, the sense definitions and usage examples from the old time period are concatenated. These concatenations and all usage examples from the new time period are then embedded in a shared vector space by a transformer model.

In the second step, the new usage examples are clustered. For each cluster C, an old word sense s_{old} is assigned to all corresponding usage examples if the cosine similarity $\cos(\mathbf{s}_{old}, \mathbf{c})$ between the old sense embedding $\mathbf{s}_{old}$ and a cluster embedding $\mathbf{c}$ is greater than a threshold $\tau \in [0, 1]$. If no old sense satisfies this condition, a new sense s_{novel} is assigned to all usage examples in the cluster.

This final step is solved in a greedy manner: Once an old sense is assigned to a cluster C_i, it is removed from a list of candidate senses S and cannot be assigned to any other cluster C_j, even if $\cos(\mathbf{s}_i, \mathbf{c}_j) > \cos(\mathbf{s}_i, \mathbf{c}_i)$. This poses a problem if word senses are split into multiple clusters.

The following subsections propose methods to alleviate this weakness of the baseline approach. The impact of each described method on the system performance is summarized in Section 5.

4.2 Cluster Merging

A straightforward technique to improve the alignment of old senses and new usage examples is to keep the set of candidate senses S fixed and assign

Model	Finnish ARI	Finnish F_1	Russian ARI	Russian F_1
Baseline	*0.022*	*0.222*	**0.098**	*0.274*
Merge-1	0.420	0.557	*0.052*	0.428
Merge-5	0.420	0.557	0.058	0.428
Merge-1c	**0.437**	**0.570**	0.071	0.447
Merge-5c	**0.437**	**0.570**	0.077	**0.449**

Table 1: Development scores at a fixed similarity threshold $\tau = 0.3$. Where Affinity Propagation is used, the model name indicates the number of ensembled clusterings and the usage of cosine similarity affinity. Highest scores are indicated in bold, lowest scores in italics.

Embedding	Finnish ARI	Finnish F_1	Russian ARI	Russian F_1
LEALLA-large	0.437	0.570	0.077	*0.449*
LaBSE	*0.277*	*0.462*	0.081	0.572
Finnish-Paraphrase	0.561	**0.676**	—	—
Sentence RuBERT	—	—	*0.056*	0.608
Multi-Paraphrase	0.554	0.661	0.118	**0.612**
Multi ⊕ LaBSE	**0.572**	0.669	**0.120**	0.603

Table 2: Development scores at a fixed similarity threshold $\tau = 0.3$ for different sentence embeddings, based on the best models in Table 1. Highest scores are indicated in bold, lowest scores in italics.

each cluster C to the sense with the greatest similarity, provided that the similarity is greater than the previously chosen threshold τ. The similarity is computed between the sense embedding $\mathbf{s}$ and the cluster mean $\bar{\mathbf{c}}$ to capture the overall semantics of C. Thus, the sense alignment step is defined as:

$$s_C = \begin{cases} \underset{s \in S}{\operatorname{argmax}} \cos(\mathbf{s}, \bar{\mathbf{c}}), & \cos(\cdot) \geq \tau \\ s_{novel}, & otherwise \end{cases} \quad (1)$$

As each old sense can now be mapped to multiple clusters, this alignment is equivalent to the merging of clusters when their similarities with the same old sense are sufficiently large. This reduces the granularity of old sense clusters. In a second pass, each novel sense cluster center is considered a novel sense embedding and novel sense clusters are merged by the same criterion based on pairwise cosine similarities. A conceptual such merging in two dimensions is depicted in Figure 1.

4.3 Two-Stage Ensembling

In addition to merging clusters with respect to the similarity with the same old sense, we propose two methods to ensemble results at different stages of the algorithm: The ensembling of embedding models and the ensembling of clusterings.

The ensembling of n models is straightforward and can be solved via the concatenation

$$\mathbf{e} = \mathbf{e}_1 \oplus \ldots \oplus \mathbf{e}_n \quad (2)$$

of each model output $\mathbf{e}_i$ which is then used as the input to the alignment step of the algorithm.

A crucial part of the alignment step is the clustering of modern usage examples. Some clustering algorithms such as K-means (Lloyd, 1982) and Affinity Propagation (Frey and Dueck, 2007) are initialized using a random seed r based on which they can converge to different local minima. We mitigate resulting errors by clustering the input embeddings multiple times using different random seeds r_i and selecting the final cluster assignments via a majority vote. Reproducibility is ensured by fixing the initial random seed r_0 and incrementing it for the subsequent clusterings, i.e., $r_i = r_0 + i$.

5 Results and Discussion

The AXOLOTL-24 baseline uses LEALLA-large (Mao and Nakagawa, 2023) in the embedding step, a lightweight language-agnostic sentence transformer distilled from LaBSE (Feng et al., 2022), and clusters these embeddings with Affinity Propagation (Frey and Dueck, 2007) using the negative Euclidean distance as the cluster affinity. We begin our study by comparing the baseline with our approach based on LaBSE embeddings on the Finnish and Russian development sets in Table 1. We generally prioritize the ARI since the F_1 score only quantifies the classification of old word senses. While the cluster merging significantly improves the ARI and F_1 score for Finnish, there is a slight trade-off between them in the Russian dataset where a greatly increased F_1 score comes at the cost of a decreased ARI. The ensembling of clusterings does not affect Finnish but leads to better results for Russian. The scores further increase when using the cosine similarity as the cluster affinity.

We further evaluate additional language-specific and language-agnostic sentence embeddings from the Hugging Face Hub in Table 2: a Finnish paraphrasing model[2] (Kanerva et al., 2021), Sentence RuBERT[3] (Kuratov and Arkhipov, 2019), and a multilingual paraphrasing model[4] (Reimers and Gurevych, 2019). Interestingly, we observe that multilingual models can outperform language-

[2]TurkuNLP/sbert-cased-finnish-paraphrase

[3]DeepPavlov/rubert-base-cased-sentence

[4]sentence-transformers/paraphrase-multilingual-mpnet-base-v2

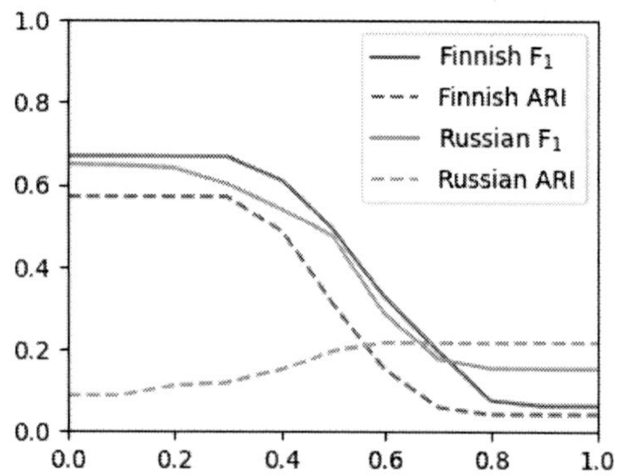

Figure 2: Threshold analysis on the development sets of both languages. ARI and F1 on the y-axis are mapped against different similarity thresholds τ on the x-axis.

specific ones, in particular, a concatenation of the multilingual paraphrasing model and LaBSE. Thus, we consider this embedding to generalize best and choose it for further experiments. We do not observe any improvement when concatenating a third model.

Next, we analyze how well the system performs for different similarity thresholds τ in Figure 2. It shows different behavior for the two datasets: Increasing τ leads to a decreasing F_1 in both languages but to a decreasing ARI for Finnish and an increasing ARI for Russian. This indicates that initial old sense clusters are too granular in both languages, whereas old and novel sense clusters are less discriminative in Russian as novel senses tend to get merged into old ones, reducing the overall clustering quality when the similarity threshold is set too small. Thus, increasing τ increases the proportion of granular novel sense clusters to coarse-grained old sense clusters. We find that the preset threshold $\tau = 0.3$ used by the baseline and our previous experiments is a reasonable choice, as the Finnish scores are stable up to this value. For Russian, a slightly higher threshold of $\tau = 0.4$ or $\tau = 0.5$ might be preferred to account for a greater ARI without sacrificing too much F_1. We choose τ for Finnish and Russian based on this graph but suggest cross-validation as a more robust method to choose the parameter for unseen data. For German, which has no development set, we select the same parameter as for Finnish since the different performance on Russian can possibly be attributed to its often noisy or missing word usage examples in the old period.

Finally, for further analysis, we skip the clustering step and assign a single most probable old sense to each target word. The result is surprising: While we achieve an ARI of merely 0.015 on Russian, we outperform our method on Finnish with an ARI of 0.614 and an F_1 score of 0.680. We attribute this anomaly to the quality of the dataset, as the numbers of senses per target word and usage examples per word sense are imbalanced, including several words with only one sense. However, this characteristic also reveals a weakness in our algorithm: Clusters are often aligned with an old sense in the first pass even though the word has no documented old sense. Possible improvements are a combination of both passes into one or the usage of two different similarity thresholds for old and novel senses.

ARI			
System	Finnish	Russian	German
Baseline	0.023	0.079	0.022
deep-change	0.638	0.059	0.543
Ours (old)	0.596	0.043	0.298
Ours (new)	0.578	0.130	0.298
F_1			
System	Finnish	Russian	German
Baseline	0.230	0.260	0.130
deep-change	0.756	0.750	0.745
Ours (old)	0.655	0.661	0.608
Ours (new)	0.655	0.563	0.608

Table 3: ARI and F_1 scores of the baseline, the winning team deep-change, our submission to the shared task, and our updated system on the three test datasets.

Our final results are summarized in Table 3. In our submission to the shared task, we tuned the similarity thresholds less carefully, used $\tau = 0.1$ for all three test sets, and did not cluster the Finnish dataset. The new system uses $\tau = 0.2$ for Finnish and German, and $\tau = 0.45$ for Russian. It does not affect our ranking on the leaderboards.

6 Conclusion

We presented a simple method to discriminate word senses on diachronic corpora by clustering usage examples and merging the resulting clusters if either their similarity with a known word sense or their mutual similarities are sufficiently large. It depends on a similarity threshold τ that can be tuned on annotated data. The resulting system performs best when embedding usage examples and word sense definitions with two different multilingual models and thus adapts well to different languages.

However, there is room for improvement. For the proposed algorithm, we suggest the usage of two different similarity thresholds for old and novel sense cluster merging. We further see a weakness in prioritizing the disambiguation of old word senses while solving the induction of novel word senses as a subsequent step.

We support the publication of a similar, better-normalized dataset for improved comparability between languages.

Limitations

The AXOLOTL-24 Shared Task takes a step from the pure quantification of semantic change to more interpretable results by assigning concrete word senses to groups of word usage examples and simultaneously identifying word usages with no recorded definition. The presented results do not go beyond the scope of this shared task. There may be limitations in the comparability between languages due to significant amounts of noise and imbalance in the provided dataset. Furthermore, the evaluation does not take the absence of recorded word senses in the new period into account and thus does not consider the full spectrum of semantic change observable in the data. These aspects should be investigated further in future research.

Acknowledgments

We thank the anonymous reviewers for their valuable feedback. This research was partially supported by SVV project number 260 698 and Horizon Europe grant agreement number 101061016.

References

Mariia Fedorova, Timothee Mickus, Niko Tapio Partanen, Janine Siewert, Elena Spaziani, and Andrey Kutuzov. 2024. AXOLOTL'24 shared task on multilingual explainable semantic change modeling. In *Proceedings of the 5th Workshop on Computational Approaches to Historical Language Change*, Bangkok. Association for Computational Linguistics.

Fangxiaoyu Feng, Yinfei Yang, Daniel Cer, Naveen Arivazhagan, and Wei Wang. 2022. Language-agnostic BERT sentence embedding. In *Proceedings of the 60th Annual Meeting of the Association for Computational Linguistics (Volume 1: Long Papers)*, pages 878–891, Dublin, Ireland. Association for Computational Linguistics.

Brendan J. Frey and Delbert Dueck. 2007. Clustering by passing messages between data points. *Science*, 315(5814):972–976.

Jenna Kanerva, Filip Ginter, Li-Hsin Chang, Iiro Rastas, Valtteri Skantsi, Jemina Kilpeläinen, Hanna-Mari Kupari, Jenna Saarni, Maija Sevón, and Otto Tarkka. 2021. Finnish paraphrase corpus. In *Proceedings of the 23rd Nordic Conference on Computational Linguistics (NoDaLiDa)*, pages 288–298, Reykjavik, Iceland (Online). Linköping University Electronic Press, Sweden.

Anna Karnysheva and Pia Schwarz. 2020. TUE at SemEval-2020 task 1: Detecting semantic change by clustering contextual word embeddings. In *Proceedings of the Fourteenth Workshop on Semantic Evaluation*, pages 232–238, Barcelona (online). International Committee for Computational Linguistics.

Yuri Kuratov and Mikhail Arkhipov. 2019. Adaptation of deep bidirectional multilingual transformers for russian language. *Preprint*, arXiv:1905.07213.

Andrey Kutuzov and Mario Giulianelli. 2020. UiO-UvA at SemEval-2020 task 1: Contextualised embeddings for lexical semantic change detection. In *Proceedings of the Fourteenth Workshop on Semantic Evaluation*, pages 126–134, Barcelona (online). International Committee for Computational Linguistics.

Andrey Kutuzov, Lilja Øvrelid, Terrence Szymanski, and Erik Velldal. 2018. Diachronic word embeddings and semantic shifts: a survey. In *Proceedings of the 27th International Conference on Computational Linguistics*, pages 1384–1397, Santa Fe, New Mexico, USA. Association for Computational Linguistics.

S. Lloyd. 1982. Least squares quantization in pcm. *IEEE Transactions on Information Theory*, 28(2):129–137.

Zhuoyuan Mao and Tetsuji Nakagawa. 2023. LEALLA: Learning lightweight language-agnostic sentence embeddings with knowledge distillation. In *Proceedings of the 17th Conference of the European Chapter of the Association for Computational Linguistics*, pages 1886–1894, Dubrovnik, Croatia. Association for Computational Linguistics.

Timothee Mickus, Kees Van Deemter, Mathieu Constant, and Denis Paperno. 2022. Semeval-2022 task 1: CODWOE – comparing dictionaries and word embeddings. In *Proceedings of the 16th International Workshop on Semantic Evaluation (SemEval-2022)*, pages 1–14, Seattle, United States. Association for Computational Linguistics.

Nils Reimers and Iryna Gurevych. 2019. Sentence-BERT: Sentence embeddings using Siamese BERT-networks. In *Proceedings of the 2019 Conference on Empirical Methods in Natural Language Processing and the 9th International Joint Conference on Natural Language Processing (EMNLP-IJCNLP)*, pages 3982–3992, Hong Kong, China. Association for Computational Linguistics.

Dominik Schlechtweg. 2023. *Human and Computational Measurement of Lexical Semantic Change*. Ph.D. thesis, University of Stuttgart, Stuttgart, Germany.

Dominik Schlechtweg, Barbara McGillivray, Simon Hengchen, Haim Dubossarsky, and Nina Tahmasebi. 2020. SemEval-2020 task 1: Unsupervised lexical semantic change detection. In *Proceedings of the Fourteenth Workshop on Semantic Evaluation*, pages 1–23, Barcelona (online). International Committee for Computational Linguistics.

Hinrich Schütze. 1998. Automatic word sense discrimination. *Computational Linguistics*, 24(1):97–123.

Kaitao Song, Xu Tan, Tao Qin, Jianfeng Lu, and Tie-Yan Liu. 2020. Mpnet: Masked and permuted pre-training for language understanding. In *Advances in Neural Information Processing Systems*, volume 33, pages 16857–16867. Curran Associates, Inc.

Historical Ink: Semantic Shift Detection for 19th Century Spanish

Tony Montes[1] **Laura Manrique-Gómez**[2] **Rubén Manrique**[1]
[1] Systems and Computing Engineering Department, Universidad de los Andes
[2] History and Geography Department, Universidad de los Andes
Bogotá D.C.
{t.montes, l.manriqueg, rf.manrique}@uniandes.edu.co

Abstract

This paper explores the evolution of word meanings in 19th-century Spanish texts, with an emphasis on Latin American Spanish, using computational linguistics techniques. It addresses the Semantic Shift Detection (SSD) task, which is crucial for understanding linguistic evolution, particularly in historical contexts. The study focuses on analyzing a set of Spanish target words. To achieve this, a 19th-century Spanish corpus is constructed, and a customizable pipeline for SSD tasks is developed. This pipeline helps find the senses of a word and measure their semantic change between two corpora using fine-tuned BERT-like models with old Spanish texts for both Latin American and general Spanish cases. The results provide valuable insights into the cultural and societal shifts reflected in language changes over time[1].

1 Introduction

The study of how word meanings evolve over time, influenced by social, historical, and political factors, is a fundamental pursuit within linguistics and natural language processing. This evolution poses challenges in detection and interpretation, often addressed through Semantic Shift Detection (SSD) task, also known as Lexical Semantic Change Detection task (LSCD) (Montanelli and Periti, 2023; Hu et al., 2021). Traditionally reliant on manual methods such as discourse analysis, recent computational linguistics advancements have revolutionized this field. These approaches streamline analysis and open doors to interdisciplinary research applications spanning sociology, history, and beyond, offering invaluable insights into cultural and societal shifts using digitized corpora.

In 2013, static word embeddings, also known as word vector representations, were first introduced by Mikolov et al. (2013) using the bag-of-words and skip-gram architectures. These embeddings represent words as static vectors that remain unchanged and are based on their surrounding words. Hamilton et al. (2016) first proposed using these embeddings for the SSD task by employing diachronic word2vec static embeddings to measure word meaning changes across consecutive decades. Various approaches have been explored to automate this task effectively. Montanelli and Periti (2023) proposed using contextual embeddings instead to capture multiple meanings assigned to the same word due to polysemy and homonymy, which static embeddings cannot achieve. This was accomplished by comparing multiple BERT-like Language Models (Devlin et al., 2018) such as XLM-RoBERTa.

In this paper, we focus on two things: crafting a 19th-century Spanish corpus (C_{old}) from sources spanning 1800 to 1914 and creating a customizable pipeline for assessing the SSD task. Utilizing this pipeline, we analyze the semantic changes of a set of target words, for both the global context and the specific Latin-American context. We explore a variety of known and novel solutions for the SSD task by comparing the 19th-century Spanish corpus with the Spanish portion of the "EUBookShop" corpus as the modern corpus (C_{new}) (Cañete, 2019)[2].

2 Related Work

Recent advances in Semantic Shift Detection have leveraged many computational approaches based on natural language processing techniques. Contextual embeddings, capable of capturing multiple-word usages and meanings, have been used in most of the state-of-the-art solutions, summarized by Montanelli and Periti (2023) who defines a classification framework based on three dimensions

[1]The pipeline and code can be found at https://github.com/historicalink/SSD-Old-Spanish

[2]This portion was taken from the large Spanish corpus available at https://huggingface.co/datasets/josecannete/large_spanish_corpus

Proceedings of the 5th Workshop on Computational Approaches to Historical Language Change, pages 29–41

of analysis: meaning representation (*form-* and *sense-oriented* approaches), time awareness (*time-oblivious* and *-aware*) and learning modality (*supervised* and *unsupervised*, referencing to the injection of external knowledge support like a dictionary), useful for *Contextualized Semantic Shif Detection*.

Martinc et al. (2020) and Giulianelli et al. (2020) explore transformer-based BERT models for detecting semantic change. Martinc et al. use contextualized embeddings to capture shifts in word usage over time, outperforming traditional techniques like Word2Vec and Glove by leveraging BERT's dynamic word representations. Giulianelli et al. (2020) adopt an unsupervised approach, obtaining and clustering word representations to measure change over time, aligning with human judgments. Both studies underscore the effectiveness of BERT-based models in identifying and analyzing diachronic linguistic changes.

Although most of the research in the field of semantic change has been done on a wide scope of languages, Spanish hasn't played such an important role in this field, except for some research, like LSCDiscovery in Spanish, a task presented by Zamora-Reina et al. (2022). This task has facilitated the development and evaluation of SSD systems in this language, accompanied by an unannotated Spanish corpus for both modern and old texts, which has a size of $22M$ and $13M$ tokens respectively. Additionally, the task paper highlighted effective techniques and approaches within the solutions. The most successful solution for the LCSDiscovery task was GlossReader, developed by Rachinskiy and Arefyev (2022), which involved fine-tuning XLM-RoBERTa, a Language Model trained on more than 100 languages, with old English datasets and employing the model zero-shot cross-lingual transferability of the model to build contextualized embeddings for Spanish, and using this fine-tuned model for SSD tasks. This approach has demonstrated good performance, especially in avoiding issues associated with word form bias and labor-intensive annotation requirements. These advancements underscore the increasing significance and potential of computational methodologies in enhancing our comprehension and automation of semantic shifts in multiple languages.

Also, Hu et al. (2021) present a set of methodological considerations for low-resource languages such as 15th-century Spanish, where a lower amount of data is available, and the data is not as clean as in other high-resource languages such as English and Mandarin Chinese, stating that common SSD techniques are also useful for these cases, but must be used carefully, under a set of considerations.

3 Data

Selecting the data is a crucial step for the reliability of the results. The LSCDiscovery shared task provides a useful corpus for old Spanish texts within the years 1810-1906, with a size of $13M$ tokens (Zamora-Reina et al., 2022). However, this paper aims to construct a larger old Spanish corpus, also adding more presence from Latin-American countries. The main sources selected and filtered for this corpus were **Project Gutenberg**[3] which was filtered by language and by the given date ranges (1800-1914), **The British Library books**[4] (portion from 1800-1899) which was also filtered by language (British Library Labs, 2021), and the **LatamXIX**[5] dataset from the *Historical Ink* project which contains Latin American texts from newspapers within years 1845-1899 (Manrique-Gómez et al., 2024).

3.1 Cleaning

The cleaning step is essential for The British Library and Project Gutenberg datasets since some texts from these sources consisted solely of chapter, book, or newspaper titles, or were filled with numbers and other characters that added noise to the dataset. In the case of the LatamXIX dataset, these noisy rows were already filtered and complemented with an LLM OCR correction process that corrected many OCR errors within the corpus, making it cleaner and more fittable for the SSD task, as it preserves better semantic meaning for words and less noise.

For The British Library books, an initial filter was applied using word confidence information to retain only those books with a mean OCR word confidence higher than 0.5. This experimental threshold was set to balance data loss (2.26% of rows) and text quality. After conducting several revisions with different examples, it was observed that this threshold maintained a high standard of text quality. Therefore, it was selected as the optimal balance

[3]Available at https://www.gutenberg.org/browse/languages/es

[4]Available at https://huggingface.co/datasets/TheBritishLibrary/blbooks

[5]Available at https://huggingface.co/datasets/Flaglab/latam-xix

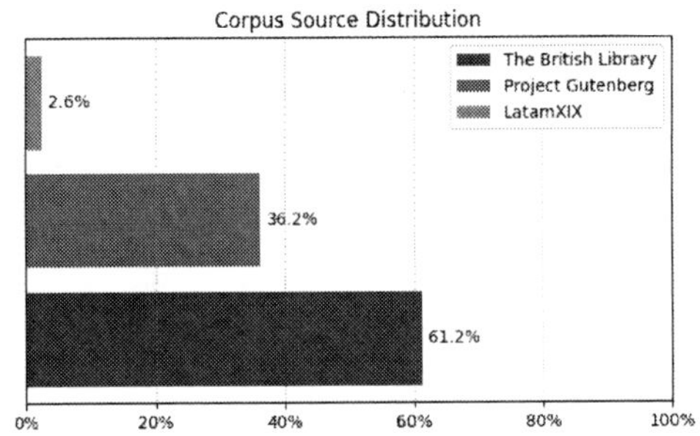

Figure 1: Final corpus distribution by source. The percentage is computed over the total number of rows of the whole C_{old} chunked corpus

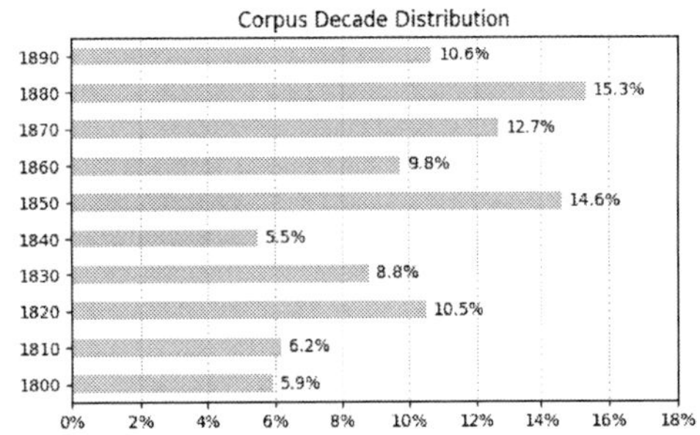

Figure 2: Final corpus distribution by decade. The percentage is computed over the total number of rows of the whole C_{old} chunked corpus

Feature	Value
Size	$\sim 865MB$
Rows	$1,141,490$
Words	$\sim 125M$
Tokens	$\sim 160M$
Years Range	1800 - 1914

Table 1: Final C_{old} chunked corpus information

Feature	Value
Size	$\sim 27MB$
Rows	29.972
Words	$\sim 4.5M$
Tokens	$\sim 5.7M$
Years Range	1845 - 1899

Table 2: Final C_{old} Latin-American portion chunked corpus information

between data retention and textual accuracy.

Same as in Manrique-Gómez et al. (2024), the cleaning steps to perform were:

1. Remove duplicates and empty rows within the whole dataset. 6.94% of rows were removed.

2. Filter out rows where over 50% of the characters are non-alphabetic, including spaces. 0.92% of rows were removed.

3. Remove the rows with 4 or fewer tokens. Samely, a new tokenizer was trained with a vocabulary size of 52,000, trained from the BETO pre-trained tokenizer (Cañete et al., 2020). 0.50% of rows were removed.

These filters were applied to minimize the risk of compromising the results due to noise in the dataset.

3.2 Chunking

As the historical texts from the corpus come from books and newspapers, many are very large, or some are very short with an average of $\sim$ 110 words and $\sim$ 140 tokens per text. For BERT-like models, the maximum sequence length consists of 512 tokens, which is not enough for very large texts like the current corpus texts.

Because of this, it's necessary to chunk the large texts within the dataset in a number shorter than 512 tokens. A much lower number was selected to make the chunked corpus fit for many different Language Models (LMs), for instance, a maximum of 256 tokens per text chunk, where a token was measured by training a new tokenizer over the cleaned version of the corpus[6].

During this step, over 67.6% of the rows were chunked, adding 460,543 new rows. Each row was transformed into a part of a paragraph or left as a whole paragraph (no chunking) with no more than 256 tokens while preserving as much semantic meaning as possible. The preservation of semantic meaning in the chunked segments was achieved by splitting through punctuation marks and common paragraph-sentence separators. The rows distribution and corpus information can be found in Figures 1, 2, and Table 1 respectively. Also, the information on the Latin-American portion of the corpus can be found in Table 2.

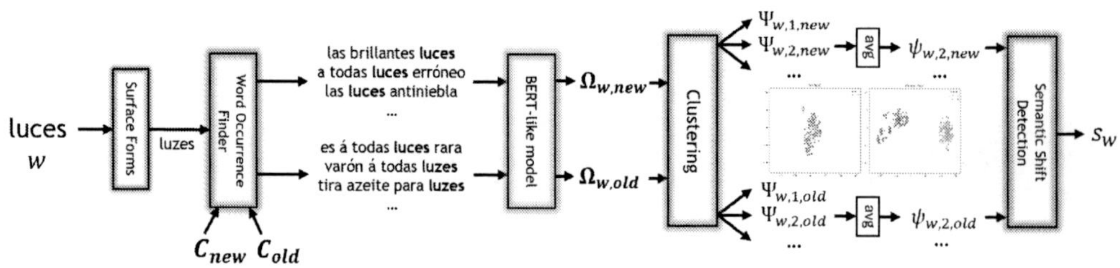

Figure 3: Historical Ink SSD Pipeline Architecture

4 Methodology

To achieve effectively the desired task, and be able to perform a quality analysis of the results, we have defined the pipeline observed in Figure 3, with the following steps:

1. Find the occurrences of a given word w in C_{old} and C_{new} corpora.
2. Retrieve the word embeddings in the found occurrences, using a BERT-like language model.
3. Cluster the word usage by its meaning (sense), and average to get the centroids of the clusters.
4. Perform the SSD task to identify lost/gained senses and measure the semantic change of the word (s_w).

It's important to note that the pipeline was designed as a flexible and reusable solution for various contexts and configurable stages. Beyond analyzing the specific case of 19th-century Spanish, we propose a modular, plug-and-play pipeline with numerous adjustable stages. Each component of the pipeline can be used independently and configured for different use cases, ensuring versatility and adaptability for further research or applications.

4.1 Find the Occurrences

Given corpora C_{old} and C_{new}, finding all texts where a word w is used is straightforward when looking for *exact occurrences*. However, this task becomes more complex with inflectional variations typical of languages like Spanish. For example, the word "crear" (to create) may appear as "creaste" (you created) or "creado" (created). Stemming can help by extracting the base form of the word, but it may lose some contextual meanings.

Also, in old Spanish, language rules have changed significantly, as noted by Montgomery (1966). These changes are detectable using the semi-automated framework presented as part of the Historical Ink project (Manrique-Gómez et al., 2024), which extracts useful lists of *surface forms* (i.e. specific appearance of a word in a given context) for words that underwent orthographic changes in 19th-century Latin-American Spanish (e.g., "luces" historically written as "luzes").

To address these challenges, we propose a method to find occurrences of a given word w in diachronic corpora C_{old} and C_{new}. This method organizes all word's expected usages and tokenizes both the word and the searching text, searching for each subword within a list of different orthographic forms of writing a given word.

For example, the word "gente" would be searched in C_{old} as "gente", "jente" (surface form), "gent", or "jent" in that order. This method relies heavily on the tokenizer, so using one trained in the specific language is recommended for better performance.

4.2 Word Embeddings

For the SSD task, contextual embeddings are very useful as they can capture the evolving meaning of words over time. By considering the surrounding context of a word within a sentence or document, contextual embeddings can provide an enhanced representation of its semantics, enabling the detection of particular shifts in meaning. In particular, there are some BERT-like LMs trained on Spanish corpora. Some of the most representative are BETO: Spanish Bert[7] in both uncased and cased versions (Cañete et al., 2020), Multilingual BERT[8] in both uncased and cased versions, which has an

[6]The final corpus can be found at https://huggingface.co/datasets/Flaglab/spanish-corpus-xix in all its three versions: "original", "cleaned", and "chunked"

[7]Available at https://huggingface.co/dccuchile/bert-base-spanish-wwm-cased

[8]Available at https://huggingface.co/google-bert/bert-base-multilingual-cased

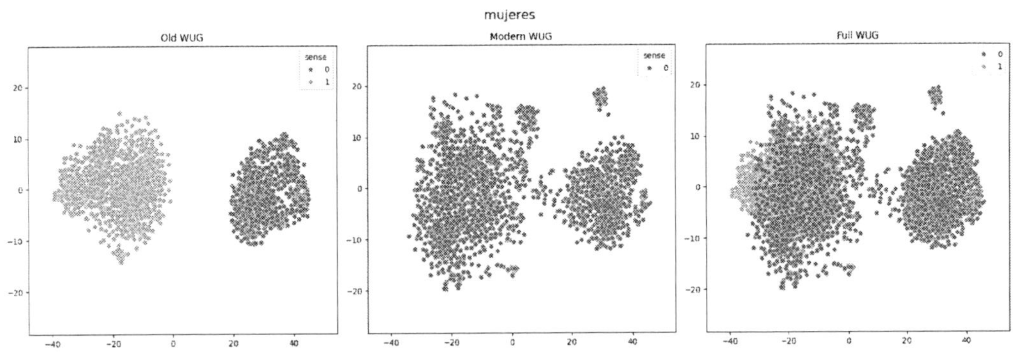

Figure 4: DWUG of the word "mujeres" (women), using the whole corpus fine-tuned model embeddings, the T-SNE dimensionality reduction algorithm, and the KMeans clustering algorithm (with the silhouette metric). Each color represents a meaning (cluster) of the word. The color changes between the left (old corpus) and center (modern corpus) images illustrate the overall semantic change between the two diachronic corpora.

important portion of training in Spanish (Devlin et al., 2018), and AlBERT Spanish version[9]. All these models are BERT-based and have the same maximum sequence length of 512 tokens, BERT has an embedding size of 768, while ALBERT has a more compact embedding size of 128.

For this paper, we performed the SSD task using the mentioned LMs. Some were trained with the whole 19th-century Spanish corpus, while others were trained only with the Latin-American portion of the dataset. We fine-tuned these models using the specific corpus for each case, employing the Masked Language Modeling (MLM) task. In this task, 15% of the corpus tokens were randomly masked, and the model learned to predict the masked tokens based on their context. This approach ensured that the model learned the unique linguistic style of each corpus, enabling it to generate word embeddings that accurately reflect the corpus' linguistic patterns, which is essential for detecting semantic shifts.

During the training phase, an Adam optimizer with a learning rate of 2×10^{-5} was employed, and the training proceeded with a batch size of 32, during a total of 5 epochs. Due to the low number of epochs, no Early Stopping was required, and the chosen parameters led to good resource utilization. The training time with the given batch size depended on the model but was on average 47 hours for the whole C_{old} corpus, and 1 hour and 20 minutes for the Latin-American portion. The training was performed on an A40 GPU.

[9]Available at https://huggingface.co/dccuchile/albert-base-spanish

4.3 Clustering

We applied a joint clustering approach, combining both corpora within the same set of embeddings before clustering. Given two corpus C_{old} and C_{new}, and a particular word w, the sets $\Omega_{w,old}$ and $\Omega_{w,new}$ are defined as the set of word embeddings generated in each corpus respectively, for the word w.

The clustering algorithm is meant to find the different meanings of a word within a given period, and overall the whole timespan of both C_{old} and C_{new} periods. This generates a well-known Diachronic Word Usage Graph (DWUG) for the word in both periods (Schlechtweg et al., 2021), allowing to perform the semantic shift detection and change measurement between *old* and *new* periods, as seen in Figure 4, where each color refers to a word meaning.

The particular algorithms used were Affinity Propagation and KMeans with an automatic K finder under a certain score function such as silhouette score or inertia. The main problem with KMeans are words with a single meaning across the whole timespan. As common KMeans K-evaluation metrics are not fittable for one-cluster evaluation, so it wouldn't be possible to validate if the best number of clusters should be just one. As this occurs for many of the target words selected for analysis, a very good alternative for it is the Affinity Propagation (AP) clustering algorithm with a damping parameter of 0.975; this parameter was selected through a test with different values and a manually-driven evaluation of the number of clusters automatically selected by the algorithm. Selecting a high damping value for the AP algorithm leads to a more stable selection of the number of clusters as the requirements for new cluster creation are more strict, which is expected for this case.

The T-SNE dimensionality reduction algorithm was used to plot the DWUGs shown in this paper, with a perplexity of 50, which proved the best for better cluster space separation. For words with a lower number of found occurrences in the dataset, a lower perplexity was employed for its representation.

4.4 Semantic Shift Measurement

Once clustering is performed, the measurement for Semantic Shift is straightforward. There are two main divisions of the SSD task which are Binary Change Detection (BCD) and Graded Change Detection (GCD) (Zamora-Reina et al., 2022), where Graded Change Detection is the most common and useful, but also the most challenging task for change classification, which consists of ranking a list of target words based on their degree of change (Periti and Tahmasebi, 2024).

The consolidation of techniques for measuring semantic shift detection has been a high-growth area, with the proposal of many different techniques, some of them comparing sets of embeddings (e.g. the clusters), and others comparing individual embeddings (e.g. the centroids). Montanelli and Periti (2023) present a survey that compiles many of the most used state-of-the-art techniques for grading the semantic shift of a word between two temporal-different corpora, classifying them between form- and sense-based approaches.

Given m number of clusters (senses) for the word w, returned by the clustering algorithm, we define $\Psi_{w,s,t}$ as the cluster with the sense s for the word w in the period t, such that all the senses compound the whole set of embeddings.

$$\Omega_{w,t} = \bigcup_{s=1}^{m} \Psi_{w,s,t} \quad \forall t = \{new, old\} \tag{1}$$

For these clusters, a centroid embedding is computed as the average:

$$\psi_{w,s,t} = \text{avg}(\Psi_{w,s,t}) \quad \forall t = \{new, old\} \tag{2}$$

Finally, two different formulas were taken from Montanelli and Periti (2023) to measure the semantic shift f, based on the cosine similarity function (CS). With this shift, for each word, we would have as many semantic shifts f as the number of clusters given by the algorithm (m), so we could determine which senses have had a diachronic shift and which haven't, for each word.

Cosine Distance (CD):

$$f_{CD}(w, s) = 1 - CS(\psi_{w,s,old}, \psi_{w,s,new}) \tag{3}$$

Inverted similarity over Word Prototype (PRT):

$$f_{PRT}(w, s) = \frac{1}{CS(\psi_{w,s,old}, \psi_{w,s,new})} \tag{4}$$

It should be noted that if a sense is not present within a period, whether old or new period, f_{CD} should be 1.0, meaning a complete change of the given sense. If the sense is absent from the embeddings of the old period ($\Psi_{w,s,old} = \emptyset$), it means that the sense was gained in modern Spanish; otherwise, if the sense only exists in the embeddings of the old period ($\Psi_{w,s,new} = \emptyset$), it means that the sense was lost in modern Spanish, as seen in Figure 4 where the sense 1 (orange color) is not present in the modern WUG.

For this task, it is crucial to consider the frequency of points per cluster within each period. If a cluster has significantly fewer points in a period, specifically less than 10% of the total, we classify these points as either misclassifications or obsolete words. This allows us to treat the cluster as a gained or lost sense. We chose this threshold based on testing with few known examples, where it provided the best performance in detecting gained and lost senses.

5 Evaluation and Model Selection

As mentioned, several pre-trained Language Models (LMs) are available for large Spanish corpora. We needed an evaluation method to select the best model for our analysis. The LSCDiscovery shared task (Zamora-Reina et al., 2022) provides over 65,000 annotated examples for 100 target words using the DURel framework proposed by Schlechtweg et al. (2018). This annotated corpus is highly useful for evaluating the LMs, as its time period is within the 19th century. Even though the LSCDiscovery task differs from the one in this paper, it offers a valuable benchmark. Our task focuses on detecting the different meanings of a word in a diachronic corpora and measuring their

LM		Average		Clustering			Non-Clustering	
#	Name	Clustering	All	AP	KM inertia	KM silhouette	CD	PRT
1	BETO cased FT	0.5799	0.6017	**0.6124**	0.5598	0.5676	0.6285	0.6402
2	**BETO cased LFT**	0.5872 (1)	0.6064	0.5853	0.5815	0.5947	0.6307	0.6396
3	BETO cased	0.5832	0.6041	0.5600	0.5790	**0.6107**	0.6302	0.6405
4	BETO uncased FT	0.5578	0.5837	0.5442	0.5579	0.5714	0.6224	0.6227
5	BETO uncased LFT	0.5658	0.5890	0.5594	0.5676	0.5703	0.6223	0.6255
6	BETO uncased	**0.5862 (3)**	0.6043	0.5916	0.5819	0.5850	0.6167	0.6463
7	mBERT cased LFT	0.5806	0.5951	0.5692	0.5788	0.5939	0.6163	0.6172
8	mBERT cased	0.5782	0.5949	0.5675	0.5808	0.5863	0.6100	0.6297
9	mBERT uncased LFT	0.5593	0.5929	0.553	0.5633	0.5615	0.6405	0.6464
10	mBERT uncased	0.5762	0.6065	0.5523	0.5924	0.5839	**0.6457**	0.6581
11	AlBERT LFT	0.5717	0.5928	0.5731	0.5796	0.5624	0.6160	0.6328
12	AlBERT	**0.5869 (2)**	**0.6132**	0.5758	**0.5992**	0.5857	0.6373	**0.6682**

Table 3: LM benchmark through the LSCDiscovery (Zamora-Reina et al., 2022) F1 of the Binary Change Detection task. Each model was fine-tuned for the Latin-American corpus (LFT) and both BETO-cased and uncased models were also fine-tuned for the whole corpus (FT), comparing also with non-fine-tuned versions.

semantic shift over time. By comparing with the LSCDiscovery task, we ensure a rigorous evaluation, confirming that the models are robust and effective across various contexts and not overly tailored to a single specific task.

The task's corpus includes pairs of sentences rated from 1 to 4, where 1 indicates identical word usage and 4 indicates completely different usage (Schlechtweg et al., 2018). To evaluate the models, we converted this numerical assessment into a binary evaluation: ratings 1-2 indicated no semantic change, while ratings 3-4 indicated a semantic change. We then defined five specific methods to classify a pair of word uses as either semantic change (1) or no change (0). Among these, two methods — *cosine distance* (CD) and *inverted similarity over word prototype* (PRT) — were tested purely for task purposes. However, the methods of primary importance for this paper are those related to sense clustering.

The three clustering-based evaluation methods consist of grouping all the embeddings of the occurrences of a word, as mentioned in the SSD section. Then, given two uses, if they do not belong to the same cluster, a semantic change is indicated (1); otherwise, no semantic change is indicated (0). This was evaluated using Affinity Propagation and KMeans (with silhouette and inertia metrics) methods. Finally, the model with the best average results across the three clustering methods was selected. The benchmark results can be seen in Table 3.

While the results provide valuable insights into the models' capabilities, they should not be directly compared to those from the LSCDiscovery leaderboard (Zamora-Reina et al., 2022). Instead, they serve as an effective benchmark for assessing how well the LMs perform in detecting semantic changes within our specific historical context. The differences in tasks and the method approaches for our study reflect that direct comparisons with LSCDiscovery scores are not applicable.

Given the results, the best-performing model was BETO fine-tuned on the Latin American dataset[10]. A possible explanation for this is that the Latin American portion of the corpus underwent an additional step of LLM OCR correction, which removed OCR-related errors and produced cleaner text. This likely reduced noise and improved the quality of fine-tuning. Additionally, BETO was trained solely in Spanish, unlike multilingual BERT, which was trained in many different languages. According to (Cañete et al., 2020), this single-language focus tends to result in better performance compared to multilingual models. This model was the one used for evaluating the target words and creating the DWUGs presented in appendix C.

[10]Fine-tuned model was uploaded to HuggingFace and is available at `https://huggingface.co/Flaglab/beto-cased-finetuned-xix-latam`

6 Results

The results of the trained model focus on a specific group of 255 target words[11] selected for their historical significance and relevance to generate hypotheses about potential semantic shifts over time, confirming the consistency of the results. Some examples of the DWUGs analyzed in this section are available in Appendix C for both AP and KMeans.

One of the main results of this research was to highlight the success and failure cases for both AP and KMeans clustering algorithms, as both were used to compute the senses of all 255 words. Affinity Propagation (AP) performed poorly in many cases where it couldn't detect multiple usages of a word, such as "grave" (serious/bass), or detected many different senses for other words, such as "honor" (honour), as shown in Figure C2. However, it effectively detected single-sense words, a task that KMeans wasn't capable of due to metrics used to choose the best K. However, KMeans performed very well in most cases, effectively detecting and clustering the senses of multi-meaning words over time.

As displayed in Figure C2, some words like "rey" (king) and "usurer" (usurer) present neither polysemy nor notable historical changes. However, the term "mujeres" (women), as shown in Figure 4, shows a change in modern usage. This finding is particularly interesting in the context of both historical discourse analysis in gender studies and historical linguistics studies, as it is an example of computational verification.

The semantic transformation of the word women, as plotted in Figure 4 and in Appendix B, primarily pertains to the antiquated use of "mujeres" designating a particular group of female individuals. In 19th-century Spanish, lexical tradition mandated the rigorous use of masculine forms of nouns and adjectives as the universal form, encompassing both genders (feminine and masculine) (Porto-Dapena, 1975). Thus, the word "hombres" (men) could be used as a synonym for humanity, while the use of "mujeres" (women) was more likely to be reserved for describing a private group of women. Twentieth-century gender studies introduced a unified meaning to the word "mujeres". Joan W. Scott famously stated that "-Women's experience- or -women's culture- exists only as the expression of female particularity in contrast to male universality" (Scott, 1988). This idea explains the rupture in the modern usage of the word women towards the relational concept of gender in the 20th century (Lux and Pérez, 2020).

Consequently, the term "mujeres" evolved from a specific designation to a broader and more inclusive reference, reflecting significant social and cultural shifts in gender discourse. As we have observed, the contemporary usage of "mujeres" tends to encompass all women more generically, since it was not until the 20th century that historical consideration began to differentiate "women" as a collective separate from "men". In the past, the term was used to refer to a distinct group of women, thereby distinguishing women from other plural nouns such as men, children, or even animals. Modern usage of "women" almost exclusively serves to differentiate women from men.

Other insightful results demonstrate both how the polysemy of words changes over time, as seen in examples in Appendix A, and the particularities of word semantics diachronically used in Latin American Spanish. Historical linguistics studies acknowledge "El español de América" as a main Spanish variant, for which corpus studies are yet to be conducted. Newspapers are recognized as a legitimate source for exploring the particularities of linguistic variants (Gutiérrez Maté and Diez del Corral Areta, 2023). Hence, the LatamXIX dataset we used to model the quantitative experiments might initiate a triangulation with new regional research. For example, we have observed how the term "infancia" (infancy/childhood), as depicted in Figure C1, was predominantly used in the 19th century as an abstract reference to the nascent phase of objects, entities, or people. This suggests a metaphorical use of the word, indicative of a broader, symbolic interpretation of "infancy" or "early development" during this era.

Newly formed Latin American nations in the 19th century viewed themselves as children recently independent from their mother, metropolitan Spain. Consequently, the term "infancia de la patria" (infancy of the nation) described the contradictory and highly unstable political and social times experienced in Latin America during that era. These old meanings have largely been supplanted by the modern understanding of "childhood", which specifically refers to the population segment of children. These results align with the

[11]From all 255 words, only 233 had enough occurrences in the modern corpus. The DWUGs and SSD for both AP and KMeans algorithms are available in the notebook https://colab.research.google.com/drive/1eaULQocxyuCNX0ftBvDJwe8nfpEi5s6i

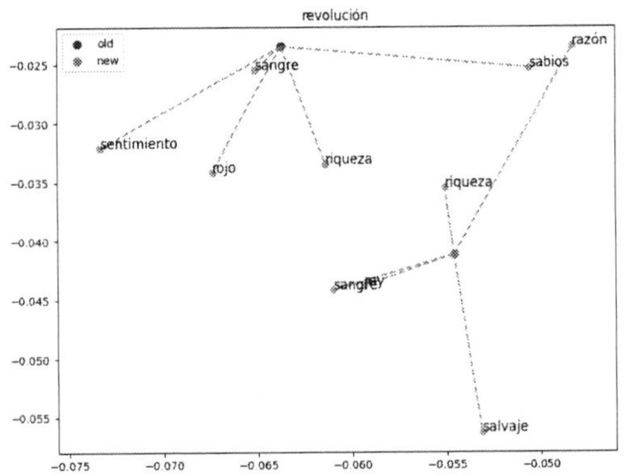

Figure 5: Diachronic comparison of word "revolución" (revolution) and its related words, between the old and the modern period using PCA dimensionality reduction algorithm.

second wave of human rights in the 20th century, which expanded the 19th century's initial civil rights to include specific rights for various western population groups, such as children and women.

Words like "sentimiento" (sentiment) have lost one of their historical meanings, as illustrated in Figure C1. In contemporary usage, "sentimiento" serves as a synonym for the feelings experienced by an individual or group of people. However, one of its older meanings has almost disappeared. In the 19th century, "sentimiento" was used to describe the expression of a person's correctness, effectively acting as a synonym for morality, or even referring to someone's elevated religious or artistic spirit. On the other hand, the term "sublime" (sublime or elevated) has largely fallen out of use and is scarcely found in the modern dataset, as depicted in Figure C1. Appendix B contains examples of the 255 words' semantic shift detection outputs, including other examples such as "luces" (ideas/lights) and "servidores" (servants/servers).

Finally, word comparison also proves highly valuable for numerous diachronic analyses. In each period, the most representative sense of a word is determined based on its frequency dominance among other senses. Then, its sense cluster centroid is computed to allow comparison between words. Within the set of 255 words, the 5 words exhibiting the highest cosine similarity to this centroid are selected, indicating their related usage contexts. For example, as observed in Figure 5, the word "revolución" (revolution) historically exhibited close associations with the words blood, richness, feeling, wise, and red. In contemporary contexts, however, the term "revolución" is linked to terms like king, reason, and savage, and it remains related to blood and richness in different proportions, with blood now more distant and richness closer.

This study provides significant insights into the SSD of 19th-century Spanish words, utilizing computational linguistics to uncover shifts in word meanings relevant to both global and Latin American contexts. By developing a specialized corpus and employing methods such as fine-tuning BERT-like models and diachronic word embeddings, we achieved a nuanced analysis of historical semantic changes. Our examination of selected words reveals the relation between societal, cultural, and political events and the shift of words' semantic meaning over time.

The application of SSD and modern computational techniques highlights the evolution of linguistic analysis from manual to systematic approaches, enhancing the accuracy of semantic shift detection and deepening our understanding of language as a dynamic entity. This study's interdisciplinary implications are notable, offering potential benefits to fields like history, sociology, and digital humanities, where these insights can provide deeper context to historical cultural shifts.

Looking ahead, the methodologies and findings of this project can serve as a framework for future research in other languages and periods, suggesting a scalable approach to historical linguistics and semantic analysis. The flexible and reusable pipeline developed here can be adapted for various contexts and stages. Future research could apply this pipeline with modified parameters or data for different use cases or languages, to prove its performance on different contexts.

However, an evaluation of the selected models for the Latin-American corpus, particularly for clustering, is still needed. An annotated dataset similar to the given in the AXOLOTL-24 shared task (Fedorova et al., 2024), but for Latin-American Spanish, would be highly beneficial. Such a dataset, with examples of specific word usages, their periods, and a gold standard for word senses, would enable a more focused assessment of the models beyond the task evaluation presented in Table 3.

7 Acknowledgements

We would like to thank the three anonymous reviewers from the ACL 2024 LChange'24 conference for their helpful feedback and suggestions.

References

British Library Labs. 2021. Digitised books. c. 1510 - c. 1900. JSONL (OCR derived text + metadata).

José Cañete. 2019. Compilation of large spanish unannotated corpora.

José Cañete, Gabriel Chaperon, Rodrigo Fuentes, Jou-Hui Ho, Hojin Kang, and Jorge Pérez. 2020. Spanish pre-trained bert model and evaluation data. In *PML4DC at ICLR 2020*.

Jacob Devlin, Ming-Wei Chang, Kenton Lee, and Kristina Toutanova. 2018. BERT: pre-training of deep bidirectional transformers for language understanding. *CoRR*, abs/1810.04805.

Mariia Fedorova, Timothee Mickus, Niko Tapio Partanen, Janine Siewert, Elena Spaziani, and Andrey Kutuzov. 2024. AXOLOTL'24 shared task on multilingual explainable semantic change modeling. In *Proceedings of the 5th Workshop on Computational Approaches to Historical Language Change*, Bangkok. Association for Computational Linguistics.

Mario Giulianelli, Marco Del Tredici, and Raquel Fernández. 2020. Analysing lexical semantic change with contextualised word representations. In *Proceedings of the 58th Annual Meeting of the Association for Computational Linguistics*, pages 3960–3973, Online. Association for Computational Linguistics.

Miguel Gutiérrez Maté and Elena Diez del Corral Areta. 2023. El español en américa (III): de las independencias a nuestros días. variedades andinas y caribeñas. In *Lingüística histórica del español / The Routledge Handbook of Spanish Historical Linguistics*, pages 539–545. Routledge, London.

William L. Hamilton, Jure Leskovec, and Dan Jurafsky. 2016. Cultural shift or linguistic drift? comparing two computational measures of semantic change. *CoRR*, abs/1606.02821.

Hai Hu, Patrícia Amaral, and Sandra Kübler. 2021. Word embeddings and semantic shifts in historical spanish: Methodological considerations. *Digital Scholarship in the Humanities*, 37(2):441–461.

Martha Lux and María Cristina Pérez Pérez. 2020. Los estudios de historia y género en américa latina. *Historia Crítica*, 1.

Laura Manrique-Gómez, Tony Montes, and Rubén Manrique. 2024. Historical Ink: 19th century Latin American spanish corpus with LLM OCR correction.

Matej Martinc, Syrielle Montariol, Elaine Zosa, and Lidia Pivovarova. 2020. Capturing evolution in word usage: Just add more clusters? In *Companion Proceedings of the Web Conference 2020*, WWW '20. ACM.

Tomas Mikolov, Kai Chen, Greg Corrado, and Jeffrey Dean. 2013. Efficient estimation of word representations in vector space. *arXiv:1301.3781*.

Stefano Montanelli and Francesco Periti. 2023. A survey on contextualised semantic shift detection. *Preprint*, arXiv:2304.01666.

Thomas Montgomery. 1966. On the development of spanish y from "et". *Romance Notes*, 8(1):137–142.

Francesco Periti and Nina Tahmasebi. 2024. A systematic comparison of contextualized word embeddings for lexical semantic change. *Preprint*, arXiv:2402.12011.

José A. Porto-Dapena. 1975. En torno a las entradas del "diccionario" de rufino josé cuervo. *Boletín del Instituto Caro y Cuervo*, 30(1).

Maxim Rachinskiy and Nikolay Arefyev. 2022. GlossReader at LSCDiscovery: Train to select a proper gloss in English – discover lexical semantic change in Spanish.

Dominik Schlechtweg, Sabine Schulte im Walde, and Stefanie Eckmann. 2018. Diachronic usage relatedness (DURel): A framework for the annotation of lexical semantic change. In *Proceedings of the 2018 Conference of the North American Chapter of the Association for Computational Linguistics: Human Language Technologies, Volume 2 (Short Papers)*, pages 169–174, New Orleans, Louisiana. Association for Computational Linguistics.

Dominik Schlechtweg, Nina Tahmasebi, Simon Hengchen, Haim Dubossarsky, and Barbara McGillivray. 2021. DWUG: A large resource of diachronic word usage graphs in four languages. In *Proceedings of the 2021 Conference on Empirical Methods in Natural Language Processing*, pages 7079–7091, Online and Punta Cana, Dominican Republic. Association for Computational Linguistics.

Joan Scott. 1988. *Gender and the politics of history*. Columbia University Press, New York, NY.

Frank D. Zamora-Reina, Felipe Bravo-Marquez, and Dominik Schlechtweg. 2022. LSCDiscovery: A shared task on semantic change discovery and detection in spanish.

A Usage Examples per Sense

Infancia: The word has presented a semantic shift as shown in Figure C1

Sense 0 in New-"Adopción derechos del niño, protección de la infancia, tráfico de personas".

Sense 1 in Old-"Los pueblos, como los hombres, tienen su infancia, embrion todavía entre nosotros, período delicado y peligroso, en el que todo exceso é indiscreción trastorna el organismo é impide el desarrollo, si es que no lo destruye." "Escamilla, por ejemplo, se casó desde la infancia con una matrona llamada Portería del Congreso de Escamilla: lleva dos apellidos, esta señora, no porque sea bigama, (pues no ha tenido mas que un solo marido) sino porque su papà es el señor Congreso, un viejo, mui necio."

Sentimiento: The word has presented a semantic shift as shown in Figure C1

Sense 0 in New- "65% de la personas que expresan un sentimiento personal de temor o esperanza". "Reforzar entre los europeos el sentimiento de pertenencia a una misma Comunidad".

Sense 1 in Old- "Será un gran artista de mucho sentimiento, posee una rica voz, si la educa, y tiene mucho aplomo en las tablas, es feo, pero simpático". "Una forma de expresión nueva, en la que brillaban un profundo sentimiento poético y una suerte de ingenuidad". "Que el divino arte de la música, lenguaje de la inteligencia y del sentimiento, ejerce sobre todos los hombres una influencia poderosa, que al mismo tiempo que atempera las pasiones, despierta las ideas de moralidad y de sociabilidad". "Republicano de ideas y de sentimiento, ha sabido armonizar sus opiniones políticas con sus creencias".

Sublime: The word presented polysemy in the past but is no longer in use as shown in Figure C1

Sense 0 in Old-"Hé aquí un epitafio sublime; la madre que busca al hijo bajo la sombra de los laureles, en la soledad de la muerte como dos almas inseparables, siempre unidas, siempre amantes".

Sense 1 in Old- "Bolívar, el del genio sublime que todo lo abarcó, que todo lo comprendió, y á quien debieron su existencia y su gloria, en menos de un cuarto de siglo, la mayor parte de las nacionalidades del Nuevo Mundo".

Sense 2 in Old- "á veces las leyes naturales- puede sí ejercer el sublime ministerio de aliviar (obra divina, según Hipócrates) y consolar á los que sufren."

Servidores: The word gained a new sense as shown in Figure C1

Sense 0 in Old-"Era allí donde se alojaba el Cacique, su familia y sus principales servidores". "a depositar- sus votos en favor de los buenos y leales servidores de la causa".

Sense 0 in New- "si la joven no está en un convento, rodearla de servidores que la acompañen por todas partes". "La Comisión y nosotros somos los servidores de los ciudadanos de nuestros Estados miembros".

Sense 1 in New- "la adquisición o el alquiler de ordenadores personales, servidores y microordenadores". "operación de los sistemas y de la red, y servidores para bases de datos, la Web, el FTP".

B SSD Examples

Some of the SSD results chosen were selected from Affinity Propagation algorithm clusterization, particularly those with only one sense such as "rey" and "usurero".

	Word	Sense	CD	PRT	gained/lost Sense
AP	Rey	0	0.005	1.005	
	Usurero	0	1.0	∞	**lost**
KMeans	Luces	0	0.012	1.012	
	Luces	1	0.012	1.013	
	Infancia	0	0.017	1.017	
	Infancia	**1**	1.0	∞	**gained**
	Sentimiento	**0**	1.0	∞	**gained**
	Sentimiento	1	0.003	1.003	
	Sublime	**0**	1.0	∞	**lost**
	Sublime	**1**	1.0	∞	**lost**
	Sublime	**2**	1.0	∞	**lost**
	Servidores	0	0.043	1.045	
	Servidores	**1**	1.0	∞	**gained**

Table B1: SSD for some of the 255 target words; the ones mentioned in the paper, and others added in the appendix DWUGs.

C DWUGs Examples

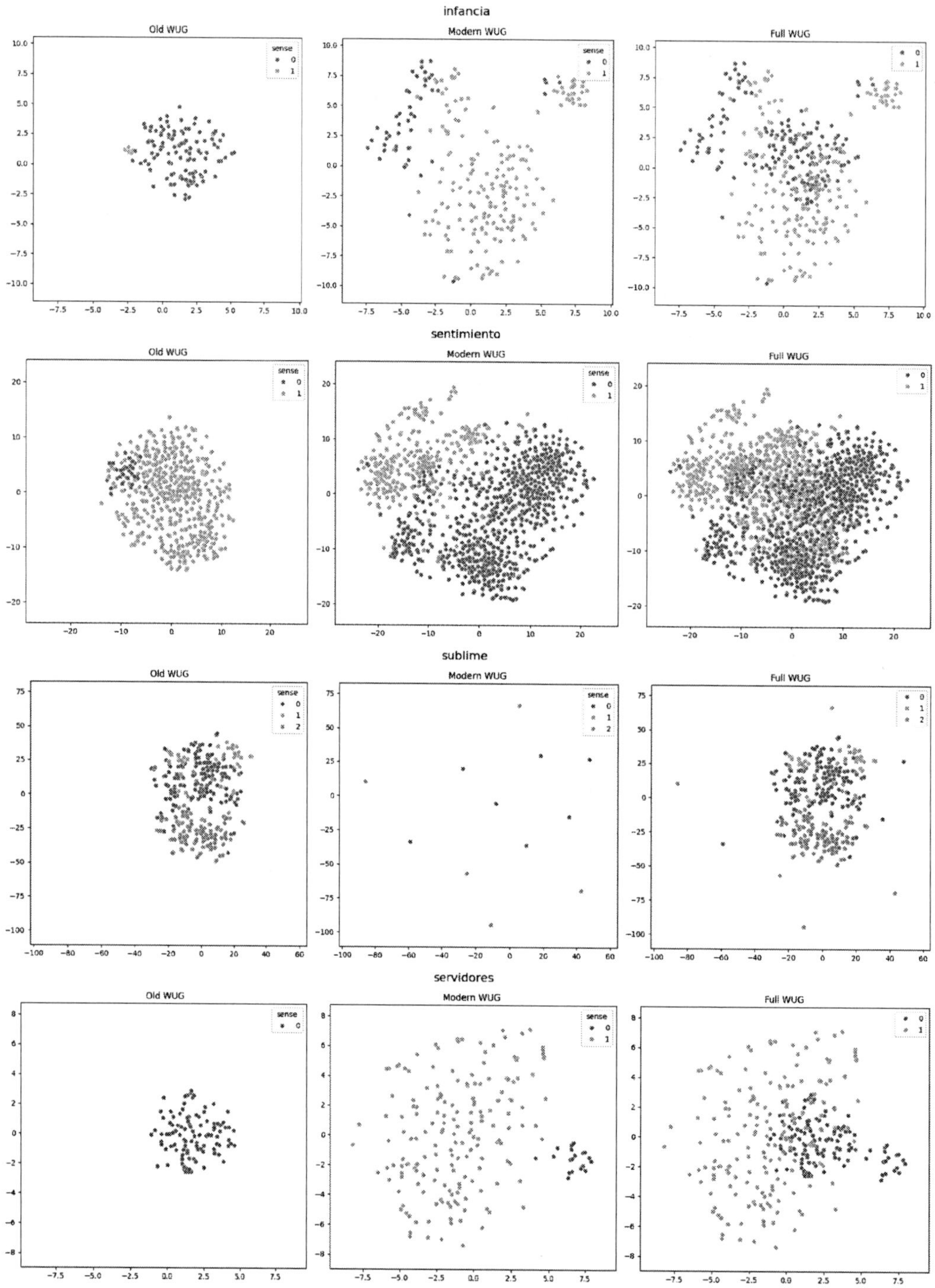

Figure C1: DWUG using the Latin American portion of the corpus fine-tuned model embeddings, the T-SNE dimensionality reduction algorithm, and the **KMeans** clustering algorithm (with the silhouette metric). All words are correctly clustered.

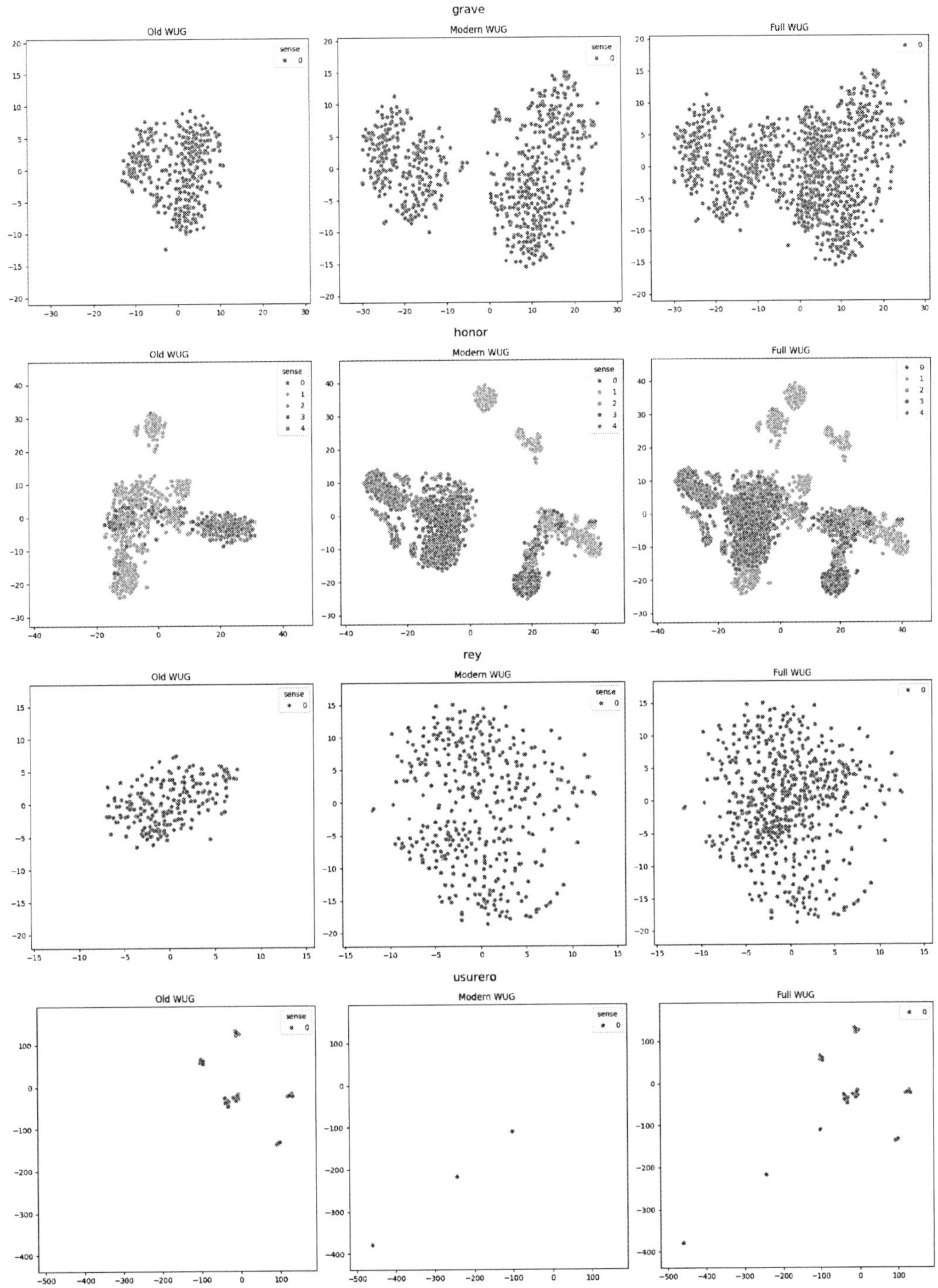

Figure C2: DWUG using the Latin American portion of the corpus fine-tuned model embeddings, the T-SNE dimensionality reduction algorithm, and the **Affinity Propagation** clustering algorithm. Words "grave" and "honor" are wrong clustered, and words "rey" and "usurero" are correctly clustered.

Presence or Absence: Are Unknown Word Usages in Dictionaries?

Xianghe Ma[1] **Dominik Schlechtweg**[2] **Wei Zhao**[3]
[1]University of Heidelberg [2]University of Stuttgart [3]University of Aberdeen
xianghe.ma@stud.uni-heidelberg.de
dominik.schlechtweg@ims.uni-stuttgart.de
wei.zhao@abdn.ac.uk

Abstract

There has been a surge of interest in computational modeling of semantic change. The foci of previous works are on detecting and interpreting word senses gained over time; however, it remains unclear whether the gained senses are covered by dictionaries. In this work, we aim to fill this research gap by comparing detected word senses with dictionary sense inventories in order to bridge between the communities of lexical semantic change detection and lexicography. We evaluate our system in the AXOLOTL-24 shared task for Finnish, Russian and German languages (Fedorova et al., 2024b). Our system is fully unsupervised. It leverages a graph-based clustering approach to predict mappings between unknown word usages and dictionary entries for Subtask 1, and generates dictionary-like definitions for those novel word usages through the state-of-the-art Large Language Models such as GPT-4 and LLaMA-3 for Subtask 2. In Subtask 1, our system outperforms the baseline system by a large margin, and it offers interpretability for the mapping results by distinguishing between matched and unmatched (novel) word usages through our graph-based clustering approach. Our system ranks first in Finnish and German, and ranks second in Russian on the Subtask 2 test-phase leaderboard. These results show the potential of our system in managing dictionary entries, particularly for updating dictionaries to include novel sense entries. Our code and data are made publicly available[1].

1 Introduction

Meaning changes over time have been a subject of research for many years in historical linguistics (e.g. Blank, 1997; Geeraerts, 2020). Researchers use linguistic tools and methods to identify gained and lost meanings of headwords, and more importantly to interpret these changes by categorizing the types of changes and detecting social and cultural forces driving the changes.

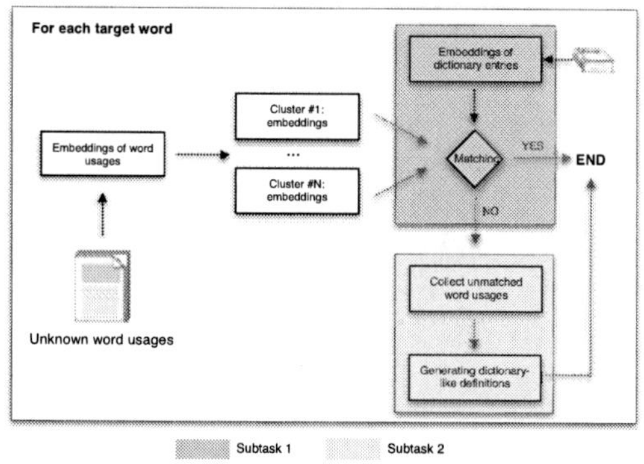

Figure 1: An illustration of the workflow for the two AXOLOTL-24 subtasks. Unknown word usages refer to usages found at a later time period, and their mappings with dictionary sense entries are unknown.

Recently, there has been scholarly interest in computational modeling of meaning changes as cost-efficient alternatives to labor-intensive linguistic tools and methods. As a result, a plateau of research outputs has been made, including shared tasks and datasets (e.g. Schlechtweg et al., 2020; Kutuzov and Pivovarova, 2021; Zamora-Reina et al., 2022; Chen et al., 2023; Schlechtweg et al., 2024a), models (Eger and Mehler, 2016; Hamilton et al., 2016a,b; Martinc et al., 2020; Kaiser et al., 2021; Montariol et al., 2021a; Teodorescu et al., 2022; Cassotti et al., 2023; Ma et al., 2024), tools (Schlechtweg et al., 2024b), and relevant workshops[2]. For instance, SemEval2020 Task 1 (Schlechtweg et al., 2020), a seminal work on this topic, introduces the first task and datasets on unsupervised lexical semantic change detection in English, German, Swedish and Latin languages. Further extensions include DIACR-Ita for Italian

[1]https://github.com/xiaohemaikoo/axolotl24-ABDN-NLP

[2]https://www.changeiskey.org/event/2024-acl-lchange/

Proceedings of the 5th Workshop on Computational Approaches to Historical Language Change, pages 42–54
August 15, 2024 ©2024 Association for Computational Linguistics

(Basile et al., 2020), RuShiftEval for Russian (Kutuzov and Pivovarova, 2021), and LSCDiscovery for Spanish (Zamora-Reina et al., 2022).

The immediate impact of these research outputs might be on the lexicography industry. Lexicographers rely on collocations and grammatical patterns to identify novel meanings that are not included in dictionaries, and add these identified meanings into the next iteration of dictionary updates (Kilgarriff et al., 2010). However, the process of doing so is costly and time-consuming. For instance, in 2023, the Oxford English Dictionary created about 1,700 new meanings[3], with the help of hundreds of language specialists for English alone. Recently, the AXOLOTL-24 shared task has connected lexical semantic change detection with dictionary entries. Instead of just detecting meaning change, the shared task aims to align dictionary sense entries with each word usage. This is particularly useful for managing dictionary entries, e.g., to identify and collect novel meanings not covered by dictionaries (Erk, 2006; Lautenschlager et al., 2024).

In this work, we participate in two AXOLOTL-24 subtasks for Finnish, Russian and German languages. The tasks include (a) bridging diachronic word uses and a synchronic dictionary and (b) definition generation for novel word senses. The first subtask aims to predict mappings between dictionary meaning entries and word usages while the second task plans to produce dictionary-like definitions for those unmatched usages with novel word meanings not covered by dictionaries. In the following, we outline the components of our system:

- For Subtask 1, we keep the workflow of the AXOLOTL-24 baseline system unchanged, which includes three components: producing embeddings for word usages, clustering these embeddings, and mapping between dictionary meaning entries and the resulting clusters. However, we make modifications to each component. The component-wise system comparison is presented in Table 1.

- For Subtask 2, unlike the baseline system, which requires costly model training for generating dictionary-like definitions for unmatched word usages, our system is training-free and does so by just prompting Large Language Models such as GPT-4 (Achiam et al., 2023) and LLaMA-3[4]. We provide the system comparison in Table 2.

[3] https://www.oed.com/information/updates

2 Related Work

This section reviews semantic change detection and discuss its potential connections with dictionaries.

Lexical Semantic Change Detection (LSCD) focuses on the automatic identification of shifts in word meanings over time. For instance, the word 'chill' used to mean 'cold' for individuals growing up in the 60s, but for those in the 90s, it means 'relaxed'. Many works proposed to detect meaning shifts by using static or contextualized embeddings (Eger and Mehler, 2016; Hamilton et al., 2016a,b; Martinc et al., 2020; Gonen et al., 2020; Kaiser et al., 2021; Montariol et al., 2021a; Teodorescu et al., 2022; Homskiy and Arefyev, 2022). Most work in LSCD has been done on an unsupervised task formulation (Schlechtweg et al., 2020) which neither involved a dictionary, nor providing interpretation or qualification of detected sense changes. While early work on static embeddings (Kim et al., 2014; Hamilton et al., 2016c) could qualify changes to a certain extent through nearest neighbors, it usually did not provide sense clusters in a dictionary-like manner. More recent work straightforwardly enables the induction of sense clusters through clustering of contextualized embeddings (Giulianelli et al., 2020; Kudisov and Arefyev, 2022; Montariol et al., 2021b; Arefyev and Bykov, 2021). More recently, Ma et al. (2024) presented a graph-based clustering approach to detect gained word senses with low frequency, and offered interpretability by visualizing cross-language semantic changes. The works by Giulianelli et al. (2023); Fedorova et al. (2024a) offer new ways of interpretability such as automatically generating sense definitions for usages from clusters. For an overview of recent model architectures incl. clustering approaches, see Zamora-Reina et al. (2022).

LSCD and dictionaries. The above-described approaches all have in common that they do not involve a dictionary in their task formulation. However, a variety of dictionaries is available for different languages and time periods (e.g. Dal, 1955; Paul, 2002; OED, 2009) providing valuable information characterizing a language stage on the lexical level. Thus, a possible alternative task formulation for LSCD is to start from an existing dictionary

[4] https://llama.meta.com/llama3/

and compare corpus usages against the dictionary entries in order to find usages not covered by the dictionary (Erk, 2006; Lautenschlager et al., 2024).

3 AXOLOTL-24 Shared Task

Participants are asked to solve the two subtasks:

- **Subtask 1 - bridging diachronic word uses and a synchronic dictionary**: This task is to identify mappings between dictionary entries and the word usages of each target word, i.e., that the task asks to detect whether each word usage has a novel sense or not, meaning that it is not (or is) recorded in dictionaries.
- **Subtask 2 - definition generation for novel word senses**: This task builds upon the mapping results of Subtask 1. It aims to generate dictionary-like definitions for the unmatched word usages discovered in Subtask 1, i.e., that these usages contain novel senses not covered by dictionaries.

An example for the Finnish target word 'palaus' is illustrated in Figure 2. Participants are provided with the mappings of usages at an earlier time period to dictionary entries (sense glosses) while the mappings for a later time period is unknown. Subtask 1 asks participants to predict which sense gloss Usage 3 belongs to. If a system predicts Usage 3 to have a novel sense not covered by existing sense glosses, then Subtask 2 asks to generate the gloss for the novel sense.

[Gloss 1]: kääntymys, hengellinen kääntyminen

[Gloss 2]: kuumuus

[Word Usage 1] (<1700): anna minulle yxi oikea catumus ia synnistä palaus.

[Word Usage 2] (<1700): Coska nyt Pauali cocosi ydhen coghon Risuija ia pani ne Tulen päle, edesmateli yxi Kyykerme palaudhesta.

[Word Usage 3] (>1700): Jumala on itze joca meisä sen suuren Palauxen ja muutoxen toimitta

[Mapping]: (Usage 1, Gloss 1),
(Usage 2, Gloss 2),
(Usage 3, [Gloss 1, Gloss 2, Unknown])

Figure 2: A running example for the target word 'palaus' from the Finnish test set. The first two usages (before 1700) belong to the earlier time period while the last one belongs to the later.

4 Our Systems

4.1 Subtask 1

Workflow. We reuse the workflow of the AXOLOTL-24 baseline system, which includes the following three components that are executed sequentially:

- **Producing embeddings of word usages**: This component aims to encode the usages of a target word.
- **Clustering embeddings**: This component is to partition the resulting embeddings of a target word into clusters. Each cluster contains embeddings with similar meanings.
- **Mapping between dictionary sense entries and clusters**: This component is to align dictionary sense entries with the resulting clusters. If the semantic meaning represented by a cluster is present in dictionaries, then we assign the dictionary entry to that cluster. Otherwise, a novel meaning is said to be identified. This implies the need for dictionary updates to include new sense entries.

Baseline. The baseline system proposes an unsupervised approach that does not rely on training data, i.e., the lack of mappings between word usages at an earlier time period and dictionary sense entries, to predict mappings for unknown word usages at a later period. The idea for the baseline system to implement the workflow is the following: For each target word, the baseline system begins with collecting all the relevant corpus usages available at an earlier time period. If corpus usages are unavailable[5], the system resorts to using dictionary definitions of the target word as substitutes. Secondly, the system aims to encode the meanings of the target word in various corpus usages. However, doing so is not trivial, as the positions of the target word in corpus usages are not always given in the AXOLOTL-24 datasets. Moreover, for morphologically rich languages, the automatic process of locating the target word in word usages is inaccurate. Thus, the baseline system approaches the meaning of a target word by using the sentence encoder LEALLA (Mao and Nakagawa, 2023) to produce the embedding for the entire word usage.

[5]For the Russian datasets in the AXOLOTL-24 shared task, some corpus usages in the 19th century are missing.

Components	Baseline	Our System
Embedding	word usages	word usages and words
Clustering	Affinity Prop.	Neighbor-based clustering
Mapping	first-indexed emb.	average emb.

Table 1: Component-wise comparison between the baseline and our system in Subtask 1.

After collecting word usage embeddings, the baseline system leverages a popular clustering approach known as Affinity Propagation (Frey and Dueck, 2007) to group word usage embeddings into several clusters. Each cluster contains multiple embeddings with similar meanings.

Lastly, to map between dictionary sense entries with unknown usages of a target word at a later time period, the baseline system proposes to align dictionary entries with the collective meaning of each cluster. In particular, for each cluster, the system chooses the embedding of the first-indexed usage of the target word in the AXOLOTL-24 datasets as the collective meaning represented by that cluster. It then computes the cosine similarity between that word usage embedding and the embedding of each dictionary entry (i.e., sense gloss). If the similarity score surpasses a predefined threshold, then all the word usages within that cluster are said to be matching that dictionary entry.

Our submitted system. Just like the baseline system, our system also does not rely on training data to predict mappings between unknown usages at a later time period and dictionary entries. However, we make substantial changes to each component of the workflow.

For each target word, we produce word usage embeddings[6] by using m-BERT (Devlin et al., 2019) to encode various corpus usages of the target word. Moreover, we create a vocabulary containing all the words available in the entire corpus, together with their average BERT-based word embeddings over their occurrences in the corpus. We take all the word usage embeddings of a target word and the vocabulary as input to derive a 3-layer semantic graph for each target word through our clustering method. Each semantic graph contains the following elements:

- **Root node** represents the average word usage embedding over all the usages of a target word in the corpus.
- **Nodes on the second layer** are centroids of each sense cluster, i.e., the average of word usage embeddings within each cluster.
- **Nodes on the third layer** are k-nearest neighbors to each cluster centroid.

[6]For our system, a word usage embedding is defined as the average of all m-BERT word embeddings in a corpus usage.

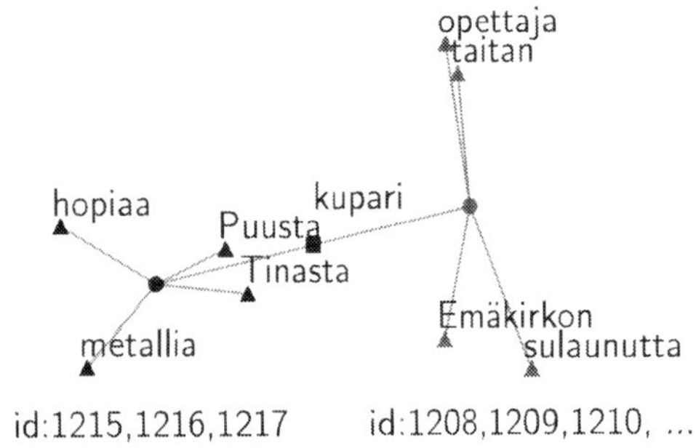

Figure 3: An illustration of our semantic graph for the Finnish target word 'kupari' (root node in the graph), together with two subtrees separating two meaning clusters. One cluster represents the meaning related to a metal (in black) that is covered by dictionaries while the other represents the novel meaning 'the recipient of metals as currency' (in blue) that is not. Each cluster contains 4-nearest neighboring words, together with their corpus usage IDs, to interpret the collective meaning of the cluster.

Note that our clustering only operates on embeddings, and the nodes on the second layer are built upon the clustering result. We introduce such a graph as a visualization tool after clustering to separate sense clusters and the corresponding word usages. See a two-dimensional illustration in Figure 3—where the graph separates a recorded word sense from an unrecorded (novel) sense, together with their word usages from the Finnish AXOLOTL-24 dev set.

Lastly, to map dictionary entries to clusters, our system differs from the baseline: Instead of choosing the first-indexed word usage embedding as the collective meaning of a cluster, our system does so by using the average word usage embedding. Here, we briefly outline our clustering approach. For further details, we refer to Ma et al. (2024).

Clustering. For each target word w, we denote $\mathcal{C}_w = \{c_1, c_2, \ldots, c_n\}$ as a word cloud consisting of a set of d-dimensional embeddings. Each embedding represents a corpus usage of the target word, and n denotes the number of word usages available in a given corpus that contain that target word. We aim to partition $\mathcal{C}_w$ into m clusters. Each cluster contains a subset of $\mathcal{C}_w$ representing embeddings of word usages with similar meanings. Our clustering method is illustrated in Algorithm 1. We choose our clustering over the baseline Affinity Propagation (Frey and Dueck, 2007) because target words in the AXOLOTL-24 datasets have 2-23 usages on average (c.f. Table 3), i.e., they only have low-frequency senses; in such a setup, our clustering largely outperforms Affinity Propagation (see Table 11 in Ma et al. (2024)). We present our clustering details in the following:

Algorithm 1 Our clustering method

Require: $\mathcal{C}_w = \{c_i\}_{i=1}^n$ as a set of word usage embeddings representing various usages of a target word w, t_{sc} as the maximum distance between similar clusters.

Initial centroids of clusters: $\mathcal{P}_w = \{p_i | p_i = c_i\}_{i=1}^n$
while $\min_{p_i \in \mathcal{P}_w, p_j \in \mathcal{P}_w, i \neq j} d(p_i, p_j) < t_{sc}$ **do**
  $\mathcal{P}_w = (\mathcal{P}_w \setminus \{p_i, p_j\}) \cup \{\frac{p_i + p_j}{2}\}$
end while
return $\mathcal{P}_w$

Our clustering method is similar to the bottom-up agglomerative clustering (Sibson, 1973) but differs in that we use a neighbor-based metric[7] to handle low-frequency clusters. The idea is the following: We start by treating each embedding as a separate cluster, and then iteratively merge two clusters when their centroids are of a distance smaller than the distance threshold t_{sc} until no further pairs of such similar clusters can be found. Following Ma et al. (2024), we use a neighbor-based distance metric in the clustering process to compute distances between clusters. Both the distance threshold and the number of nearest neighbors are hyperparameters, which we tune on dev sets.

Importantly, using a neighbor-based distance metric in the clustering process is crucial for handling many low-frequency word senses in the AXOLOTL-24 datasets. Ma et al. (2024) showed that using such a metric to compute distances between clusters is a contributing factor to identify

[7]For agglomerative clustering, the distance between two clusters is calculated as the average pairwise distance between usage pairs based on their embeddings. For us, each pairwise distance is calculated as the bipartite matching score over k-nearest neighbors of a word usage and those of another.

Components	Baseline	Our System
Collection	collect the mapping results of Subtask 1	
Generation	finetune XGLM	prompte LLMs

Table 2: Component-wise comparison between the baseline and our system in Subtask 2.

low-frequency sense clusters. The reason for this is the following: for a low-frequency sense with few word usages, relying on those usages to decide whether they should form a standalone low-frequency cluster or be merged into another cluster can be unreliable. However, with k-nearest neighbors of those usages participating (i.e., additional information provided) in the decision making, the decision becomes more reliable.

Lastly, for mapping, we select the average usage embedding (i.e., cluster centroid) as the collective meaning of a cluster, and compare that embedding with dictionary entries. We choose the average embedding over the embedding of the first-indexed usage of a target word (see Table 1) because the first-indexed choice is almost random. We use the average embedding to eliminate such randomness.

4.2 Subtask 2

Workflow. Our submitted system follows the workflow of the AXOLOTL-24 baseline that includes the two sequential components below:

- **Collecting unmatched word usages.** This component aims to collect word usages with novel senses not found in dictionaries. Doing so is straightforward: The mapping results from Subtask 1 include word usages that match dictionary entries, as well as unmatched (novel) usages. Here, we only collect those unmatched usages. We note that the system performance in Subtask 1 immediately impacts the quality of this component.
- **Generating definitions.** This component takes unmatched word usages as input and generates their dictionary-like definitions.

Baseline. The baseline system proposes a supervised approach that trains a generative model on train sets, i.e., the mappings between dictionary entries and matched word usages, in order to generate definitions for unmatched word usages. In particular, the system takes a target word and its matched word usages as input, and dictionary definitions of these word usages as the ground-truth output. The system uses the generative model XGLM (Lin et al., 2022) to encode the input and fine-tunes its model parameters by minimizing the cross-entropy loss in a way to make the generated definitions as close as possible to the ground-truth counterparts. Note that the fine-tuning process of the baseline is costly as it is executed separately for each language.

Our submitted system. Unlike the baseline system, our system is fully unsupervised[8]. After collecting unmatched word usages we prompt Large Language Models (LLMs) to generate definitions for these word usages. We experiment with several LLMs including open-source and commercial models (LLaMA and GPT). Figure 6 (appendix) illustrates the prompt to instruct GPT-3.5-turbo[9] to generate English definitions.

5 Experiments

Datasets. The shared task provides datasets for the two subtasks for Finnish, Russian and German languages. These datasets contain dictionary entries such as headwords (target words), the definitions of their meanings, word usages, the positions of the headwords within word usages, and time period (indicating whether word usages belong to an earlier or later time period).

For Finnish, the dataset is curated from Vanhan kirjasuomen sanakirja (Dictionary of Old Literary Finnish)[10] and is split into train, dev and test sets. It includes word usages from earlier and later time periods (before 1700 and after 1700). For Russian, the dataset from an earlier time period is sourced from Explanatory Dictionary of the Living Great Russian Language (Dal, 1955) while the dataset from a later period is from CODWOE (Mickus et al., 2022). Again, the dataset is divided into train, dev and test sets. For German, the dataset is collected from DWUG DE Sense (Schlechtweg, 2023). The German dataset is only available in the test phase, meaning that no train and dev sets are provided. This setup is to put submitted systems to test in handling an unseen language. We provide data statistics for the AXOLOTL24 shared task in Table 3, where the data from earlier and later time periods are treated as two separate corpora.

Implementation details in Subtask 1. The baseline system is unsupervised, although it still requires a number of hyperparameters. These hyperparameters include a threshold for the minimum similarity between a word usage and a dictionary definition based on their embeddings, as well as parameters required by Affinity Propagation, such as the choice of distance metrics to compute distances between clusters and the number of clustering iterations. The baseline system sets the similarity threshold to 0.3 and keeps the default parameters of Affinity Propagation unchanged for all languages. For our submitted system, two predefined hyperparameters are needed: the similarity threshold as for the baseline system, and the number of nearest neighbors required for generating a semantic graph and computing distances between clusters. After tuning on the development sets, we set the similarity threshold to 0.5 and the number of nearest neighbors to 5 for all languages. On a side note, the baseline system uses the sentence-level encoder LEALLA (Mao and Nakagawa, 2023) to produce word usage embeddings while our system uses the word-level encoder m-BERT (Devlin et al., 2019) to produce both word and word usage embeddings.

Implementation details in Subtask 2. The baseline system is supervised and finetunes the model parameters of XGLM (Lin et al., 2022) in the task of generating definitions for word usages. Doing so requires several hyperparameters, including learning rate and weight decay for the Adam optimizer (Kingma and Ba, 2014), and the number of epochs for training. The baseline system uses the default parameters of the Adam optimizer and sets the number of epochs to 1. Our submitted system, on the contrary, is fully unsupervised. For each target word, we take a set of word usages identified by our clustering approach in Subtask 1 and prompt LLMs to generate a collective definition for the usages of the target word. A predefined prompt is needed and we provide it in Figure 6. For LLMs, we experiment with GPT-3.5-turbo and GPT-4-turbo, LLaMA-2-7B and LLaMA-3-8B.

Prompt engineering. Note that our prompt is created from scratch and refined on a small selection of random instances in the development sets, meaning that our prompt is not optimal for the entire sets in any language. Our refinement process starts with an English prompt to instruct LLMs to generate Finnish, Russian and German definitions; however, LLMs often generate English def-

[8]Our system based on LLMs is unsupervised in that it does not rely on training data; however, the training data for pre-training LLMs include many human-annotated data.

[9]`https://platform.openai.com/docs/models/gpt-3-5-turbo`

[10]`https://kaino.kotus.fi/vks/`

Languages	Corpus #1 Period ($t-1$)	#usages	avg/u	max/u	min/u	Corpus #2 Period (t)	#usages	avg/u	max/u	min/u	#targets
Finnish (train)	1543-1650	45897	10	272	1	1700-1750	47242	11	214	2	4289
Finnish (dev)	1543-1650	3203	12	338	1	1700-1750	3351	12	266	2	254
Finnish (test)	1543-1650	3461	12	137	1	1700-1750	3264	11	114	2	275
Russian (train)	1800-1900	1912	2	12	1	1950-present	4581	5	19	1	924
Russian (dev)	1800-1900	421	2	11	1	1950-present	1605	8	30	1	201
Russian (test)	1800-1900	424	2	10	1	1950-present	1702	8	32	2	211
German (test)	1800–1899	584	24	25	20	1946–1990	568	23	25	14	24

Table 3: Statistics of the AXOLOTL-24 datasets. '#targets' denotes the number of target words; '#usages' means the total usage count of target words; 'avg/u' indicates the average usage count of each target word; 'max/u' indicates the maximum usage count per target word; 'min/u' indicates the minimum usage count per target word.

Systems	#Entries	Finnish ARI	Finnish macro-F1	Russian ARI	Russian macro-F1	German ARI	German macro-F1
deep-change(1)	17	**0.649**	**0.760**	**0.247**	0.640	0.322	0.510
deep-change(2)	16	**0.649**	**0.760**	0.048	**0.750**	**0.521**	**0.740**
Holotniekat	4	0.596	0.630	0.043	0.660	0.298	0.610
ABDN-NLP (Ours)	2	0.553	0.590	0.009	0.570	0.102	0.300
Baseline	5	0.023	0.230	0.079	0.260	0.022	0.130

Table 4: Results on the test-phase leaderboard for AXOLOTL-24 Subtask 1.

initions for non-English word usages; we address this by translating the English prompt into Finnish, Russian and German via Google Translate. Other factors for refinement include (a) the length of a definition, (b) determining when to stop generation in order to ensure that generated definitions are comparable in length to the ground-truth counterparts, and (c) the number of word usages for LLMs to generate a collective definition.

Evaluation. For Subtask 1, the Adjusted Rand Index (ARI) (Hubert and Arabie, 1985) and macro-F1 score are the two evaluation metrics for reporting and comparing system performances. ARI calculates how much a pair of word usages from the predictions belong to the same sense ID (or different sense IDs) as they should, while the macro-F1 score computes the precision and recall of word usages for each sense ID and then averages these scores across all sense IDs. Note that F1 only considers old senses in the "new" time period, meaning that mappings of word usages to novel senses are not evaluated. ARI considers both novel and old senses in the "new" time period.

For Subtask 2, generated definitions for those usages with novel senses are compared to their ground-truth counterparts by computing similarities between definition pairs. The AXOLOTL-24 shared task uses both lexical-based and embedding-based metrics to compute definition pair similarities. The metrics considered are BLEU (Papineni et al., 2002) and BERTScore (Zhang* et al., 2020). Other metrics appropriate for doing so include MoverScore (Zhao et al., 2019), BlonDe (Jiang et al., 2022) and DiscoScore (Zhao et al., 2023). The latter two metrics have shown to be well-suited for computing long-text pair similarities, particularly useful when dealing with lengthy definitions.

6 Results

We present the results of our systems and analyses on LLMs. Case studies are shown in Appendix A.

Subtask 1. We made two submissions for Subtask 1, with minor difference between them. The only difference is that the second submission includes additional predictions for the unseen German language. Table 4 compares the results of our system and other teams. We see that our system, based on the unsupervised graph-based clustering approach, outperforms the unsupervised baseline system by a large margin in all the languages. We observe a big performance drop for the German language compared to other two languages. One of the reasons for this is due to historical data issues. Unlike the Russian and Finnish corpus usages—which have been carefully preprocessed by AXOLOTL-24 organizers, German usages are not cleaned up and contain spelling variations (e.g., *nöthig* instead of *nötig*), OCR errors, escaping double quotes and

Systems	#Entries	Finnish BLEU	Finnish BERTScore	Russian BLEU	Russian BERTScore	German BLEU	German BERTScore
ABDN-NLP (Ours)	3	**0.107**	**0.706**	0.027	0.677	0.000	**0.714**
TartuNLP	1	0.028	0.679	**0.587**	**0.869**	**0.010**	0.630
t-montes	7	0.023	0.675	0.027	0.656	**0.010**	0.650
Baseline	6	0.033	0.403	0.005	0.377	0.000	0.490

Table 5: Results on the test-phase leaderboard for Subtask 2. Our post-evaluation results are underlined.

others. These issues would incur out-of-vocabulary tokens, potentially resulting in poor performance.

Lastly, our system performs poorly in terms of ARI on both Russian and German test sets, despite having better scores in macro-F1. The performance gap between F1 and ARI attributes to the scope mismatch between the two metrics: new sense IDs are excluded when computing F1, whereas both old and novel sense IDs are considered when computing ARI. This means unlike ARI, F1 would not penalize wrong prediction of novel sense IDs. As a result, although our system performs poorly for novel sense predictions in Russian (see the ARI_new result in Table 6), the F1 result (F1=0.570) is still quite high.

Metrics	Finnish	Russian	German
macro-F1	0.590	0.570	0.300
ARI	0.596	0.043	0.298
ARI_new	0.633	0.039	0.524
ARI_old	0.619	0.754	0.260

Table 6: Post-evaluation results of our system on the test-phase leaderboard for AXOLOTL-24 Subtask 1. ARI_new considers new sense IDs only, while ARI_old focuses on old sense IDs.

Note that the results from our system and other teams are not directly comparable as the system details of other teams are missing. For instance, it remains unclear whether their systems are unsupervised or not. Overall, we see the deep-change system achieves the best performance in all the three languages (including the unseen German language where train and dev sets are unavailable); however, their achievement is made through a total of 33 submissions and the leaderboard only reports their best performance; this indicates overfitting.

Subtask 2. We refined our prompts for instructing GPT-3.5-turbo. This results in three submissions we made for Subtask 2, where the prompts in our final submission yield the best performance on the randomly selected instances from the Finnish and Russian dev sets. Note that the final prompts are the Finnish, Russian and German translations from the English version (see Figure 6).

LLMs	Finnish BLEU	Finnish BERTScore	Russian BLEU	Russian BERTScore
Baseline	**0.248**	0.607	**0.886**	0.595
GPT-3.5-turbo	0.022	0.640	0.035	0.676
GPT-4-turbo	0.025	**0.658**	0.036	**0.678**
LLaMA-2-7B	0.013	0.611	0.024	0.604
LLaMA-3-8B	0.013	0.603	0.021	0.601

Table 7: Comparing LLMs on the dev set in Subtask 2.

Despite not using train sets, our unsupervised system, based on GPT-3.5-turbo, considerably outperforms the supervised baseline system in all setups (see Table 5). This might be because the train sets are not large enough for fine-tuning XGLM (Lin et al., 2022). When compared with other teams, our system ranks first for Finnish and German, and ranks second for Russian. Again, it is unclear whether other teams take advantage of the train sets, and thus the direct comparison with other systems is not meaningful.

Comparison of LLMs. Figure 7 compares the results of several LLMs. Overall, we observe that our unsupervised system based on LLMs greatly outperforms the supervised baseline system in terms of BERTScore. However, our system performs worse than the baseline in BLEU. This is because our generated definitions are not lexically but semantically similar to their ground-truth counterparts. The reason for this is the following: BLEU cannot recognize text pair similarity when there is no lexical overlap between them (Reiter, 2018). This is particularly problematic when dealing with morphologically rich languages like Russian and Finnish. In such languages, high-quality generated definitions might differ greatly from ground-truth definitions in morphological forms; in this case, BLEU would wrongly assign low scores to high-quality definitions due to the absence of lexical overlap. This is demonstrated by our results, where BLEU scores (0.02-0.03) mean very few lexical overlaps between the generated and ground-truth definitions while BERTScore (0.65-0.67) suggest that definition pairs are indeed semantically similar.

Additionally, we observe the supervised baseline system performs best in terms of BLEU, particularly for Russian. This means the generated definitions are lexically similar to the ground-truth. This might be attributed to the memorization of training sets. We see that many ground-truth definitions contain words from corpus usages. During training, the baseline system might have learned to prioritize the use of words from corpus usages when generating definitions. Lastly, although GPT-4-turbo has shown to greatly outperform GPT-3.5-turbo in many NLP tasks, we demonstrate that the superiority of GPT-4-turbo is not considerable in Subtask 2, especially for Russian, so is the case for LLaMA-2-7B and LLaMA-3-8B.

7 Limitations

Dataset size. The datasets provided in the shared task are quite small and contain very few word usages for each headword on average. This is indeed expected as the datasets are sourced from handcrafted dictionaries where lexicographers only collect a small number of word usages for each dictionary sense entry due to the costly mapping process. Here we argue that it would be better to use such datasets only for evaluation purposes, rather than for dividing them into train sets. Furthermore, we call for an additional database containing a large amount of word usages for each headword to support the development of unsupervised systems, as we see their potential demonstrated by our unsupervised system, which greatly outperformed the supervised baseline system in Subtask 2.

Text encoder. Our system relies on m-BERT (Devlin et al., 2019), a text encoder invented five years ago, to produce embeddings for both word usages and words in Subtask 1. In recent years, many text encoders (Ni et al., 2022; Neelakantan et al., 2022) have been introduced and shown to perform much better than m-BERT in various NLP tasks. Other encoders such as XL-LEXEME (Cassotti et al., 2023) specialized in capturing lexical semantic changes also meet our needs.

Data contamination. The works by Balloccu et al. (2024); Ravaut et al. (2024) show that the results of LLMs can be misleading due to the data contamination issue, i.e., that test sets are included in the training data of LLMs. This issue might be present in the AXOLOTL-24 test sets for the two reasons: (a) the source base of the test sets is publicly accessible and (b) LLMs do not document their training data at all. Thus, it is unclear whether the headwords, word usages, and definitions in the test sets have been exposed to LLMs. Future work should design a measure to calculate data contamination rates of LLMs on the AXOLOTL-24 datasets.

8 Conclusions

In this work, we presented our system that automates the process of identifying novel word meanings not covered in dictionaries and generating their definitions. We evaluated our system in the AXOLOTL-24 shared task. Our results show that supervision is not always useful: Without access to train sets, our unsupervised system still greatly outperforms the supervised baseline system, as well as other team submissions in Subtask 2—which demonstrates the potential of LLMs in generating definitions for novel word usages; however, the uncertainty as to whether the AXOLOTL-24 test sets are included in the training data for pre-training LLMs calls for careful investigation in the future.

Acknowledgements

We thank the anonymous reviewers for their thoughtful feedback that greatly improved the texts. Dominik Schlechtweg has been funded by the research program 'Change is Key!' supported by Riksbankens Jubileumsfond (under reference number M21-0021).

References

Josh Achiam, Steven Adler, Sandhini Agarwal, Lama Ahmad, Ilge Akkaya, Florencia Leoni Aleman, Diogo Almeida, Janko Altenschmidt, Sam Altman, Shyamal Anadkat, et al. 2023. Gpt-4 technical report. *arXiv preprint arXiv:2303.08774*.

Nikolay Arefyev and Dmitrii Bykov. 2021. An interpretable approach to lexical semantic change detection with lexical substitution. volume 2021-June, pages 31–46.

Simone Balloccu, Patrícia Schmidtová, Mateusz Lango, and Ondrej Dusek. 2024. Leak, cheat, repeat: Data contamination and evaluation malpractices in closed-source LLMs. In *Proceedings of the 18th Conference of the European Chapter of the Association for Computational Linguistics (Volume 1: Long Papers)*, pages 67–93, St. Julian's, Malta. Association for Computational Linguistics.

Pierpaolo Basile, Annalina Caputo, Tommaso Caselli, Pierluigi Cassotti, and Rossella Varvara. 2020. Overview of the EVALITA 2020 Diachronic Lexical Semantics (DIACR-Ita) Task. In *Proceedings of the 7th evaluation campaign of Natural Language Processing and Speech tools for Italian (EVALITA 2020)*, Online. CEUR.org.

Andreas Blank. 1997. *Prinzipien des lexikalischen Bedeutungswandels am Beispiel der romanischen Sprachen*. Niemeyer, Tübingen.

Pierluigi Cassotti, Lucia Siciliani, Marco DeGemmis, Giovanni Semeraro, and Pierpaolo Basile. 2023. XL-LEXEME: WiC pretrained model for cross-lingual LEXical sEMantic changE. In *Proceedings of the 61st Annual Meeting of the Association for Computational Linguistics (Volume 2: Short Papers)*, pages 1577–1585, Toronto, Canada. Association for Computational Linguistics.

Jing Chen, Emmanuele Chersoni, Dominik Schlechtweg, Jelena Prokic, and Chu-Ren Huang. 2023. ChiWUG: A graph-based evaluation dataset for Chinese lexical semantic change detection. In *Proceedings of the 4th Workshop on Computational Approaches to Historical Language Change*, pages 93–99, Singapore. Association for Computational Linguistics.

VI Dal. 1955. Explanatory dictionary of the living great russian language.

Jacob Devlin, Ming-Wei Chang, Kenton Lee, and Kristina Toutanova. 2019. BERT: Pre-training of deep bidirectional transformers for language understanding. In *Proceedings of the 2019 Conference of the North American Chapter of the Association for Computational Linguistics: Human Language Technologies, Volume 1 (Long and Short Papers)*, pages 4171–4186, Minneapolis, Minnesota. Association for Computational Linguistics.

Steffen Eger and Alexander Mehler. 2016. On the linearity of semantic change: Investigating meaning variation via dynamic graph models. In *Proceedings of the 54th Annual Meeting of the Association for Computational Linguistics (Volume 2: Short Papers)*, pages 52–58, Berlin, Germany. Association for Computational Linguistics.

Katrin Erk. 2006. Unknown word sense detection as outlier detection. In *Proceedings of the Human Language Technology Conference of the NAACL, Main Conference*, pages 128–135, New York City, USA. Association for Computational Linguistics.

Mariia Fedorova, Andrey Kutuzov, Nikolay Arefyev, and Dominik Schlechtweg. 2024a. Enriching word usage graphs with cluster definitions. In *The 2024 Joint International Conference on Computational Linguistics, Language Resources and Evaluation*.

Mariia Fedorova, Timothee Mickus, Niko Tapio Partanen, Janine Siewert, Elena Spaziani, and Andrey Kutuzov. 2024b. AXOLOTL'24 shared task on multilingual explainable semantic change modeling. In *Proceedings of the 5th Workshop on Computational Approaches to Historical Language Change*, Bangkok. Association for Computational Linguistics.

Brendan J Frey and Delbert Dueck. 2007. Clustering by passing messages between data points. *science*, 315(5814):972–976.

Dirk Geeraerts. 2020. *Semantic Change*, chapter 1. American Cancer Society.

Mario Giulianelli, Marco Del Tredici, and Raquel Fernández. 2020. Analysing lexical semantic change with contextualised word representations. In *Proceedings of the 58th Annual Meeting of the Association for Computational Linguistics*, pages 3960–3973, Online. Association for Computational Linguistics.

Mario Giulianelli, Iris Luden, Raquel Fernandez, and Andrey Kutuzov. 2023. Interpretable word sense representations via definition generation: The case of semantic change analysis. In *Proceedings of the 61st Annual Meeting of the Association for Computational Linguistics (Volume 1: Long Papers)*, pages 3130–3148, Toronto, Canada. Association for Computational Linguistics.

Hila Gonen, Ganesh Jawahar, Djamé Seddah, and Yoav Goldberg. 2020. Simple, interpretable and stable method for detecting words with usage change across corpora. In *Proceedings of the 58th Annual Meeting of the Association for Computational Linguistics*, pages 538–555, Online. Association for Computational Linguistics.

William L. Hamilton, Jure Leskovec, and Dan Jurafsky. 2016a. Cultural shift or linguistic drift? comparing two computational measures of semantic change. In *Proceedings of the 2016 Conference on Empirical Methods in Natural Language Processing*, pages 2116–2121, Austin, Texas. Association for Computational Linguistics.

William L. Hamilton, Jure Leskovec, and Dan Jurafsky. 2016b. Diachronic word embeddings reveal statistical laws of semantic change. In *Proceedings of the 54th Annual Meeting of the Association for Computational Linguistics (Volume 1: Long Papers)*, pages 1489–1501, Berlin, Germany. Association for Computational Linguistics.

William L Hamilton, Jure Leskovec, and Dan Jurafsky. 2016c. Diachronic word embeddings reveal statistical laws of semantic change. *arXiv preprint arXiv:1605.09096*.

Daniil Homskiy and Nikolay Arefyev. 2022. Deep-Mistake at LSCDiscovery: Can a multilingual word-in-context model replace human annotators? In *Proceedings of the 3rd International Workshop on Computational Approaches to Historical Language*

Change, Dublin, Ireland. Association for Computational Linguistics.

Lawrence Hubert and Phipps Arabie. 1985. Comparing partitions. *Journal of classification*, 2:193–218.

Yuchen Jiang, Tianyu Liu, Shuming Ma, Dongdong Zhang, Jian Yang, Haoyang Huang, Rico Sennrich, Ryan Cotterell, Mrinmaya Sachan, and Ming Zhou. 2022. BlonDe: An automatic evaluation metric for document-level machine translation. In *Proceedings of the 2022 Conference of the North American Chapter of the Association for Computational Linguistics: Human Language Technologies*, pages 1550–1565, Seattle, United States. Association for Computational Linguistics.

Jens Kaiser, Sinan Kurtyigit, Serge Kotchourko, and Dominik Schlechtweg. 2021. Effects of pre- and post-processing on type-based embeddings in lexical semantic change detection. In *Proceedings of the 16th Conference of the European Chapter of the Association for Computational Linguistics: Main Volume*, pages 125–137, Online. Association for Computational Linguistics.

Adam Kilgarriff, Pavel Rychlỳ, et al. 2010. Semi-automatic dictionary drafting. In *A Way with Words*, pages 299–312.

Yoon Kim, Yi-I Chiu, Kentaro Hanaki, Darshan Hegde, and Slav Petrov. 2014. Temporal analysis of language through neural language models. In *LTCSS@ACL*, pages 61–65. Association for Computational Linguistics.

Diederik P Kingma and Jimmy Ba. 2014. Adam: A method for stochastic optimization. *arXiv preprint arXiv:1412.6980*.

Artem Kudisov and Nikolay Arefyev. 2022. BOS at LSCDiscovery: Lexical substitution for interpretable lexical semantic change detection. In *Proceedings of the 3rd International Workshop on Computational Approaches to Historical Language Change*, Dublin, Ireland. Association for Computational Linguistics.

Andrey Kutuzov and Lidia Pivovarova. 2021. Rushifteval: a shared task on semantic shift detection for russian. In *International Conference on Computational Linguistics and Intellectual Technologies: Dialogue 2021*. Redkollegija sbornika.

Jonathan Lautenschlager, Simon Hengchen, and Dominik Schlechtweg. 2024. Detection of non-recorded word senses in english and swedish. *Preprint*, arXiv:2403.02285.

Xi Victoria Lin, Todor Mihaylov, Mikel Artetxe, Tianlu Wang, Shuohui Chen, Daniel Simig, Myle Ott, Naman Goyal, Shruti Bhosale, Jingfei Du, Ramakanth Pasunuru, Sam Shleifer, Punit Singh Koura, Vishrav Chaudhary, Brian O'Horo, Jeff Wang, Luke Zettlemoyer, Zornitsa Kozareva, Mona Diab, Veselin Stoyanov, and Xian Li. 2022. Few-shot learning with multilingual generative language models. In *Proceedings of the 2022 Conference on Empirical Methods in Natural Language Processing*, pages 9019–9052, Abu Dhabi, United Arab Emirates. Association for Computational Linguistics.

Xianghe Ma, Michael Strube, and Wei Zhao. 2024. Graph-based clustering for detecting semantic change across time and languages. In *Proceedings of the 18th Conference of the European Chapter of the Association for Computational Linguistics (Volume 1: Long Papers)*, pages 1542–1561, St. Julian's, Malta. Association for Computational Linguistics.

Zhuoyuan Mao and Tetsuji Nakagawa. 2023. LEALLA: Learning lightweight language-agnostic sentence embeddings with knowledge distillation. In *Proceedings of the 17th Conference of the European Chapter of the Association for Computational Linguistics*, pages 1886–1894, Dubrovnik, Croatia. Association for Computational Linguistics.

Matej Martinc, Syrielle Montariol, Elaine Zosa, and Lidia Pivovarova. 2020. Capturing evolution in word usage: just add more clusters? In *Companion Proceedings of the Web Conference 2020*, pages 343–349.

Timothee Mickus, Kees Van Deemter, Mathieu Constant, and Denis Paperno. 2022. Semeval-2022 task 1: CODWOE – comparing dictionaries and word embeddings. In *Proceedings of the 16th International Workshop on Semantic Evaluation (SemEval-2022)*, pages 1–14, Seattle, United States. Association for Computational Linguistics.

Syrielle Montariol, Matej Martinc, and Lidia Pivovarova. 2021a. Scalable and interpretable semantic change detection. In *Proceedings of the 2021 Conference of the North American Chapter of the Association for Computational Linguistics: Human Language Technologies*, pages 4642–4652, Online. Association for Computational Linguistics.

Syrielle Montariol, Matej Martinc, and Lidia Pivovarova. 2021b. Scalable and interpretable semantic change detection. In *2021 Annual Conference of the North American Chapter of the Association for Computational Linguistics*.

Arvind Neelakantan, Tao Xu, Raul Puri, Alec Radford, Jesse Michael Han, Jerry Tworek, Qiming Yuan, Nikolas Tezak, Jong Wook Kim, Chris Hallacy, et al. 2022. Text and code embeddings by contrastive pre-training. *arXiv preprint arXiv:2201.10005*.

Jianmo Ni, Gustavo Hernandez Abrego, Noah Constant, Ji Ma, Keith Hall, Daniel Cer, and Yinfei Yang. 2022. Sentence-t5: Scalable sentence encoders from pre-trained text-to-text models. In *Findings of the Association for Computational Linguistics: ACL 2022*, pages 1864–1874, Dublin, Ireland. Association for Computational Linguistics.

OED. 2009. *Oxford English Dictionary*. Oxford University Press.

Kishore Papineni, Salim Roukos, Todd Ward, and Wei-Jing Zhu. 2002. Bleu: a method for automatic evaluation of machine translation. In *Proceedings of the 40th annual meeting of the Association for Computational Linguistics*, pages 311–318.

Hermann Paul. 2002. *Deutsches Wörterbuch: Bedeutungsgeschichte und Aufbau unseres Wortschatzes*, 10. edition. Niemeyer, Tübingen.

Mathieu Ravaut, Bosheng Ding, Fangkai Jiao, Hailin Chen, Xingxuan Li, Ruochen Zhao, Chengwei Qin, Caiming Xiong, and Shafiq Joty. 2024. How much are llms contaminated? a comprehensive survey and the llmsanitize library. *arXiv preprint arXiv:2404.00699*.

Ehud Reiter. 2018. A Structured Review of the Validity of BLEU. *Computational Linguistics*, 44(3):393–401.

Dominik Schlechtweg. 2023. *Human and Computational Measurement of Lexical Semantic Change*. Ph.D. thesis, University of Stuttgart, Stuttgart, Germany.

Dominik Schlechtweg, Barbara McGillivray, Simon Hengchen, Haim Dubossarsky, and Nina Tahmasebi. 2020. SemEval-2020 task 1: Unsupervised lexical semantic change detection. In *Proceedings of the Fourteenth Workshop on Semantic Evaluation*, pages 1–23, Barcelona (online). International Committee for Computational Linguistics.

Dominik Schlechtweg, Shafqat Mumtaz Virk, and Nikolay Arefyev. 2024a. The LSCD benchmark: a testbed for diachronic word meaning tasks. *arXiv preprint arXiv:2404.00176*.

Dominik Schlechtweg, Shafqat Mumtaz Virk, Pauline Sander, Emma Sköldberg, Lukas Theuer Linke, Tuo Zhang, Nina Tahmasebi, Jonas Kuhn, and Sabine Schulte im Walde. 2024b. The DURel annotation tool: Human and computational measurement of semantic proximity, sense clusters and semantic change. In *Proceedings of the 18th Conference of the European Chapter of the Association for Computational Linguistics: System Demonstrations*, pages 137–149, St. Julians, Malta. Association for Computational Linguistics.

Robin Sibson. 1973. Slink: an optimally efficient algorithm for the single-link cluster method. *The computer journal*, 16(1):30–34.

Daniela Teodorescu, Spencer von der Ohe, and Grzegorz Kondrak. 2022. UAlberta at LSCDiscovery: Lexical semantic change detection via word sense disambiguation. In *Proceedings of the 3rd Workshop on Computational Approaches to Historical Language Change*, pages 180–186, Dublin, Ireland. Association for Computational Linguistics.

Frank D. Zamora-Reina, Felipe Bravo-Marquez, and Dominik Schlechtweg. 2022. LSCDiscovery: A shared task on semantic change discovery and detection in Spanish. In *Proceedings of the 3rd Workshop on Computational Approaches to Historical Language Change*, pages 149–164, Dublin, Ireland. Association for Computational Linguistics.

Tianyi Zhang*, Varsha Kishore*, Felix Wu*, Kilian Q. Weinberger, and Yoav Artzi. 2020. Bertscore: Evaluating text generation with bert. In *International Conference on Learning Representations*.

Wei Zhao, Maxime Peyrard, Fei Liu, Yang Gao, Christian M. Meyer, and Steffen Eger. 2019. MoverScore: Text generation evaluating with contextualized embeddings and earth mover distance. In *Proceedings of the 2019 Conference on Empirical Methods in Natural Language Processing and the 9th International Joint Conference on Natural Language Processing (EMNLP-IJCNLP)*, pages 563–578, Hong Kong, China. Association for Computational Linguistics.

Wei Zhao, Michael Strube, and Steffen Eger. 2023. DiscoScore: Evaluating text generation with BERT and discourse coherence. In *Proceedings of the 17th Conference of the European Chapter of the Association for Computational Linguistics*, pages 3865–3883, Dubrovnik, Croatia. Association for Computational Linguistics.

A Appendix

Case studies. Figures 4 and 5 compare generated and ground-truth definitions for the two target words sampled from the Russian dev set. For the first target word, the generated definition by GPT-3.5-turbo is quite similar to the ground-truth definition. We suspect that the word 'radioactive' in the corpus usage suggests that the location is likely to be a burial ground. We test this hypothesis by removing the word 'radioactive' and prompting GPT-3.5-turbo again: the generation definition then becomes "a burial ground or cemetery" (English translation)—which is too general and refers to a non-metaphorical scenario where people are buried underground, whereas "radioactive burial ground" could mean metaphorically a site for disposing of radioactive waste.

Consider the second word, which is computer slang meaning "to make something inaccessible". Interestingly, GPT-3.5-turbo did not provide any guess on the definition of the word usage, and just acknowledged that this is a Russian word without giving further details. This could be because GPT-3.5-turbo lacks knowledge of the cybersecurity term 'DDoS' (it means a denial-of-service attack), and thus it did not provide any guess for the definition. This analysis, however, is only based on two cases. Future work could include a due diligence investigation of wrongly generated definitions, such as categorizing incorrect definitions.

#A usage for the word: [могильник]

Якобы тут, возле Черниховки, находится радиоактивный могильник.

(English Translation): Allegedly here, near Chernikhovka, there is radioactive burial ground.

[Generated Definition by GPT-3.5-turbo]:
Могильник - место захоронения радиоактивных отходов или погибших.

(English Translation): Burial ground - a burial place for radioactive waste or dead.

[Ground-truth Definition]:
спец. место захоронения радиоактивных отходов; специальное сооружение для такого захоронения.

(English Translation): Special burial site for radioactive waste; special structure for such burial.

[Evaluation]: BLEU: 21.2 BERTScore: 0.79

Figure 4: A well-generated definition in Russian.

A usage for the headword: [положить]

Также впустую ушли две недели ддоса главной страницы пикаперов, хотя форум положить удалось.

(English Translation): Also, two weeks of DDoSing the main page were wasted pick-up artists' pages, although they managed to put down the forum.

[Generated Definition by GPT-3.5-turbo]:
язык, используемый в России и других странах.

(English Translation): A language used in Russia and other countries.

[Ground-truth Definition]:
комп. жарг. привести в нерабочее состояние, «уронить», сделать недоступным что-либо.

(English Translation): A computer slang referring to something inoperative and inaccessible.

[Evaluation]: BLEU: 3.38 BERTScore: 0.59

Figure 5: A poorly-generated definition in Russian.

Our prompt. Figure 6 illustrates the prompt used to instruct GPT-3.5-turbo to generate definitions in English.

[Instruction]:
Imagine that you are a lexicographer, given a headword {target_word} in {lang}, write the dictionary definition of its usage in the following quotations:

1. First quotation
2. Second quotation

[Requirements]:
The definition you create should be brief. A maximum of ten words is allowed. The definition ends at the first period.

[Response]:
Definition (string): {definition}

Figure 6: An illustration of our prompt used to instruct GPT-3.5-turbo to generate dictionary-like definitions, where 'quotation' is synonymous of 'word usage'.

Towards a GoldenHymns Dataset for Studying Diachronic Trends in 19th Century Danish Religious Hymns

Ea Lindhardt Overgaard
School of Communication and Culture
Aarhus University
elt@cc.au.dk

Pascale Feldkamp
Center for Humanities Computing
Aarhus University
pascale.moreira@cc.au.dk

Yuri Bizzoni
Center for Humanities Computing
Aarhus University
yuri.bizzoni@cc.au.dk

Abstract

Religious hymns represent a particularly complex literary domain, due to their specialized registry and context, which remain understudied in computational linguistics, especially in less-resourced languages. We introduce GoldenHymns(S), a novel dataset of Danish historical religious hymns (1798–1873). To allow for a comparison with existing NLP tools' performances, the GoldenHymns(S) dataset is enriched with modernized Danish versions as well as English translations of the hymns. To further the study of sentiment changes in Danish religious texts - a particularly relevant aspect of their development - we also provide verse-level valence annotations by human experts, and we examine the effect of language change and specificity on the performance of contemporary Danish sentiment analysis tools. The dataset is the first resource for evaluating and enhancing the performance of sentiment analysis within the realm of historical religious poetry in the Danish language.

1 Introduction

Historical texts present a challenge for the performance of computational models, especially in under-resourced languages (Schmidt et al., 2021; Zilio et al., 2024). Danish religious hymns represent just such a challenge for computational tools. The hymnal tradition has a central place in Danish culture (Nielsen, 2020), and the official hymn books, which disseminates and curates the hymnal heritage, is the most widely distributed book in the poetry genre in Denmark (Sandstrøm, 2007). Communal singing ("fællessang") remains popular, continually drawing on and revitalizing the hymnal heritage (Baunvig, 2020), especially the production of central hymnists of the late 18th and 19th century. It is a common interpretation that older hymns depict a dualistic view of the world, where a dominant eschatological understanding highlights earthly instances more negatively and religious instances more positively than in newer hymns. A hymn dataset provided with valence scores makes investigations in such polarity shifts possibly both regarding certain religious concepts within the hymns as well as general sentiment structures in the chronology of the hymns. During the 19th century, a historically critical period for Danish society (Glenthøj and Ottosen, 2021) and culture alike (Mortensen et al., 2006),[1] a long line of hymnists and poets took up the endeavor to boost Danish literature and contribute to official church hymn books,[2] which theologians and civil servants wished to "express happy feelings" (Kjærgaard, 2003). Hymnists brought deism and Enlightenment ideals into a new Christian outlook (Baunvig and Nielbo, 2023; Nielsen, 2020), which echoes in the continued publication of official hymn books to this day. This change in mood in 19th century hymns remains relatively unexplored, with studies focusing on individual authors over historical trends (Baunvig, 2023), especially in traditional humanities research (Elbek, 1959).

In this paper, we present two main contributions to the quantitative exploration of historical sentiment changes in religious hymns:

1) We present a new dataset – the GoldenHymns(S)[3] – of Danish historical religious hymns

[1]The period is known as *the Danish Golden Age* for its cultural and political productivity.

[2]Official church hymn books were released in Denmark in 1569.

[3]The "Small" (S) designation reflects its current composition of 65 hymns, with plans for expansion in the future.

Proceedings of the 5th Workshop on Computational Approaches to Historical Language Change, pages 55–61
August 15, 2024 ©2024 Association for Computational Linguistics

with human-annotated valence scores. [4]

2) We evaluate different sentiment analysis (SA) tools on the dataset. To distinguish the effects of language change on the systems' performance, we repeat our experiments on a version translated into modern Danish.

2 Related Works

2.1 Available resources

There are currently three datasets for Danish hymns available. The first is the work of one author, N.F.S. Grundtvig (CGR, 2019), where the hymnal collection is only a subset of the full authorship of Grundtvig. The second dataset indexes hymnal books and bibles related to the reformation era (DSLDK, 2021), spanning from 1529 to 1569 – where only the latter collection, from 1569, is an authorized hymnal book.[5] A third dataset consists of the hymns from the most recent authorized Danish hymnal book of 2002 (By-, Land- og Kirkeministeriet and Vajsenhus, 2002). Beyond the most modern one, the existing datasets treat one authorship or specific period. As such, there is to the best of our knowledge no dataset that facilitates the study of diachronic change in the genre.

The second (Reformation) dataset does enable study of the development of a (limited) period, as well as comparative analysis of historical characteristics and registry of religious Danish in the genre. Yet, the hymns included in the dataset feature comprehensive orthographic deviations (compared to modern Danish), posing a challenge to human annotators with its 16th century Danish, possibly resulting in low levels of agreement between annotators.

With the GoldenHymns(S) dataset, we thus supplement available Danish resources, facilitating both diachronic study and supplying texts that have been modernized and annotated by scholars experienced with the linguistic registry.

2.2 Sentiment Analysis of historical texts

While the study of sentiment has come to be a central approach in computational literary studies (Rebora, 2023), its applications to Danish literature – especially historical – are relatively rare. Though significantly less resourced than English, there is no obvious issue halting the use of SA tools in the Danish language and literature: Danish dictionary-based tools show comparable performance (Schneidermann and Pedersen, 2022), and a tool like Sentida has been validated against human scores of text (chunks) across domains, showing a robust performance for fiction (Lauridsen et al., 2019). Still, there is no comprehensive Danish SA benchmark, and the performance is generally evaluated on modern Danish across (few) domains. Assessing the performance of SA models on historical Danish and Norwegian literary texts, Allaith et al. (2023) found that multilingual transformer models outperformed models trained on modern Danish as well as classifiers based on Danish lexical resources. Schmidt et al. (2021) similarly found that transformers did best on historical German drama. Testing dictionary-based methods on historical German plays, Schmidt and Burghardt (2018) found that dictionaries did well when extending their lexica with historical variants. They also found an issue with low levels of agreement between annotators who were not used to the historical register – foregrounding the importance of using annotators experienced with the register of the period and domain. Toft (2023) addressed how modernizing historical Danish hymns improved the performance of Danish NLP tools achieving significant improvements in the accuracy of automatic annotating of POS-tags using models like DaCy and SpaCy, underscoring the importance of either normalizing historical language or adapting NLP techniques when working with historical texts.

	No.	Vs	Words	$\bar{x}$ Vs	Period
Hymns	65	1,914	10,303	32.9	1798-1873

Table 1: Presenting the dataset: The total number of verses (Vs) and words, mean ($\bar{x}$) number of verses per hymn, and timeframe.

3 Dataset

The dataset consists of 65 Danish hymns collected at random from three different official hymnal books from the years 1798 (n=35), 1857 (n=17), and 1873 (n=13) (psa, 1798, 1857, 1873). Popular hymns from earlier periods might be included in these collections, but following Danish tradition, hymns in the hymnals were edited from their authentic version into a version that fitted the church at the time. Each hymn is then edition-specific and

[4]The dataset is available at: `https://github.com/EaLindhardt/GoldenHymns-S-`

[5]In Denmark, authorized hymnal books have been published since 1569, meaning they are approved by the Danish Crown, and should by law be used in the Danish National Church.

represents the associated hymnal. The hymns are characterized by their metrical structure (verses, rhymes, etc.), their poetic language style (exclamations, figurative language), and their archaic and formal language - e.g., the use of Latinized "est" for "is" ("er"). Each hymn is coupled with its modernized version and English translation (which maintain the original verse style and syntactical structure), as well as a sentiment score per verse.

Hymns are challenging for SA due to their register. Their poetic and figurative language, often embodies subtle emotional tones, as well as the cultural and religious contexts they refer to (Skovsted et al.; Nielsen, 2020). Due to the poetic style, the sentiment analysis is based on dividing the hymns into verses (Table 1). Our unit of analysis was verses since the fundamental unit of poetry is the verse, rather than the sentence. A syntactically sound sentence might thus not be present in every verse, which further challenges sentimental interpretations.

By including both original and modernized versions of the hymns in the dataset we allow observations on how modernizing the hymns affects Danish sentiment analysis. Furthermore, by including validated English translations, we provide accessibility for English-speaking researchers and cross-linguistic comparability (e.g. comparing English SA model performance). Examples of verses from the dataset is shown in Table 2, with examples of the original verse, its modernization and its English translation.

Sentence	Score
J Mistvivl, Angest, Smerte (M) I mistvivl, angst og smerte (En) In doubt, anxiety, and pain	2.0
Ungdomsliv i Morgenrøden (M) Ungdomsliv i morgenrøden (En) Youthful life in the morning's red glow	7.0

Table 2: Example of a positive and negative sentence (original, modernized and English translation) with the human mean score.

4 Methods

We provide an overview of how the dataset was supplemented and annotated for valence (by human annotators and automatic systems). We then show a use-case of the valence annotation, comparing human to automatic scores – both overall for original and modernized versions of the hymns and for each of the hymn book collections separately – to examine systems' performance and how it may vary throughout the period covered by our data.

4.1 Modernization and translation

Beyond the original hymn texts, the dataset includes modernized versions and English translations of each verse following the original verse and syntactical structure. The verses were modernized by two scholars, who prompted ChatGPT 3.5,[6] and subsequently validated each output verse manually against the original to ensure that spelling and vocabulary were updated, keeping semantic and syntactical changes to a minimum. English translations were created by using Google Translate, and then again manually revised and validated by two bilingual experts.

4.2 Human Sentiment Annotation

Danish language and literature scholars (n=2)[7] read and scored all 1,914 verses – defined by line breaks – on a 0 to 10 valence scale: 0 signifying the lowest, and 10 the highest valence (for example sentences see Table 2). Here, valence was intended as the sentiment expressed by the verse. Annotators were instructed to try reporting on the sentiments embedded in the verse, i.e., to think about the valence of each verse individually, not overthinking context.

We report a relatively high inter-rater correlation, with a Spearman's r between their scores of 0.726 – high considering the fragmentary nature of the text rated (verses, not sentences) and considering that humans rarely have an agreement higher than 80% for tasks like positive/neutral/negative tagging (Wilson et al., 2005) or 0.80 Krippendorff's α for continuous scale polarity annotation of non-fiction texts (Batanović et al., 2020).[8]

4.3 Automatic Annotation

We used several models on Danish sentiment analysis, both transformer- and dictionary-based (the latter of which are usually also rule-based), to score the verses in the hymns for valence. Dictionary-based methods remain popular due to their transparency and versatility, and appear to perform well

[6]The prompt was: "Oversæt til moderne dansk retstavning", i.e. "translate to modern Danish spelling".

[7]The annotators (MA and PhD in literature) were native Danish speakers and had domain knowledge in 19th century Scandinavian literature and historical religious hymns.

[8]For a discrete sentiment annotation task similar to the one presented here – albeit on modern fiction – Bizzoni and Feldkamp (2023) report a Spearman correlation between annotators (n=2) of 0.624.

	Alex.inst.	Senda	RoBERTa	Asent	Afinn	Sentida
Hymns original	0.39	0.32	0.39	0.40	0.39	**0.49**
Hymns modernized	0.42	0.35	0.46	0.41	0.40	**0.53**

Table 3: Sentiment analysis of hymns: Spearman correlation between scores on the **original** (above) and **modernized lines** (below) to the human mean scores (annnotated on the original lines). Transfomer-based systems are on the left, and dictionary and rule-based systems are on the right. For the correlations, all pvalues are <0.01.

	Alex.inst.	Senda	RoBERTa	Asent	Afinn	Sentida
1798	0.29 (0.36)	0.30 (0.36)	0.36 (0.40)	0.35 (0.33)	0.36 (0.34)	**0.43 (0.44)**
1857	0.39 (0.36)	0.36 (0.38)	0.43 (0.51)	0.41 (0.42)	0.38 (0.39)	**0.49 (0.53)**
1873	0.43 (0.48)	0.30 (0.33)	0.37 (0.46)	0.40 (0.44)	0.40 (0.44)	**0.51 (0.56)**

Table 4: Sentiment analysis over time: Spearman correlation between scores on the **original** and **modernized lines** (in parentheses) to the human mean scores for each hymn-collection individually (1798, 1857, and 1873). Transfomer-based systems on the left, dictionary and rule-based systems on the right. For the correlations, all pvalues are <0.01.

on literary texts (Bizzoni and Feldkamp, 2023). We test sentiment dictionaries that have had a wide application in Danish. Our chosen dictionary-based tools were:

Afinn: A valence dictionary without rules, created from Twitter data and various open sources.[9] The dictionary includes many inflections of the same lemma. Valence scores range from -5 to +5.

Sentida: A rule-based system inspired by the English VADER, considering negations, adverb modifiers, and more.[10] Sentida integrates the Afinn dictionary with the 10,000 most frequent Danish lemmas, which were manually annotated by the authors (Lauridsen et al., 2019). It relies on stemming to find matching dictionary entries during inference. Valence scores range from -5 to +5.

Asent: A rule-based system that is part of the DaCy suite (asent_da_v1), a comprehensive NLP toolkit for Danish.[11] It uses the Afinn dictionary by default and adds rules for handling negations, modifiers, intensifiers, etc. Scores range from -1 to +1.

Moreover, we use more recent Transformer-based models, which are becoming popular and show potential applied to literary texts (Elkins, 2022) and historical literary texts (Allaith et al., 2023). We chose to use two off-the-shelf models currently developed for Danish SA, as well as one widely used multilingual model, RoBERTa xlm, which has shown a good performance on literary prose (Bizzoni and Feldkamp, 2023):[12]

Senda:[13] was specifically created for Danish. It is based on the Roberta architecture and pretrained on an extensive collection of Danish texts.

Alexandra Institute sentiment base:[14] represents another Danish-oriented transformer model fine-tuned for sentiment analysis tasks. This model is provided by the Alexandra Institute.

RoBERTa xlm multilingual base sentiment:[15] uses cross-lingual training techniques, designed to enhance its capacity for understanding and processing multiple languages by transferring knowledge. This method allows the model to apply skills from one language to another, which can improve its generalization in sentiment analysis. However, this may limit its effectiveness with language-specific nuances, particularly in specialized domains.

We opted to exclude GPT models or new generation LLMs at this stage. Generative models like GPT suffer from increased opacity even with respect to traditional transformers and, in the case of the largest models, are trained on unknown data. Most importantly, GPTs' generative nature makes any application dependent on prompting, which introduces a level of variability and inconsistency that would complicate our results. While this was

[9] https://github.com/fnielsen/afinn

[10] https://github.com/Guscode/Sentida

[11] https://centre-for-humanities-computing.github.io/DaCy

[12] We maintained all presets as the default when applying these models, so that the hyperparameters are as specified in the documentation of the individual model (see the model hyperlinks).

[13] https://huggingface.co/larskjeldgaard/senda

[14] https://huggingface.co/alexandrainst/da-sentiment-base

[15] https://huggingface.co/cardiffnlp/twitter-xlm-roberta-base-sentiment

not a problem in the text modernization phase, as it made sense to review and correct the result, we opted to stick to tools specifically trained to return an SA output from a text, leaving the introduction of generative models to a later phase.

5 Results

We report the performance (Spearman's *rho*) of system sentiment scores compared to human scores in Table 3. It appears that dictionary-based tools (Afinn, Sentida and Asent) perform comparable to or – in the case of Sentida – better than transformer-based methods. Moreover, all methods improve when applied to modernized texts, against the original text, with the biggest improvements observed for Sentida (+0.04) and RoBERTa (+0.07). Across the collections, published in 1798, 1857, and 1873, models generally improve over time. Notably this trend is weakened – though not gone – when applied to the modernized versions of the text (Table 4). Irrespective of the year of publication, Sentida continues to perform the best in this genre.

Among transformer-based models, the Alexandra Institute and RoBERTa xlm models appear to perform best, and the consistency of their performance over time appears only slightly worse than dictionary-based models (e.g., a 0.12 point difference for the Alexandra Institute model, and an 0.8 point difference for Sentida when contrasting coefficients of the earliest and the latest collection).

6 Discussion and Conclusions

Contrary to previous findings on modern narrative (Bizzoni and Feldkamp, 2023) and historical drama and narrative texts (Allaith et al., 2023; Schmidt et al., 2021), where multilingual transformer-based models appeared to perform best, we find that dictionary-based methods outperform transformer-based models in this domain. Transformer-based models may depend more heavily on the presence of syntactically sound phrases (which are not always extant in hymn verses), and be impaired by a verse-level tokenization of the hymns, worsening their performance. It is interesting to note that systems that put particular emphasis on the valence of individual words appear to perform better in contexts – such as a single poetic verse – where semantic blow of single words is more central. An intriguing observation of this study is the overall improvement of models through time, which also holds true when applying the models to modernized verses. It is possible that hymns evoke sentiment differently through time, with hymnists changing their affective strategies, so that factors like the level of language concreteness, which has been shown to elude SA models and impact perceived sentiment in literary texts (Bizzoni and Feldkamp, 2024), might change through time.

Studies on sentiment analysis (SA) within the domain of historical hymns can contribute to the broader field of SA in literary genres. Hymns, with their consistent and limited themes, use of topics and metaphors, serve as a good starting point for exploring SA in poetry in general. This consistency provides a controlled environment to refine and test SA methodologies, as the genre is quite accessible to machine processing, which can then be applied to more complex and varied literary forms. Insights gained from SA in hymn literature not only enhance our understanding of emotional expression in religious and historical texts but also offer valuable methodologies that can be adapted for other literary genres. For instance, the success of dictionary-based models in outperforming transformer-based models within the context of hymn analysis suggests that traditional, lexicon-driven approaches may have advantages in certain types of literary analysis such as poetis genres. This could be due to the repetitive and formulaic nature of hymns, which might be better captured by dictionary-based models. By starting with hymns, researchers can develop robust techniques that address the unique challenges of poetic texts, such as figurative language and complex emotional expressions. These techniques can then be extended to analyze sentiment in a wide range of literary genres, from classical poetry to modern prose, thus enriching the field of SA in literature as a whole.

Overall, insights from the current study show ample reason to work towards expanding this dataset in the future, both in terms of size and temporal range. Future work might test the improvement of SA tools' performance when supplying lexica of historical language variants, and examine the development in hymnal sentiment across time generally or in connection with certain concepts. We also plan to work on larger datasets and to fine-tune models on this kind of sentiment annotations. Finally, an undoubtedly interesting next step would be that of testing the behaviour of generative large language models on the task, both in terms of similarity with human judgments and in terms of prompt-dependent variability.

References

1798. *Evangelisk-kristelig Psalmebog til Brug ved Kirke- og Huus-Andagt.* Kongl. Vaisenhus, Kiøbenhavn.

1857. *Nyt Tillæg til evangelisk-christelig Psalmebog.* Kongl. Vaisenhus, Kiøbenhavn.

1873. *Tillæg til Psalmebog for Kirke- og Huus-Andagt.* Kongl. Vajsenhuses Forlag, Kjøbenhavn.

Ali Allaith, Kirstine Degn, Alexander Conroy, Bolette Pedersen, Jens Bjerring-Hansen, and Daniel Hershcovich. 2023. Sentiment Classification of Historical Danish and Norwegian Literary Texts. In *Proceedings of the 24th Nordic Conference on Computational Linguistics (NoDaLiDa)*, pages 324–334, Tórshavn, Faroe Islands. University of Tartu Library.

Vuk Batanović, Miloš Cvetanović, and Boško Nikolić. 2020. A versatile framework for resource-limited sentiment articulation, annotation, and analysis of short texts. *PLoS ONE*, 15(11):e0242050.

Katrine F. Baunvig and Kristoffer Nielbo. 2023. Benign Structures. The Worldview of Danish National Poet, Pastor, and Politician N.F.S. Grundtvig (1783-1872). *Digital Humanities in the Nordic and Baltic Countries Publications*, 5(1):1–10. Number: 1.

Katrine Frøkjær Baunvig. 2020. Forestillede fællesskabers virtuelle sangritualer: Forskningsprojekt vil kaste lys over den kulturelle betydning af den virtuelle fællessang under corona-tiden. *Tidsskriftet SANG*, 1(1):40–45. Number: 1.

Katrine Frøkjær Baunvig. 2023. A Computational Future? Distant Reading in the Historical Study of Religion. In *Stepping Back and Looking Ahead: Twelve Years of Studying Religious Contact at the Käte Hamburger Kolleg Bochum*, pages 325–352. Brill. Section: Stepping Back and Looking Ahead: Twelve Years of Studying Religious Contact at the Käte Hamburger Kolleg Bochum.

Yuri Bizzoni and Pascale Feldkamp. 2023. Comparing transformer and dictionary-based sentiment models for literary texts: Hemingway as a case-study. In *Proceedings of the 3rd International Workshop on Natural Language Processing for Digital Humanities*, pages 219–226, Tokyo, Japan. Association for Computational Linguistics.

Yuri Bizzoni and Pascale Feldkamp. 2024. Below the sea (with the sharks): Probing textual features of implicit sentiment in a literary case-study. In *Proceedings of the Third Workshop on Understanding Implicit and Underspecified Language*, pages 54–61, Malta. Association for Computational Linguistics.

By-, Land- og Kirkeministeriet and Det Kgl. Vajsenhus. 2002. Den danske salmebog online.

CGR. 2019. Salmer Dataset. Centre for Grundtvig Research (CGR), GitHub repository.

DSLDK. 2021. Salmer Dataset. Society for Danish Language and Literature (DSLDK), GitHub repository.

Jørgen Elbek. 1959. Grundtvig og de latinske salmer. *Grundtvig-Studier*, 12(1):7–64.

Katherine Elkins. 2022. *The Shapes of Stories: Sentiment Analysis for Narrative*. Cambridge University Press.

Rasmus Glenthøj and Morten Nordhagen Ottosen. 2021. *Union eller undergang: kampen for et forenet Skandinavien.* Gads Forlag.

Jørgen Kjærgaard. 2003. *Salmehåndbog*. Det Kgl. Vajsenhus' Forlag.

Gustav Aarup Lauridsen, Jacob Aarup Dalsgaard, and Lars Kjartan Bacher Svendsen. 2019. SENTIDA: A New Tool for Sentiment Analysis in Danish. *Journal of Language Works - Sprogvidenskabeligt Studentertidsskrift*, 4(1):38–53. Number: 1.

Klaus P. Mortensen, May Schack, and Annemette Sørensen, editors. 2006. *Dansk litteraturs historie*. Gyldendal.

Marita A. Nielsen. 2020. Salmesprog. In *Dansk Sproghistorie Bind 4. Sprog i brug*. Aarhus University Press and Society for Danish Language and Literature (DSLDK).

Simone Rebora. 2023. Sentiment Analysis in Literary Studies. A Critical Survey. *Digital Humanities Quarterly*, 17(2).

Bjarne Sandstrøm. 2007. Salmen - fra kampsang til lovprisning. In V. A. Pedersen, M. Schack, and K. P. Mortensen, editors, *Dansk Litteraturs Historie 1100-1800*. Gyldendal.

Thomas Schmidt and Manuel Burghardt. 2018. An Evaluation of Lexicon-based Sentiment Analysis Techniques for the Plays of Gotthold Ephraim Lessing. In *Proceedings of the Second Joint SIGHUM Workshop on Computational Linguistics for Cultural Heritage, Social Sciences, Humanities and Literature*, pages 139–149, Santa Fe, New Mexico. Association for Computational Linguistics.

Thomas Schmidt, Katrin Dennerlein, and Christian Wolff. 2021. Using Deep Learning for Emotion Analysis of 18th and 19th Century German Plays. In Manuel Burghardt, Lisa Dieckmann, Timo Steyer, Peer Trilcke, Niels-Oliver Walkowski, Joëlle Weis, and Ulrike Wuttke, editors, *Fabrikation von Erkenntnis: Experimente in den Digital Humanities*, pages 1–32. Melusina Press.

Nina Schneidermann and Bolette Pedersen. 2022. Evaluating a New Danish Sentiment Resource: the Danish Sentiment Lexicon, DSL. In *Proceedings of the 2nd Workshop on Sentiment Analysis and Linguistic Linked Data*, pages 19–24, Marseille, France. European Language Resources Association.

Morten Skovsted, Mads Djernes, Kirsten Nielsen, Martin Horsntrup, and Hanne J. Jakobsen. Hvad gør en ny salme til en god salme? *Salmedatabasen*.

Ea Lindhardt Toft. 2023. 1500-talssalmer og danske sprogmodeller. *19. Møde om Udforskningen af Dansk Sprog*.

Theresa Wilson, Janyce Wiebe, and Paul Hoffmann. 2005. Recognizing Contextual Polarity in Phrase-Level Sentiment Analysis. In *Proceedings of Human Language Technology Conference and Conference on Empirical Methods in Natural Language Processing*, pages 347–354, Vancouver, British Columbia, Canada. Association for Computational Linguistics.

Leonardo Zilio, Rafaela Radünz Lazzari, and Maria Jose Bocorny Finatto. 2024. NLP for historical Portuguese: Analysing 18th-century medical texts. In *Proceedings of the 16th International Conference on Computational Processing of Portuguese*, pages 76–85, Santiago de Compostela, Galicia/Spain. Association for Computational Lingustics.

A Feature-Based Approach to Annotate the Syntax of Ancient Chinese

Chenrong Zhao
Department of Chinese Language and Literature / Peking University
crzhao@pku.edu.cn

Abstract

This paper is concerned with annotating the syntax of ancient Chinese, which is a series of languages in the same development process. The major challenge is to ensure the annotations of languages at different stages are comparable. To this end, we propose a feature-based approach that integrates the deductive feature design from the Chomskyan school and the inductive feature design from traditional philological studies. We demonstrate the effectiveness of our approach by annotating a collection of representative sentences that cover various linguistic phenomena that are extensively discussed in the literature. As a result, we establish a corpus of 673 (for now) ancient Chinese sentences paired with syntactic analyses, covering from 700s B.C.E. to 1900s C.E. The corpus can be utilised as a guideline for future large-scale TreeBanking.

1 Introduction

This paper proposes a feature-based method for annotation that makes the evolution of functional categories and structures in different language systems comparable. A fundamental methodology for diachronic linguistics, the comparative method (Meillet, 1925; Hoenigswald, 1950, 1965; Harris and Campbell, 1995) that identifies and explains form-meaning pairs (i.e., phonological and semantic correspondences) mainly in phonology and morphology among languages from different places or eras, encounters challenges in the field of syntax at the very beginning step of establishing corresponding sets. Various attempts have been made to identify relatively fixed comparable components within the evolving and generative (and therefore infinite) set of sentences (Winter, 1984; Rankin, 2017). One approach considers categories as fundamental, but lexical categorization and the functions of categories vary across languages or in different language periods. Another influential approach is the Parameter Comparative Method (PCM; Guardiano et al., 2016; Longobardi, 2014, 2017; Crisma et al., 2020) that splits the parts of speech (POS; Lyons, 1968) i.e., word categories into syntactic features. It offers a more nuanced comparative framework for understanding syntactic functions across diverse languages based on streamlined parameters in phylogenetic comparisons, but it falls short on languages without morphological markers, such as Chinese.

A distinct perspective on features is needed to address the deficiency. In addition to formal features encoded by morphology (Chomsky, 1995; Adger and Svenonius, 2011), the categorial features (Chomsky, 1970) encompass information of syntactic position, which serves as a crucial foundation for the syntax of languages without formal markers. Another feature, individuation (Bisang, 1999, 2002; Imai and Mazuka, 2003) characterises syntactic functional components, which may be integrated with lexical formally in these languages. Moreover, the particularities of syntactic representation in specific languages are deeply considered. Drawing on Chinese as an example, we annotate features for structures and functional components that underwent significant changes during the language's evolution over two millennia. Our proposed features can represent and effectively differentiate typical instances across different stages.

As we further develop this annotation approach into a large-scale endeavour, we could model language systems across different eras and extract patterns in functional features, revealing deeper rules of language development beyond traditional studies focused on individual structures.

2 Feature Design

Our proposed features aim to rectify the common oversight of languages lacking morphological markers. This in turn facilitates the comparative

Proceedings of the 5th Workshop on Computational Approaches to Historical Language Change, pages 62–71
August 15, 2024 ©2024 Association for Computational Linguistics

analysis of syntactic evolution across different periods for such languages.

2.1 From Categories to Features

The cornerstone of language syntactic modelling lies in annotated databases, where syntactic information such as POS tags, categories, and syntactic functions are marked. Drawing on theoretical research and linguistic practice, we propose that features can serve as the foundation for such annotations, striking a balance between inductive and deductive approaches while also accounting for the influence of both syntax and lexicon on grammar rules.

Annotation of POS is challenging for languages like Chinese due to their flexibility. According to (Rijkhoff and van Lier, 2013), FLEXIBLE LANGUAGES have word classes covering functions associated with multiple traditional categories (verbs, nouns, and adjectives). "Traditional word classes", also known as "semantic categories", as suggested by (Rauh, 2010), vary in distribution across languages. In actual analysis, "word classes" are often distinguished semantically, while syntactic classes focus on functions and positions. It is tricky to establish a satisfactory category system following the principle of syntactic categories due to the "flexible" nature of languages like Chinese, where words can appear in various positions without markers.

In response to challenges in categories, linguistic theories have shifted towards lexicalized approaches, seen in frameworks like LFG (Kaplan et al., 1981; Bresnan et al., 2015) and HPSG (Pollard and Sag, 1988, 1994). The Borer–Chomsky Conjecture (BCC; Borer, 1984) pursued the possibility that the syntactic functions of vocabulary are carried by the lexical themselves in the form of features. The feature system and its values not only avoid the problem of classification while describing the syntactic function of the lexicon but also present a more systematic picture of syntactic evolution by means of the temporal change of feature values. However, the interpretable and uninterpretable feature structure in the minimalist program associated with lexical entries (Baker, 2008) barely suits isolating languages like Chinese; neither do the features or parameters have been highly developed in historical linguistics like PCM, for the widely accepted feature system is based on inflectional languages, while Chinese lacks formal inflexion. Therefore, we propose a feature system that mainly contains [±N], [±V] and [±IND(ividuation)] that concerns whether words can be anchored to the real world when used grammatically (represented by the feature of individuation). When features are correlated with functional components (Borer, 1984; Fukui, 1988), this method enables comparisons not only across different stages of the same language but also across different languages. This section will provide details on the feature system.

2.2 Features: [±N], [±V] and [±IND]

Flexible languages—take Chinese, especially ancient Chinese, as an example—have rather vague boundaries between nouns, verbs, and adjectives. Here is a typical example[1]:

(1) ěr (尔) yù (欲) Wú wáng (吴王) wǒ (我) hū (乎) ?
2PRON want king of Wú 1PRON Q?
"Do you want to make me be (like) the king of Wu?"

The categorical features [±N] and [±V], proposed by (Chomsky, 1970), delineating categories based on feature restrictions, address the problem. Despite the lack of morphological inflexion for ϕ features in Chinese, the relatively strict word order (Sun and Givón, 1985; Sun, 1996; Rijkhoff and van Lier, 2013; Van Lier et al., 2013) of Chinese sentences, typically following the SVO sequence, allows for determinations of [±N] and [±V]. For instance, in Example (1), 吴王 *(Wú wáng)* precedes the pronoun 我 *(wǒ)* indicating it was used as a verb[2].

The combination of [±N], [±V] and [±F] (functional) distinguishes thematic categories from functional categories[3] (Chomsky, 1970; Grimshaw, 2000). However, in ancient Chinese, where functional categories were less developed, many func-

[1]In this sentence, 吴王 *(Wú wáng)* is a proper noun (refers to the certain king of 吴 (Wú) who was assassinated), yet could still take an object and express causative meaning. The shift of semantics (if there is one) without any morphological representation is periphrastic for containing a complex argument structure of "make (into)".

[2]In our annotation, 吴王 *(Wú wáng)* is tagged as [+N], [+V], [-IND], [+VBLZ], where [+N] and [+V] aligns with the adjectives in Chomsky (1970), while [+VBLZ] represents "verbalisation", indicating the noun here means to make somebody be 吴王 *(Wú wáng)*. [-VBLZ] is used to express the opposite of verbalisation – nominalisation. These usages are common in ancient Chinese.

[3]Every thematic category would exhibit the [–F] feature, while every functional category would exhibit the [+F] feature. Thematic categories include verbs, nouns, adjectives and prepositions. Functional categories include inflexions, determiners, degree adverbs, and complementizers.

tional features, like ϕ features and TAM (tense, aspect, and mood), were carried by lexical items. The process of grammaticalization involves the emergence of these functional features as independent from lexical items, resulting in the formation of functional categories.

The mixed state of functional and thematic categories can be described from the point of view of INDIVIDUATION. Specifically, when a thematic category enters a sentence, it has to be individuated in some manner. Individuation (Imai and Mazuka, 2003) serves to anchor objects or events, indicating grammatical information regarding whether an object is identifiable and a motion is anchored[4]. While nouns are generally individuated by the determiner (or classifiers in certain languages) (Chierchia, 1998; Davidse, 2004; Zhang, 2013), the individuation of verbs includes all the components that wrap around the outside of the verb to make it legitimately used, like TAM, little v, etc.. We can draw the mapping relations of categories and the three features [±N], [±V], [±IND], with an additional [±VBLZ] in table 1. The feature [+VBLZ] represents "verbalised actuation" that refers to the action of making the object to be a particular role or status, and "verbalised conation" refers to the action of regarding the object as treating someone. [-VBLZ] mainly denotes the nominalizers in ancient Chinese.

Categories	Features			
	N	V	IND	VBLZ
CommonNoun	+	-	-	/
Copula	+	-	-	/
Pronoun, ProperNoun	+	-	+	/
NominalClassifier, Quantifier	+	-	+	/
Adjective	+	+	-	/
MotionVerb	-	+	-	/
Preposition	-	+	-	/
ModalVerb	-	+	+	/
VerbalClassifier, Disposal, Passive, Tense/Aspect, v(所 suǒ)	-	+	+	/
Sentence-finalParticle (SFP)	-	-	+	/
CoordinateMarker	-	-	-	/
Modifier-introducingParticle	+	±	-	/
VerbalisedActuation	+	+	-	+
VerbalisedConation	+	-	-	+
Nominaliser (者 zhě, 之 zhī)	+	-	-	-

Table 1: Features of common categories in Chinese at different times

[4]The feature is effective, especially in languages lacking inflexion, but it could also be used on morphological languages, for it is based on cognitive theory (c.f. Langacker (1991))

2.3 [±IND]: Case Study on Nominal Features

The [±IND] feature will be further illustrated through changes in the annotation of quantifiers within the domain of nouns.

In Mandarin Chinese, there are primarily two major categories of noun forms. One type requires a classifier when modified by a numeral, while the other functions directly as an argument without requiring a classifier. As shown in example (7) and (3).

(2) sān (三) (běn (本) shū (书)
three CL books
"three books"

(3) bān (搬) zhuō zi (桌子)
move table
"move the table (at the corner)/moving tables (is a simple job)"

In the nominal domain, the most significant change is the emergence of classifiers (Wei, 2000). Therefore, to depict the diachronic evolution of noun representations in Chinese, it is necessary to account for the function of classifiers. As is shown above, classifiers are obligatory when nouns are quantified by numbers, therefore they are numeral classifiers as Allan (1977) proposed and followed by others (Croft, 1994; Craig, 1994; Grinevald, 2000; Aikhenvald, 2000). Classifiers bear the features [+N, -V, +IND], where the [+N] and [-V] are projected from N. In sentence (7), the noun takes the features [+N, -V, -IND], while the combination of the [-IND] feature and the [+IND] feature of the classifier 本 (*běn*) results in the entire expression being marked as [+IND], meaning that the noun 书 (*shū*) is instantiated of the concept of book, and is individuated from other books.

Following the principles of generative linguistics, determining the syntactic position of classifiers is necessary. Under the influence of the DP (Determiner Phrase) hypothesis (Abney, 1987), a prevailing view among scholars suggests a developmental tendency of classifiers in Chinese to adopt the functional role of the determiner (D), as evidenced by specific instances of classifier usage in certain dialects (Cheng and Sybesma, 1999, 2005; C-TJ et al., 2009; Gebhardt, 2011; Li, 2013). For example, the classifier 只 (*tsəʔ*) in sentence (4) (Li and Bisang, 2012) does not appear with numbers and indicates definiteness. There are also numerous opponents to this viewpoint, with the majority arguing that such usage is constrained by other factors.

For instance, Wu and Bodomo (2009) suggests that definiteness is not an inherent attribute of Chinese classifiers. The definite reading in examples like (4) is provided by the context.

(4) tsəʔ (只) kiu (狗) ɕan kan (像看) san (生)
CL dog look-like have
mao biŋ (毛病) die (喋)
sickness PFV
"This dog looks ill." Fuyang (Wu dialect)

Due to the relatively weak syntactic constraints on nominal expressions in Chinese, we argue that feature selection should be guided by communicative needs. The concept of communicative needs reminds us to prioritise aspects in Chinese speakers' cognition that are more readily conceptualised, thus exhibiting greater universality and systematicity. From the functional perspective, individuation, the pragmatic function of numeral classifiers, is defined as "to establish a sensory perception as an individual by actualizing the inherent properties which constitute its conceptual unity" (Bisang, 1999, 2002), contrasting with "identification". The concept of "identification" here, which differs from the function of DP (determiner phrase), does not explicitly treat an object as an individual. For instance, it's conceivable to associate a sensory perception with the concept of, for example, an "apple" without explicitly delineating its inherent boundaries (Bisang, 2002).

The function of individuation, expressed through classifiers, emerged only after Middle Chinese. Before the appearance of individual classifiers, numerals directly modified nouns in Archaic Chinese, similar to English. According to Huang (1964); Li (2000) and others, it is commonly accepted that the evolution of classifiers progressed through four stages: from "noun + numeral" or "numeral + noun"[5], to "noun + numeral + noun", further evolving into "noun + numeral + classifier", and ultimately forming structures like "numeral + classifier + noun". The forms in the second and third stages serve as transitional forms, leading to the emergence of classifiers in Modern Chinese, where classifiers originated from nouns occupying the same position. As for the structure of "numeral + classifier + noun" phrases in Mandarin Chinese, some scholars propose that it stems from the repositioning of "numeral + classifier" from "noun + numeral + classifier" structures (Wang, 1957), as shown in (5), while others argue that after the formation of classifiers, "numeral + classifier + noun" structures directly replaced "numeral + noun" (Yang, 1993; Zhang, 2010).

(5) $[_{NumP}$ numeral classifier$]_i$ noun t_i

To describe the noun forms in different periods of Chinese, it is crucial to address the question: did individuation exist in Archaic Chinese before the emergence of individual classifiers? If so, how was this function realised grammatically? If in Mandarin Chinese, common nouns behave akin to mass nouns in English, such as "water", requiring individuation through classifiers to serve as arguments, then common nouns in Archaic Chinese exhibited characteristics of count nouns. With the emergence and development of classifiers, bare nouns and numeral-noun structures tended to convey generic reference (He et al., 2011; Krifka et al., 1995) and individuated reference, respectively. In other words, before the emergence of classifiers, Chinese nouns lacked gender, number, and case markings, with generic and individuated references both conveyed by bare nouns without formal distinction. We argue that in Archaic Chinese, the grammaticalization level of the noun domain was low, and the individuation function was not yet fully isolated from count nouns. The distinction between the nominal domain and the verbal domain was also not clear. At this stage, it is challenging to assign specific word-class labels with external distinctiveness and internal consistency, let alone functional categories. This is why we propose the use of feature marking. In the feature system we proposed, nouns in numeral-noun and noun-numeral structures in Archaic Chinese possess the feature [+IND], inherited from count nouns. Before the emergence of individual classifiers, countable nouns, proper nouns, demonstrative pronouns, and personal pronouns all bore the [+IND] feature. However, with the development of quantifiers, this feature shifted to functional elements like classifiers and pronouns, while lexical elements such as common nouns and proper nouns became [-IND]. For instance, in Mandarin Chinese, classifiers are now obligatory before proper nouns, as illustrated in example (8).

(6) sān[+N, -V, +NUM] (三)
three

[5] In Archaic Chinese, both forms existed: the former was primarily used for counting, while the latter tended to convey predication (Cheng, 2015). These meanings were inherently inclined, as Yao (2008) pointed out.

rén[+N, -V, +IND] (人)
person
"three persons" Archaic Chinese

(7) sān[+N, -V, +NUM] (三)
three
gè[+N, -V, +IND] (个)
CL
rén[+N, -V, -IND] (人)
person
"three persons" Mandarin Chinese

(8) yī (一) gè (个) yuè liang (月亮)
one CL moon
"one moon/the moon"

These features are deductively constructed to represent lexical and functional categories while inductively drawing from linguistic insights, thus covering a wider range of interconnected phenomena and a flexible, appropriate representation of syntactic information.

3 Test Suite

The three-feature annotation can be applied to a representative test suite that covers typical changing structures in Chinese based on Wei (2000), ensuring the feasibility of the annotation method with minimal annotation required.

Utilising prior research on classical Chinese syntax, we have created a test suite of 673 sentences spanning three major historical periods, annotated with syntactic structures and features from 82 literary sources. The research-oriented dataset spans from the East-Zhou dynasty (which began in the 700s B.C.E.) to the Qing dynasty (which ended in the 1900s C.E.), encompassing influential documents and Chinese classics widely referenced by scholars and native speakers. According to the periodization of Chinese historical syntax by Pan (1982), these materials can be categorised into three stages, as shown in Table 2.

Stage	#Book	#Sent
Archaic Chinese (700s B.C.E.–1 C.E.)	10	33
Middle Chinese (200s C.E.–900s C.E.)	19	87
Early Mandarin (1000s C.E.–1900s C.E.)	53	553
Total	82	673

Table 2: Distribution of test suite sentences.

These linguistic phenomena signify significant grammatical shifts in ancient Chinese over time, extensively explored in traditional research. Wei (2000) evaluates the frequency of certain typical phenomena at different times to determine the exact period when the reanalysis and analogy happened. The phenomena examined by Wei (2000) cover changes related to nominal and verbal domains. Nominal expressions include the development of suffixes, plural markers, 3rd personal pronouns, classifiers and quantifiers that modify N. Verbal expressions include the changes of actualisation, perfective marker, passive structure, disposal marker, etc.. The test suite encompasses crucial processes of reanalysis wherein these items (including lexical and functional) and structures undergo transformation.

In the nominal domain, aside from the grammaticalization of pronouns and classifiers, noun affixes in word formation (子 *(zi),* 儿 *(er),* 头 *(you),* etc.) and morphology (们 *(men)*) formed. Specifically, the test suite covers pronouns that have been largely simplified since Middle Chinese compared with those in Archaic Chinese (Wei, [1990] 2004), as well as the third-person pronouns that formed in Middle Chinese (Wang, 1945; Wei, [1990] 2004). The emergence of individual classifiers and plural affix 们 *(men)* are included in the test suite as well.

The aforementioned functional categories originate from the development of nouns, while other functional categories stem from the evolution of verbs. For instance, 了 *(le)* (perfective marker) evolves from verbs denoting completion, 着 *(zhe)* (durative marker) evolves from verbs indicating attachment, and 过 *(guo)* (past tense marker) derives from verbs conveying experiential meanings. Another typical change, complex predicates that express action results or depict the degree of a state, originates from the development of coordinated verbs. The special sentence structures, such as 把 *(bǎ)*, 被 *(bèi)*, and 比 *(bǐ)*, all function as action verbs capable of taking objects in Archaic Chinese.

Furthermore, the grammaticalization of the particles 的/地/得 *(de)* indicating modification relationships, prepositions, and conjunctions has intensified.

These selected representative instances of structures have reflected the significant changes across different periods in the Chinese language system. This ensures the accuracy and professionalism of manual annotations and enables the extraction of units that effectively characterise Chinese syntactic structures. In the following sections, we will present our data annotated by the features.

4 Related Works

The previously annotated corpora included partial syntactic information that mainly relied on POS tags, which are not comparable for diachronic variations. Moreover, there is a lack of detailed syntactic relations among components across different periods.

Due to the extensive timespan of Chinese, it's challenging to employ unified annotation rules, yet inconsistent rules hinder comparisons across different periods of the language system. For example, the biggest annotated corpus, Academia Sinica tagged corpus adopts the second strategy to pursue annotation accuracy, while the POS tags designed for early languages may not be suitable for languages that have changed in later periods. Moreover, the flexibility of word classes in Chinese (Rijkhoff and van Lier, 2013)—where nouns, verbs, and adjectives lack clear boundaries—poses challenges in establishing a theoretical basis for categorization when tagging POS. In contrast, features are more suitable than POS tags for comparing syntactic systems across languages, which had been successfully put into practice by the PCM. However, the PCM primarily focuses on verifying and quantifying phylogenetic relations among languages, and the features proposed by the PCM are not precise enough to describe the historical evolution in languages outside the Indo-European language family.

The scarcity of functional markers in Chinese, particularly evident in ancient times compared to languages with rich morphological markings, further increases the difficulty of syntactic analysis and annotation. For inflected languages, lexical categories and functional information can be validated through morphological markings, making it easier to correspond to diachronic changes in morphological markers. For instance, syntactic information in Middle Portuguese(Rocio et al., 2003)[6] is mapped based on Modern Portuguese.

While addressing the above issues with the three-feature annotation, we also annotate syntactic structures, supplementing syntactic information beyond lexicons. In languages like English with mature annotation standards such as Taylor et al. (2003), historical data annotated with syntactic treebanks have seen significant development, for instance, the Penn-Helsinki Parsed Corpus of Middle English (PPCME; Taylor and Kroch, 1994). However, there is still a lack of comprehensive development in non-inflectional languages like Chinese.

An annotated corpus that facilitates comparisons of syntactic changes across different periods and reflects the development process of functional categories is required for depicting diachronic syntax.

5 Annotation examples

Syntax information is conveyed through both lexicon and structure. In this regard, we are employing the three-feature standard to annotate vocabulary while referencing the phrase structure grammar (Gazdar, 1985) to annotate syntactic trees. This approach represents our endeavour to further construct a large-scale diachronic treebank training set. We will illustrate our annotation method through the development of resultative predicates and passive constructions, demonstrating that the data collected in the test set encompasses typical instances of structural changes in Chinese across various periods.

One of the most noticeable structural changes in VP is the development of complex predicates. The structure contains a verb and a postverbal constituent that modifies the verb, expressing the result, manner, or degree. The structure of VP changed from figure 1 and 2 (Archaic Chinese) to figure 3 (Middle Chinese [7]).

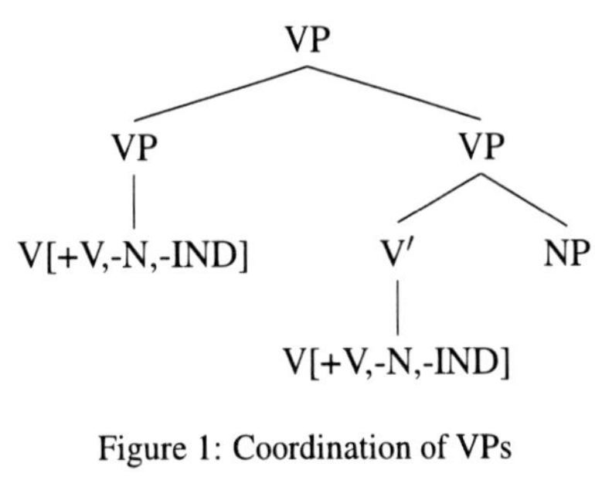

Figure 1: Coordination of VPs

[6]MPPT (Mediaeval Portuguese Partial Treebank) uses the tagging resources of modern Portuguese as part of the training materials for automatic tagging of mediaeval Portuguese.

[7]The period depicted in the illustration signifies the theoretical emergence of resultative complements, a topic that has sparked debate among scholars regarding its specific historical emergence. In this context, we refer to the perspectives of scholars such as (Wang, 1957; Ota, [1958] 1987; Mei, 1991; Wei, 2000).

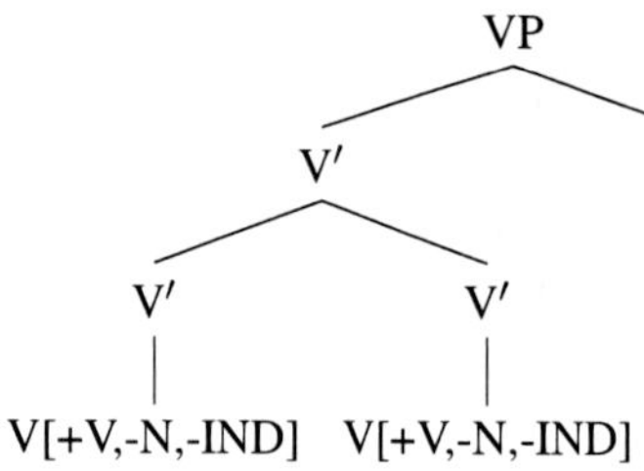

Figure 2: Coordination of V′s

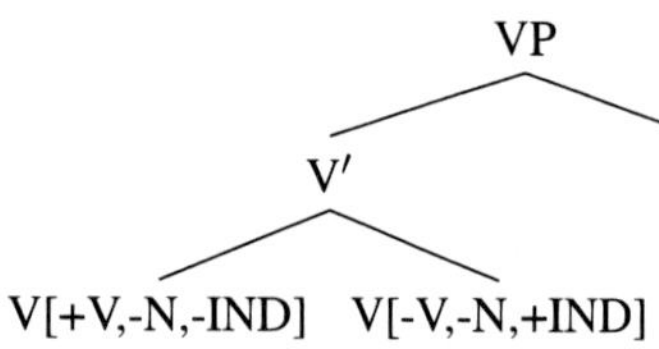

Figure 3: Complex predicate structure (Coordination of Vs)

The patterns demonstrate the development of complex predicate structures. During this process, the ability of the second verb to take a complement gradually diminishes until it merges with the first verb in the third stage. For instance, the *shā* in (9) and (10) is an action verb indicating killing, while that in (11) is a degree adverb representing the degree of the predicate. This process involves the merging of two VPs, i.e. two predicates. When two verbs are adjacent, the second verb gradually loses its function as a verb, therefore, the feature becomes [-V]. Adjacent to the first verb in the linear sequence, the second verb undergoes structural reanalysis, merging into a single VP with the first verb. Consequently, the original second verb expresses either the degree of the first verb or the resulting status, indicating a perfective predicate with a positive value for the [IND] feature.

(9) jī (击) ér (而) **shā** (杀) zhī (之) .
hit COORD kill 3PRON
"Attact and kill him." Archaic Chinese

(10) dǎ (打) **shā** (杀) qián (前) jiā (家)
hit **kill** former household
gē zi (哥子) .
boy
"Beat the boy of former family to death."
Middle Chinese

(11) é méi (娥眉) wù (误) **shā** (杀) rén (人)
pretty eyebrows impede largely people
"The pretty eyebrows (representing beauty) impeded her (entire life) to a large extent."
Middle Chinese

Generally, in the process of linguistic evolution, new linguistic forms must coexist with old forms for a certain period until they are widely accepted by the linguistic community, thus replacing the older forms. The study of the syntactic evolution of ancient Chinese is particularly concerned with this transition from the old to the new. Take the example of passive sentences and their structural analyses, *bèi* in sentence (12) is an action verb expressing to receive. In contrast, *bèi* has lost its lexical meaning and introduces the agent and indicates the passive voice in typical passive constructions like example 4. The feature [+IND] is attributed to *bèi* due to the passive voice, which also shows that the action is completed. The usage of *bèi* presented in example (14) further demonstrates its grammaticalization. Some scholars argue that this usage implies a passive subject (Jiang, 1994). In this construction, the predicate can take an object, distinguishing it from the typical passive usage described in example 4. Specifically, the subject of the expression *nà rén* ("that person", mentioned in preceding texts) undergoes an event involving the action by the agent and is directly affected by this associated event. The structures are illustrated in 4 and 5.

(12) yòu (幼) **bèi** (被) cí (慈) mǔ (母)
child receive beloved mother
sān (三) qiān (迁) zhī (之) jiào (教)
three move NMLZ education
"When I was a child, (I) received the education from (my) beloved mother by moving three times." Archaic Chinese

(13) lǎo (老) sēng (僧) **bèi** (被) rǔ (汝) qí (骑)
old monk PASS 2PRON ride
"(I,) Old monk, was ride by you." Middle Chinese

(14) **bèi** (被) Wǔsōng (武松) bù (不)
PREP PN NEG
guǎn (管) tā (他)
take-care 3PRON
"Wǔsōng does not take care of him."
被武松不管他。 Early Mandarin

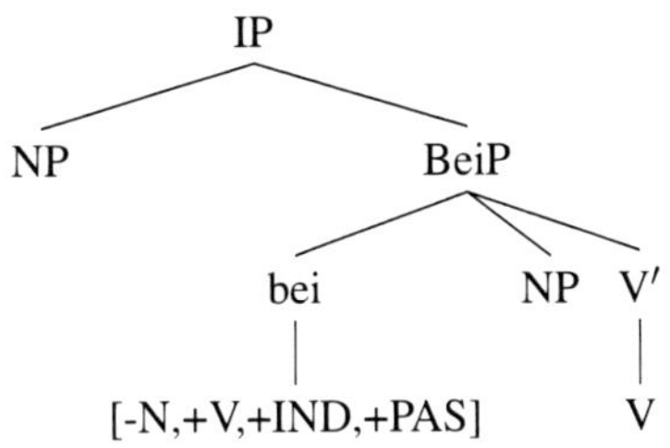

Figure 4: Passive constructions: "bèi" as a passive marker

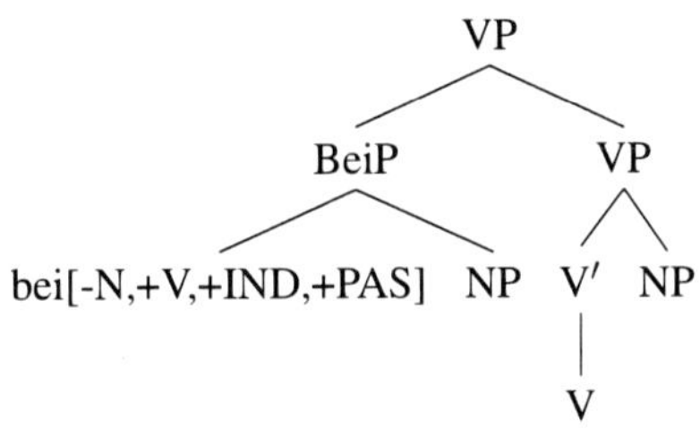

Figure 5: Passive constructions: "bèi" as a preposition

6 Conclusion

The feature annotation system is based on intuitions from a philological study of ancient Chinese syntax evolution, as well as features from both formal and functional grammar. The materials annotated are typical examples representing the process of Chinese syntactic evolution. This approach ensures annotation effectiveness and feasibility when data volume is limited. Our proposed three-feature system aligns well with the flexible characteristics of Chinese parts of speech, minimising researcher bias while expressing all known syntactic and semantic information. The simplicity and cross-temporal, cross-linguistic comparability of our feature labels make them suitable for languages like Chinese lacking morphological markers and adaptable for inflected languages as well.

References

Steven P Abney. 1987. The English noun phrase in its sentential aspect. Ph.D. thesis, Massachusetts Institute of Technology.

David Adger and Peter Svenonius. 2011. Features in minimalist syntax. The Oxford handbook of linguistic minimalism, 1:27–51.

Alexandra Y Aikhenvald. 2000. Classifiers: A typology of noun categorization devices. OUP Oxford.

Keith Allan. 1977. Classifiers. Language, 53(2):285–311.

Mark C Baker. 2008. The macroparameter in a microparametric world. In Theresa Biberauer, editor, The limits of syntactic variation. Amsterdam: John Benjamins Pub.

Walter Bisang. 1999. Classifiers in east and southeast asian languages: Counting and beyond. TRENDS IN LINGUISTICS STUDIES AND MONOGRAPHS, 118:113–186.

Walter Bisang. 2002. Classification and the evolution of grammatical structures: a universal perspective. STUF-Language Typology and Universals, 55(3):289–308.

Hagit Borer. 1984. Parametric Syntax: Case Studies in Semitic and Romance Languages. Foris Publications.

Joan Bresnan, Ash Asudeh, Ida Toivonen, and Stephen Wechsler. 2015. Lexical-Functional Syntax, 2 edition. Blackwell Textbooks in Linguistics. Wiley-Blackwell, Chichester, England.

Huang C-TJ, Li A, and Li Y. 2009. The Syntax of Chinese. Cambridge University Press.

Lisa Lai-Shen Cheng and Rint Sybesma. 1999. Bare and not-so-bare nouns and the structure of np. Linguistic inquiry, 30(4):509–542.

Lisa Lai-Shen Cheng and Rint Sybesma. 2005. Classifiers in four varieties of chinese. Handbook of comparative syntax, pages 259–292.

Wenwen Cheng. 2015. Cong chutu wenxian kan "shu + liang + ming" jiegou de lishi xingcheng guocheng [the forming of the structure "numeral + quantifier + noun" in excavated documents] 从出土文献看"数+量+名"结构的历时形成过程. Guhanyu Yanjiu [Research in Ancient Chinese Language] 古汉语研究, (4):14–21.

Gennaro Chierchia. 1998. Reference to kinds across language. Natural language semantics, 6(4):339–405.

Noam Chomsky. 1970. Remarks on nominalistion. In R. Jacobs and P. S. Rosenbaum, editors, Readings in English Transformational Grammar.

Noam Chomsky. 1995. The Minimalist Program. Cambridge University Press.

Colette G Craig. 1994. Classifier languages. The encyclopedia of language and linguistics, 2:565–569.

Paola Crisma, Cristina Guardiano, Giuseppe Longobardi, et al. 2020. Syntactic diversity and language learnability. Studi e saggi linguistici, 58(2):99–130.

William Croft. 1994. Semantic universals in classifier systems. Word, 45(2):145–171.

Kristin Davidse. 2004. The interaction of quantification and identification in English determiners. Language, culture and mind, pages 507–533.

Naoki Fukui. 1988. Deriving the differences between english and japanese: A case study in parametric syntax. English Linguistics, 5:249–270.

Gerald Gazdar. 1985. Generalized phrase structure grammar. Harvard University Press.

Lewis Gebhardt. 2011. Classifiers are functional. Linguistic Inquiry, 42(1):125–130.

Jane Grimshaw. 2000. Locality and extended projection. AMSTERDAM STUDIES IN THE THEORY AND HISTORY OF LINGUISTIC SCIENCE SERIES 4, pages 115–134.

Colette Grinevald. 2000. A morphosyntactic typology of classifiers. Systems of nominal classification.

Cristina Guardiano, Dimitris Michelioudakis, Andrea Ceolin, Monica Alexandrina Irimia, Giuseppe Longobardi, Nina Radkevich, Giuseppina Silvestri, Ioanna Sitaridou, et al. 2016. South by southeast. a syntactic approach to greek and romance microvariation. L'Italia dialettale, 77:95–166.

Alice C Harris and Lyle Campbell. 1995. Historical syntax in cross-linguistic perspective, volume 74. Cambridge University Press.

C He, Y Jiang, et al. 2011. Nominative xp-de and semantics of-de. (Contemporary linguistics), 13(1):49–62.

Henry M Hoenigswald. 1950. The principal step in comparative grammar. Language, pages 357–364.

Henry M Hoenigswald. 1965. Language change and linguistic reconstruction. University of Chicago Press, Chicago.

Zaijun Huang. 1964. Cong jiawen, jinwen liangci de yingyong kaocha hanyu liangci de qiyuan yu fazhan [a study of the origin and develpment of classifiers in chinese, beginning from their use in the oracle bone insceiptions and metal inscriptions] 从甲文、金文量词的应用考察汉语量词的起源与发展. Zhongguo Yuwen, 133(6).

Mutsumi Imai and Reiko Mazuka. 2003. Re-evaluating linguistic relativity: Language-specific categories and the role of universal ontological knowledge in the construal of individuation. Language in mind: Advances in the study of language and thought, pages 429–464.

Shaoyu Jiang. 1994. Jindai Hanyu Yanjiu Gaikuang [A Survey Study on Early Mandarin] 近代汉语研究概况. Beijing: Peking University Press.

Ronald M Kaplan, Joan Bresnan, et al. 1981. Lexical-functional grammar: A formal system for grammatical representation. Massachusetts Institute Of Technology, Center For Cognitive Science.

M. Krifka, F. Pelletier, G. Carlson, and A. 1995. ter meulen. The Generic Book [C]. Chicago: The University of Chicago Press, 1-124.

R. Langacker. 1991. Foundations of Cognitive Grammar. Vol. 2. Descriptive Application, volume 2. Stanford University Press, Stanford.

Xuping Li. 2013. Numeral Classifiers in Chinese. Mouton de Gruyter, Berlin.

Xuping Li and Walter Bisang. 2012. Classifiers in sinitic languages: From individuation to definiteness-marking. Lingua, 122(4):335–355.

Yuming Li. 2000. Kaobei xing liangci ji qi zai hanzangyuxi liangci fazhan zhong de diwei [The copying type quantifiers and their position in the development of quantifiers in the Sino-Tibetan language family] 拷贝型量词及其在汉藏语系量词发展中的地位. Zhongguo Yuwen 中国语文, (1):27–34.

Giuseppe Longobardi. 2014. Theory and experiment in parametric minimalism. Language description informed by theory. Amsterdam: John Benjamins, pages 217–262.

Giuseppe Longobardi. 2017. Principles, Parameters, and Schemata: A Constructivist UG. Linguistic Analysis, 41(3 & 4):517–558.

John Lyons. 1968. Introduction to theoretical linguistics, volume 510. Cambridge university press.

Tsu-lin Mei. 1991. The development of predicate-complement structure based on *V-shā*, *V-sǐ* in the han dynasty. Yuyanxue Luncong [Essays on Linguistics], 16:169–171.

Antoine Meillet. 1925. La méthode comparative en linguistique historique. Aschehoug, Paris.

Tatsuo Ota. [1958] 1987. A Historical Grammar of Modern Chinese. Peking University Press.

Yunzhong Pan. 1982. Hanyu Yufa Shi Gaiyao[Outline of Historical grammar of Chinese] 汉语语法史概要. Zhongzhou Chinese Classics Publishing House.

Carl Pollard and Ivan A Sag. 1988. Information-based syntax and semantics: Vol. 1: fundamentals. Center for the Study of Language and Information.

Carl Pollard and Ivan A Sag. 1994. Head-driven phrase structure grammar. University of Chicago Press.

Robert L. Rankin. 2017. The Comparative Method, chapter 1. John Wiley Sons, Ltd.

Gisa Rauh. 2010. Syntactic categories: Their identification and description in linguistic theories. OUP Oxford.

Jan Rijkhoff and Eva van Lier. 2013. Flexible word classes: Typological studies of underspecified parts of speech. OUP Oxford.

Vitor Rocio, Mário Amado Alves, J Gabriel Lopes, Maria Francisca Xavier, and Graça Vicente. 2003. Automated creation of a Medieval Portuguese partial treebank. In Treebanks, pages 211–227. Springer.

Chao-Fen Sun and Talmy Givón. 1985. On the so-called SOV word order in Mandarin Chinese: A quantified text study and its implications. Language, pages 329–351.

Chaofen Sun. 1996. Word-order change and grammaticalization in the history of Chinese. Stanford University Press.

Ann Taylor and Anthony S Kroch. 1994. The penn-helsinki parsed corpus of middle english. MS. University of Pennsylvania, page 30.

Ann Taylor, Mitchell Marcus, and Beatrice Santorini. 2003. The penn treebank: an overview. Treebanks: Building and using parsed corpora, pages 5–22.

Eva Van Lier, Jan Rijkhoff, et al. 2013. Flexible word classes in linguistic typology and grammatical theory. Flexible word classes. Typological studies of underspecified parts of speech, pages 1–30.

Li Wang. 1945. Zhongguo Yufa Lilun [Theory of Grammar in Chinese] 中国语法理论. Zhonghua Book Company.

Li Wang. 1957. Hanyushi Gao [A Draft History of the Chinese Language] 汉语史稿. Number v. 1 in . China Science Publishing Media Ltd.

Peiquan Wei. [1990] 2004. Han Wei Liuchao Chengdaici Yanjiu [Studies on Pronouns in the Eastern Han and Six Dynasties] 汉魏六朝称代词研究. Language and Linguistics. Institute of Linguistics, Academic Sinica.

Peiquan Wei. 2000. Donghan wei jin nanbeichao zai yufa shi shang de diwei [the position of the Eastern Han and Six Dynasties in the history of Chinese grammar] 东汉魏晋南北朝在语法史上的地位. Chinese Studies 汉学研究, 18:199–230.

Werner Winter. 1984. Reconstructional comparative linguistics and the reconstruction of the syntax of undocumented stages in the development of languages and language families. Mouton Publishers.

Yicheng Wu and Adams Bodomo. 2009. Classifiers≠ determiners. Linguistic Inquiry, 40(3):487–503.

Jianguo Yang. 1993. Jindai Hanyu Yinlun [An introduction to Early Mandarin] 近代汉语引论. Huangshan Publishing House.

Zhenwu Yao. 2008. "Hanyu 'shu + liang + ming' geshi de laiyuan" duhou [After reading 'the origin of the 'number + quantifier + noun' format in Chinese'] 《汉语"数+量+名"格式的来源》读后. Zhongguo Yuwen 中国语文, (3):247–253.

Cheng Zhang. 2010. Fazhan chuqi de hanyu mingliangci tedian—handai liangci yanjiu [the characteristics of measure words in early Chinese development: A study of measure words in the Han dynasty] 发展初期的汉语名量词特点—汉代量词研究. Journal of Chinese Language History 汉语史学报, (1):120–130.

Niina Ning Zhang. 2013. Classifier Structures in Mandarin Chinese, volume 263. Walter de Gruyter.

AXOLOTL'24 Shared Task on Multilingual Explainable Semantic Change Modeling

Mariia Fedorova[♠] **Timothee Mickus**[♡] **Niko Partanen**[♡]
Janine Siewert[♡] **Elena Spaziani**[♣] **Andrey Kutuzov**[♠]

[♠]University of Oslo [♡]University of Helsinki [♣]Sapienza University of Rome

[♠]{mariiaf, andreku}@ifi.uio.no [♡]firstname.lastname@helsinki.fi
[♣]elena.spaziani@uniroma1.it

Abstract

This paper describes the organization and findings of AXOLOTL'24, the first multilingual explainable semantic change modeling shared task. We present new sense-annotated diachronic semantic change datasets for Finnish and Russian which were employed in the shared task, along with a surprise test-only German dataset borrowed from an existing source. The setup of AXOLOTL'24 is new to the semantic change modeling field, and involves subtasks of identifying unknown (novel) senses and providing dictionary-like definitions to these senses. The methods of the winning teams are described and compared, thus paving a path towards explainability in computational approaches to historical change of meaning.

1 Introduction

One area of linguistic inquiry that has traditionally been very challenging is the study of linguistic change: documenting how languages evolve and how meaning can shift requires fine-grained judgments, careful design of sense inventories and the exhaustive survey of all existing historical material. The novel possibilities that technological breakthroughs open up should also lead us to develop more ambitious research goals and projects: one such prospect is the automation of diachronic word sense annotation and explanation, a task we dub *explainable semantic change modeling*.

Explainable semantic change modeling can be broken down into two sub-tasks:

(i) Finding target word usages corresponding to newly gained senses;

(ii) Providing human-readable descriptions (such as definitions) of the gained senses.

In this paper, we summarize the organization and findings of the LChange'24 shared task, dubbed AXOLOTL'24, ('**A**scertain and e**X**plain **O**verhauls of the **L**exicon **O**ver **T**ime at **L**Change'**24**').[1] The AXOLOTL'24 shared task constitutes the first formalization and evaluation of **explainable** semantic change modeling systems. It focused on three languages: Old Literary Finnish ('Finnish' below), Russian, and German, with this third language being provided as a test-only surprise language. Languages in AXOLOTL'24 were selected so as to evaluate systems across varying conditions and to avoid excessive emphasis on English which one can often observe in semantic change research.

The AXOLOTL'24 shared task, by testing and evaluating explainable semantic change modeling systems, allows us to push the state of the art in challenging scenarios involving novel tasks, ranging from semantic change detection to definition modeling, and extreme data scarcity.

AXOLOTL'24 involved participants across 6 teams, and their results show that explainable semantic change modeling is far from being solved – be it in terms of detecting novel senses of highly polysemous words or generating glosses for novel senses from scratch;[2] see Section 5 for detailed results of the shared task. Still, we expect that AXOLOTL'24 findings will pave the way for developing more robust computational systems dealing with diachronic semantic change. We also hope it will serve as a step towards building bridges between NLP and historical linguistics communities.

2 Prior work and state of the field

Diachronic semantic change modeling (Kutuzov et al., 2018; Tahmasebi et al., 2021), sometimes also called 'lexical semantic change detection' (LSCD) can be described as an NLP field which attempts to develop computational approaches to historical semantics and to operationalize the notion of 'semantic shifts'. As an empirical field, it regularly sanity checks itself by organizing shared tasks aimed at objective comparing of approaches

[1] https://github.com/ltgoslo/axolotl24_shared_task

[2] We use the terms 'gloss' and 'definition' interchangeably.

Proceedings of the 5th Workshop on Computational Approaches to Historical Language Change, pages 72–91
August 15, 2024 ©2024 Association for Computational Linguistics

to various problems within semantic change modeling. One can mention SemEval 2020 Task 1 (Schlechtweg et al., 2020) for English, German, Latin and Swedish; DIACR-Ita for Italian (Basile et al., 2020); RuShiftEval for Russian (Kutuzov and Pivovarova, 2021); LSCDiscovery for Spanish (Zamora-Reina et al., 2022), etc.

But up to now, semantic change related shared tasks focused on evaluating the systems regarding their ability to **detect** the mere fact of change or its degree (by classifying or ranking target words). They did not challenge the participants to provide **explanations** on what exactly has changed in the semantics of the target words. It actually has been acknowledged for several years already as one of the 'gaps' in the field (Hengchen et al., 2021). The AXOLOTL'24 shared task aims at filling this gap.

Obviously, 'explanations' of semantic change can take different forms. One option is to automatically detect **types** of change; see one of possible categorizations in Blank and Koch (1999) and a recent computational approach in Cassotti et al. (2024). However, we choose another type of explanations, based on **senses** as discrete units of meaning. AXOLOTL'24 is focused on identifying and describing newly gained senses of the target words with human-interpretable definitions. After the first attempts on computational diachronic sense tracing in Mitra et al. (2014), the notion of senses has somewhat disappeared from the focus of the field. Very recently, the unknown sense detection task has again showed up in the attention of the LSCD community (Lautenschlager et al., 2024), in line with our shared task.

AXOLOTL'24 focus on explaining novel senses links it to the **contextualized definition generation** field (Noraset et al., 2017; Mickus et al., 2022; Gardner et al., 2022) and its LSCD applications (Giulianelli et al., 2023; Fedorova et al., 2024).

3 Data

The AXOLOTL'24 shared task challenged the participants with usage collections in three languages: Finnish, Russian and German. Each usage (sample) is a sentence containing a target word and belonging to one of two time periods, dubbed 'old' and 'new' (for different languages, the actual time periods were different). Importantly, each usage is also annotated with the sense of the target word, sense identifiers standardized across the time periods.

Finnish and Russian datasets came with the training and development data splits which were made available to the participants from the very beginning of the shared task. German dataset featured only the test split, and this 'surprise language data' was made available to the participants only at the AXOLOTL'24 test phase.

Language	Period	Train	Dev	Test
Finnish	New	47 242	3 351	3 264
	Old	45 897	3 203	3 461
	Total	93 139	6 554	6 725
Russian	New	4 581	1 605	1 702
	Old	1 912	421	424
	Total	6 493	2 026	2 126
German	New	—	—	568
	Old	—	—	584
	Total	—	—	1 152

Table 1: Number of samples in AXOLOTL'24 splits.

Language	Train	Dev	Test
Finnish	4 289	254	275
Russian	924	201	211
German	—	—	24

Table 2: Number of target words in AXOLOTL'24 splits.

Table 1 shows the general statistics of the AXOLOTL'24 datasets in terms of the number of usages (samples), while Table 2 shows the number of target words for each language and data splits. A brief description of the structure of the data files is provided in Appendix A.1.

3.1 Finnish

Data sources. The Dictionary of Old Literary Finnish (henceforth DOLF; Institute for the Languages of Finland, 2023) was used as the data source for Finnish. This dictionary has been in construction for several decades already and is one of the major Finnish dictionary projects of national importance, alongside the Dictionary of Finnish Dialects. The DOLF is currently progressing in the letter *P*, and new versions with extended coverage are released annually. Each headword in the dictionary can contain multiple senses and sub-senses (we systematically selected the most specific subsense as the gloss). They are illustrated with examples, which contain source information, including a coarse publication date, author and publishing place, among others. The sentences taken as examples stem from an extensive bibliography[3] of source materials in Old Literary Finnish (Institute for the Languages of Finland, 2013).

Along the website interface of the DOLF website, the lexicographic data are also available as a CC-BY licensed XML data package. The latter was used in our data preparation; we consulted the online version to ensure the structure was parsed correctly. We extracted a total of 150 867 items (unique combinations of words, glosses and usage examples), across 33 826 senses (unique combinations of headwords and glosses) and 22 917 headwords. The structure of the XML file is closely connected to the online version of the dictionary, with emphasis on visual layout of the dictionary. In the README file of the XML data package it is specified that the two versions are identical. The XML data was parsed at the example sentence level and each example was associated with metadata of the current word article. Most important for our purposes was the publishing year, which was used to divide the examples into different periods. The original data is divided into five time periods (1543–1599, 1600–1649, 1650–1699, 1700–1749, and 1750–1810), which we have merged into two, corresponding to the 'old' and 'new' time periods (**1543–1699** and **1700–1810**).

The headwords as well as the definitions are given in the modern standard language, while examples of usage are provided in original spelling. Especially in the older data, this can differ substantially from the current standard, as illustrated by the following example, where a) shows the original example and b) the normalized modern spelling:

a) *waicka wiele kymmenen Mieste ydhes Hones ylitzieisit, pite heiden quitengin cooleman*

b) *Vaikka vielä kymmenen miestä yhdessä huoneessa ylitsejäisi(vä)t, pitää heidän kuitenkin kuoleman.* ("Even if ten men remained in one room, they would still have to die.")

Data annotation. The dataset used in the shared task was extracted from the DOLF XML data package in as complete form as possible. It was not marked in the DOLF which word in the example sentence the entry was concerning. We tried to detect the correct word in the sentence automatically using Levenshtein distance. The result was relatively clean, especially for the newer parts of the data, but it was obvious that further verification was needed. The position of the correct word was verified manually for all sentences in the validation and test splits of the dataset. The final dataset contained the lemma, its realization in the sentence in a given word form and the position of that form in the sentence. The manual annotation was done by two individuals who coordinated together the annotation conventions. Conventions were developed to mark words that were adjacent to punctuation or otherwise not continuous, i.e. when parts of a compound word were split apart from one another.

[3] https://kaino.kotus.fi/vks/?p=references

3.2 Russian

Data sources. The Russian data sources were Dal's Explanatory Dictionary of the Living Great Russian Language (Dal, 1909) for the 'old' time period (roughly **XIX century**) and Wiktionary-based CoDWoE (Mickus et al., 2022) for the 'new' time period (roughly **modern Russian**). We used the TEI-encoded version of the Dal's Dictionary (Mikhaylov and Shershneva, 2018). Our criteria for selecting target words were that (i) they be present in both Dal and CoDWoE; (ii) they be defined and polysemous in Dal; and (iii) at least one of their senses had at least two examples in CoDWoE. We further ensured that the final set of examples was at least twice as large as the final set of senses.

Dal did not always provide examples for every sense, and even when it did, all examples were merged into one line per sense. This and higher granularity of senses in CoDWoE (which is discussed in the next paragraph) caused data imbalance between old and new time periods and could be the reason for the higher share of novel senses in the Russian dataset than e.g. in German (which covers approximately the same centuries, so distance between time periods is unlikely to cause the difference in the number of novel senses). This imbalance has made it difficult to solve the task for systems that heavily relied onto WSD and tended to assign old senses to most usages. We discuss it in more details in Section 5.

Data annotation. Since there existed no mapping between Dal senses and CoDWoE senses, we had to create such a mapping manually.

We needed an automatic alignment of the sense definitions from the two datasets to ease the mapping task. In order to develop a method for such an alignment, we manually annotated a subset of randomly sampled target words. We sampled 50 words and selected those with ≥ 2 old senses, which gave us 228 pairs of definitions of the same or different senses from the two datasets. The annotation task was to yield a binary judgment about whether the two definitions mean the same. The inter-rater agreement between the two annotators according to Krippendorff's α was 0.74 which is substantial (Artstein and Poesio, 2008).

Then we encoded all definitions by sentence-transformers (Reimers and Gurevych, 2020)[4] and calculated cosine similarity for each pair of Dal's and CoDWoE definitions. These similarities were used as an input feature to train a decision tree classifier predicting one of two classes ('same sense' and 'not the same sense'). The trained classifier was employed to predict mappings between Dal and CoDWoE sense definitions for all Russian target words. But its quality was by no means sufficient to produce gold data; thus, all the mappings were manually checked in the following procedure.

For each target word, a human annotator was shown all its sense definitions from Dal. For each of these senses, the annotator had to choose all CoDWoE definitions with the same meaning (from the list of all CoDWoE senses for this target word). The sense pairs predicted by the classifier as 'same sense' were pre-selected, and the annotator could leave them as is or change at will. The annotation was conducted by three native Russian speakers, with each instance annotated by only one of them, due to the size and time constraints.

Since CoDWoE senses are usually more granular than those in Dal, it was allowed to map more than one CoDWoE definition to a Dal definition, but not vice versa. For example, words denoting plants usually have one sense in Dal, which is separated into two senses (a plant itself and its seeds) in CoDWoE. The annotators had to map both CoDWoE senses to the Dal sense in this case. However, in the cases where a Dal's sense definition was broader than all CoDWoE definitions, the meanings missing in CoDWoE were ignored and the Dal's definition was still mapped to the CoDWoE definitions. Thus, the mapping was always one-to-many in the direction from Dal to CoDWoE. It could have been done in many other ways, but in AXOLOTL'24, we assumed that the 'old' Dal's dictionary is a trusted source and focused on cases of words acquiring novel senses.

During the manual mapping of senses, some words were dismissed, if it was not possible to understand their meaning because of parsing errors in the TEI-encoded Dal. The most common parsing error was incorrect split of the article into a definition and examples. What's more, the original articles were often organized in such a way that it would be difficult or impossible to split them automatically (no definition, but example only instead of it; difference between an example and a definition denoted only by a formatting style which could be broken when digitizing etc.); some of such instances were fixed manually in the post-processing stage, see the details in the next section.

Data post-processing. Both automated and manual data processing were deemed necessary to improve the overall quality of the Russian dataset. First, in accordance with the overarching interest of this task in semantic change rather than mere formal change, all the examples were automatically converted from the XIX century spelling to modern standard Russian orthography. Furthermore, quotation marks were standardized and stress marks were removed. Since the CoDWoE dataset had been pretokenized and punctuation symbols were separate tokens, the white spaces introduced by this tokenization were removed.

All Dal's definitions were replaced with the CoDWoE definitions, if they existed for a specific sense. We discussed the possibility of using Dal's definitions in cases when there were several CoDWoE senses for one overarching Dal sense, but this would unfairly penalize the participants in Subtask 2, so we used the first CoDWoE definition in such cases. Although some of these usages got too narrow definitions with a slightly different meaning, we assume that it affects participants less than if they had to create systems that would be able to produce correct definitions both in the XIX century Russian and modern Russian.

The cases of obviously wrong annotations (where an annotator erroneously selected the same CoDWoE sense for multiple Dal senses) were removed, and the target words with no old usages left after that were dropped.

Finally, parsing errors, mostly found in the definitions from the old time period, and other irregularities (e.g., redundant or erroneous instances; redundant punctuation; metadata) were addressed manually, when possible. A more comprehensive

[4]https://huggingface.co/sentence-transformers/distiluse-base-multilingual-cased-v1

description of the irregularities is provided in Appendix A.2. Sizes of the resulting dataset splits after all fixes and removals are shown in Tables 1 and 2. See Appendix A.3 for additional statistics.

3.3 German

German was a surprise language introduced in the test phase only in order to evaluate the systems' ability to handle a language unseen before.

Data source. The German test split is a version of the DWUG DE Sense dataset (Schlechtweg, 2023). It already contained all the information of interest to AXOLOTL'24; the 'old' time period included usages from the **XIX century**, while the 'new' time period included usages from **1946-1990**. We did not use the cleaned majority voting sense labels provided within the dataset, but instead inferred the senses ourselves from raw annotations, using less strict filtering. The only post-processing step was removing senses for which definitions were missing or contained only 'others'[5].

4 AXOLOTL'24 organization

So as to provide participants with a manageable workload, we elected to frame the task as two complementary sub-tasks or tracks: the first focused on identifying old and gained senses, whereas the second pertained to elucidating the gained senses. See Appendix B for illustrative examples.

4.1 Subtask 1. Bridging diachronic word uses and a synchronic dictionary

In this first subtask, the participants were offered two sets of word usages belonging to different time periods. In addition to this, they were provided with a set of dictionary entries (sense inventory) for the target words describing their senses in the old time period (accompanied by definitions). The task consisted in finding usages of the target words belonging to newly gained senses, i.e., senses not covered by the provided sense inventory, as well as usages belonging to the previously existing senses.

The underlying assumption is that sense definitions from the dictionary, even though not always covering all word senses even from the same time period, may still be a useful additional source of information. Since a part of this subtask is to map word usages to the dictionary senses, it is very much related to Word Sense Disambiguation (WSD). But in addition, the usages in word senses absent from the dictionary should be grouped into novel sense clusters. This makes this subtask also similar to Word Sense Induction (WSI).

Evaluation. The participants' test data looked like a set of target words with two sets of per-word entries, from the 'old' and 'new' time periods, where each entry was a target word usage, the target word itself and the time period label. The entries from the 'old' time period also contained sense identifiers (with definitions). Participants were expected to predict a sense identifier for every entry of the 'new' time period (either re-using an identifier from the 'old' time period or adding a novel one). Systems' performance was measured by 1) Adjusted Rand Index (ARI) (Steinley, 2004) for all 'new' entries, and 2) macro-F1 for 'new' entries with previously existing senses. The choice of the metrics is explained by the necessity to evaluate the ability of the systems to both 1) correctly cluster a set of usages into senses, independent of whether these senses are old or novel (evaluated by ARI) *and* 2) correctly identify the usages belonging to the specific old senses (measured by F1). Using only one of these metrics would turn Subtask 1 into either a WSI or WSD task correspondingly. Thus, we decided to use both metrics, although it obviously leads to the absence of one defining score (as shown in Section 5, a submission can be top-performing when measured with F1, but not with ARI, and vice versa). The final scores were computed as the average across all the target words.

Baseline system. Participants were provided with a very basic baseline system, which worked as follows: the old glosses were merged with their examples (if any), then both the resulting old senses and new examples were encoded with a sentence embedding model (we used `LEALLA-large` (Mao and Nakagawa, 2023)[6] because we wanted to avoid using the same model as during data processing and because it supports all three of our languages).

The encoded new examples were clustered using Affinity Propagation (Frey and Dueck, 2007). For each cluster, we assumed the first example encountered in the dataset and belonging to this cluster to be the prototypical one (although using centroids would be possibly a safer choice) and calculated its cosine similarity to all of the old senses (gloss and example pairs). If the similarity was above a

[5] https://github.com/ltgoslo/axolotl24_shared_task/tree/main/data/german

[6] https://huggingface.co/setu4993/LEALLA-large

pre-defined threshold of 0.3 (it was chosen manually after analyzing the first 5 target words from the Russian dataset sorted alphabetically before train-validation-test splitting; none of those words was present later in the test split), we mapped the current cluster to this sense. If the similarity was below the threshold for all the old senses, the baseline system made a decision that the current cluster of new examples represents a novel sense.

4.2 Subtask 2. Definition generation for novel word senses

The second aspect that explainable semantic change modeling encompasses is producing explanations of how lexical meanings have changed: the goal behind explainable semantic change modeling is not only to detect semantic change, but also provide insights on what this change consists in. Remark that our emphasis here is on *providing* explanations, not necessarily *creating them from scratch*: in other words, it would be equally appropriate to generate explanations on the fly or to retrieve existing ones in the form of glosses from an external lexical resource. Subtask 2 of AXOLOTL'24 therefore challenged participants to submit appropriate descriptions (definitions) of gained senses.

In our case, as we elected to use lexicographic data, this second subtask connects with a broader group of NLP tasks, ranging from definition modeling (the task focused on generating lexicographic definitions; Noraset et al., 2017) to definition extraction (retrieving existing text segments that can be used as definitions; Spala et al., 2020).

Evaluation. Two organizational factors shaped how Subtask 2 submissions would be evaluated. The first of these, owed to our use of lexicographic data to set up this shared task (Section 3), was that gold sense descriptions were to be formatted as lexicographic definitions. We therefore expected participants to submit human readable explanations matching these targets. A fair assessment of how appropriate the submitted definition is would therefore require some semantic similarity metric between two pieces of text, which calls for the use of NLG metrics for ranking submissions. In short, we treat this second subtask as a variant of definition modeling. We elect as our primary metric BERTScore (Zhang et al., 2020), as it was found to most closely align with human judgments for factual correctness out of an array of standard NLG metrics (Segonne and Mickus, 2023). We also included BLEU (Papineni et al., 2002; Post, 2018), given its broad prevalence in NLG studies.

The second aspect that weighs on our evaluation approach is that the AXOLOTL'24 focuses on explanations for word *senses*, not word *usages*; therefore, we expect participants to submit one explanation per sense, rather than per example of usage. This entails that we depart from the usual definition modeling framework of evaluating context-dependent productions (Gadetsky et al., 2018). In practice, we adopt a framework similar to the L-BLEU used by Mickus et al. (2022): for each target word, each of its gold definitions is mapped one by one in a greedy fashion to the hypothesis (a definition provided by the participant) that yields the highest BERTScore. This approach also allows us to ensure that participants submitting to both tracks would not be doubly penalized for providing too many or too few senses: the shape of the sense inventory was assessed in Subtask 1; the evaluation of Subtask 2 therefore limits itself to evaluating the validity of provided glosses.[7] A pseudo-code overview of the resulting evaluation procedure is provided in Appendix C.2.

Baseline system. To illustrate the intended use-case, the baseline system provided to participants focused on generating output definitions for a set of examples of usage. In practice, we fine-tune a multilingual causal language model (XGLM; Lin et al., 2021) as a Siamese network. We first embed all relevant examples of usage into sentence-level representations, by pooling over the CLM's output embeddings and applying a learned linear projection. We then prompt the same CLM to generate the lexicographic definition, using as a prefix the sentence embeddings obtained in the previous step.

5 AXOLOTL'24 results

The shared task was organized into three stages occurring from February till April 2024. The **training phase** lasted from February 4 till March 25; participants had access to training and development data splits for Finnish and Russian and could evaluate their development set predictions by submitting them to Codalab. The **evaluation phase** lasted from March 25 till April 9; participants had access

[7]Note that the separation of our task in two subtasks entails that evaluation across subtasks is not strictly consistent. A cluster of usages can be mapped to an optimal target sense S_A for Subtask 1 while the corresponding explanation submitted to Subtask 2 may be assigned to some other target S_B.

Team	Fi-Ru-De	Fi-Ru	Fi	Ru	De
Deep-change	**41.3**	**34.9**	**63.8**	5.9	**54.3**
Holotniekat	31.2	32.0	59.6	4.3	29.8
TartuNLP	31.0	26.8	43.7	9.8	39.6
IMS_Stuttgart	28.7	27.4	54.8	0.0	31.4
ABDN-NLP	22.1	28.1	55.3	0.9	10.2
WooperNLP	18.7	28.0	42.8	**13.2**	0.0
Baseline	4.1	5.1	2.3	7.9	2.2

Table 3: Subtask 1 evaluation phase results (ARI $\times 100$)

Team	Fi-Ru-De	Fi-Ru	Fi	Ru	De
Deep-change	**75.0**	**75.3**	**75.6**	**75.0**	**74.5**
Holotniekat	64.1	65.8	65.5	66.1	60.8
TartuNLP	59.0	59.5	55.0	64.0	58.0
ABDN-NLP	48.7	58.0	59.0	57.0	30.0
IMS_Stuttgart	43.1	32.8	65.5	0.0	63.8
WooperNLP	31.6	47.5	50.3	44.6	0.0
Baseline	20.7	24.5	23.0	26.0	13.0

Table 4: Subtask 1 evaluation phase results (F1 $\times 100$)

to the testing splits for Finnish, Russian and German, but references were hidden and participants had to submit predictions for these splits to Codalab. The current **post-evaluation phase** started on April 9; testing splits have been published in full together with references and evaluation scores for all submissions from the evaluation phase. The official AXOLOTL'24 leaderboards are now frozen, but Codalab post-evaluation tasks are available.[8]

In the evaluation phase, AXOLOTL'24 received submissions from six different teams. All six participated in Subtask 1,[9] but only three also submitted predictions for Subtask 2.[10] Teams were ranked by their highest scoring submissions averaged over all three AXOLOTL'24 languages. For convenience, we refer to average scores across languages as 'Fi-Ru-De' (Finnish, Russian & German) and 'Fi-Ru' (Finnish & Russian) in what follows. See more details about the teams' approaches in Appendix C.

5.1 Subtask 1.

For the Subtask 1, we keep separate leaderboards for ARI (Table 3) and F1 (Table 4), since these metrics focus on very different aspects of the task, and it does not make sense to average across them.

One can observe an interesting discrepancy in the Subtask 1 evaluation results when measured by ARI and macro-F1. In the WSI part (evaluated by ARI), **Deep-change** (Kokosinskii et al., 2024) is the best on average, but is outperformed on the Russian data by three other teams, including the baseline system. The best ARI score for Russian (13.2) is achieved by the **WooperNLP** team. However, the **Deep-change** team is a winner across all languages in the WSD part (evaluated by F1).

Deep-change seems to be a pure WSD system (it has detected no novel senses at all for all three languages) and nothing in its method description explains how it could detect novel senses; in fact, its high result may be explained by a lower share of novel senses in Finnish (14%) and German (21%), compared to Russian (57%). Thus, if a system classified correctly only the samples belonging to old senses across three languages, it was still able to outperform (by F1) the systems that tried to predict novel senses (and had a harder task, since they had to choose among larger number of classes). Among the teams which did predict novel senses, the one ranked highest both by ARI and F1 is **Holotniekat** (Brückner et al., 2024). Note that we considered for the leaderboards only one best submission from each team, ranked highest by the sum of all metrics; thus, if an approach identified more novel senses, but produced more sense classification errors, it could have been ranked lower (if a system chooses among much more classes than were present in the gold data, the probability of a mistake is higher than for a system choosing among less classes, even in the case of random choice) .

Another reason for differences in ARI between **Deep-change** and **WooperNLP** on the Russian data may be different assumptions made by the two teams about the distribution of unique senses per word. For more than half of the target words, **Deep-change** infers one sense only, while the dataset was constructed in such a way that all target words are polysemous; the maximum number of **Deep-change**'s senses is 10, which is almost two times less than in the gold data. Although **WooperNLP**'s numbers of senses per word are also different from the gold ones, and the cases with one sense per word also occur, they differ less (more details in Appendix C.5). Both systems produced at least one wrong prediction for all target words.

The **WooperNLP**'s system is able to estimate the degree of polysemy in Russian words: 15% of the target words got the correct number of clusters and 89% of the target words got ≤ 3 redundant or missing senses. For example, the target word 'драить' correctly got 4 senses, but some samples with 3 different senses ('to scrub', 'to criticize severely', 'to

[8] `codalab.lisn.upsaclay.fr/competitions/18570`, `codalab.lisn.upsaclay.fr/competitions/18572`

[9] `codalab.lisn.upsaclay.fr/competitions/18009`

[10] `codalab.lisn.upsaclay.fr/competitions/18008`

inflate sails') were merged into one. **Deep-change** incorrectly predicted one sense for this target word (which was wrong for all usages, since all of them had novel senses).

However, the **WooperNLP**'s system may fail to distinguish between separate senses correctly, which results in lower F1 score. An example where **Deep-change** got higher F1 score despite incorrectly predicting one sense only is the word 'мёд' ('honey'). The gold data contained two new usages with the sense '*sweet sirup-like liquid produced by bees from nectar of flowers of melliferous plants*' (this was also the only old sense), two new usages with the sense '*metaphorical: about something pleasant, causing pleasure*' and one new usage with the sense '*archaic: an alcoholic drink, produced by fermentation from honey, water and fruit juice*'. The **Deep-change**'s system assigned the first sense to all new usages, which is correct in two cases. The **Wooper-NLP**'s system correctly detected that the new usages have three different senses, but incorrectly assigned novel senses to the usages with the old one.

Taking classification of new examples with old senses into account made Subtask 1 more similar to pure WSD than LSCD, and this may be disappointing, since we did not aim to create yet another shared task on WSD; the approach used by **Deep-change** has already proved its efficiency on it (Blevins and Zettlemoyer, 2020). But in the real-world task of updating a dictionary, the system would be required to do WSD as well (predicting many novel senses without being able to spot and differentiate old senses is not very useful practically). It is not yet completely clear what metrics could be used in the future to avoid this pitfall, but we believe that in the end using two independent metrics helped us to at least spot the problem.

5.2 Subtask 2.

For Subtask 2, we average across BLEU and BERTScore (Table 5), since they aim at measuring the same aspects of the task. BLEU scores are very low (≤ 0.11) for all systems and languages, except in one case: **TartuNLP** (Dorkin and Sirts, 2024) for Russian (BLEU = 0.587). BERTScores range from 0.630 to 0.869. See the full results in Appendix C.4.

There are several reasons why the two metrics appear to have different behaviors, despite being designed to evaluate the same aspect of the submissions – namely the adequacy of the submitted outputs as textual replacements for the gold explanations. First, as per Algorithm 1, we align targets and hypotheses based on BERTScores, rather than BLEUs, which is beneficial to BERTScores but detrimental to BLEUs. Second, BLEU and BERTScore are computed in very distinct ways: the former is based on n-gram overlaps whereas the latter is derived from cosine similarity scores between hypothesis and target contextual embeddings. Given the languages of interest include morphologically rich languages with varying degrees of support from the NLP community, it makes sense to expect divergences between BLEU and BERTScore assessments. Third, automatic NLG metrics exhibit various degrees of correlation with human judgments (Freitag et al., 2021; Segonne and Mickus, 2023); empirically establishing which metric is most appropriate for explainable semantic change modeling was not feasible, given the novelty of the task. It is crucial to investigate this point further in future studies.

Team	Fi-Ru-De	Fi-Ru	Fi	Ru	De
TartuNLP	**46.7**	**54.1**	35.4	**72.8**	32.0
WooperNLP	34.0	34.6	34.9	34.2	**33.0**
ABDN-NLP	25.3	37.9	**40.7**	35.2	0.0
Baseline	21.8	20.5	21.8	19.1	24.5

Table 5: Subtask 2 results (average of BLEU and BERTScore, $\times 100$).

In Subtask 2, the **TartuNLP** team topped the leaderboard on average, but mostly because of its very high results on Russian. For Finnish, it was outperformed by **ABDN-NLP** (Ma et al., 2024a), and for German by **WooperNLP**. An important caveat is due here: the AXOLOTL'24 evaluation script for Subtask 2 does not penalize the participants for skipping some of the target words, even if the gold data lists them as gaining senses in the 'new' time period. BLEU and BERTScore are computed as an average across all the target words with gained senses which are present in both reference data and the system's submission ('redundant' target words in the submission are ignored). Thus, a system's coverage of Subtask 2 target words can be different. And it was: although most systems did submit gained sense definitions for (almost) all gold target words, the **ABDN-NLP** team is a notable exception. Its Subtask 2 best submission covered only 1% of the gold target words for Finnish and 3% for Russian. In practice, it means the evaluation metrics for this team were computed on *one* and *six* words correspondingly, so these results should be taken cautiously.[11] Table 6 shows the coverage percentages for all teams and languages.

The extremely high performance of the **TartuNLP** solution for Subtask 2 in Russian is explained by its use of a GlossBERT (Huang et al., 2019) model, fine-tuned with adapters to match usage examples to definitions from Wiktionary. Since the majority of the gold Russian definitions from the AXOLOTL'24 'new' time period had the same source, the **TartuNLP** system was choosing from a limited set of definitions for every target word. This also allowed it to submit predicted definitions very similar to the gold ones on the surface level (as measured by BLEU), unlike other systems.

On the other hand, gold definitions for Finnish and German did not come from Wiktionary. As such, many of the mistakes in German and Finnish submissions by **TartuNLP** appear to be mismatches between the lexicographic resources employed by them and the ones we used to create AXOLOTL'24 data. One clear example is that our German dataset marks senses of words used in idiomatic expression. The target word *Fuß* ('foot') being glossed as *Angst bekommen* ('become afraid') owing to the context *kalte Füße bekommen* ('to get cold feet') does not match the Wiktionary standards, and **TartuNLP**'s system therefore retrieves glosses matching the literal sense of *Fuß*. Another case concerns morphologically close words, such as the two deverbals *Schmiere* ('grease, cream', feminine) and *Schmieren* ('lubrication, greasing', and figuratively 'bribe', neuter) are grouped as a single entry in the AXOLOTL'24 dataset but map to different headwords in Wiktionary. As a result, the **ABDN-NLP** and **WooperNLP** teams topped the Subtask 2 leaderboard for Finnish and German, by prompting GPT 3.5 for definitions. In fact, ignoring Russian results would lead to ranking **WooperNLP** and **TartuNLP** equally.

A manual inspection of **ABDN-NLP** and **WooperNLP**'s Russian GPT3.5 answers suggests they suffer from various grammatical errors and input copying, which may result in overly narrow or semantically inadequate definitions and in paraphrases instead of definitions. Selected examples can be found in Appendix C.6. Thus, although GPT3.5's Russian definitions can seem semantically close to references, many of them appear of limited practical use.

To sum up, the task of providing definitions for the gained senses turned out to be quite challenging **unless** one is using a lexical database already containing all possible glosses. However, even without access to such a database, one can produce more or less acceptable definitions with a large generative language model and a good prompt. Although these definitions will not exactly reproduce the gold ones, they will be similar semantically, and this is true for all three languages under analysis. Still, we would like to see more approaches to this task, yielding better results across multiple languages.

6 Conclusions

We described the organization and findings of AXOLOTL'24, the first multilingual explainable semantic change modeling shared task. The shared task consisted of two subtasks, with the first one focusing on spotting examples containing target words in novel (unknown) senses, thus involving elements from both word sense disambiguation and word sense induction. The second subtask required the participants to provide dictionary-like definitions for these novel senses, as an attempt to explain them. Both subtasks proved to be challenging; one important finding is that systems relying on masked language models specifically fine-tuned on a set of curated sense definitions are most robust across languages and tasks. However, systems which attempt to infer sense knowledge directly from a large generative LM do not fall far behind; this observation complements nicely the findings of Periti et al. (2024). Also, most systems demonstrated good cross-lingual capabilities, being able to produce satisfactory predictions for a surprise language (German) without any training data.

For AXOLOTL'24, we created sense-annotated diachronic semantic change datasets for Finnish and Russian (and a re-formatted version of an existing German dataset), using publicly available sources. These resources can be used to evaluate future approaches or train relevant models. Although not completely free from errors, they are still an important contribution of ours to the LSCD research community; these datasets are now publicly available in AXOLOTL'24 GitHub repository.

[11]This single Finnish definition is not entirely unreasonable: the word *likempää*, glossed as *tarkemmin, paremmin* ('more precisely, better') in the DOLF, is predicted to mean *lähempänä, likempänä, lähempänä* ('closer, closer, closer').

Limitations

While an ideal end-to-end setup for explainable semantic change modeling would involve starting from two raw corpora embodying two specific chronological states of a given language, such a setup would complicate the establishment of a gold standard. As a simplifying assumption, we therefore construct datasets around sets of usage examples manually annotated according to an external sense inventory. This allows us to provide a verified benchmark to compare systems against, but comes at the expense of the thoroughness of our evaluation — some semantic shifts necessarily fall beyond the scope of the inventories we consider, and our implementation of the semantic change modeling task has to be understood as a heuristic overview rather than a definitive and thorough outlook on diachronic linguistic change. AXOLOTL'24 is only a preliminary step towards creating systems able to automatically explain the nature of diachronic semantic shifts. Still, we hope its results will be of immediate practical use.

Ethics Statement

We do not anticipate any significant ethical impact from this work. It is important to mention that all the annotations for data processing were conducted by the paper authors — voluntarily and without any monetary compensation.

Acknowledgments

We would like to thank the LChange'24 workshop organizers for hosting AXOLOTL'24. We would also like to sincerely thank all the AXOLOTL'24 participants for their efforts, questions, discussions and criticisms, which helped to improve the shared task a lot. The computations were performed on resources provided by Sigma2 – the National Infrastructure for High-Performance Computing and Data Storage in Norway. Andrey Kutuzov has received funding from the European Union's Horizon Europe research and innovation program under Grant agreement No 101070350 (HPLT). We acknowledge the help of Pavel Suvorkov who has done much for the Russian dataset preparation.

References

Ron Artstein and Massimo Poesio. 2008. Survey article: Inter-coder agreement for computational linguistics. *Computational Linguistics*, 34(4):555–596.

Pierpaolo Basile, Annalina Caputo, Tommaso Caselli, Pierluigi Cassotti, and Rossella Varvara. 2020. DIACR-Ita@ EVALITA2020: Overview of the EVALIATA2020 diachronic lexical semantics (DIACR-Ita) task. *Evaluation Campaign of Natural Language Processing and Speech Tools for Italian.*

Andreas Blank and Peter Koch. 1999. *Historical semantics and cognition*, volume 13. Walter de Gruyter.

Terra Blevins and Luke Zettlemoyer. 2020. Moving down the long tail of word sense disambiguation with gloss informed bi-encoders. In *Proceedings of the 58th Annual Meeting of the Association for Computational Linguistics*, pages 1006–1017, Online. Association for Computational Linguistics.

Christopher Brückner, Leixin Zhang, and Pavel Pecina. 2024. Similarity-based cluster merging for semantic change modeling. In *Proceedings of the 5th Workshop on Computational Approaches to Historical Language Change*, Bangkok. Association for Computational Linguistics.

Pierluigi Cassotti, Stefano De Pascale, and Nina Tahmasebi. 2024. Using synchronic definitions and semantic relations to classify semantic change types. *Preprint*, arXiv:2406.03452.

Pierluigi Cassotti, Lucia Siciliani, Marco DeGemmis, Giovanni Semeraro, and Pierpaolo Basile. 2023. XL-LEXEME: WiC pretrained model for cross-lingual LEXical sEMantic changE. In *Proceedings of the 61st Annual Meeting of the Association for Computational Linguistics (Volume 2: Short Papers)*, pages 1577–1585, Toronto, Canada. Association for Computational Linguistics.

Alexis Conneau, Kartikay Khandelwal, Naman Goyal, Vishrav Chaudhary, Guillaume Wenzek, Francisco Guzmán, Edouard Grave, Myle Ott, Luke Zettlemoyer, and Veselin Stoyanov. 2020. Unsupervised cross-lingual representation learning at scale. In *Proceedings of the 58th Annual Meeting of the Association for Computational Linguistics*, pages 8440–8451, Online. Association for Computational Linguistics.

Vladimir Dal. 1909. Explanatory dictionary of the living great Russian language ed. by Boduen de Kurtene [Tolkovy slovar zhivogo velikorusskogo yazyka, pod red. I. A. Boduena de Kurtene].

Aleksei Dorkin and Kairit Sirts. 2024. TartuNLP @ AXOLOTL-24: Leveraging classifier output for new sense detection in lexical semantics. In *Proceedings of the 5th Workshop on Computational Approaches to Historical Language Change*, Bangkok. Association for Computational Linguistics.

Mariia Fedorova, Andrey Kutuzov, and Yves Scherrer. 2024. Definition generation for lexical semantic change detection. *Preprint*, arXiv:2406.14167.

Markus Freitag, Ricardo Rei, Nitika Mathur, Chi-kiu Lo, Craig Stewart, George Foster, Alon Lavie, and Ondřej

Bojar. 2021. Results of the WMT21 metrics shared task: Evaluating metrics with expert-based human evaluations on TED and news domain. In *Proceedings of the Sixth Conference on Machine Translation*, pages 733–774, Online. Association for Computational Linguistics.

Brendan J Frey and Delbert Dueck. 2007. Clustering by passing messages between data points. *Science*, 315(5814):972–976.

Artyom Gadetsky, Ilya Yakubovskiy, and Dmitry Vetrov. 2018. Conditional generators of words definitions. In *Proceedings of the 56th Annual Meeting of the Association for Computational Linguistics (Volume 2: Short Papers)*, pages 266–271, Melbourne, Australia. Association for Computational Linguistics.

Noah Gardner, Hafiz Khan, and Chih-Cheng Hung. 2022. Definition modeling: Literature review and dataset analysis. *Applied Computing and Intelligence*, 2(1):83–98.

Mario Giulianelli, Iris Luden, Raquel Fernandez, and Andrey Kutuzov. 2023. Interpretable word sense representations via definition generation: The case of semantic change analysis. In *Proceedings of the 61st Annual Meeting of the Association for Computational Linguistics (Volume 1: Long Papers)*, pages 3130–3148, Toronto, Canada. Association for Computational Linguistics.

Simon Hengchen, Nina Tahmasebi, Dominik Schlechtweg, and Haim Dubossarsky. 2021. Challenges for computational lexical semantic change. In *Computational approaches to semantic change / Tahmasebi, Nina, Borin, Lars, Jatowt, Adam, Yang, Xu, Hengchen, Simon (eds.)*, pages 341–372. Language Science Press, Berlin.

Neil Houlsby, Andrei Giurgiu, Stanislaw Jastrzebski, Bruna Morrone, Quentin De Laroussilhe, Andrea Gesmundo, Mona Attariyan, and Sylvain Gelly. 2019. Parameter-efficient transfer learning for NLP. In *Proceedings of the 36th International Conference on Machine Learning*, volume 97 of *Proceedings of Machine Learning Research*, pages 2790–2799. PMLR.

Luyao Huang, Chi Sun, Xipeng Qiu, and Xuanjing Huang. 2019. GlossBERT: BERT for word sense disambiguation with gloss knowledge. In *Proceedings of the 2019 Conference on Empirical Methods in Natural Language Processing and the 9th International Joint Conference on Natural Language Processing (EMNLP-IJCNLP)*, pages 3509–3514, Hong Kong, China. Association for Computational Linguistics.

Institute for the Languages of Finland. 2013. Corpus of Old Literary Finnish.

Institute for the Languages of Finland. 2023. Vanhan kirjasuomen sanakirja [Dictionary of Old Literary Finnish]. Digital resource. Last update 24.11.2023. Accessed 24.11.2023.

Denis Kokosinskii, Mikhail Kuklin, and Nikolay Arefyev. 2024. Deep-change at AXOLOTL-24: Orchestrating WSD and WSI models for semantic change modeling. In *Proceedings of the 5th Workshop on Computational Approaches to Historical Language Change*, Bangkok. Association for Computational Linguistics.

Andrey Kutuzov, Lilja Øvrelid, Terrence Szymanski, and Erik Velldal. 2018. Diachronic word embeddings and semantic shifts: a survey. In *Proceedings of the 27th International Conference on Computational Linguistics*, pages 1384–1397, Santa Fe, New Mexico, USA. Association for Computational Linguistics.

Andrey Kutuzov and Lidia Pivovarova. 2021. RuShiftEval: a shared task on semantic shift detection for Russian. *Computational linguistics and intellectual technologies: Papers from the annual conference Dialogue*.

Jonathan Lautenschlager, Emma Sköldberg, Simon Hengchen, and Dominik Schlechtweg. 2024. Detection of non-recorded word senses in English and Swedish. *Preprint*, arXiv:2403.02285.

Xi Victoria Lin, Todor Mihaylov, Mikel Artetxe, Tianlu Wang, Shuohui Chen, Daniel Simig, Myle Ott, Naman Goyal, Shruti Bhosale, Jingfei Du, Ramakanth Pasunuru, Sam Shleifer, Punit Singh Koura, Vishrav Chaudhary, Brian O'Horo, Jeff Wang, Luke Zettlemoyer, Zornitsa Kozareva, Mona T. Diab, Veselin Stoyanov, and Xian Li. 2021. Few-shot learning with multilingual language models. *CoRR*, abs/2112.10668.

Xianghe Ma, Dominik Schlechtweg, and Wei Zhao. 2024a. Presence or absence: Are unknown word usages in dictionaries? In *Proceedings of the 5th Workshop on Computational Approaches to Historical Language Change*, Bangkok. Association for Computational Linguistics.

Xianghe Ma, Michael Strube, and Wei Zhao. 2024b. Graph-based clustering for detecting semantic change across time and languages. In *Proceedings of the 18th Conference of the European Chapter of the Association for Computational Linguistics (Volume 1: Long Papers)*, pages 1542–1561, St. Julian's, Malta. Association for Computational Linguistics.

Zhuoyuan Mao and Tetsuji Nakagawa. 2023. LEALLA: Learning lightweight language-agnostic sentence embeddings with knowledge distillation. In *Proceedings of the 17th Conference of the European Chapter of the Association for Computational Linguistics*, pages 1886–1894, Dubrovnik, Croatia. Association for Computational Linguistics.

Timothee Mickus, Kees Van Deemter, Mathieu Constant, and Denis Paperno. 2022. Semeval-2022 task 1: CODWOE – comparing dictionaries and word embeddings. In *Proceedings of the 16th International Workshop on Semantic Evaluation (SemEval-2022)*, pages 1–14, Seattle, United States. Association for Computational Linguistics.

S. Mikhaylov and D. Shershneva. 2018. Dictionary aggregator Vyshka. Dictionaries. In *Komp'juternaja Lingvistika i Intellektual'nye Tehnologii*, pages 490–500.

Sunny Mitra, Ritwik Mitra, Martin Riedl, Chris Biemann, Animesh Mukherjee, and Pawan Goyal. 2014. That's sick dude!: Automatic identification of word sense change across different timescales. In *Proceedings of the 52nd Annual Meeting of the Association for Computational Linguistics (Volume 1: Long Papers)*, pages 1020–1029, Baltimore, Maryland. Association for Computational Linguistics.

Thanapon Noraset, Chen Liang, Lawrence Birnbaum, and Doug Downey. 2017. Definition modeling: Learning to define word embeddings in natural language. In *AAAI*.

Kishore Papineni, Salim Roukos, Todd Ward, and Wei-Jing Zhu. 2002. Bleu: a method for automatic evaluation of machine translation. In *Proceedings of the 40th Annual Meeting of the Association for Computational Linguistics*, pages 311–318, Philadelphia, Pennsylvania, USA. Association for Computational Linguistics.

Francesco Periti, Haim Dubossarsky, and Nina Tahmasebi. 2024. (chat)GPT v BERT dawn of justice for semantic change detection. In *Findings of the Association for Computational Linguistics: EACL 2024*, pages 420–436, St. Julian's, Malta. Association for Computational Linguistics.

Matt Post. 2018. A call for clarity in reporting BLEU scores. In *Proceedings of the Third Conference on Machine Translation: Research Papers*, pages 186–191, Brussels, Belgium. Association for Computational Linguistics.

Maxim Rachinskiy and Nikolay Arefyev. 2022. GlossReader at LSCDiscovery: Train to select a proper gloss in English – discover lexical semantic change in Spanish. In *Proceedings of the 3rd Workshop on Computational Approaches to Historical Language Change*, pages 198–203, Dublin, Ireland. Association for Computational Linguistics.

Nils Reimers and Iryna Gurevych. 2020. Making monolingual sentence embeddings multilingual using knowledge distillation. In *Proceedings of the 2020 Conference on Empirical Methods in Natural Language Processing (EMNLP)*, pages 4512–4525, Online. Association for Computational Linguistics.

Dominik Schlechtweg. 2023. *Human and computational measurement of lexical semantic change*. Ph.D. thesis, University of Stuttgart.

Dominik Schlechtweg, Barbara McGillivray, Simon Hengchen, Haim Dubossarsky, and Nina Tahmasebi. 2020. SemEval-2020 task 1: Unsupervised lexical semantic change detection. In *Proceedings of the Fourteenth Workshop on Semantic Evaluation*, pages 1–23, Barcelona (online). International Committee for Computational Linguistics.

Vincent Segonne and Timothee Mickus. 2023. Definition modeling : To model definitions. generating definitions with little to no semantics. In *Proceedings of the 15th International Conference on Computational Semantics*, pages 258–266, Nancy, France. Association for Computational Linguistics.

Sasha Spala, Nicholas Miller, Franck Dernoncourt, and Carl Dockhorn. 2020. SemEval-2020 task 6: Definition extraction from free text with the DEFT corpus. In *Proceedings of the Fourteenth Workshop on Semantic Evaluation*, pages 336–345, Barcelona (online). International Committee for Computational Linguistics.

Douglas Steinley. 2004. Properties of the Hubert-Arable adjusted Rand index. *Psychological methods*, 9(3):386.

Nina Tahmasebi, Lars Borin, Adam Jatowt, Yang Xu, and Simon Hengchen, editors. 2021. *Computational approaches to semantic change*. Language Science Press, Berlin.

Viktor V. Vinogradov. 1977. *Izbrannye trudy: leksikologija i leksikografija*. Nauka.

Frank D. Zamora-Reina, Felipe Bravo-Marquez, and Dominik Schlechtweg. 2022. LSCDiscovery: A shared task on semantic change discovery and detection in Spanish. In *Proceedings of the 3rd Workshop on Computational Approaches to Historical Language Change*, pages 149–164, Dublin, Ireland. Association for Computational Linguistics.

Tianyi Zhang, Varsha Kishore, Felix Wu, Kilian Q. Weinberger, and Yoav Artzi. 2020. BERTScore: Evaluating Text Generation with BERT. In *International Conference on Learning Representations*.

A Dataset details

A.1 Dataset files structure

Training and development sets are structured as tab-separated-values (TSV) files. Every row corresponds to one usage example.

The files contain 9 named columns, as follows:

- `usage_id`: usage IDs, unique across all AXOLOTL'24 data, templated as `<dataset>_<language>_<row number>`, e.g. `dev_ru_0`
- `word`: target word
- `orth`: the target word in an old spelling (if applicable)
- `sense_id`: unique ID of the sense in which the target word is used in the current example usage

- `gloss`: definition of the sense
- `example`: usage example of the target word, usually a sentence, but can also be longer or shorter
- `indices_target_token`: automatically produced character offsets for the target word in its usage example, if applicable
- `date`: a coarse-grained date of attestation of the usage example (year, if applicable)
- `period`: indicator of the usage example belonging to the first ('old') or the second ('new') time period; thus, can take either the value of 'old' or the value of 'new'.

The test splits in the test folder have `sense_id` and gloss fields empty for the usages from the 'new' time period. The participants' task is to fill in the `sense_id` values in Subtask 1 and the definitions for the novel senses in Subtask 2.

Note that target words are split-specific, that is, a target word occurring in the training set will never occur in the development and test sets, and vice versa.

A.2 Irregularities and manual post-processing of Russian data

An examination of the Russian development and test sets revealed that the extracted data, particularly from Dal, exhibited certain irregularities, which could be grouped into three main categories.

The first category pertains the definition being merged with the example of a given target word, appearing in this combined format both in the `gloss` and in the `example` fields. As the phenomenon was solely related to the instances from the old time period, it can be reasonably attributed to two key elements in Dal's Dictionary: its non-prescriptivist nature and its macro-structure ordering (alphabetical and nesting, whereby related words are grouped within the same entry. For further details on the Dictionary's distinctive characteristics, see Vinogradov (1977)). These factors give rise to the absence of clear boundaries between headwords, definitions and examples, which in turn may lead to incorrect parsing. The issue was addressed by properly reconstructing both fields.

The second category relates to incorrect or incomplete definitions. This issue was particularly prevalent in the old time period, due to both the aforementioned parsing errors and the occasional lack of comprehensive information in Dal. Incorrect instances were either corrected, thus restoring the original definition found in Dal, or eliminated. The latter was the case when the definitions did not correspond to the target word (they corresponded to different dictionary entries or to different words within the same entry due to nesting) or were merely erroneous (e.g., definitions split into two instances; redundant instances, etc.). Incomplete instances could feature either wrongly parsed or vague definitions already present in Dal which were attributed to various target words (e.g. 'действие по глаголу' 'action according to the verb'). In such cases, the definition was either restored to its original condition or manually completed, adding further information. Nevertheless, some glosses from the new time period were also affected, presenting overly narrow definitions for the corresponding examples. This specific issue originated as a byproduct of the annotation process, where a narrower definition of the new time period corresponded to a broader definition in the old time period. As a result, the definitions were manually broadened.

The third category concerns the examples in the old time period having the target word omitted or incorrect. When the issue was caused by the lack of information in Dal it was not addressed.

A.3 Statistics

The kernel density estimation plots in Figures 1a to 1c show the distributions of the number of unique senses per target word for all languages and time periods in all data splits. A value of the 'Density' axis in these (and other figures in this appendix) can be roughly understood as an approximate probability of having a value given on the x-axis, e.g. in Figure 1b the probability of having 5 unique senses per word is about 0.05 for the Russian development split, new time period. The figures were produced using the `kdeplot()` method of `seaborn`[12].

One can see the difference across the languages and time periods. While the number of senses is approximately the same in the new and old time periods of Finnish, in Russian it is notably less in the old time period. The number of new senses in Russian is higher than in Finnish. Most words in all three languages have less than 10 senses (which may explain the choice of cluster number by some

[12] https://seaborn.pydata.org/generated/seaborn.kdeplot.html

participants), but extreme cases of ≥ 20 senses also occur (and should have been taken into account).

Figure 2 shows the distribution of the number of examples per target word across the whole AXOLOTL'24 dataset. Again, there is less difference between the time periods in Finnish (which is expected, since the samples come from the same dictionary). Having much less examples for the old time period in Russian may explain lower results for it in Subtask 1, when measured by ARI.

B Subtasks illustrative outline

As mentioned above, for a given `word` in the test set a `sense_id`, a `gloss` and an `example` were provided in the old `period`; while in the new `period` only `examples` were available. The Russian `word` 'экспресс' (*means of transport; combined bet; express mail*) serves as an illustrative example:

a) **`word`**: экспресс; **`sense_id`**: ekspress_IMBVcXtuQEw; **`gloss`**: транспортное средство (поезд, судно, автобус и т. п.); идущее с повышенной скоростью и с остановками лишь на крупных станциях (means of transport (train, ship, bus etc.); traveling at an increased speed, stopping only at major stations); **`example`**: поезд-экспресс, особенно скорый, курьерский. (express train, especially fast, express); **`period`**: old.

b) **`word`**: экспресс; **`sense_id`**: ? ; **`gloss`**: ? ; **`example`**: ехал я в экспрессе, в спальном вагоне. (I was traveling by an express train, in a sleeping car); **`period`**: new.

c) **`word`**: экспресс; **`sense_id`**: ? ; **`gloss`**: ? ; **`example`**: А вот другому клиенту этого букмекера не повезло. Он отдал 700 тыс. рублей на экспресс, в который включил ставку на «Лион» с форой (0). Результат для игрока печальный. (But the other client of this bookmaker was unlucky. He placed 700 thousand rubles on a combined bet, in which he included a bet on "Lyon" with betting odds (0). The result for the player is unfortunate); **`period`**: new.

d) **`word`**: экспресс; **`sense_id`**: ? ; **`gloss`**: ? ; **`example`**: В этом ночном экспрессе, который отличался от всех остальных поездов довоенным комфортом, — в маленьких купе поскрипывали настоящие кожаные ремни, тускло блестели медные пепельницы, проводники разносили крепкий кофе, — в этом поезде по коридору Скандинавия-Швейцария практически ездили теперь лишь одни дипломаты. (In this night train, which distinguished itself from all other trains by its pre-war comfort, real leather belts creaked in small compartments, copper ashtrays glistered dully, conductors carried strong coffee, - in this train, almost only diplomats traveled along the Scandinavia-Switzerland passage then); **`period`**: new.

e) **`word`**: экспресс; **`sense_id`**: ? ; **`gloss`**: ? ; **`example`**: — Во-первых, как только попадешь в восемьдесят второй год, так сразу опиши подробно все, что ты здесь видел, и пошли мне экспрессом в Отрадное. (First of all, as soon as you get into the year 82, write in details what you see and send it to me in Otradnoe by express mail); **`period`**: new.

In Subtask 1 the goal was to discover new senses, assigning to the usages in the new period a new sense ID, or using the same sense ID if no new senses were detected. The gold data for 'экспресс' indicate two novel senses, c) and e), in the new period:

a) **`sense_id`**: ekspress_IMBVcXtuQEw

b) **`sense_id`**: ekspress_IMBVcXtuQEw

c) **`sense_id`**: ekspress_ao65pt5Rcys

d) **`sense_id`**: ekspress_IMBVcXtuQEw

e) **`sense_id`**: ekspress_u4-6oODM_fk

The predictions made by both **WooperNLP** and **Deepchange**, for instance, entail the old sense only (sense ID: ekspress_IMBVcXtuQEw), which is overextended to all usages, decreasing ARI.

In subtask 2, the aim was to generate definitions for the novel senses which were supposedly discovered in subtask 1, however the two subtasks could be solved independently. Below are shown the gold definitions of the word 'экспресс' for the five usages above:

a) **`gloss`**: транспортное средство (поезд, судно, автобус и т. п.); идущее с повышенной скоростью и с остановками лишь на крупных станциях (means of transport (train, ship, bus etc.); traveling at an increased speed, stopping only at major stations)

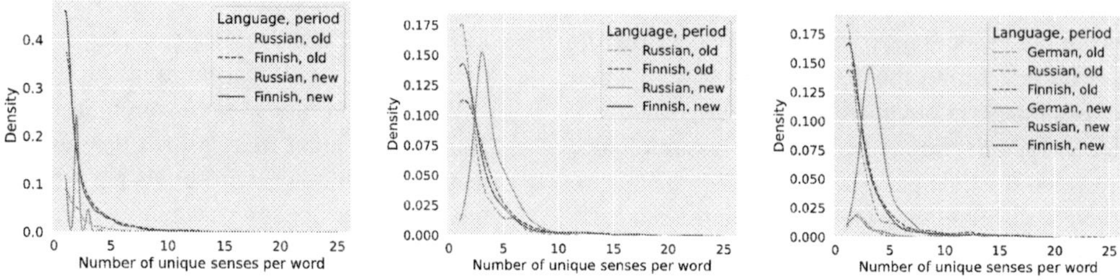

(a) Train splits (b) Development splits (c) Test splits

Figure 1: Distribution of the number of unique senses per target word in the AXOLOTL'24 datasets. Cases with more than 25 senses clipped.

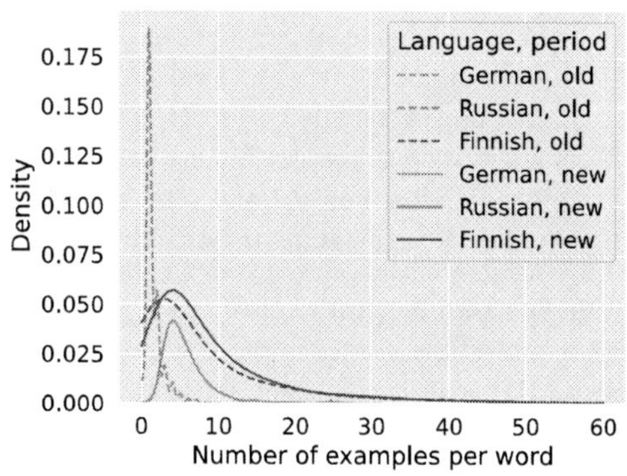

Figure 2: Distribution of the number of examples per target word.

b) **gloss**: транспортное средство (поезд, судно, автобус и т. п.); идущее с повышенной скоростью и с остановками лишь на крупных станциях (means of transport (train, ship, bus etc.); traveling at an increased speed, stopping only at major stations)

c) **gloss**: спец. ставка на несколько независимых исходов событий (spec. bet on several independent outcomes)

d) **gloss**: транспортное средство (поезд, судно, автобус и т. п.); идущее с повышенной скоростью и с остановками лишь на крупных станциях (means of transport (train, ship, bus etc.); traveling at an increased speed, stopping only at major stations)

e) **gloss**: разг. срочное почтовое отправление (coll. express mail)

The definitions could be either generated *ex nihilo* or based on existing ontologies. For example, with regard to the sense c), the definition that **TartuNLP** presented is identical to the gold definition, while **WooperNLP** generated a new definition: 'Экспресс - комбинированную ставку, в которой несколько событий объединены в одну ставку. В данном примере клиент сделал экспресс-ставку, включив в нее ставку на футбольную команду «Лион» с форой (0). Однако, результат ставки оказался неудачным для игрока'

(Express - a combined bet in which several events are combined into one bet. In this example, the client placed a combined bet, including a bet on the Lyon football team with betting odds (0). However, the result of the bet was unsuccessful for the player").

C Supplementary details on subtask results

C.1 Methods used by participants for Subtask 1

The **Deep-change** (Kokosinskii et al., 2024) approach to Subtask 1 involved classification over senses from the 'old' time period, using a fine-tuned GlossReader model (Rachinskiy and Arefyev, 2022). It was fine-tuned on the concatenation of Russian and Finnish AXOLOTL'24 training sets and the English SemCor corpus (on which the original GlossReader was trained). In another submission, **Deep-change** used outlier detection to find novel senses. For German, they used the same system as for Russian. Although this submission achieved lower average score, it is more interesting scientifically, since it did predict some novel senses and got high ARI on the Russian test dataset.

The **WooperNLP** approach was to 1) augment the test data with GPT3.5; 2) produce contextualized embeddings for all the instances with a BERT-like model; 3) cluster the instance embeddings into sense groups.

Holotniekat (Brückner et al., 2024) described their method as follows: '*We extend the baseline system by assigning senses to clusters in a non-greedy manner and reducing the cluster granularity. In a first pass, we merge multiple clusters if the same old sense is their best candidate. In a second pass, we repeat this procedure for the remaining clusters and novel senses, assuming the cluster centroids to be the embeddings of novel glosses. Glosses and usage examples are embedded using a concatenation of two different multilingual sentence transformers.*'

ABDN-NLP (Ma et al., 2024a) described their method as follows: '*For Subtask 1, we reuse the workflow of the baseline system, which includes three components: producing embeddings for word usages, clustering these embeddings, and mapping of dictionary meaning entries to the resulting clusters. But we make modifications to each component. For the embedding component, we use embeddings of both words and word usages to construct a semantic tree representation for each target word. For the clustering component, we replace Affinity Propagation with Neighbor-based clustering (Ma et al., 2024b) to deal with low-frequency sense clusters. For mapping, we map dictionary entries to the average embedding (rather than the embedding of the first-indexed usage) of each cluster in order to eliminate randomness. For Subtask 2, unlike the baseline system, which requires costly model training for generating dictionary-like definitions for new word usages, our system is training-free and does so by just prompting Large Language Models such as GPT-4 and LLaMA-3*'.

IMS Stuttgart described their method as follows: '*USD to WSD, WSI. Firstly we create XL-LEXEME (Cassotti et al., 2023) sense embeddings based on augmented glosses. Then we classify usages into unknown vs. known sense under a task called USD, by comparing their embeddings (also computed with XL-LEXEME) with the sense embeddings from step 1. We compare usage and sense embeddings by employing Spearman Correlation as a distance metric and by setting a similarity threshold as a decision boundary. We also replace orthography of the inflected target word in the usage with the base form of the target word (calling this SUB method). We only compare usage embeddings to already known sense id embeddings. We use WSD (word sense disambiguation) to classify the predicted from USD known senses and WSI (word sense induction) to cluster predicted unknown sense into new sense id clusters. For clustering a hierarchical flat clustering technique is used with cosine as a metric and clustering threshold of 0.1 (we need to experiment here definitely).*'

Tartu-NLP (Dorkin and Sirts, 2024) described their method as follows: '*GlossBERT (Huang et al., 2019) with XLM-RoBERTa (Conneau et al., 2020) as the base model for both subtasks. In other words, we treat both as binary classification of gloss/example sentence pairs. New senses are identified using an arbitrary threshold for the classifier probability. So, if all known glosses are below the probability threshold for a given usage example, then this is a new sense. We fine-tune bottleneck adapters (Houlsby et al., 2019) for each language instead of full fine-tuning. I suppose, this doesn't actually play a key role in the solution, but it did allow us to spend less time on training.*'

For more details about the methods, we refer the reader to the participants' papers.

C.2 Subtask 2 evaluation algorithm

Algorithm 1 Subtask 2 evaluation for one target word

Require: Y, set of target sense explanations
$\hat{Y}$, set of predicted sense explanations

$s \leftarrow 0$
while $Y \neq \emptyset$ and $\hat{Y} \neq \emptyset$ **do**
  $y_a, \hat{y}_b \leftarrow \underset{y^* \in Y,\, \hat{y}^* \in \hat{Y}}{\text{argmax}} \text{ BertScore}(y^*, \hat{y}^*)$
  $s \leftarrow s + \text{BertScore}(y_a, \hat{y}_b)$
  $Y \leftarrow Y \setminus \{y_a\}$
  $\hat{Y} \leftarrow \hat{Y} \setminus \{\hat{y}_b\}$
end while
$s \leftarrow s / \min(|Y|, |\hat{Y}|)$
return s

The procedure for attributing the average sense-level BERTScore for a given target word during our evaluation procedure is outlined in Algorithm 1. Simply put, it amounts to (i) greedily selecting the pair of target and predicted explanations that yield the highest BERTScore; (ii) adding that score to a running sum s; (iii) discarding the corresponding target and prediction; (iv) repeating steps i–iii until no such pair can be formed; (v) normalizing the running sum by the number of pairs formed. After the targets and predictions were paired using BERTScore, they were additionally evaluated with BLEU, likewise macro-averaged across target words.

C.3 Subtask 2 target word coverage

Team	Finnish	Russian	German
TartuNLP	87	86	50
WooperNLP	100	91	100
ABDN-NLP	1	3	—
Baseline	100	100	100

Table 6: Subtask 2: systems' coverage of target words with newly gained senses (percents).

In Table 6, we show the coverage of subtask 2 systems (viz., the proportion of changed senses for which a gloss was provided). In practice, our decision to not penalize incorrect sense inventory shape in Subtask 2 led to a wide variety in terms of coverage, with **ABDN-NLP** displaying an especially poor coverage. We recommend that future works on explainable semantic change modeling properly penalize incorrect sense inventory shapes, e.g. by introducing a penalty on coverage. The scoring script used in the AXOLOTL'24 shared task provides an implementation of an intersection-over-union penalty designed to penalize sense inventories with too few or too many senses.

C.4 Subtask 2 rankings per metric

Team	Fi-Ru-De	Fi-Ru	Fi	Ru	De
TartuNLP	**72.6**	**77.4**	67.9	**86.9**	63.0
WooperNLP	66.0	66.6	67.5	65.6	**65.0**
ABDN-NLP	46.1	69.2	**70.6**	67.7	0.0
Baseline	42.3	39.0	40.3	37.7	49.0

Table 7: BERTScores (×100)

Team	Fi-Ru-De	Fi-Ru	Fi	Ru	De
TartuNLP	**20.8**	**30.8**	2.8	**58.7**	**1.0**
WooperNLP	0.2	2.5	2.3	2.7	**1.0**
ABDN-NLP	4.5	6.7	**10.7**	2.7	0.0
Baseline	1.3	1.9	3.3	0.5	0.0

Table 8: BLEUs (×100)

In the main text, we focus only on rankings derived from average BLEU and BERTScore as they are meant to assess the same aspect of the shared task. On the other hand, the two metrics need not always agree, and it is therefore more prudent to assess each separately. Tables 7 and 8 respectively assess BERTScores and BLEUs for all best submissions: we can observe how BLEUs are systematically extremely low, aside from the retrieval system of **TartuNLP** for Russian; whereas the divergence in BERTScores is less pronounced.

C.5 Deep-change and WooperNLP at Subtask 1

Figure 3 shows how the distribution of number of unique senses per target word (in both time periods) differs in the **Deep-change**'s and **WooperNLP**'s submissions and in the gold data. Figures 4 to 6 show the same information, but as histograms. Table 9 shows minimum, mean and maximum of this distribution.

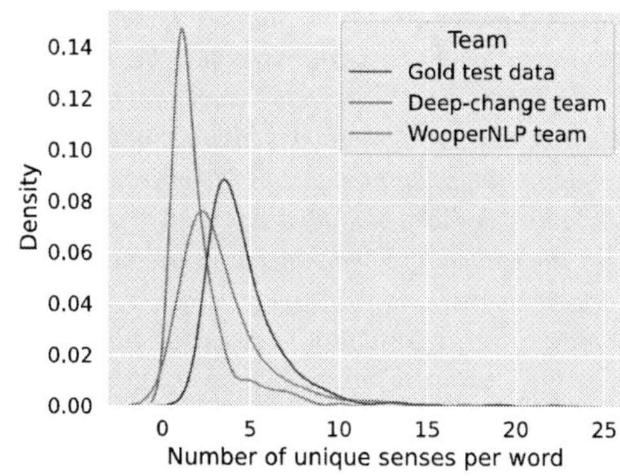

Figure 3: Distribution of number of unique senses per target word in the Russian gold test data, the winner team's prediction and the best predictions for Russian by ARI (the WooperNLP team).

Team	Min	Max	Mean
Gold test data	2	19	4.6
Deep-change	1	10	2
WooperNLP	1	22	3.5

Table 9: Number of unique senses per word in Russian predictions, descriptive statistics.

C.6 Subtask 2 examples

The example below shows a definition of the Russian verb 'драить' in the sense of 'to scrub' (used in its past simple form 'драил') from the **WooperNLP**'s submission (**ABDN-NLP** did not generate a definition for it):

a) **Context:** 'Сачков драил шкуркой бензинопровод: как у всякого механика, у него чесались руки, когда он видел кусочек меди или латуни.'

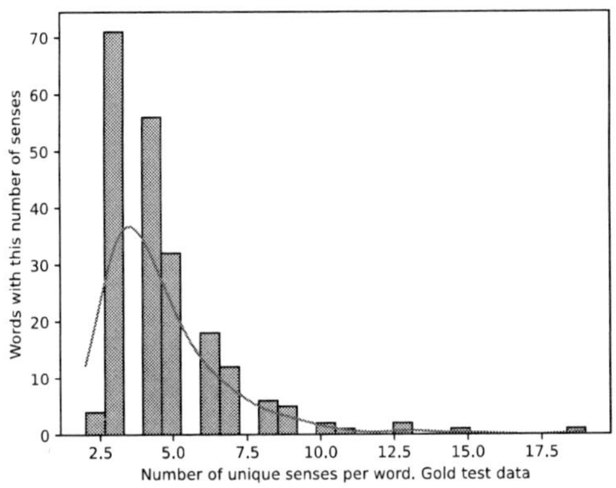

Figure 4: Number of unique senses per word in Russian, the gold test data.

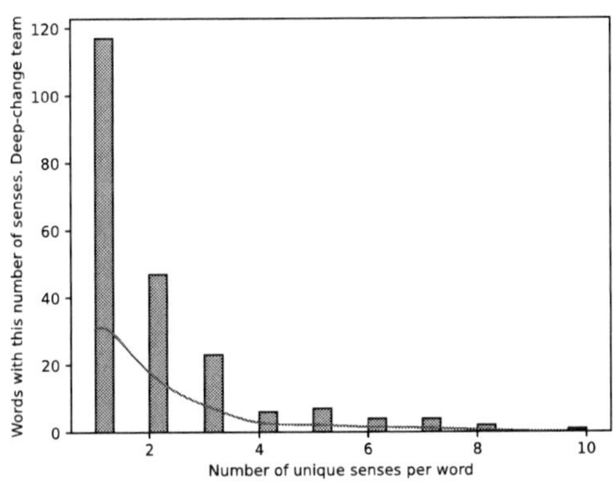

Figure 5: Number of unique senses per word in Russian, the Deep-change team.

> "Sachkov scrubbed the petrol conductor with a sandpaper; like every mechanic, he itched, when he saw a piece of copper or brass."

b) **Definition:** 'Драил - инструмент, используемый для обработки поверхностей, снятия заусенцев, шлифовки и полировки металлических изделий. В данном контексте, сачков драил шкуркой бензинопровод, означает, что механик использовал драил с шкуркой для обработки поверхности бензинопровода из меди или латуни.'

> "Scrubbed is an instrument, used for refinement of surfaces... In the given context, sachkov scrubbed the petrol conductor with a sandpaper, means that the mechanic used scrubbed with a sandpaper for refinement the petrol conductor surface of copper or brass."

The following mistakes were made by GPT in this

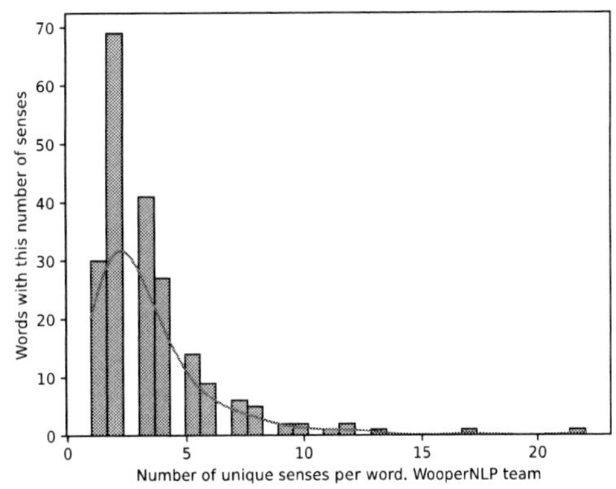

Figure 6: Number of unique senses per word in Russian, the WooperNLP team.

short definition:

- 'драил' is only a past simple form of a verb and can never be used as a noun;
- the model doesn't stop after producing the definition, but continues with an explanation
- 'сачков' ('sachkov') starts from a lowercase letter although it is a surname and must start with an uppercased one
- the verb 'означает' ('means') requires a subject that is missed in the model's answer.

The next example shows definitions of the word 'месть' ('revenge') by both systems. The **ABDN-NLP**'s definition is correct, although contains an error, most likely originating from the model's multilinguality: in English, 'commit' can be used both with 'crime' and 'offense', while in Russian it is used with 'crime' only. The **WooperNLP**'s definition is entirely wrong because it is generated not for the word 'месть', but for the word 'вместе' ('together'), which also occurs in the example. A possible reason can be that revenge is plural in this example, which is a rare case in Russian as well as in English.

a) **Context:** И в душе Лиды ответно что-то замерло и задрожало, в желании расстаться с грустной и нежной благодарностью за пережитые вместе наслаждения, без всяких местей, злоб и ненавистей.

> 'And in response something froze and began to tremble in Lida's soul, in the desire to part with sad and tender gratitude for the pleasures lived through together, without any revenges, angers and hatreds.'

b) **ABDN-NLP definition:** Месть - возмездие за совершенное преступление или обиду

'Revenge is retribution for the committed crime or offence'

c) **WooperNLP definition:** Совместно, вместе с кем-то или чем-то. В данном контексте означает пережитые совместно события, радости или удовольствия.

'Together with someone or something. In the given context means events, gladnesses or pleasures lived through together.'

The next examples show definitions of the word 'травля' in the senses 'baiting' and 'bullying'. Both systems correctly separated these senses in Subtask 1, but in Subtask 2, **ABDN-NLP**'s system generated almost equal definitions for them. Also using 'slander' with 'over' in its second definition is correct in English, but not in Russian. **WooperNLP**'s definitions are correct semantically, but the first one includes unnecessary details (and 'decreasing insects' again looks like a loan translation from English) and the second one is too narrow, because bullying is not something specific for Nekrasov only.

a) **Context:** Он здраво оценил собственные перспективы и занялся старым промыслом — травлей бытовых насекомых.

"He evaluated his perspectives reasonably and engaged in old trade - baiting domestic insects."

b) **ABDN-NLP definition:** Травля - уничижительное обращение, издевательство или преследование

"Baiting is disparaging handling, humiliation or stalking"

c) **WooperNLP definition:** Травля бытовых насекомых - это процесс уничтожения или контроля насекомых, которые могут быть вредными или неприятными для человека в его доме или других помещениях. Это может включать использование химических средств, ловушек, уловителей или других методов для устранения или снижения насекомых.

"Baiting of domestic insects is a process of destroying or controlling insects which may be harming or unpleasant for a human in their house or other locations. This may include usage of chemical means, traps, catchers or other methods for removal or decreasing insects."

a) **Context:** 'Говорили о том, что началась настоящая травля Некрасова в печати.'

"There were talks that real bullying of Nekrasov began in press"

b) **ABDN-NLP definition:** Травля - систематическое преследование, унижение или клевета над кем-либо

"Bullying is systematic stalking, humiliation or slander over someone"

c) **WooperNLP definition:** Травля - систематическое и агрессивное осуждение, оскорбления и нанесение ущерба репутации Некрасова в печати.

"Bullying is systematic and aggressive condemnagaination, insulting and doing damage to Nekrasov's reputation in press."

As far as Finnish goes, a close inspection of **TartuNLP**'s top scoring submission reveal a few interesting trends. In particular, a manual inspection of the top 10 and bottom 10 target words as ranked by their BERTScores does not suggest that the metric is primarily sensitive to semantic adequacy: 9 out of the top 10 items correspond to submissions with some degree of semantic inadequacy, versus 5 out of the bottom 10 items. The metric appears more sensitive to matters of fluency: A number of predictions among the 10 lowest scoring target words in terms of BERTScore contain an overabundance of parentheses, such as:

a) **TartuNLP definition:** *( ) ("aste")*

'( ) ("degree")'

We furthermore observe cases where a morphologically related modern word is produced (a documented heuristic in definition modeling; Segonne and Mickus, 2023), regardless of the meaning. For instance, the word *osoitella* is defined as follows:

a) **TartuNLP definition:** *( ) osoittaa*

'( ) to show/point/indicate'

b) **Reference definition:** *matkia, jäljitellä; noudattaa jonkun tai jonkin esimerkkiä* 'to mimic, imitate, follow someone's example'

Other cases pertain to senses that are inappropriate for the Old Literary Finnish data at hand, as the entry pertains to an idiomatic or specific usage of the word. For instance, the word *korjata* ('collect, correct'), is used in the idiomatic expression *korjata luunsa* or *korjata luitansa* (lit., 'collect one's bones'), which is glossed *mennä tiehensä* ('to go one's way'). On the other hand, the predictions provided by **TartuNLP** all pertain to the literal, non-idiomatic usage:

a) **TartuNLP definition 1:** *oikaista virheellisyys, korvata virheellinen tai huono oikealla tai paremmalla*

   'correct something wromg, replace something wrong or bad with something correct or better'

b) **TartuNLP definition 2:** *kerätä tai ottaa talteen*

   'collect or take into one's safekeeping'

c) **TartuNLP definition 3:** *saattaa ehyeksi, toimivaksi*

   'make whole, functioning'

This mismatch echoes our earlier remarks on German; nonetheless this particular target word was scored highly by the evaluation script of AXOLOTL'24.

Overall, this manual inspection reveals two key points worth keeping in mind in future work on explainable semantic change modeling: (i) BERTScore seems at times more sensitive to fluency characteristics than semantic aspects; and (ii) a tighter control on the contents of resources to weed out idiomatic expressions might bring about a different picture than what we summarized in this paper.

D Shared task logo

The shared task logo in Figure 7 is provided as a recompense for the reader who did trudge through the 9 pages of appendix material. We are proud to indicate it received a stamp of approval from one of our anonymous reviewers.

Figure 7: AXOLOTL'24 shared task logo

Improving Word Usage Graphs with Edge Induction

Bill Noble
University of Gothenburg
bill.noble@gu.se

Francesco Periti
University of Milan
francesco.periti@unimi.it

Nina Tahmasebi
University of Gothenburg
nina.tahmasebi@gu.se

Abstract

This paper investigates *edge induction* as a method for augmenting Word Usage Graphs, in which word usages (nodes) are connected through scores (edges) representing semantic relatedness. Clustering (densely) annotated WUGs can be used as a way to find senses of a word without relying on traditional word sense annotation. However, annotating all or a majority of pairs of usages is typically infeasible, resulting in sparse graphs and, likely, lower quality senses. In this paper, we ask if filling out WUGs with edges *predicted* from the human annotated edges improves the eventual clusters. We experiment with edge induction models that use structural features of the existing sparse graph, as well as those that exploit textual (distributional) features of the usages. We find that in both cases, inducing edges prior to clustering improves correlation with human sense-usage annotation across three different clustering algorithms and languages.

1 Introduction

Recently, Word Usage Graphs (WUGs) have emerged as a new paradigm in the computational study of lexical semantic change (Schlechtweg et al., 2021b). For a given target word (lexeme), a word usage graph consists of a set of *usages*,[1] along with humanly generated *relatedness scores* for some subset of the pairs of usages. Together, the usages (nodes) and relatedness scores (edges) form a weighted graph. Graph clustering techniques can be used to discover word senses, where each cluster of usages is understood to be a distinct sense of the target word.

This procedure relies on a simpler human annotation task than assigning a sense from a fixed inventory to each usage, thus allowing us to obtain more annotations with the same number of annotation hours. Moreover, since no sense inventory is required, new or otherwise undocumented senses can be discovered by the procedure. These two factors make WUG annotation particularly useful in applications involving Lexical Semantic Change (LSC), since they make it more feasible to cover a large vocabulary and consider novel or unattested historical senses.

The SemEval-2020 task on Unsupervised Lexical Semantic Change Detection used Diachronic Word Usage Graphs (DWUGs) to develop LSC evaluation datasets for four languages, namely English, German, Swedish, and Latin (Schlechtweg et al., 2020). The use of DWUGs for this purpose has since been adopted in LSC benchmarks for Italian (Basile et al., 2020), Russian (Kutuzov and Pivovarova, 2021), Spanish (Zamora-Reina et al., 2022), Norwegian (Kutuzov et al., 2022), Chinese (Chen et al., 2023), Japanese (Ling et al., 2023), and most recently Slovenian (Pranjić et al., 2024). Each benchmark consists of a diachronic corpus and a set of target words over which human annotation was conducted.

While WUG annotation is less burdensome than traditional word sense annotation, the creation of reliable benchmarks over multiple time periods, still requires a substantial annotation effort. A complete graph on N usages has $(N \cdot (N-1))/2$ edges and, since sense frequency distributions can be highly skewed, sampling a small number of usages does not ensure a representative sample of senses. Thus far, this issue has been addressed by creating simplified LSC benchmarks with reduced annotated edges over two time periods (with the exception of Kutuzov and Pivovarova (2021), who created a benchmark over three time periods). Additionally, as word senses are automatically derived from relatedness judgments of sparse graphs, the evaluation of approaches to LSC is typically conducted through *Graded Change Detection* (i.e., ranking the target words by the degree of semantic change across the corpus) regardless of *Word Sense Induc-*

[1] Contexts drawn from a corpus including the target word.

Proceedings of the 5th Workshop on Computational Approaches to Historical Language Change, pages 92–107
August 15, 2024

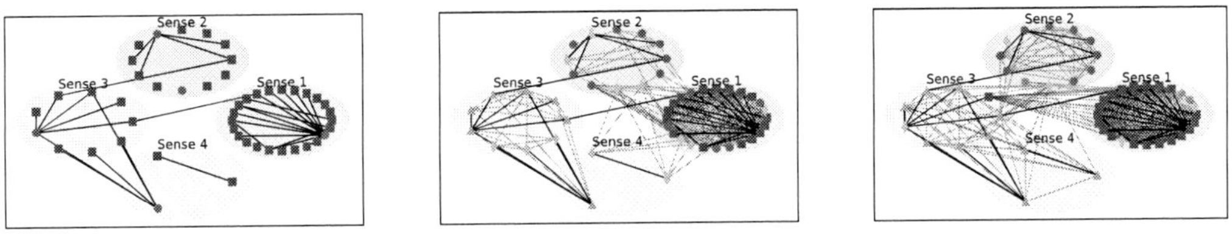

(a) Sparse usage relatedness judgments from human annotators (ARI=0.06)

(b) Missing edges inferred with graph-structural features (ARI=0.37)

(c) Missing edges inferred with structural and textual features (ARI=0.62)

Figure 1: The WUGs for *ausspannen*. Only positive (weight $\geq$ 2.5) edges are shown. Colored regions (labeled Sense 1–4) correspond to human usage-sense annotation, while node colors correspond to clusters found by the `SBM-binomial` model using three different sets of edges: (a) only the human-annotated edges, (b) augmented with induced edges (gray) using *structural evidence*, and (c) augmented edges induced with *structural and textual evidence*. ARI scores indicate correlation with human usage-sense annotation. This example is drawn from Experiment 3 which is described in Section 6.3.

tion (i.e., assessing the quality of word meaning derived by computational models). As a result, more and more so-called *form-based* approaches to LSC have been developed to quantify change. These models sidestep the fundamental aspect of sense modeling that connects LSC to other relevant NLP tasks such as Word Sense Disambiguation and Induction (Periti and Tahmasebi, 2024; Aksenova et al., 2022), and which would make the results of an LSC detection model more interpretable. For example, the SOTA approach to LSC (known as APD) currently consists in measuring the degree of change as average pairwise distance between the contextualized embeddings for a given word (Giulianelli et al., 2020).[2]

In this paper, we investigate *edge induction* as a methodology for augmenting human relatedness judgments in the creation of WUGs, with the goal of reducing the annotation effort required to derive high-quality WUGs. We investigate the following research questions:

RQ1 Can edge induction reduce the human annotation burden required to produce high-quality WUGs?

RQ2 What are the relative contributions of graph-based (structural) and usage-based (contextual) features in WUG edge prediction?

In addition to considering the classification performance of edge induction models, we assess the *quality* of augmented WUGs in terms of how well their node clusters correspond to human-annotated word senses.

[2]We refer the reader to Periti and Montanelli (2024); Tahmasebi et al. (2021); Kutuzov et al. (2018); Tang (2018) for extensive overviews.

2 Related work

In the Word in-Context (WiC) task (Pilehvar and Camacho-Collados, 2019; Loureiro et al., 2022), a model is expected to determine, if two usages of a target word are *related* or *unrelated*. As this is similar to WUG annotation, recent work has shown that large language models such as GPT and BERT can be used as *computational annotators* of DWUGs, reducing the burden of annotation through WiC assessments (Periti and Tahmasebi, 2024; Periti et al., 2024).

This work is similarly motivated. However in contrast to WiC, edge induction leverages a (partial) WUG annotated by humans to infer missing edges, instead of solely relying on models' assessments of relatedness. For example, given a WUG where usage pairs $\langle u, v \rangle$ and $\langle v, w \rangle$ are known to be related, an edge induction model may infer that usages u and w are also related, based on the information provided by the partial graph (see Figure 2a). We use the term *structural features* to denote predictive features derived from the partial graph, and *contextual features* to refer to textual features of the usage applicable in the standard WiC task.

3 Edge induction models

A WUG can be regarded as a weighted graph, with a set of nodes (usages) N, and a weight function $W : E \mapsto \{1, 2, 3, 4\}$,[3] where the domain of W is a subset of pairs of nodes in N; i.e., $E \subseteq \mathcal{E}$, where $\mathcal{E}$ is the set of edges on the complete graph K_N.

[3]These weights correspond to the Likert scale provided to human annotators: *unrelated*, *distantly related*, *closely related*, and *identical*. In some cases, we allow other values in $[1, 4]$, as when the graph is constructed with relatedness scores aggregated over multiple annotator judgments.

An edge induction model is a function that finds a $W' : E' \mapsto \{1, 2, 3, 4\}$ such that $E' \supset E$, while retaining $E' \subseteq \mathcal{E}$. The intended interpretation is that W' *extends* W in such a way that (potentially) uses information encoded in W to induce values $W'(u, v)$ for edges missing from the domain of W.

The simplest operationalization of edge induction is as *classification*, such that, given $\langle u, v\rangle \in \mathcal{E}$, the classifier features can be computed from W (structural features), and potentially some other auxiliary information (as in the case of our textual features). Since our experimental focus is on features, all of the induction models we experiment with in this paper are four-way multi-class logistic regression models provided with different combinations of structural and textual features (described below).

xl-lexeme-cos XL-Lexeme (Cassotti et al., 2023) is an XLM-R-based model trained on a large multilingual corpus of combined WiC datasets. It uses a Siamese architecture similar to sentence BERT (Reimers and Gurevych, 2019), but with the target word marked off by special tokens. The model is trained to minimize the contrasting loss (Hadsell et al., 2006) between pairs of usage embeddings, with cosine distance used as the underlying distance function.

For a pair of usages u and v, let

$$x^{\text{xl-lex}}_{\langle u,v\rangle} = \delta^{\cos}(\mathbf{u}, \mathbf{v}), \quad (1)$$

where $\delta^{\cos}$ is cosine distance and $\mathbf{u}$ and $\mathbf{v}$ are the XL-Lexeme embeddings of usages u and v computed with the lemma of the WUG in question marked as the target.[4]

Since XL-Lexeme is currently state-of-the-art in the WiC task (Periti and Tahmasebi, 2024), we use $x^{\text{xl-lex}}_{\langle u,v\rangle}$ to investigate the predictive contribution of contextual features in our experiments.

log-triangle Intuitively, we should be able to infer something about missing edges based on the edges that have been annotated. This feature works on the intuition of "completing the triangle" between u and v based on the known edges. Suppose we have another usage w and, following Figure 2a, let $x = W(u, w)$ and $z = W(w, v)$ and suppose we know that $x = z = 4$ (i.e,. both pairs $\langle u, w\rangle$ and $\langle w, v\rangle$ are closely related), we might expect that u and v are closely related too and therefore assign $W'(u, v) = \hat{y} := 4$. In fact, given that $x = 4$ we might generalize to expect that $y = z$. However, this is less true when $x = 3$. And when both x and z are 1 or 2, it is difficult to say what can be inferred about y. Moreover, as in Figure 2b, we may have multiple intermediary w_i's that we want to use to "complete the triangle" and aggregate the information provided by their conjunction — pure heuristics won't get us very far.

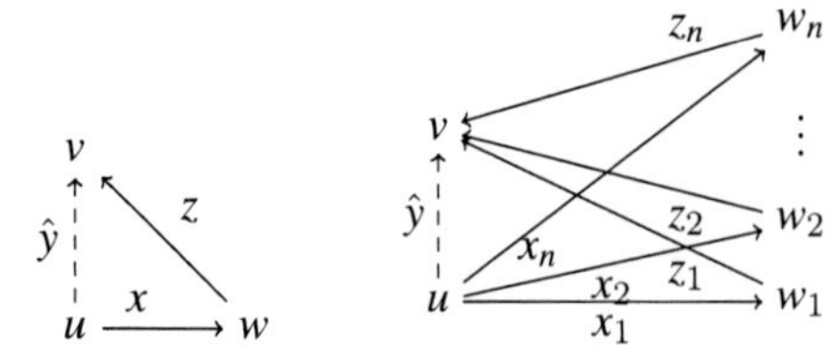

(a) (b)

Figure 2: Setup for *triangle path count edge* induction. The value of the missing edge ($\hat{y}$) can be inferred from the weights along each of the known paths $\{(x_1, z_1), ..., (x_n, z_n)\}$ from u to v.

The general case is described by Figure 2. There is no edge between usages u and v, but we do have edges between u and some number of other usages $w_1, w_2, ..., w_n$ and edges between each w_i and v. We define the *triangle path count* as a count vector of the weights along all the length-2 paths from u to v. Formally,

$$\mathbf{x}^{\text{tri}}_{\langle u,v\rangle}[i] = \sum_{w_j} \{1 \mid \langle W(u, w_j), W(w_j, v)\rangle = p_i\}, \quad (2)$$

where p_i indexes the set of the possible length-2 paths of weights (i.e., permutations of $\{1, 2, 3, 4\}$). If all counts $\mathbf{x}^{\text{tri}}_{\langle u,v\rangle}[i] = 0$, then $\mathbf{x}^{\text{tri}}_{\langle u,v\rangle}$ is undefined — assuming that the domain of W is constructed from independently distributed samples from $\binom{N}{2}$, the fact that there is no length-2 path between u and v doesn't tell us anything about what $W'(u, v)$ should be.

To account for the fact that each additional path of a given type likely provides marginally less predictive information about the correct label for $\langle u, v\rangle$, we use the point-wise log of the triangle path count as input features to the logistic regression model.[5]

[4] Note that $x^{\text{xl-lex}}_{\langle u,v\rangle}$ is a scalar value, meaning that the regression model using only this feature essentially finds data-driven thresholds that segment $[-1, 1]$ (the range of $\delta^{\cos}$) into four bins corresponding to the edge annotation schema.

[5] A more natural way to account for this diminishing information content would be with a Multinomial Naive Bayes model, that operates on $\mathbf{x}^{tri}$, however we found the classification performance of that model to be similar to that of the logistic regression model using the log-count feature. For

$$\mathbf{x}^{\text{log-tri}}_{\langle u,v\rangle}[i] = \log(\mathbf{x}^{\text{tri}}_{\langle u,v\rangle}[i] + 1) \tag{3}$$

log-triangle+xl-lexeme-cos Finally, the model that combines textual and and structural features simply uses the concatenation of `xl-lexeme-cos` and the `log-triangle` features:

$$\mathbf{x}^{\text{log-tri+xl-lex}}_{\langle u,v\rangle} = \mathbf{x}^{\text{log-tri}}_{\langle u,v\rangle} \oplus [x^{\text{xl-lex}}_{\langle u,v\rangle}] \tag{4}$$

3.1 Iterated inference

Models that use $\mathbf{x}^{\text{log-tri}}$ (and $\mathbf{x}^{\text{log-tri+xl-lex}}$) have undefined features when there are no length-2 paths from u to v. Suppose we have a trained classifier C which, given an existing weight function W and auxiliary information A, predicts new weights; i.e., $C_{W,A} : N \times N \mapsto [1,4]$. Letting W^0 be the initial weight function and $E^0 = \mathrm{Dom}(W^0)$ be the edges for which we have ground-truth weights, we infer edges in stages as follows:

$$W^i(u,v) = \begin{cases} W^0(u,v) & \text{if } \langle u,v\rangle \in E^0 \\ C_{W^{i-1},A}(u,v) & \text{otherwise.} \end{cases} \tag{5}$$

In other words, we preserve all of the original (ground-truth) edge weights while updating inferred weights with new predictions at each iteration. Other schemes are of course possible, but this one seeks a balance between propagating information from the larger graph at each iteration and remaining grounded in the seed edges (hopefully avoiding excessive error propagation).

3.2 Levels of stratification

There are several choices for how to divide the predictive domain of each classifier. Intuitively, we would expect words to behave similarly with respect to the inferential evidence provided by the $\mathbf{x}^{\text{log-tri}}$ and $x^{\text{xl-lex}}$ features.

But there might be differences across words (especially considering that different words have different patterns of polysemy and part-of-speech) and across languages. Given a limited annotation budget, it would be beneficial to share training data as much as possible. We experiment with three schemes:

word-level A classifier is trained based on the training edges for each word, regardless of language. At inference time, edges are inferred using the word-specific classifier with the same *seen* edges initializing the graph.

language-level Training data is merged across words in a given language. At inference time, the language-specific classifiers are used to predict edges for words in the corresponding language. Graphs are initialized with the word-specific *seen* edges, which may be the edges from the training set (as in Section 6.1) or edges from new words from the same language that weren't seen at train time (as in Section 6.3).

cross-lingual Only one classifier is trained using data from all training words. As before, the classifier can be used to infer edges in WUGs for words both inside or outside of the training set.

3.3 Evaluation: Correlation with human annotators

We evaluate edge induction models by their weighted average pairwise Spearman correlation with human annotators, defined as follows:

$$\frac{\sum_{h\in H} \rho(y_h, \hat{y}_{m,h})}{\sum_{h\in H} \mid y_h \mid}, \tag{6}$$

where y_h is the sequence judgments by annotator h, $\hat{y}_h$ is the corresponding sequence of model predictions on the same items, and ρ is the Spearman correlation coefficient.

Pairwise Spearman correlation is a common metric for evaluating agreement among annotators of usage relatedness (e.g., Erk et al., 2013; Schlechtweg et al., 2021b). We use this metric to evaluate our edge induction models in order to assess how well they perform as computational annotators.

4 Clustering

Correlation Clustering has traditionally been used with sparsely human-annotated WUGs. For example, to identify senses forming the basis of the SemEval-2020 bencmark (Schlechtweg et al., 2020). We also experiment with two varieties of *Stochastic Block Model* (SBM; Holland et al., 1983), a family of generative models which may better accommodate the uncertainty introduced by computationally-annotated edges.

In an SBM, an edge between nodes u and v is determined by a random variable which depends

this reason and because the logistic regression model is more readily compatible with additional features, we only report the results of the logistic regression models.

on the blocks that u and v belong to. The parameters of the distributions that generate edges between pairs of blocks and the block membership of nodes can be jointly inferred through Bayesian non-parametric inference. In this way, SBMs can discover both *assortative* block structures (clusters), in which nodes belonging to the same block are more likely to have an edge, as well as other more general relationships between blocks, as expressed though the graph's edges.

The Hierarchical SBM (Peixoto, 2014) generalizes the SBM by imposing an additional block structure on the first-order blocks. The inferred relationship between— and membership in— second-order blocks allows the model to find informative priors for the first-order blocks. In principle the model can be nested to an arbitrary depth. In practice Peixoto (2014) provides methods to infer the hierarchical structure.[6] One benefit of using hierarchical models is they they can find smaller well-defined blocks compared to vanilla SBM. This is particularly advantageous to our use-case, since sense distributions are known to be highly skewed (Kilgarriff, 2004).

In both standard and hierarchical SBM, block membership determines the likelihood of an edge between two nodes. Unknown values aside, WUGs are complete graphs — the *existence* of an edge is not informative for finding a good clustering. For that reason, we experiment with two SBM variants that can be adapted to our situation.

sbm-binomial The weighted SBM (Aicher et al., 2015; Peixoto, 2018) draws edge weights from a distribution in the exponential family. As with the SBM, these distributions are parametrized by the block membership of the nodes. Schlechtweg et al. (2021a) found the Binomial distribution to have the best fit to WUG edge weights.

sbm-layers We also experiment with an approach that uses the layered model of Peixoto (2015). In this model, each of the four edge weights are treated as a different *type* of edge. The generative process allows the the edge likelihood between blocks to be treated independently for each block while the blocks (clusters) themselves are inferred jointly.

In all of our experiments that use SBM models, we cluster according to the most frequently-assigned blocks over 10 000 samples from the agglomerative Markov chain Monte Carlo algorithm, after first minimizing the entropy of the model.[7]

correlation Correlation clustering (Bansal et al., 2004) scores possible partitions according to the difference between the sum of positive edges *across* clusters and sub of the weight of negative edges *within* clusters. Following (Schlechtweg et al., 2021b), we shift all of the edge weights by 2.5 so that edges weighted 1 and 2 are negative and edges weighted 3 and 4 are positive. We also use their implementation of the cluster search, which uses simulated annealing to approximate an optimal solution.

4.1 Evaluation: Adjusted Rand Index

For two partitions of the same set, the Rand Index (RI; Rand, 1971) measures the proportion of pairs of items that either appear in the same or different clusters in both partitions. RI is a measure of correlation between partitions that, crucially, doesn't rely on any explicit alignment of clusters. The Adjusted Rand Index (ARI; Hubert and Arabie, 1985) accounts for the possibility that pairs of items are assigned together or apart at random by normalizing with the expected value of the RI.

5 Data

Our experiments draw on two sets of WUGs. We use the German `DWUG_DE` dataset (Schlechtweg et al., 2022, v2.3.0). In particular, we use the subset of this data which is additionally annotated with usage-sense annotations (24 of 50 lemmas and 50 of 200 usages per lemma). In contrast to the usage-usage annotation used to construct the WUGs, the usage-sense annotation (Schlechtweg, 2023) was carried out in the traditional way where annotators select a sense from a predefined list of senses. This will allow to evaluate how well the derived WUG clusters correlate with traditional sense annotation. Each usage was annotated by 3 annotators and we use the sense annotated by a majority (2) as the ground-truth. Usages where the annotators disagree (83 out of 1200) are excluded from the correlation analysis.

Additionally, the `resampled` dataset is a larger dataset of WUGs (Schlechtweg et al., 2024)[8] from three languages (German, English, and Swedish),

[6]Both of our SBM models use hierarchical implementations from `graph-tool.skewed.de` (v.2.45).

[7]We use `minimize_nested_blockmodel_dl` with default parameters.

[8]https://www.ims.uni-stuttgart.de/data/wugs

which are much more densely annotated with usage-usage edges. This allows us to experiment with the effect of different amounts of ground-truth data (Sections 6.1 and 6.2).

In Section 6.3, we use the German portion of the DWUG_DE corpus that *doesn't* overlap with the sense-annotated lemmas to test the usefulness of edge induction in a simulated low-data scenario.

Some of the data contains overlapping human usage-usage annotation. In all of our experiments, we use the median (rounded up to the nearest integer) of these judgments as the ground-truth edge scores for clustering and training edge induction models. For testing the edge induction models, we use the disaggregated judgments to compute annotator-wise correlations of the model prediction with human judgments (see Section 3.3).

6 Experiments

Given limited human usage-sense annotation, we conduct two stages of experiments. First (Section 6.1), we use the densely annotated `resampled` WUGs to test how well edge induction models recover edge weights given different amounts of usage-usage annotation for training and graph initialisation. Likewise (Section 6.2), we test the robustness of different clustering methods with respect to recovering sense clusters with limited usage-usage annotated data. Next (Section 6.3) we construct a more realistic scenario in which pre-trained edge induction models are used to predict edges in sparsely-annotated WUGs of "new" words. These enriched graphs are then clustered and compared to human usage-sense annotations.

Ultimately the end-to-end results (correlation with human sense annotation) are what matter, but considering the intermediate results will allow us to better explain the final performance and make recommendations that generalize to more WUG creation scenarios (for example, given different annotation budgets).

6.1 Experiment 1: Edge induction performance

For 5 different folds, we reserve 10% of the edges in each `resampled` WUG for testing. Of the remaining edges, for each fold, we train classifiers with different amounts of training data, from 50 to 300 annotated edges, using each of the stratification schemes described in Section 3.2. At inference time, we initialize the graphs with the edges that were seen during training and infer the remaining edges, including the edges in the respective test set. For models that use $\mathbf{x}^{\text{tri}}$ and $\mathbf{x}^{\text{tri+xl-lex}}$, four rounds of inference are performed.

The results are shown in Figure 3. Overall, the results are good. In the best cases, our models roughly achieve parity with human-human agreement for a moderate number ground-truth of edges (see (Schlechtweg et al., 2021b)), and have decent agreement in low-data scenarios.

The models that combine textual and structural features (i.e., $\mathbf{x}^{\text{tri+xl-lex}}$) perform best for all but the smallest number of ground-truth edges, especially in the language-level and cross-lingual case. It's important to consider that the number of ground-truth edges are reported *per word*, so at 50 ground-truth edges, the cross-lingual model has many more training examples than any of the individual word-level models. However, this is exactly the point of training models at higher levels of stratification, since it makes quality inference more efficient in terms of annotation effort.

We also see that iterated inference does make a difference. For word-level models the performance actually degrades at higher inference interactions, suggesting that the model may suffer from some degree of error propagation. This is not the case with language-level and cross-lingual models, which have richer training sets: subsequent inference iterations do improve the performance, though there is not much change after the second round for the combined model. Crucially, subsequent rounds also have better predictive *coverage*, since the triangle count-based models are unable to make an edge prediction when there is no length-2 path between the corresponding nodes. For the purposes of the clustering, this means that later inference rounds should almost always be preferred, especially in the language-level and cross-lingual setups.

6.2 Experiment 2: Clustering robustness

In this experiment, we use the same data, folds, and training limits as in Experiment 1, this time experimenting with clustering results. The goal of this experiment is to observe the stability of each clustering algorithm given different numbers of ground-truth edges. We perform this experiment as a precursor to clustering on induced edges, since it will provide context for any clustering improvements stemming from edge induction. Each of the algorithms we experiment with is designed to work on graphs with missing edges, so it is important to

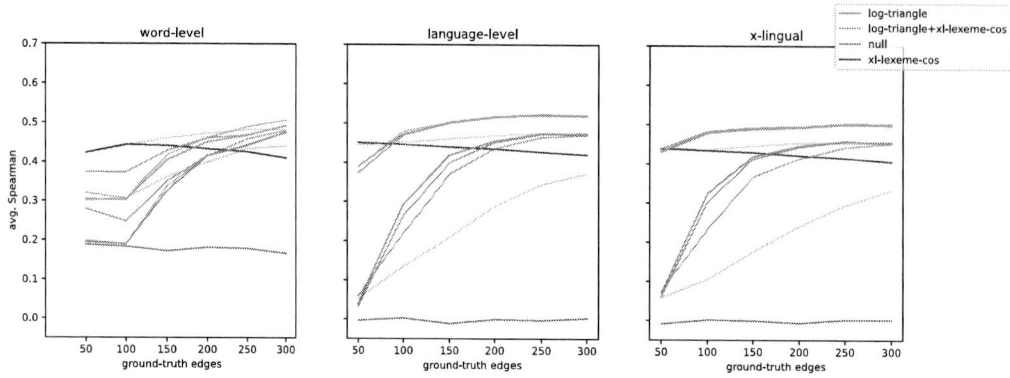

Figure 3: Weighted average Spearman correlations between model predictions and human annotations (see Section 3.3). Here, the scores are computed by considering annotations from all lemmas together, and then averaged over 5 folds. For models using `log-triangle` features, inference iterations are shown with increasingly saturated lines, with iteration 4 being the most saturated. A proportional random baseline (gray) is show for comparison. Analogous to the models, label proportions are computed at the word, language and cross-lingual level. Language-specific results are provided in Appendix A.

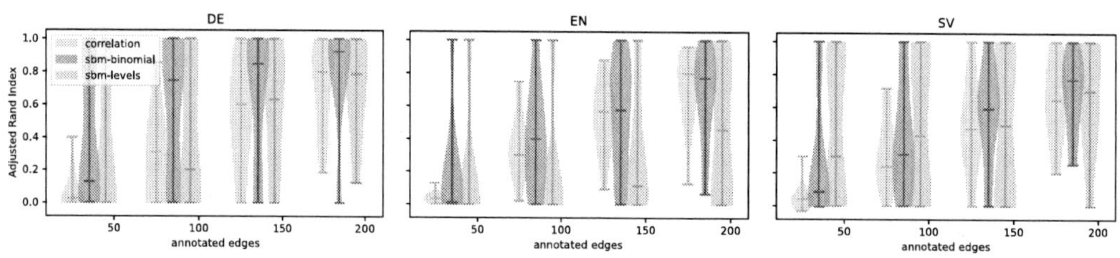

Figure 4: ARI spread over lemmas (first averaged over 5 folds), for different number of edge annotations. For each algorithm the ARI is computed with respect to the clusters achieved by the same clustering algorithm provided with 300 annotations These results are only useful to compare across algorithms insofar as they give an idea of how quickly the algorithm converges to a clustering result.

understand how much the results change for WUGs with different amounts of missing data. For each algorithm, we compute the ARI between clusters produced with 50 to 200 ground-truth edges and clusters produced by the same algorithm with 300 ground-truth edges.

The results are presented in Figure 4. Naturally, all methods produce clusters more similar to the 300-edge clusters when provided with higher numbers of ground-truth edges. With 50 ground-truth edges, clustering is very poor across all clustering algorithms for the majority of words. The results using the `sbm-binomial` method improve fastest with increasing numbers of ground-truth edges, and at 200 edges, it performs best on German and Swedish, while `correlation` performs best for English.

Even at the highest number edges, though, there is a wide spread of performance across words. It is important to interpret all of these results bearing in mind that the ARI is compared to clusters produced by the same algorithm, just with more data. For an extrinsic validation of the clusters, we must turn to Experiment 3, which compares clusters to human-annotated sense data.

6.3 Experiment 3: Realistic scenario

Experiment 3 imitates a scenario in which one has (1) a number of "new" words with very limited edge annotation, and (2) another collection of words with larger and more densely annotated WUGs.

For the sparsely-annotated data, we draw from `DWUG DE`, selecting the 24 words that have been annotated with sense data. For each word, we construct graphs with only the 50 usages that were annotated with sense data and all of the annotated edges that include only those usages (median 55 edges per word; see Appendix B for word-level

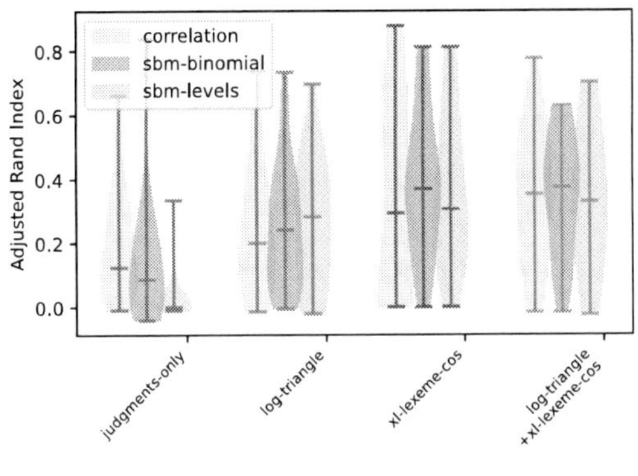

Figure 5: ARI of WUG clusters versus human sense annotation. Spreads are shown over lemmas (N=24). The judgments-only column shows clustering of the graphs based on human usage-usage annotation alone, while the other columns show the effect of adding predicted edges. Disaggregated results for the $\mathbf{x}^{\text{tri+xl-lex}}$ models can be found in Appendix C.

counts) The densely-annotated data, is drawn from the full set of usages of lemmas in DWUG_DE that *don't* overlap with the words annotated for sense (26 words). We reserve 10% of the edges for testing and train language-level classifiers on the remainder.

We then predict edges on the sparsely-annotated WUGs and compare the clusters to human-annotated sense data. As a baseline, we compute clusters for the graphs with only ground-truth edges. For each edge induction model, we compute clusters using the graph enriched with predicted edges (retaining the ground-truth edges that exist).

The results (Figure 5) show clear improvements over the sparse graph clusters for all induction models and clustering algorithms. The `sbm-binomial` algorithm performs slightly better than the `correlation` clustering algorithm on graphs with edges induced by models that include the $x^{\text{xl-lex}}$. Moreover, there is a tighter spread in performance across words for the `sbm-binomial` algorithm.

In cases where $x^{\text{xl-lex}}$ isn't used, `sbm-layers` performs best on average.

In all cases, there are still some words where the correlation with human sense annotation is very poor, median but performance can be improved greatly by using induced edges.

7 Conclusion

In this paper we investigate the question of whether missing edges in WUGs can be induced using information derived from the existing human annotated edges. Our final goal is to improve downstream clustering performance by using only as much human annotation as is needed. To set the stage, we first explore how well edge induction models that exploit structural and textual features correlate with human WUG annotation for different amounts of ground-truth data (Section 6.1). Then, we characterize the stability of clustering algorithms, finding notable differences in the clusters as more ground-truth edges are added across all 3 algorithms (Section 6.2). Finally, we conduct an experiment showing that edge induction models can be used to improve the clustering of sparse WUGs even when they are trained on data from a completely disjoint set of lemmas (Section 6.3). These results show that edge induction can be a valuable tool for improving the quality of sense clusters inferred from sparsely-annotated WUGs. This can allow researchers and lexicographers to cover a larger set of lemmas on a limited annotation budget. It also points to annotation strategies that strategically use triangles to maximize the utility of each human annotation.

Importantly, we saw that both structural (graph-based) and contextual (language model-based) features contribute to the WUG quality improvements resulting from augmenting with induced edges. This is significant since there may be situations when it is desirable to avoid the possibility of introducing historical biases with language model-derived features.

This work leaves room for further improvements on edge induction and clustering in WUGs. The iterated inference strategy described in Section 3.1 is just one of many possible strategies for incorporating distant graph information while minimizing error propagation. More principled approaches, such as Message Passing Neural Networks (Gilmer et al., 2017; Zhang and Chen, 2018) should also be investigated. Likewise, some versions of the Stochastic Block Model (i.e., Peixoto, 2019) can account for missing edges, which theoretically makes joint induction of edges and clusters possible, though no implementation currently exists for weighted networks.

8 Limitations

A notable limitation of the results in Section 6.3 stems from the use of usage-sense annotation for evaluation. One of the motivations for WUGs is that they can be used to discover unattested word senses. By its nature, usage-sense annotation assumes a fixed sense inventory — it could simply be that some of the senses discovered by the clustering process were not present in the sense inventory used for annotation, either because they were missing or because the clusters capture a more fine-grained notion of sense. Nevertheless correlation with usage-sense annotation is an important way to validate that usage clusters correspond to what we think of as word senses.

Finally, in this work, our investigation is confined to English, Swedish, and German WUGs. Since these languages are all closely related, the cross-lingual results should be interpreted with that in mind. Otherwise, our proposed methods are language-agnostic, and we do not anticipate significant challenges in adapting them to other languages.

Acknowledgments

This work has in part been funded by the research program Change is Key! supported by Riksbankens Jubileumsfond (under reference number M21-0021). The computational resources were provided by the National Academic Infrastructure for Supercomputing in Sweden (NAISS), partially funded by the Swedish Research Council through grant agreement no. 2022-06725.

References

Christopher Aicher, Abigail Z. Jacobs, and Aaron Clauset. 2015. Learning latent block structure in weighted networks. *Journal of Complex Networks*, 3(2):221–248.

Anna Aksenova, Ekaterina Gavrishina, Elisei Rykov, and Andrey Kutuzov. 2022. RuDSI: Graph-based word sense induction dataset for Russian. In *Proceedings of TextGraphs-16: Graph-based Methods for Natural Language Processing*, pages 77–88, Gyeongju, Republic of Korea. Association for Computational Linguistics.

Nikhil Bansal, Avrim Blum, and Shuchi Chawla. 2004. Correlation Clustering. *Machine Learning*, 56(1):89–113.

Pierpaolo Basile, Annalina Caputo, Tommaso Caselli, Pierluigi Cassotti, and Rossella Varvara. 2020. DIACR-Ita@ EVALITA2020: Overview of the EVALITA2020 DiachronicLexical Semantics (DIACR-Ita) Task. In *Proceedings of the Evaluation Campaign of Natural Language Processing and Speech Tools for Italian (EVALITA)*, Online. CEUR-WS.

Pierluigi Cassotti, Lucia Siciliani, Marco DeGemmis, Giovanni Semeraro, and Pierpaolo Basile. 2023. XL-LEXEME: WiC pretrained model for cross-lingual LEXical sEMantic changE. In *Proceedings of the 61st Annual Meeting of the Association for Computational Linguistics (Volume 2: Short Papers)*, pages 1577–1585, Toronto, Canada. Association for Computational Linguistics.

Jing Chen, Emmanuele Chersoni, Dominik Schlechtweg, Jelena Prokic, and Chu-Ren Huang. 2023. ChiWUG: A Graph-based Evaluation Dataset for Chinese Lexical Semantic Change Detection. In *Proceedings of the 4th Workshop on Computational Approaches to Historical Language Change*, pages 93–99, Singapore. Association for Computational Linguistics.

Katrin Erk, Diana McCarthy, and Nicholas Gaylord. 2013. Measuring word meaning in context. *Computational Linguistics*, 39(3):511–554.

Justin Gilmer, Samuel S. Schoenholz, Patrick F. Riley, Oriol Vinyals, and George E. Dahl. 2017. Neural Message Passing for Quantum Chemistry. *arXiv:1704.01212 [cs]*.

Mario Giulianelli, Marco Del Tredici, and Raquel Fernández. 2020. Analysing Lexical Semantic Change with Contextualised Word Representations. In *Proceedings of the 58th Annual Meeting of the Association for Computational Linguistics*, pages 3960–3973, Online. Association for Computational Linguistics.

Raia Hadsell, Sumit Chopra, and Yann LeCun. 2006. Dimensionality Reduction by Learning an Invariant Mapping. In *2006 IEEE Computer Society Conference on Computer Vision and Pattern Recognition (CVPR 2006), 17-22 June 2006, New York, NY, USA*, pages 1735–1742. IEEE Computer Society.

Paul W. Holland, Kathryn Blackmond Laskey, and Samuel Leinhardt. 1983. Stochastic blockmodels: First steps. *Social Networks*, 5(2):109–137.

Lawrence Hubert and Phipps Arabie. 1985. Comparing partitions. *Journal of Classification*, 2(1):193–218.

Adam Kilgarriff. 2004. How Dominant Is the Commonest Sense of a Word? In *Text, Speech and Dialogue*, Lecture Notes in Computer Science, pages 103–111, Berlin, Heidelberg. Springer.

Andrey Kutuzov, Lilja Ovrelid, Terrence Szymanski, and Erik Velldal. 2018. Diachronic Word Embeddings and Semantic Shifts: a Survey. In *Proceedings of the 27th International Conference on Computational Linguistics*, pages 1384–1397, Santa Fe, New

Mexico, USA. Association for Computational Linguistics.

Andrey Kutuzov and Lidia Pivovarova. 2021. Three-part Diachronic Semantic Change Dataset for Russian. In *Proceedings of the 2nd International Workshop on Computational Approaches to Historical Language Change 2021*, pages 7–13, Online. Association for Computational Linguistics.

Andrey Kutuzov, Samia Touileb, Petter Mæhlum, Tita Enstad, and Alexandra Wittemann. 2022. NorDiaChange: Diachronic Semantic Change Dataset for Norwegian. In *Proceedings of the Thirteenth Language Resources and Evaluation Conference*, pages 2563–2572, Marseille, France. European Language Resources Association.

Zhidong Ling, Taichi Aida, Teruaki Oka, and Mamoru Komachi. 2023. Construction of Evaluation Dataset for Japanese Lexical Semantic Change Detection. In *Proceedings of the 37th Pacific Asia Conference on Language, Information and Computation*, pages 125–136, Hong Kong, China. Association for Computational Linguistics.

Daniel Loureiro, Aminette D'Souza, Areej Nasser Muhajab, Isabella A. White, Gabriel Wong, Luis Espinosa-Anke, Leonardo Neves, Francesco Barbieri, and Jose Camacho-Collados. 2022. TempoWiC: An Evaluation Benchmark for Detecting Meaning Shift in Social Media. In *Proceedings of the 29th International Conference on Computational Linguistics*, pages 3353–3359, Gyeongju, Republic of Korea. International Committee on Computational Linguistics.

Tiago P. Peixoto. 2014. Hierarchical Block Structures and High-Resolution Model Selection in Large Networks. *Physical Review X*, 4(1):011047.

Tiago P. Peixoto. 2015. Inferring the mesoscale structure of layered, edge-valued, and time-varying networks. *Physical Review E*, 92(4):042807.

Tiago P. Peixoto. 2018. Nonparametric weighted stochastic block models. *Physical Review E*, 97(1):012306.

Tiago P. Peixoto. 2019. Network Reconstruction and Community Detection from Dynamics. *Physical Review Letters*, 123(12):128301.

Francesco Periti, Haim Dubossarsky, and Nina Tahmasebi. 2024. (Chat)GPT v BERT Dawn of Justice for Semantic Change Detection. In *Findings of the Association for Computational Linguistics: EACL 2024*, pages 420–436, St. Julian's, Malta. Association for Computational Linguistics.

Francesco Periti and Stefano Montanelli. 2024. Lexical semantic change through large language models: a survey. *ACM Comput. Surv.*, 56(11).

Francesco Periti and Nina Tahmasebi. 2024. A Systematic Comparison of Contextualized Word Embeddings for Lexical Semantic Change. In *Proceedings of the 2024 Conference of the North American Chapter of the Association for Computational Linguistics: Human Language Technologies (Volume 1: Long Papers)*, pages 4262–4282, Mexico City, Mexico. Association for Computational Linguistics.

Mohammad Taher Pilehvar and Jose Camacho-Collados. 2019. WiC: The Word-in-Context Dataset for Evaluating Context-Sensitive Meaning Representations. In *Proceedings of the 2019 Conference of the North American Chapter of the Association for Computational Linguistics: Human Language Technologies, Volume 1 (Long and Short Papers)*, pages 1267–1273. Association for Computational Linguistics.

Marko Pranjić, Kaja Dobrovoljc, Senja Pollak, and Matej Martinc. 2024. Semantic change detection for slovene language: a novel dataset and an approach based on optimal transport.

William M. Rand. 1971. Objective Criteria for the Evaluation of Clustering Methods. *Journal of the American Statistical Association*, 66(336):846–850.

Nils Reimers and Iryna Gurevych. 2019. Sentence-BERT: Sentence Embeddings using Siamese BERT-Networks. In *Proceedings of the 2019 Conference on Empirical Methods in Natural Language Processing and the 9th International Joint Conference on Natural Language Processing (EMNLP-IJCNLP)*, pages 3982–3992, Hong Kong, China. Association for Computational Linguistics.

Dominik Schlechtweg. 2023. *Human and Computational Measurement of Lexical Semantic Change*. doctoralThesis, University of Stuttgart.

Dominik Schlechtweg, Pierluigi Cassotti, Bill Noble, David Alfter, Sabine Schulte im Walde, and Nina Tahmasebi. 2024. More DWUGs: Extending and evaluating word usage graph datasets in multiple languages.

Dominik Schlechtweg, Enrique Castaneda, Jonas Kuhn, and Sabine Schulte im Walde. 2021a. Modeling Sense Structure in Word Usage Graphs with the Weighted Stochastic Block Model. In *Proceedings of *SEM 2021: The Tenth Joint Conference on Lexical and Computational Semantics*, pages 241–251. Association for Computational Linguistics.

Dominik Schlechtweg, Barbara McGillivray, Simon Hengchen, Haim Dubossarsky, and Nina Tahmasebi. 2020. SemEval-2020 Task 1: Unsupervised Lexical Semantic Change Detection. In *Proceedings of the Fourteenth Workshop on Semantic Evaluation*, pages 1–23, Barcelona (online). International Committee for Computational Linguistics.

Dominik Schlechtweg, Barbara McGillivray, Simon Hengchen, Haim Dubossarsky, and Nina Tahmasebi. 2022. DWUG DE: Diachronic Word Usage Graphs for German.

Dominik Schlechtweg, Nina Tahmasebi, Simon Hengchen, Haim Dubossarsky, and Barbara McGillivray. 2021b. DWUG: A large Resource of Diachronic Word Usage Graphs in Four Languages. In *Proceedings of the 2021 Conference on Empirical Methods in Natural Language Processing*, pages 7079–7091, Online and Punta Cana, Dominican Republic. Association for Computational Linguistics.

Nina Tahmasebi, Lars Borin, and Adam Jatowt. 2021. *Survey of Computational Approaches to Lexical Semantic Change Detection*, pages 1–91. Language Science Press, Berlin.

Xuri Tang. 2018. A State-of-the-art of Semantic Change Computation. *Natural Language Engineering*, 24(5):649–676.

Frank D. Zamora-Reina, Felipe Bravo-Marquez, and Dominik Schlechtweg. 2022. LSCDiscovery: A Shared Task on Semantic Change Discovery and Detection in Spanish. In *Proceedings of the 3rd Workshop on Computational Approaches to Historical Language Change*, pages 149–164, Dublin, Ireland. Association for Computational Linguistics.

Muhan Zhang and Yixin Chen. 2018. Link prediction based on graph neural networks. In *Proceedings of the 32nd International Conference on Neural Information Processing Systems*, NIPS'18, pages 5171–5181, Red Hook, NY, USA. Curran Associates Inc.

A Edge induction by language

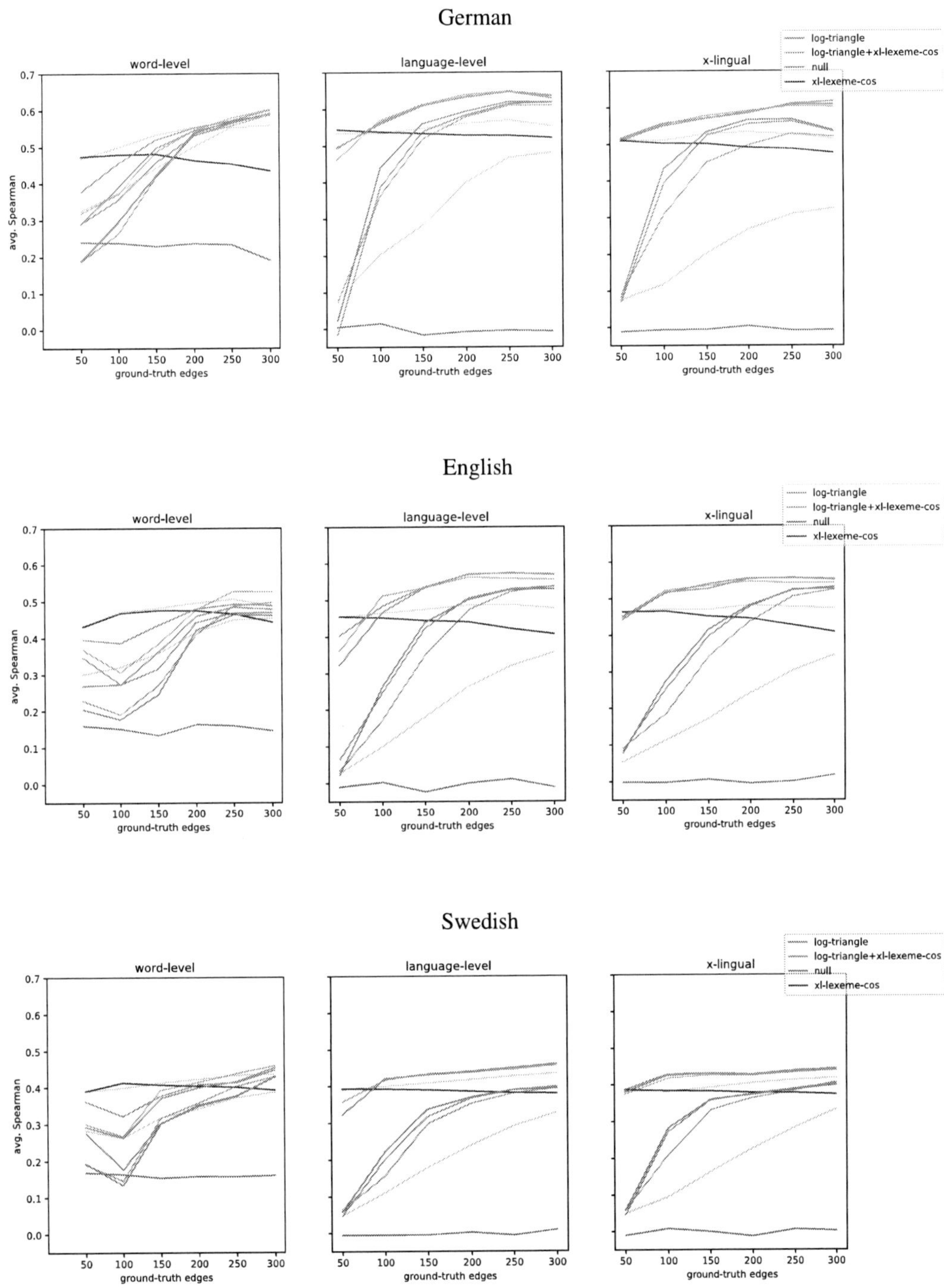

Figure 6: Weighted average Spearman correlations between model predictions and human annotations (see Section 3.3). Here, the scores are computed by considering all annotations from each respective language, and then averaged over 5 folds. For models using `log-triangle` features, inference iterations are shown with increasingly saturated lines, with iteration 4 being the most saturated.

B Experiment 3 data

lemma	usages	edges	% edges
Pachtzins	139	179	1.85
Ackergerät	153	193	1.65
Festspiel	150	193	1.72
aufrechterhalten	140	201	2.05
Ausnahmegesetz	159	202	1.60
weitgreifend	164	205	1.52
Einreichung	160	207	1.62
Unentschlossenheit	176	223	1.44
Mut	200	237	1.19
Frechheit	200	258	1.29
Kubikmeter	200	258	1.29
Truppenteil	200	258	1.29
Entscheidung	200	261	1.31
Gesichtsausdruck	200	265	1.33
Tier	200	272	1.36
Mulatte	200	276	1.38
vergönnen	200	278	1.39
Naturschönheit	198	283	1.44
Lyzeum	200	284	1.42
Behandlung	200	315	1.58
vorliegen	200	331	1.66
Tragfähigkeit	182	337	2.03
voranstellen	200	379	1.90
vorweisen	168	384	2.72
beimischen	200	594	2.97
verbauen	168	1053	7.46

Table 1: Statistics of ground truth data used for training the edge induction models used in Section 6.3.

lemma	usages	edges	% edges
Seminar	50	22	1.76
Spielball	50	26	2.08
Sensation	50	27	2.16
Engpaß	50	32	2.56
Eintagsfliege	50	42	3.36
Manschette	50	43	3.44
Armenhaus	50	44	3.52
artikulieren	50	49	3.92
Knotenpunkt	50	50	4.00
abbauen	50	50	4.00
packen	50	54	4.32
Rezeption	50	54	4.32
Mißklang	50	56	4.48
Abgesang	50	57	4.56
zersetzen	50	60	4.80
überspannen	50	68	5.44
Fuß	50	68	5.44
Titel	50	68	5.44
abgebrüht	50	76	6.08
Schmiere	50	76	6.08
Dynamik	50	81	6.48
abdecken	50	84	6.72
Ohrwurm	50	86	6.88
ausspannen	50	151	12.08

Table 2: Statistics of ground truth data used for edge induction (inference) and clustering in Section 6.3.

C Cluster characteristics

Correlation Clustering

lemma	usage-sense $H(C)$	usage-sense $\mid C \mid$	judgments only $H(C)$	judgments only $\mid C \mid$	judgments only ARI	edge induction $H(C)$	edge induction $\mid C \mid$	edge induction ARI
Spielball	0.17	2	1.17	5	0.05	0.69	4	-0.01
Rezeption	0.37	3	1.80	8	0.08	0.64	4	0.26
Sensation	0.48	3	1.67	7	0.20	1.43	6	0.23
Mißklang	0.51	3	1.46	6	-0.00	-0.00	2	-0.02
artikulieren	0.54	3	1.38	6	0.08	1.36	5	0.17
Abgesang	0.62	3	1.90	9	0.07	1.12	7	0.12
Dynamik	0.64	2	1.76	8	0.13	0.91	4	0.47
Manschette	0.64	4	0.51	4	0.06	0.76	5	0.21
zersetzen	0.68	2	0.68	3	0.34	0.67	3	0.60
Armenhaus	0.68	2	1.76	8	0.11	1.10	5	0.31
Knotenpunkt	0.68	3	1.52	8	-0.01	1.35	6	0.23
Engpaß	0.69	3	1.05	5	0.32	0.88	4	0.34
Ohrwurm	0.69	3	0.68	4	0.66	0.55	3	0.59
Eintagsfliege	0.69	3	0.94	4	0.31	0.68	3	0.50
abgebrüht	0.69	3	1.33	6	0.30	0.92	4	0.78
Titel	0.80	4	0.82	5	0.00	1.03	5	0.07
Seminar	0.92	4	1.29	5	0.12	0.88	4	0.12
packen	1.01	4	1.88	8	0.20	1.45	6	0.41
abbauen	1.04	4	0.92	4	0.32	1.17	5	0.36
ausspannen	1.18	5	1.32	6	0.47	1.23	5	0.63
überspannen	1.22	5	1.38	6	0.20	0.67	3	0.48
abdecken	1.27	6	1.43	6	0.29	0.77	4	0.48
Fuß	1.34	8	1.31	6	0.09	1.43	6	0.48
Schmiere	1.45	8	1.67	7	0.11	0.69	3	0.45

Table 3: Distributional characteristics of `correlation` clusters from Section 6.3 compared to the human *usage-sense* annotation. The *edge induction* column shows the best-performing edge induction model in terms of median ARI (`log-triangle+xl-lexeme-cos`) while *judgments only* is the result of clustering only on ground-truth usage-usage edges. $H(C)$=entropy of the sense/cluster distribution, $\mid C \mid$ = number of senses/clusters, *ARI*=ARI with usage-sense annotation.

SBM-binomial

lemma	usage-sense $H(C)$	usage-sense $\mid C \mid$	judgments only $H(C)$	judgments only $\mid C \mid$	judgments only ARI	edge induction $H(C)$	edge induction $\mid C \mid$	edge induction ARI
Spielball	0.17	2	0.37	2	0.17	0.97	3	0.08
Rezeption	0.37	3	0.85	3	0.21	1.07	4	0.26
Sensation	0.48	3	0.37	2	0.26	1.17	4	0.38
Mißklang	0.51	3	0.53	2	0.21	0.50	2	-0.02
artikulieren	0.54	3	0.23	2	0.14	1.59	5	0.14
Abgesang	0.62	3	0.67	2	0.02	1.37	4	0.08
Dynamik	0.64	2	0.47	2	-0.04	1.16	4	0.49
Manschette	0.64	4	0.67	3	0.38	1.09	4	0.30
zersetzen	0.68	2	0.37	2	0.00	1.08	4	0.60
Armenhaus	0.68	2	0.53	3	0.19	1.16	4	0.33
Knotenpunkt	0.68	3	0.33	2	0.02	1.36	4	0.22
Engpaß	0.69	3	0.17	2	-0.00	1.04	3	0.37
Ohrwurm	0.69	3	0.69	2	0.84	1.09	4	0.63
Eintagsfliege	0.69	3	0.33	2	0.02	1.27	4	0.47
abgebrüht	0.69	3	0.40	2	-0.01	1.37	5	0.60
Titel	0.80	4	0.50	2	-0.02	0.95	3	0.13
Seminar	0.92	4	-0.00	1	0.00	1.11	5	0.11
packen	1.01	4	0.40	2	0.03	1.31	4	0.44
abbauen	1.04	4	0.65	2	0.10	1.33	4	0.38
ausspannen	1.18	5	0.37	2	0.06	1.42	5	0.63
überspannen	1.22	5	0.68	3	0.13	1.29	4	0.43
abdecken	1.27	6	0.81	3	0.23	1.23	4	0.45
Fuß	1.34	8	0.70	3	0.08	1.37	4	0.35
Schmiere	1.45	8	1.21	5	0.29	1.45	5	0.52

Table 4: Distributional characteristics of `sbm-binomial` clusters from Section 6.3 compared to the human usage-sense annotation. The *edge induction* column shows the best-performing edge induction model in terms of median ARI (`log-triangle+xl-lexeme-cos`) while *judgments only* is the result of clustering only on ground-truth usage-usage edges. $H(C)$=entropy of the sense/cluster distribution, $\mid C \mid$ = number of senses/clusters, *ARI*=ARI with usage-sense annotation.

SBM-layers

lemma	usage-sense $H(C)$	usage-sense $\mid C \mid$	judgments only $H(C)$	judgments only $\mid C \mid$	judgments only ARI	edge induction $H(C)$	edge induction $\mid C \mid$	edge induction ARI
Spielball	0.17	2	-0.00	1	0.00	0.44	2	0.30
Rezeption	0.37	3	-0.00	1	0.00	0.49	3	0.70
Sensation	0.48	3	-0.00	1	0.00	0.82	3	0.45
Mißklang	0.51	3	-0.00	1	0.00	1.12	4	0.03
artikulieren	0.54	3	-0.00	1	0.00	1.33	4	0.05
Abgesang	0.62	3	-0.00	1	0.00	1.16	4	-0.02
Dynamik	0.64	2	-0.00	1	0.00	0.93	3	0.48
Manschette	0.64	4	-0.00	1	0.00	0.59	3	0.61
zersetzen	0.68	2	0.28	2	0.03	0.87	4	0.67
Armenhaus	0.68	2	-0.00	1	0.00	0.99	4	0.42
Knotenpunkt	0.68	3	-0.00	1	0.00	1.23	4	0.20
Engpaß	0.69	3	0.17	2	-0.00	0.55	2	0.16
Ohrwurm	0.69	3	0.40	2	0.08	0.53	3	0.15
Eintagsfliege	0.69	3	-0.00	1	0.00	0.89	4	0.35
abgebrüht	0.69	3	0.40	2	-0.01	1.18	4	0.57
Titel	0.80	4	-0.00	1	0.00	1.56	5	0.23
Seminar	0.92	4	-0.00	1	0.00	0.50	2	-0.01
packen	1.01	4	0.37	2	0.04	1.05	3	0.25
abbauen	1.04	4	-0.00	1	0.00	1.05	4	0.21
ausspannen	1.18	5	0.37	2	0.06	1.41	5	0.61
überspannen	1.22	5	0.10	2	0.02	0.95	3	0.38
abdecken	1.27	6	0.55	2	0.33	0.94	4	0.48
Fuß	1.34	8	-0.00	1	0.00	1.02	3	0.29
Schmiere	1.45	8	0.33	2	0.01	1.25	5	0.39

Table 5: Distributional characteristics of `sbm-levels` clusters from Section 6.3 compared to the human usage-sense annotation. The *edge induction* column shows the best-performing edge induction model in terms of median ARI (`log-triangle+xl-lexeme-cos`) while *judgments only* is the result of clustering only on ground-truth usage-usage edges. $H(C)$=entropy of the sense/cluster distribution, $\mid C \mid$ = number of senses/clusters, *ARI*=ARI with usage-sense annotation.

Towards more complete solutions for Lexical Semantic Change: an extension to multiple time periods and diachronic word sense induction

Francesco Periti*
University of Milan
Via Celoria 18
20133 Milan, Italy
francesco.periti@unimi.it

Nina Tahmasebi*
University of Gothenburg
Renströmsgatan 6
40530 Göteborg, Sweden
nina.tahmasebi@gu.se

Abstract

Thus far, the research community has focused on a simplified computational modeling of semantic change between *two time periods*. This simplified view has served as a foundational block but is not a *complete* solution to the complex modeling of semantic change. Acknowledging the power of recent language models, we believe that now is the right time to extend the current modeling to *multiple time periods* and *diachronic word sense induction*. In this position paper, we outline several extensions of the current modeling and discuss issues related to the extensions.

1 Introduction

Lexical Semantic Change (LSC) is the problem of automatically identifying words that change their meaning over time (Periti and Montanelli, 2024; de Sá et al., 2024; Tahmasebi et al., 2021; Kutuzov et al., 2018; Tang, 2018). Conceptually, this problem implicitly involves a fundamental step of *diachronic word sense induction* to distinguish each individual sense of a word over all the *multiple time periods* of interest (Periti et al., 2023; Alsulaimani and Moreau, 2023; Alsulaimani et al., 2020; Emms and Jayapal, 2016; Tahmasebi, 2013). However, the computational challenges in handling large corpora and the absence of comprehensive benchmarks have in practice led to a simplified modeling focused on *two* time periods t_1 and t_2 only. These are either modeled individually t_1, t_2 or in a single time interval $\langle t_1, t_2 \rangle$ considering all the data jointly.

Typically, approaches over two time periods are assumed to be directly extendable to real scenarios involving multiple time periods. For example, approaches designed for a single interval $\langle t_1, t_2 \rangle$, can be iteratively re-executed across multiple, contiguous intervals $\langle t_1, t_2 \rangle$, $\langle t_2, t_3 \rangle$, ..., $\langle t_{n-1}, t_n \rangle$ (Giulianelli et al., 2020). However, multiple re-executions presents a computational challenge that significantly escalates as the number of considered periods increases. Procedures that were initially considered optional steps to expedite modeling in two time periods become fundamental over multiple time periods. For instance, since words can occur thousands of times in a diachronic corpus, it becomes imperative to randomly sample a limited number of occurrences and to leverage hardware components, such as GPU processor units.

Due to the absence of diachronic lexicographic resources (e.g., dictionaries, thesauri), and the gap between a general resource and specific data, the modeling of word sense is commonly approached in an *unsupervised* manner. Clustering techniques are generally employed to aggregate usages of a specific word into clusters, with the idea that each cluster denotes a specific word meaning that can be recognized in the considered documents. However, clusters of usages (regardless of method of clustering) do not necessarily correspond to precise senses (Martinc et al., 2020), but typically represent noisy projections related to specific context (Periti and Montanelli, 2024). As a result, manual activity is always required to translate the automatically derived clusters into a *diachronic sense inventory*. This sense inventory is the basis for interpreting the identified semantic change and modeling sense evolution (see Figure 1). While automatic methods, such as keywords extraction (Kellert and Mahmud Uz Zaman, 2022), or generating definitions for word usages (Giulianelli et al., 2023), have been proposed to support cluster interpretation, a reliable interpretation still needs manual supervision. Therefore, when multiple time periods are considered, interpretability challenges increase several orders of magnitude, making the direct re-execution of existing approaches unsuitable for effectively detecting semantic change and the evolution of each individual word meaning (Periti et al., 2023, 2022).

*Authors contributed equally

Proceedings of the 5th Workshop on Computational Approaches to Historical Language Change, pages 108–119
August 15, 2024

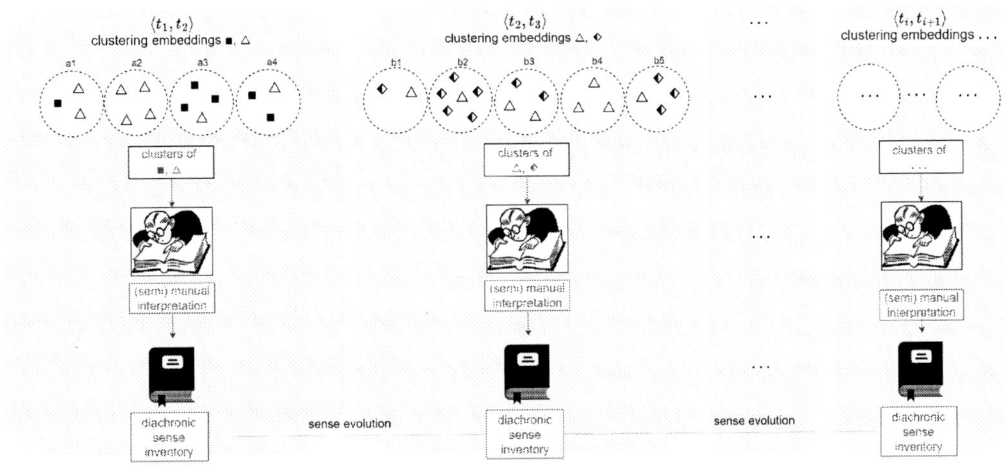

Figure 1: Word usages and their corresponding representations, for time period t_1, t_2, and t_3 are denoted with ■, △, ◆, respectively. Typically, the clustering of representations is done for individual time interval (i.e., two time periods jointly) and manual supervision is required to translate the clusters of each time interval to a diachronic sense inventory. The amount of manual supervisions increase with the number of considered time intervals.

We thus argue that the *diachronic word sense induction* over *multiple time periods* inherent to LSC requires more careful considerations compared to the simplified modeling currently done. More efforts should be devoted to develop approaches for assisting text-based researchers like linguists, historians and lexicographers as much as possible.

Our original contribution

In this paper, we discuss the complexities inherent in modeling semantic change for each word sense individually over multiple time periods. We challenge the general assumption that conventional approaches designed to address LSC over two time periods are easily extendable over multiple time periods. Because currently, contextualized embeddings represents the preferred tool for addressing LSC (Periti and Tahmasebi, 2024), we will use these as an example. Our discussion is however more general, and can be applied regardless of which model is used to represent individual word usages – such as definitions (Giulianelli et al., 2023), co-occurrence vectors (Schütze, 1998), lexical replacements (Periti et al., 2024), or bag-of-substitutes (Kudisov and Arefyev, 2022) – or sense clusters in general as in Tahmasebi and Risse, 2017.

We advocate for an alternative modeling of LSC over multiple time periods, and specifically, we present i) five distinct approaches for *tracking* semantic change and the *evolution* of word meanings; and ii) three distinct settings for assessing semantic change over time. Our work has significant implications for both the computational modeling and the creation of benchmarks, contributing to the ongoing discussion presented by Periti and Montanelli (2024); Hengchen et al. (2021); Montariol et al. (2021) on the open challenges associated with modeling semantic change.

2 Background and related work

Since SemEval-2020 (Schlechtweg et al., 2020), there is an established evaluation framework for LSC to compare the performance of various models and approaches. However, given the substantial annotation efforts required to create reliable benchmarks over multiple time periods, the framework is typically adopted to create simplified benchmarks over two time periods, with gold labels for semantic change but without diachronic sense labels (Ling et al., 2023; Chen et al., 2023; Kutuzov et al., 2022a; Zamora-Reina et al., 2022; Kutuzov and Pivovarova, 2021; Basile et al., 2020; Schlechtweg et al., 2020).[1] In such benchmarks, the LSC problem is defined as follows.

2.1 Problem statement over two time periods

Given a diachronic corpus C containing a set of documents (e.g., sentences, paragraphs) from two time periods t_1 and t_2, the current modeling of LSC involves the following evaluation tasks:

[1] Kutuzov and Pivovarova, 2021 introduced a benchmark encompassing two time intervals. However, these intervals have been treated independently, leading to their consideration as two distinct sub-benchmarks over a single time interval.

i) to quantify the semantic change of words (i.e., *Graded Change Detection*);

ii) to recognize words that change their meaning by either gaining new ones or losing old ones (i.e., *Binary Change Detection, Sense Gain Detection, Sense Loss Detection*).

Words that change their meanings by means of gaining or loosing senses will have a high degree of (graded) semantic change, while words that have a high degree of graded change do not need to have lost or gained senses.

These tasks inherently involve the modeling of word meanings across t_1 and t_2. However, due to the lack of diachronic sense labels, researchers and practitioners tend to focus on addressing tasks **i)** and **ii)** without adequately tackling the challenges associated with modeling sense evolution.

2.2 State-of-the-art approaches to LSC

Thus far, computational approaches to solve the above tasks have followed a standard receipt using a *four-step pipeline* (Periti and Montanelli, 2024). Given a corpus C spanning two time periods t_1 and t_2, and a target word w:

1) extraction of the word occurrences from both t_1 and t_2;

2) computational representation of each occurrence (the current standard is to leverage pre-trained contextualized embeddings);

3) word sense induction by aggregating embeddings with a clustering algorithm;

4) assessment of semantic change by leveraging a distance measure on the embeddings from t_1 and t_2.

Approaches are typically distinguished in *form-based* and *sense-based*. The former does not induce sense **(3)** but quantifies semantic change using **(1,2,4)**, either as a shift in the dominant meaning of w or in its degree of polysemy. There is thus no easy way to discern individual senses from the change score without integrating "close reading" by humans. Sense-based approaches remedies this by relying on all steps **(1-4)** but generally induce senses **(3)** in a *synchronic* way, without considering the temporal nature of the documents (Ma et al., 2024). That is, they consider all the documents from t_1 and t_2 available as a whole and perform a single clustering activity over the entire set of generated embeddings, regardless of their time origin.

2.3 Modeling senses through clusters

The clustering of representations via word sense induction, step **(3)** above, serves as a tool to operationalize word senses in an unsupervised fashion through unstructured text (Lake and Murphy, 2023). On one hand, this operationalization offers a flexible adaptation to the data under consideration and allows to derive senses that do not necessarily need to be aligned with available static lexicographic resources (Kilgarriff, 1997). For instance, senses derived from youth slang (Keidar et al., 2022), or scientific texts are unlikely to align with a general lexicon meant to cover the whole spectrum of a given language.

On the other hand, as computational models derive information from the contexts surrounding word tokens, sense modeling tends to emphasize word usages rather than word meanings (Tahmasebi and Dubossarsky, 2023; Kutuzov et al., 2022b). Thus, while ideally we would like each cluster to correspond to one, and only one sense, in practice, multiple clusters may correspond to different nuances of the same sense. This effect is further amplified when considering data from diverse time, domains, or genres, where distinct linguistic registers, styles, or co-occurrence patterns may results in different senses.

Additionally, the interpretation of clusters as senses requires a notion of (word) "meaning" that can both differ in the mind of humans according to social or cultural background and age, as well as in the varying usages of a word in context. Thus, the mapping of *clusters* to *senses* involves i) identifying commonalities on the usages of each cluster that may be judged differently, as well as ii) mapping these commonalities to word meanings. The outcome results in a *sense inventory*.

2.4 Modeling LSC over multiple time periods

Modeling LSC involves computationally deriving word senses progressively over time. This entails re-executing the steps **(1-4)** multiple times. At each execution i, a set of clusters is generated and humans are needed to identify and update the sense inventory. This involves mapping the clusters generated at the i-th execution to senses and aligning senses temporally.

The way senses align over time give us important insights into how word meanings change. Classifying *types* of semantic change has been long studied and different schema have been proposed (Blank,

1997; Bloomfield, 1933; Paul, 1880). Among others, common types of change include *broadening* of meaning (e.g., dog was used to refer to dogs of specific large and strong breeds), *narrowing* of meaning (e.g., `girl` was used to refer to people of either gender), *novel senses* (e.g., `rock` as a music genre) and *metaphorical* extensions (e.g., `surfing` the web). The result is a *diachronic* sense inventory with temporal information on the active senses at each time, as well as potential relationships between senses.

To facilitate the interpretation of semantic change and the evolution of word meaning, the current, *synchronic* modeling of senses can benefit from *diachronic* modeling encompassing both incremental word sense induction and cluster alignment (Kanjirangat et al., 2020). Aligning clusters computationally will allow the simultaneous interpretation of multiple clusters, thereby reducing the burden of manual supervision at each time period. Clusters aligned over time can potentially suggest the continuation of an active sense, as well as the broadening and narrowing of meanings. In contrast, clusters not aligned over time can reveal both the continuation of different senses, as well as types of semantic change, like metaphoric extension.

Thus far, word meanings have been modeled through conventional clustering algorithms such as Affinity Propagation (Martinc et al., 2020) or K-Means (Kobayashi et al., 2021). However, these algorithms were originally designed for one-time data clustering and are not inherently suited to handle temporal dynamics. Specifically, clusters generated at t_{i-1} can become mixed up when re-executing the algorithm with both previous data and new data points at time $\langle t_{i-1}, t_i \rangle$. Consequently, objects that were previously clustered together at time t_{i-1} may either remain in the same cluster or be reassigned to different clusters based on the updated data at time t_i. This dynamic nature complicates the task of tracking the history of specific clusters across different time periods, and can lead to the creation of noisy clusters, especially when new data points arrive according to a skewed distribution.

Diachronic sense clustering. Conventional unsupervised clustering algorithms do not incorporate the faithfulness properties typical in *incremental clustering* literature, where clustering activities at any given point in time should remain faithful to the already existing clusters as much as possible (Chakrabarti et al., 2006) while at the same time be flexible to fit the new data. This would avoid dramatic change in clusters from one time-step to the next that do not derive from semantic change, but from differences in the underlying documents over time (Castano et al., 2024).

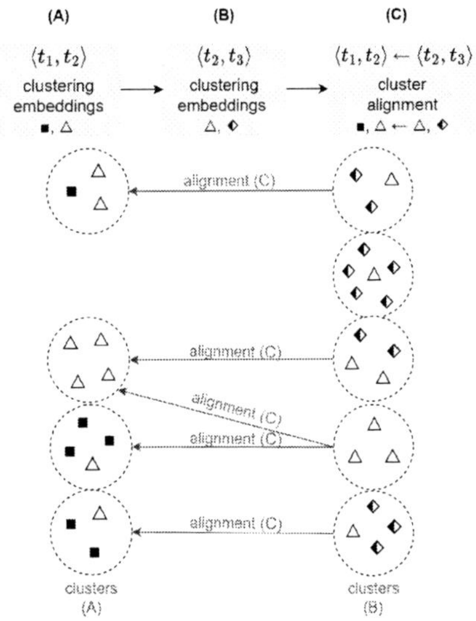

Figure 2: Clustering over consecutive time intervals.

To this end, we argue that, for each target word, modeling LSC over time should involve *monitoring* the evolution of each individual senses across all the time periods under consideration, as well as *tracing* the types of each change. However, this extension is not straightforward; instead, it requires crucial time series analysis to mitigate potential noise introduced by the predictions of computational approaches (Kulkarni et al., 2015).

Monitoring and tracing word meaning evolution and semantic change require a careful consideration in the current *four-step pipeline* of sense-based approaches. As for scalability and interpretability issues related to **(1-3)**, suggestions and workaround are discussed in Periti and Montanelli, 2024; Montariol et al., 2021. In this paper, we further discuss the extension of steps **(3)** and **(4)** when considering multiple time points. In particular, we discuss *diachronic word sense induction* in Section 3, and *semantic change assessment* in Section 4.

3 Diachronic word sense induction

For the sake of simplicity, consider a diachronic corpus C spanning three general, consecutive time periods t_1, t_2, t_3, not necessarily contiguous. This simplification does not lead to any loss of information, but serves to aid the discussion in a clear

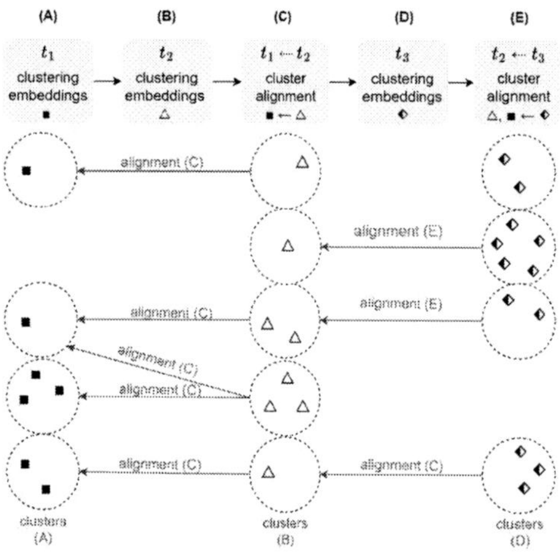

Figure 3: Clustering over consecutive time periods.

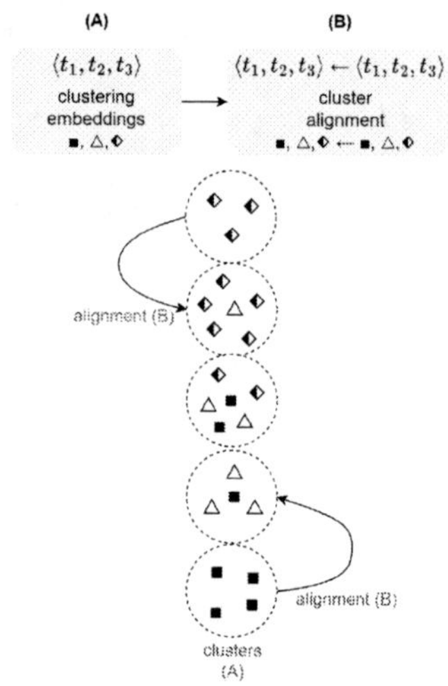

Figure 4: One-time clustering over all time periods.

and concise fashion. At the same time, three time points are easily extendable to the general case of tens or hundreds of time periods. Word usages, and their corresponding representations, for time period t_1, t_2, and t_3 are denoted with ■, △, ◆, respectively. From here on, we will use contextualized embeddings as an example for contextualized representations. In the following, we present five different approaches for monitoring the evolution of word meanings and discuss suitability, and drawbacks.

3.1 Clustering over consecutive time intervals

Clustering algorithms used for *jointly* modeling senses over two time periods t_1 and t_2 can be progressively re-executed over consecutive pairs of time periods $\langle t_1, t_2 \rangle$ and $\langle t_2, t_3 \rangle$. To facilitate the interpretation of sense evolution, a cluster alignment step is thus required between consecutive re-executions. For instance, in Figure 2, the clusters generated in step (B) are linked to those generated in step (A) through a cluster alignment step (C) (Deng et al., 2019).

When clustering over consecutive time intervals $\langle t_1, t_2 \rangle, \dots, \langle t_{n-1}, t_n \rangle$, the embeddings from $n-2$ time periods (all time periods but first and last) are clustered twice. For instance, consider the embeddings △ from t_2 in Figure 2: (A) they are first clustered with the embeddings ■ from t_1, and (B) then re-clustered with the embeddings ◆ from t_3. When a limited number of word usages is available, this approach can potentially enhance the emergence of certain senses, as patterns of embeddings from t_{i-1} are reinforced by additional evidence (if present) from t_i. However, this compromises the faithfulness property, as embeddings from t_i can be clustered differently when considered jointly with t_{i-1} compared to when considered jointly with t_{i+1} (from a past and future perspective respectively).

3.2 Clustering over consecutive time periods

When a substantial number of documents is available for each time period, there is no need to cluster the embeddings of a time *interval* as a whole. Instead, the embeddings of each time *period* can be clustered individually, and a cluster alignment algorithm can be applied progressively to link the clusters across time periods (Kanjirangat et al., 2020; Montariol et al., 2021). This approach is represented in Figure 3. Step (A), (B), and (D) represents the application of a conventional clustering algorithm over the embeddings of time period t_1, t_2, t_3, respectively. Step (C) and (E) represents cluster alignment steps to link the clusters generated through step (B) to the cluster generated through step (A), and in turn, the clusters generated through step (D) to the cluster generated through step (B) (Deng et al., 2019).

Clustering over time periods involves a similar number of clustering activities and cluster alignment steps as clustering over time intervals. However, each clustering activity is more scalable, as it involves a smaller number of embeddings.

3.3 One-time clustering over all time periods

Embeddings from all the considered time periods can be clustered jointly in one single execution. For instance, in Figure 4 step (A), embeddings

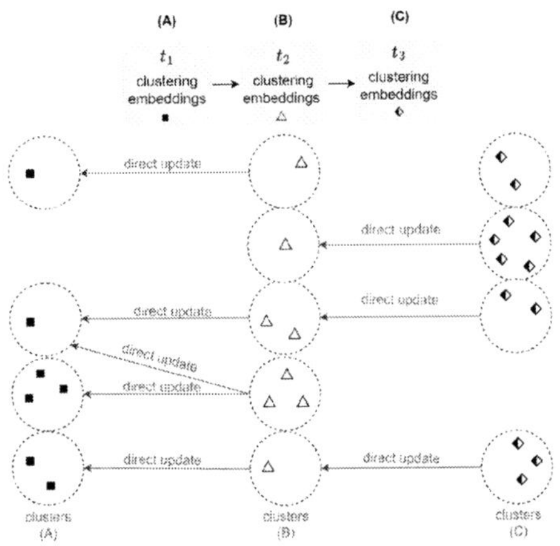

Figure 5: Incremental clustering over time periods.

■, △, ◆ are clustered together as a whole. This single clustering activity results in clusters that may include embeddings from various combinations of time periods. For example, a cluster may include embeddings from a single, all, or selected time periods. A cluster alignment step (B) can be further executed to enable the modeling of sense evolution and change type.

When dealing with hundreds of time periods and a significant number of embeddings at once, clustering can be unfeasible due to scalability issues. In real scenarios, a diachronic corpus can be *dynamic* (Periti et al., 2022), where documents from subsequent time periods are not available as a whole but are progressively added (e.g., *posts* from social networks, Kellert and Mahmud Uz Zaman, 2022; Noble et al., 2021). In such scenarios this approach is thus not suitable as it would require re-execution of the clustering from scratch when new documents are added.

Furthermore, the use of conventional clustering algorithms is generally insensitive to the order of time periods, allowing embeddings of later time periods to influence pattern of the earlier time periods. This risks leading to a global view of word meaning while precluding a local view where smaller and gradual variation of individual senses as well as small sense clusters are missed. These issues can be mitigated by considering the temporal order of documents in the clustering activity (Smyth, 1996).

3.4 Incremental clustering over time periods

Incremental clustering algorithms are designed to effectively address the temporal nature of data (Kulkarni and Mulay, 2013). Thus, they are a suitable option to model the dynamic nature of language where temporal progression is key. When employed for diachronic word sense induction, they can efficiently and directly update the prior clustering results by processing and assimilating new data into existing clusters. The word usages observed in past time periods are consolidated into a set of clusters that constitute the *memory* of the word meanings observed thus far (Periti et al., 2022). This memory then serves as a foundation for understanding subsequent word usages in the current time period. Like Figure 4, Figure 5 represents similar steps (A-C) without alignment as clusters generated in step (A-C) are directly and consecutively updated.

Some of the incremental algorithms implement the faithfulness property in an *evolutionary* way: once a cluster has been created, it can only gain new members (i.e, word usages) but can never loose any members that have already been assigned to it. Meanwhile, the word usages observed in the present must be stratified or integrated over those from the past, that is, either be placed in existing clusters, or create new clusters. Other algorithms implement the faithfulness property in a more flexible way and enable small changes in past clusters when more evidence is available.

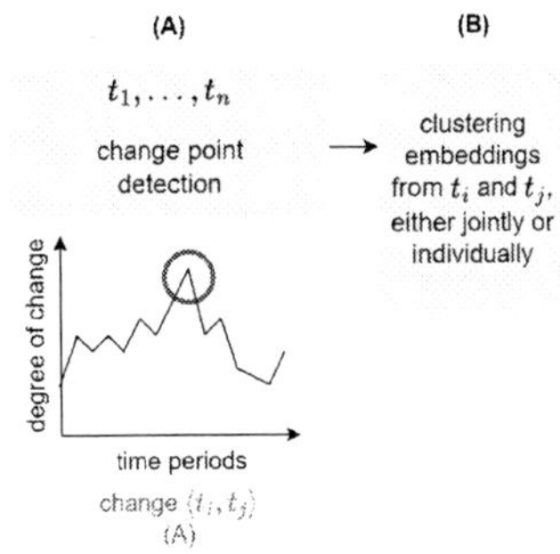

Figure 6: Scaling up with form-based approaches.

3.5 Scaling up with form-based approaches

Regardless of the complexity of each presented method, it is difficult to scale an approach to the level of whole vocabulary in a large corpus. In addition, some senses remain stable for a long time before they potentially change meaning, others never change. Therefore, clustering the senses during the stability periods of words is superfluous. To reduce computational needs and scale to the entire vocabulary, form-based approaches (without sense-induction) can be used to monitor stability allowing the use of more powerful sense-based approaches only when there is indication of change.

By considering change only in the general usage of a word, form-based approaches reduce the semantic change problem significantly. Thus, they serve for two important purposes: first, they can be used to quantify the degree of change at the vocabulary level, and thus give us the opportunity to quantify change during different time periods (e.g., before and after WWI v. WWII); secondly, they can be used to find words and periods of interest.

Such a kind of stability monitoring can be done via change point detection (Kulkarni et al., 2015) and be integrated with diachronic sense modeling as shown in Figure 6. In particular, step A involves quantifying semantic change through form-based assessment to detect change points across the entire time span covered by the corpus. Step B involves modeling each individual sense of the word around the detected change point(s) through approaches presented in Section 3.1-3.4.

4 Semantic change assessment

The diachronic word sense induction is independent from the assessment of change at the level of senses or words. While the modeling of word meaning relies on the notion of word senses, the assessment of change depends on the research questions that we want investigate. E.g., considering a perfect sense inventory we may want to ask how many meanings have been lost and gained, and if change is more evident in some time intervals compared to others. The answer to these depend on the way we assess change.

Assessment of change, like sense induction, has focused on two time intervals which is the smallest unit over which we can quantify change. However, generalizing from two intervals to multiple intervals is not trivial and needs considerations that depend heavily on the kind of research question that is being asked, as well as the kind of data available. Short-term data contra long-term data, or small contra large data require different strategies for quantifying change. Here we present some possible strategies that extend to multiple time periods.

Assessment over consecutive time intervals represents a general way to assess semantic change over time $\langle t_1, t_2 \rangle$, $\langle t_2, t_3 \rangle$, ..., $\langle t_{n-1}, t_n \rangle$. This kind of assessments can be affected by i) (random) fluctuations in the underlying corpus, where the coverage of topics can be heavily influenced by real-life events; and ii) noisy artifacts of the computational modeling, e.g., influenced by frequency. The use of time series analysis or statistical tests can reduce the effect of potential artifacts from the data and capture only significant changes evident in the time series (Liu et al., 2021; Kulkarni et al., 2015).

This assessment represents a useful solution for scenarios where the focus is on detecting immediate changes, such as in rapidly evolving fields or during specific events that might impact language usage. When comparing $\langle t_{i-1}, t_i \rangle$, the assumption is that all the active word meanings in t_i, except for the new or changed ones, are active also in t_{i-1}. However, some senses are periodic and an undesirable side-effect is that they may be detected as change each time they appear and disappear as they are not represented in t_{i-1}.

Pairwise assessment over time periods Sometimes research questions may be tailored to specific time intervals (e.g, *before* and *after* the time period t_i of the corona pandemic). Thus, this assessment aims to quantify the change across specific time intervals $\langle t_{i-1}, t_i \rangle$ and $\langle t_j, t_{j+1} \rangle$ such that $i < j$. This assessment is also useful for identifying changes in periodic senses when the periodicity of the sense is known. For example, the meaning of the term *gold* related to the Olympic games that take place every forth year.

This assessment is also useful when research questions are tailored to specific types of change irrespective of when the change occurs. For example, when a diachronic sense inventory is available, broadening or narrowing can be investigated regardless of their time-specific appearance.

When all possible time intervals are considered, this assessment is associated with a computational complexity of $\mathcal{O}(n^2)$ where n is the number of considered periods. However, it provides a broader view of how meaning evolves over different spans, capturing trends that may not be apparent in consecutive intervals. For example, gradual changes over time would not appear with assessment over consecutive time intervals as too little evidence would be present, but could appear as radical changes when larger gaps between intervals are used.

By considering all the possible time intervals it is also possible to quantify the **global** level of change over the whole corpus. This method is insensitive to the order of the time periods and is useful for capturing overarching trends and patterns in semantic change across the entire timeline.

Cumulative assessment over time When research questions focus on the novel senses gained at time period t_i, the comprehensive overview of active senses from the past must be considered $\bigcup_{j=1}^{i-1} t_j$. Instead of considering only consecutive or specific time intervals, each new time period should be compared with the full diachronic sense inventory. Cumulative assessment emphasizes the overall evolution of meaning, providing a holistic view of changes from the beginning to the end of the timeline. It is useful for consolidating the evidence across multiple time periods which would not suffice on their own. For example, when research questions focus on the novelty introduced in time period t_i compared to the past periods, the assessment of change should consider the cumulative evidence of the past as a single, large time period. Similar assessment can be employed when research questions want to compare a past time period t_i with respect to the following $\bigcup_{j=i+1}^{n-1} t_j$, until the nth time period.

5 Discussion and conclusion

Computational modeling of semantic change has long been done in a simplified way due to the challenges related to modeling senses across multiple time periods. However, sense inventories and the type of change a word exhibits, are fundamental aspects for text-based researchers like historians, linguists and lexicographers, and therefore, the full complexity of semantic change must be taken into consideration in the computational modeling. Now that we have powerful language models like GPT-4 (OpenAI, 2023) and XL-LEXEME (Cassotti et al., 2023) there are no excuses for taking a simplistic view on the modeling of semantic change.

In this paper, we have presented possible extensions to expand on the simplistic view. These extensions have equal implications both for the computational modeling as for the generation of manually annotated benchmarks which has also been done over two time periods due to the sheer volume of required annotations.

Crucial for the usefulness of semantic change studies is a *diachronic sense inventory* where the different senses are linked together to capture semantic change type and linguistic relation. It is using the diachronic sense inventory that the majority of the research questions can be answered. These pertain both to linguistic, language-level questions, but also to societal and cultural enquiries where text can be used as evidence. How to best frame and store the diachronic sense inventory is still an open issue and requires involvement from the communities around computational modeling of semantic change, word sense induction and lexical semantics in general, as well as the text-based researchers that will use the outcome.

Human supervision is necessary to develop a reliable sense inventory. As diachronic corpora can span multiple time periods and contain millions of documents, automatic supervision support is mandatory to reduce manual efforts as much as is possible. In this regard, aligning similar clusters and detecting change types to speed up the interpretation process is as crucial as it is difficult. Employing different kinds of diachronic word sense induction and assessment as outlined here, will lead to different amounts of manual interaction.

Aligning clusters over time poses a very challenging task, as some clusters may represent outliers, time intervals may be characterized by different numbers of clusters, and multiple noisy (or nuanced) clusters denoting the same meaning may emerge. As a result, the cluster alignment often involves the discretization of a fuzzy problem (Kianmehr et al., 2010), that is the creation of new global clusters that encompass sets of fuzzy clusters. Furthermore, when cluster are aligned through a posteriori step rather than being linked and updated directly, the alignment process (worst case) involves comparing each cluster with every other cluster across all time periods. This risks amplifying the potential level of noise and require intricate decisions typically taken without any theoretical basis.

Thus far, the research community has focused more on the quantification of semantic change rather than the underlying word sense induction because form-based approaches consistently outperformed sense-based approaches. However, the clustering algorithms that have been employed do not take the temporal nature of documents into consideration, and we thus argue that they are not optimal for modeling word meaning over time.

In this paper, we have outlined several possible paths forward, both in terms of diachronic word sense induction and assessment of change. We have left methods for change type detection for future work. Each proposed path is suitable for different kinds of research questions and data. For example, by clustering embeddings over a whole corpus, smaller senses that would not appear in sequential modeling can gain sufficient evidence in global clustering. Such a method is however computationally expensive. Other methods suffer from the problem that when only consecutive time periods are considered, slow and gradual shift risks being missed and over long time periods other strategies are more suitable. Among these methods, we strongly advocate for a shift towards incremental methods as these are currently the best fit to the LSC problem.

6 Limitations

This is a position paper and as such, we have not reported any experiments nor proposed concrete algorithms. Instead, we have outlined general weaknesses of the current methods in the field of computational modeling of semantic change and discussed possible ways forward. We believe that different kinds of solutions can be used for this purpose, spanning from different classes of clustering algorithms (e.g., evolutionary, Periti et al., 2023) to different classes of graphs and networks (e.g., temporal, Ma et al., 2024).

We have focused on unsupervised methods that induce senses through clustering of word representations. In particular, we have focused on contextualized representations, which represent the de facto standard, irrespective of the model that is used to generate the representations (e.g., Devlin et al., 2019; Hofmann et al., 2021; Cassotti et al., 2023). We only mention other methods such as word masking for lexical substitutions (Card, 2023; Arefyev and Zhikov, 2020) or previous paradigms such as the use of static embeddings (Shoemark et al., 2019). Typically, static embeddings, as well as methods based on SVD or PPMI (Hamilton et al., 2016), collapse all the meanings of a word into a single static vector, thus our proposals may not be considered suitable for such solutions even if dynamic word embeddings such as those presented by Bamler and Mandt (2017); Yao et al. (2018); Rudolph and Blei (2018) are used. However, we argue that the methods outlined in this paper are directly extendable to methods based on static embeddings where sense clusters are generated by looking at the top neighbors in the embedding space (Gonen et al., 2020).

We have not focused on how to detect the *type* of semantic change nor the *cause* of it, primarily due to space limitations. However, we believe that the methods outlined in this paper inherently offer ways to detect type, but not necessarily cause, of change. When we begin to target change types, we need evaluation benchmarks. Creating such benchmarks entail consolidating and digitizing the types of change offered in taxonomies as, for example, (Blank, 1997; Ullmann, 1957; Bloomfield, 1933; Stern, 1931; Bréal, 1904; Darmesteter, 1893; Paul, 1880; Reisig, 1839), such as the work started by Cassotti et al. (2024).

Acknowledgments

This work has in part been funded by the research program Change is Key! supported by Riksbankens Jubileumsfond (under reference number M21-0021).

References

Ashjan Alsulaimani and Erwan Moreau. 2023. Improving Diachronic Word Sense Induction with a Nonparametric Bayesian Method. In *Findings of the Association for Computational Linguistics: ACL 2023*, pages 8908–8925, Toronto, Canada. Association for Computational Linguistics.

Ashjan Alsulaimani, Erwan Moreau, and Carl Vogel. 2020. An Evaluation Method for Diachronic Word Sense Induction. In *Findings of the Association for Computational Linguistics: EMNLP 2020*, pages 3171–3180, Online. Association for Computational Linguistics.

Nikolay Arefyev and Vasily Zhikov. 2020. BOS at SemEval-2020 Task 1: Word Sense Induction via Lexical Substitution for Lexical Semantic Change Detection. In *Proceedings of the Fourteenth Workshop on Semantic Evaluation*, pages 171–179, Barcelona (online). International Committee for Computational Linguistics.

Robert Bamler and Stephan Mandt. 2017. Dynamic word embeddings. In *Proceedings of the 34th International Conference on Machine Learning*, volume 70 of *Proceedings of Machine Learning Research*, pages 380–389. PMLR.

Pierpaolo Basile, Annalina Caputo, Tommaso Caselli, Pierluigi Cassotti, and Rossella Varvara. 2020. DIACR-Ita@ EVALITA2020: Overview of the EVALITA2020 DiachronicLexical Semantics (DIACR-Ita) Task. In *Proceedings of the Evaluation Campaign of Natural Language Processing and Speech Tools for Italian (EVALITA)*, Online. CEUR-WS.

Andreas Blank. 1997. *Prinzipien des lexikalischen Bedeutungswandels am Beispiel der romanischen Sprachen.* Max Niemeyer Verlag, Berlin, Boston.

Leonard Bloomfield. 1933. *Language.* Holt, Rinehart and Winston, New York.

Michel Bréal. 1904. *Essai de Sémantique (Science des Significations)*. Hachette.

Dallas Card. 2023. Substitution-based Semantic Change Detection using Contextual Embeddings. In *Proceedings of the 61st Annual Meeting of the Association for Computational Linguistics (Volume 2: Short Papers)*, pages 590–602, Toronto, Canada. Association for Computational Linguistics.

Pierluigi Cassotti, Stefano De Pascale, and Nina Tahmasebi. 2024. Using Synchronic Definitions and Semantic Relations to Classify Semantic Change Types. In *Proceedings of the 62nd Annual Meeting of the Association for Computational Linguistics (Volume 1: Long Papers)*, Bangkok, Thailand. Association for Computational Lingustics.

Pierluigi Cassotti, Lucia Siciliani, Marco DeGemmis, Giovanni Semeraro, and Pierpaolo Basile. 2023. XL-LEXEME: WiC Pretrained Model for Cross-Lingual LEXical sEMantic changE. In *Proceedings of the 61st Annual Meeting of the Association for Computational Linguistics (Volume 2: Short Papers)*, pages 1577–1585, Toronto, Canada. Association for Computational Linguistics.

Silvana Castano, Alfio Ferrara, Stefano Montanelli, and Francesco Periti. 2024. Incremental Affinity Propagation based on Cluster Consolidation and Stratification.

Deepayan Chakrabarti, Ravi Kumar, and Andrew Tomkins. 2006. Evolutionary Clustering. In *Proceedings of the 12th ACM SIGKDD International Conference on Knowledge Discovery and Data Mining*, KDD '06, page 554–560, Philadelphia, PA, USA. Association for Computing Machinery.

Jing Chen, Emmanuele Chersoni, Dominik Schlechtweg, Jelena Prokic, and Chu-Ren Huang. 2023. ChiWUG: A Graph-based Evaluation Dataset for Chinese Lexical Semantic Change Detection. In *Proceedings of the 4th Workshop on Computational Approaches to Historical Language Change*, pages 93–99, Singapore. Association for Computational Linguistics.

Arséne Darmesteter. 1893. *La Vie des Mots Étudiée Dans Leurs Significations*. C. Delagrave.

Jader Martins Camboim de Sá, Marcos Da Silveira, and Cédric Pruski. 2024. Survey in characterization of semantic change.

Zhijie Deng, Yucen Luo, and Jun Zhu. 2019. Cluster Alignment With a Teacher for Unsupervised Domain Adaptation. In *2019 IEEE/CVF International Conference on Computer Vision (ICCV)*, pages 9943–9952.

Jacob Devlin, Ming-Wei Chang, Kenton Lee, and Kristina Toutanova. 2019. BERT: Pre-training of deep bidirectional transformers for language understanding. In *Proceedings of the 2019 Conference of the North American Chapter of the Association for Computational Linguistics: Human Language Technologies, Volume 1 (Long and Short Papers)*, pages 4171–4186, Minneapolis, Minnesota. Association for Computational Linguistics.

Martin Emms and Arun Kumar Jayapal. 2016. Dynamic Generative model for Diachronic Sense Emergence Detection. In *Proceedings of COLING 2016, the 26th International Conference on Computational Linguistics: Technical Papers*, pages 1362–1373, Osaka, Japan. The COLING 2016 Organizing Committee.

Mario Giulianelli, Marco Del Tredici, and Raquel Fernández. 2020. Analysing Lexical Semantic Change with Contextualised Word Representations. In *Proceedings of the 58th Annual Meeting of the Association for Computational Linguistics*, pages 3960–3973, Online. Association for Computational Linguistics.

Mario Giulianelli, Iris Luden, Raquel Fernandez, and Andrey Kutuzov. 2023. Interpretable Word Sense Representations via Definition Generation: The Case of Semantic Change Analysis. In *Proceedings of the 61st Annual Meeting of the Association for Computational Linguistics (Volume 1: Long Papers)*, pages 3130–3148, Toronto, Canada. Association for Computational Linguistics.

Hila Gonen, Ganesh Jawahar, Djamé Seddah, and Yoav Goldberg. 2020. Simple, Interpretable and Stable Method for Detecting Words with Usage Change across Corpora. In *Proceedings of the 58th Annual Meeting of the Association for Computational Linguistics*, pages 538–555, Online. Association for Computational Linguistics.

William L Hamilton, Jure Leskovec, and Dan Jurafsky. 2016. Diachronic word embeddings reveal statistical laws of semantic change. In *Proceedings of the 54th Annual Meeting of the Association for Computational Linguistics (Volume 1: Long Papers)*, pages 1489–1501.

Simon Hengchen, Nina Tahmasebi, Dominik Schlechtweg, and Haim Dubossarsky. 2021. *Challenges for Computational Lexical Semantic Change*, pages 341–372. Language Science Press, Berlin.

Valentin Hofmann, Janet Pierrehumbert, and Hinrich Schütze. 2021. Dynamic contextualized word embeddings. In *Proceedings of the 59th Annual Meeting of the Association for Computational Linguistics and the 11th International Joint Conference on Natural Language Processing (Volume 1: Long Papers)*, pages 6970–6984, Online. Association for Computational Linguistics.

Vani Kanjirangat, Sandra Mitrovic, Alessandro Antonucci, and Fabio Rinaldi. 2020. SST-BERT at SemEval-2020 Task 1: Semantic Shift Tracing by Clustering in BERT-based Embedding Spaces. In *Proceedings of the Fourteenth Workshop on Semantic Evaluation*, pages 214–221, Barcelona (online). International Committee for Computational Linguistics.

Daphna Keidar, Andreas Opedal, Zhijing Jin, and Mrinmaya Sachan. 2022. Slangvolution: A Causal Analysis of Semantic Change and Frequency Dynamics in Slang. In *Proceedings of the 60th Annual Meeting of the Association for Computational Linguistics (Volume 1: Long Papers)*, pages 1422–1442, Dublin, Ireland. Association for Computational Linguistics.

Olga Kellert and Md Mahmud Uz Zaman. 2022. Using Neural Topic Models to Track Context Shifts of Words: a Case Study of COVID-related Terms Before and After the Lockdown in April 2020. In *Proceedings of the 3rd Workshop on Computational Approaches to Historical Language Change*, pages 131–139, Dublin, Ireland. Association for Computational Linguistics.

Keivan Kianmehr, Mohammed Alshalalfa, and Reda Alhajj. 2010. Fuzzy clustering-based discretization for gene expression classification. *Knowledge and Information Systems*, 24:441–465.

Adam Kilgarriff. 1997. "I Don't Believe in Word Senses". *Computers and the Humanities*, 31(2):91–113.

Kazuma Kobayashi, Taichi Aida, and Mamoru Komachi. 2021. Analyzing Semantic Changes in Japanese Words Using BERT. In *Proceedings of the 35th Pacific Asia Conference on Language, Information and Computation*, pages 270–280, Shanghai, China. Association for Computational Lingustics.

Artem Kudisov and Nikolay Arefyev. 2022. BOS at LSCDiscovery: Lexical Substitution for Interpretable Lexical Semantic Change Detection. In *Proceedings of the 3rd Workshop on Computational Approaches to Historical Language Change*, pages 165–172, Dublin, Ireland. Association for Computational Linguistics.

Parag A. Kulkarni and Preeti Mulay. 2013. Evolve Systems using Incremental Clustering Approach. *Evolving Systems*, 4(2):71–85.

Vivek Kulkarni, Rami Al-Rfou, Bryan Perozzi, and Steven Skiena. 2015. Statistically Significant Detection of Linguistic Change. In *Proceedings of the 24th International Conference on World Wide Web*, WWW '15, page 625–635, Florence, Italy. International World Wide Web Conferences Steering Committee.

Andrey Kutuzov, Lilja Øvrelid, Terrence Szymanski, and Erik Velldal. 2018. Diachronic Word Embeddings and Semantic Shifts: a Survey. In *Proceedings of the 27th International Conference on Computational Linguistics*, pages 1384–1397, Santa Fe, New Mexico, USA. Association for Computational Linguistics.

Andrey Kutuzov and Lidia Pivovarova. 2021. Three-part Diachronic Semantic Change Dataset for Russian. In *Proceedings of the 2nd International Workshop on Computational Approaches to Historical Language Change 2021*, pages 7–13, Online. Association for Computational Linguistics.

Andrey Kutuzov, Samia Touileb, Petter Mæhlum, Tita Enstad, and Alexandra Wittemann. 2022a. NorDiaChange: Diachronic Semantic Change Dataset for Norwegian. In *Proceedings of the Thirteenth Language Resources and Evaluation Conference*, pages 2563–2572, Marseille, France. European Language Resources Association.

Andrey Kutuzov, Erik Velldal, and Lilja Øvrelid. 2022b. Contextualized Embeddings for Semantic Change Detection: Lessons Learned. In *Northern European Journal of Language Technology, Volume 8*, Copenhagen, Denmark. Northern European Association of Language Technology.

Brenden M Lake and Gregory L Murphy. 2023. Word Meaning in Minds and Machines. *Psychological Review*, 130(2):401–431.

Zhidong Ling, Taichi Aida, Teruaki Oka, and Mamoru Komachi. 2023. Construction of Evaluation Dataset for Japanese Lexical Semantic Change Detection. In *Proceedings of the 37th Pacific Asia Conference on Language, Information and Computation*, pages 125–136, Hong Kong, China. Association for Computational Linguistics.

Yang Liu, Alan Medlar, and Dorota Glowacka. 2021. Statistically Significant Detection of Semantic Shifts using Contextual Word Embeddings. In *Proceedings of the 2nd Workshop on Evaluation and Comparison of NLP Systems*, pages 104–113, Punta Cana, Dominican Republic. Association for Computational Linguistics.

Xianghe Ma, Michael Strube, and Wei Zhao. 2024. Graph-based Clustering for Detecting Semantic Change Across Time and Languages.

Matej Martinc, Syrielle Montariol, Elaine Zosa, and Lidia Pivovarova. 2020. Capturing Evolution in Word Usage: Just Add More Clusters? In *Companion Proceedings of the Web Conference 2020*, WWW '20, page 343–349, Taipei, Taiwan. Association for Computing Machinery.

Syrielle Montariol, Matej Martinc, and Lidia Pivovarova. 2021. Scalable and Interpretable Semantic Change Detection. In *Proceedings of the 2021 Conference of the North American Chapter of the Association for Computational Linguistics: Human Language Technologies*, pages 4642–4652, Online. Association for Computational Linguistics.

Bill Noble, Asad Sayeed, Raquel Fernández, and Staffan Larsson. 2021. Semantic Shift in Social Networks. In *Proceedings of *SEM 2021: The Tenth Joint Conference on Lexical and Computational Semantics*, pages 26–37, Online. Association for Computational Linguistics.

OpenAI. 2023. GPT-4 Technical Report.

Hermann Paul. 1880. *Prinzipien der Sprachgeschichte*. Niemeyer, Halle.

Francesco Periti, Pierluigi Cassotti, Haim Dubossarky, and Nina Tahmasebi. 2024. Analyzing Semantic Change through Lexical Replacements. In *Proceedings of the 62th Annual Meeting of the Association for Computational Linguistics*, Bangkok, Thailand. Association for Computational Linguistics.

Francesco Periti, Alfio Ferrara, Stefano Montanelli, and Martin Ruskov. 2022. What is Done is Done: an Incremental Approach to Semantic Shift Detection. In *Proceedings of the 3rd Workshop on Computational Approaches to Historical Language Change*, pages 33–43, Dublin, Ireland. Association for Computational Linguistics.

Francesco Periti and Stefano Montanelli. 2024. Lexical Semantic Change through Large Language Models: a Survey. *ACM Comput. Surv.* Just Accepted.

Francesco Periti, Sergio Picascia, Stefano Montanelli, Alfio Ferrara, and Nina Tahmasebi. 2023. Studying Word Meaning Evolution through Incremental Semantic Shift Detection: A Case Study of Italian Parliamentary Speeches.

Francesco Periti and Nina Tahmasebi. 2024. A Systematic Comparison of Contextualized Word Embeddings for Lexical Semantic Change. In *Proceedings of the 2024 Conference of the North American Chapter of the Association for Computational Linguistics: Human Language Technologies (Volume 1: Long Papers)*, pages 4262–4282, Mexico City, Mexico. Association for Computational Linguistics.

Karl Christian Reisig. 1839. *Professor K. Reisig's Vorlesungen Über Lateinische Sprachwissenschaft*. Verlag der Lehnhold'schen Buchhandlung.

Maja Rudolph and David Blei. 2018. Dynamic embeddings for language evolution. In *Proceedings of the 2018 World Wide Web Conference*, WWW '18, page 1003–1011, Republic and Canton of Geneva, CHE. International World Wide Web Conferences Steering Committee.

Dominik Schlechtweg, Barbara McGillivray, Simon Hengchen, Haim Dubossarsky, and Nina Tahmasebi. 2020. SemEval-2020 Task 1: Unsupervised Lexical Semantic Change Detection. In *Proceedings of the Fourteenth Workshop on Semantic Evaluation*, pages 1–23, Barcelona (online). International Committee for Computational Linguistics.

Hinrich Schütze. 1998. Automatic Word Sense Discrimination. *Computational Linguistics*, 24(1):97–123.

Philippa Shoemark, Farhana Ferdousi Liza, Dong Nguyen, Scott Hale, and Barbara McGillivray. 2019. Room to Glo: A Systematic Comparison of Semantic Change Detection Approaches with Word Embeddings. In *Proceedings of the 2019 Conference on Empirical Methods in Natural Language Processing and the 9th International Joint Conference on Natural Language Processing (EMNLP-IJCNLP)*, pages 66–76, Hong Kong, China. Association for Computational Linguistics.

Padhraic Smyth. 1996. Clustering sequences with hidden markov models. In *Advances in Neural Information Processing Systems*, volume 9. MIT Press.

Gustaf Stern. 1931. *Meaning and Change of Meaning; with Special Reference to the English Language*. Wettergren & Kerbers.

Nina Tahmasebi, Lars Borin, and Adam Jatowt. 2021. *Survey of Computational Approaches to Lexical Semantic Change Detection*, pages 1–91. Language Science Press, Berlin.

Nina Tahmasebi and Haim Dubossarsky. 2023. Computational Modeling of Semantic Change.

Nina Tahmasebi and Thomas Risse. 2017. Finding Individual Word Sense Changes and their Delay in Appearance. In *Proceedings of the International Conference Recent Advances in Natural Language Processing, RANLP 2017*, pages 741–749, Varna, Bulgaria. INCOMA Ltd.

Nina N. Tahmasebi. 2013. *Models and Algorithms for Automatic Detection of Language Evolution*. Ph.D. thesis, Gottfried Wilhelm Leibniz Universität Hannover.

Xuri Tang. 2018. A state-of-the-art of Semantic Change Computation. *Natural Language Engineering*, 24(5):649–676.

S. Ullmann. 1957. *The Principles of Semantics*. Glasgow University publications. Jackson.

Zijun Yao, Yifan Sun, Weicong Ding, Nikhil Rao, and Hui Xiong. 2018. Dynamic word embeddings for evolving semantic discovery. In *Proceedings of the Eleventh ACM International Conference on Web Search and Data Mining*, WSDM '18, page 673–681, New York, NY, USA. Association for Computing Machinery.

Frank D. Zamora-Reina, Felipe Bravo-Marquez, and Dominik Schlechtweg. 2022. LSCDiscovery: A Shared Task on Semantic Change Discovery and Detection in Spanish. In *Proceedings of the 3rd Workshop on Computational Approaches to Historical Language Change*, pages 149–164, Dublin, Ireland. Association for Computational Linguistics.

TartuNLP @ AXOLOTL-24: Leveraging Classifier Output for New Sense Detection in Lexical Semantics

Aleksei Dorkin and **Kairit Sirts**
Institute of Computer Science
University of Tartu
{aleksei.dorkin, kairit.sirts}@ut.ee

Abstract

We present our submission to the AXOLOTL-24 shared task. The shared task comprises two subtasks: identifying new senses that words gain with time (when comparing newer and older time periods) and producing the definitions for the identified new senses. We implemented a conceptually simple and computationally inexpensive solution to both subtasks. We trained adapter-based binary classification models to match glosses with usage examples and leveraged the probability output of the models to identify novel senses. The same models were used to match examples of novel sense usages with Wiktionary definitions. Our submission attained third place on the first subtask and the first place on the second subtask.

Team	ARI	F1
deep-change	**0.413**	**0.750**
Holotniekat	0.312	0.641
TartuNLP (ours)	0.310	0.590
IMS_Stuttgart	0.287	0.487
ABDN-NLP	0.221	0.431
WooperNLP	0.187	0.316
Baseline	0.041	0.207

Table 1: Overall results on the Subtask 1.

Team	Overall	BLEU	BERTScore
TartuNLP (ours)	**0.467**	**0.208**	**0.726**
WooperNLP	0.340	0.020	0.660
ABDN-NLP	0.253	0.045	0.461
baseline	0.218	0.013	0.423

Table 2: Overall results on the Subtask 2.

1 Introduction

The subject of the AXOLOTL-24 shared task (Fedorova et al., 2024) is diachronic semantic change detection and explanation. Diachronic semantic change is understood as the change in word meanings (i.e., words losing old senses and obtaining new ones) over shorter or longer periods. Accordingly, given a dataset containing usage examples from different periods (old and new), the task is to identify and define the new senses that words gain in the new time period compared to the old one.

The goal of the shared task is to implement a semantic change modeling system for two tasks:

1) Correctly assigning existing senses to target word usages and identifying novel, previously unseen senses;
2) Describing the identified novel senses.

The data in the shared task is provided in three languages: Finnish, Russian, and German (the surprise language for which only the test split is available). For each language, examples from old and new periods are given. Each data point consists of a target word and its usage example, gloss (target word definition), the period the example comes from, and usage and sense IDs. The data includes glosses for both time periods in the training and validation splits, while glosses for the new time period are not provided in the test splits. The "old" and "new" periods differ for each language. For Finnish, old texts are dated before 1700, and new ones are dated after 1700. For Russian, the old target word usages are from the 19th century, and the new data represents modern usages of words. For German, the old period is from 1800 to 1899, and the new period is from 1946 to 1990 (Schlechtweg, 2023).

Although we participated in both subtasks, we were primarily interested in the second subtask of producing definitions for new senses. We implemented a solution that matches identified novel sense usages with definitions from an external resource (Wiktionary). Our approach is based on a binary classification task to predict whether a proposed definition matches the sense under consideration. We reused this binary classification model

Proceedings of the 5th Workshop on Computational Approaches to Historical Language Change, pages 120–125
August 15, 2024 ©2024 Association for Computational Linguistics

for the second subtask of describing the identified novel senses.

Our system attained the first place on the second subtask (Table 2) and obtained competitive results on the first subtask (Table 1).

2 Methodology

We propose a simple classification-based solution for both subtasks. We adopt the GlossBERT approach (Huang et al., 2019) that treats word sense disambiguation as a sentence pair classification task, where each pair comprises a usage example and a sense definition. In turn, we frame the problem of new sense identification as the problem of matching between usage examples and sense definitions. Accordingly, the matching problem can be solved with a binary classification model that, given a usage example and a sense definition, outputs the probability of the sense definition correctly describing the usage example.

We adopt the cross-encoder model that simultaneously processes the usage examples and the sense definitions with the same model. Given a usage example and a sense inventory, we apply the classification model to predict binary probabilities for each example/sense definition combination. If the highest probability over all candidate pairs exceeds a predefined threshold, the system assigns the highest probability sense to the usage example. Otherwise, the sense used in the example is deemed to be new.

2.1 Subtask 1: Bridging Diachronic Word Uses and a Synchronic Dictionary

This subtask aims to assign a sense ID to every usage example from the new period; the sense ID may come either from the senses in the old period or, if the system identifies a novel sense, a unique new sense ID is created.

The data for the first subtask contains sense definitions and correct usages, which can be used to construct positive examples for our task formulation. However, having only positive examples for a classification model is generally insufficient. To produce negative examples, we employ a simple algorithm. We only consider words associated with at least two distinct sense IDs. For a given sense ID and its associated gloss, we create all possible combinations of the gloss with the usage examples associated with the other sense IDs of the same word (consult Appendix A for additional details). We expect that the negatives obtained with this algorithm are hard and, as such, are more useful for training that could be obtained, for instance, via random sampling.

We transform every split of every language by extending it with negative examples created with the procedure described above. For each language, we train a separate classification model on the train split and evaluate on the development split. When training and evaluating the classifier, we do not consider the period (old or new) from which the examples come. The best checkpoint for each model is selected based on the development F1 score.

Having trained the classification models, we perform inference on the test set and transform the output into the expected format. During inference, the usage examples from the old period are ignored and the classification is performed only on pairs of usage examples from the new period and sense definitions from the old period. If the highest predicted probability for a usage example is above a threshold, we assign the sense ID of the most probable sense definition to the usage example. Otherwise, a new sense ID is created. The final result submitted for evaluation contains both the predicted senses for the examples from the new period as well as the positive examples in the test split from the old period.[1]

For the surprise language—German—the training process is slightly different. No training or validation data is provided, so we train and validate the classification model on the positive and negative examples obtained from the old period in the test data. Inference, however, is exactly the same.

2.2 Subtask 2: Definition Generation for Novel Word Senses

Subtask 2 aims to define each novel sense identified in the first subtask. Despite the name of the subtask, our approach does not generate any new definitions. We also do not train any additional models. As previously mentioned, we consider this task a matching problem, except that the definitions for the novel senses are not present in the data provided in the shared task. To solve this problem, we scrape the definitions of the surface forms, for which we identified at least one example as the usage of a novel sense, from the Wiktionary. More specifically, we scrape the definitions from

[1]Since the test examples for the old period were already annotated, we simply copied their sense definitions to the submitted result file.

the language-specific Wiktionary versions for each language (i.e. Finnish,[2] Russian,[3] and German[4] Wiktionaries).

Having scraped the necessary definitions, we head straight to inference on the test set. We reuse the models and predictions from the first subtask. We collect the examples identified as the usages of the novel senses from the predictions and match them with the Wiktionary definitions using the classifier models trained in the first subtask. After that, we add the matched definitions to the predicted new senses.

2.3 Implementation Details

Different from GlossBERT (Huang et al., 2019), which is based on the BERT (Devlin et al., 2019) model, we instead use XLM-RoBERTa (Conneau et al., 2020) as the base model for our classifiers. XLM-RoBERTa is a multilingual model that includes Finnish, Russian, and German in its training data. We expect our system to benefit from the multilinguality. Instead of full fine-tuning, we opt for parameter-efficient fine-tuning. More specifically, we train bottleneck adapter (Houlsby et al., 2019) classifiers for each language. We adopted this approach because it makes our solution computationally lightweight and easily reproducible.

In GlossBERT, Huang et al. (2019) differentiate between training setups with and without weak supervision, with the former including the defined word itself in the gloss, as well as highlighting it in the usage example. According to the experimental results reported by Huang et al. (2019), weak supervision appears to bring minor improvements in sense prediction. However, we do not use weak supervision in our submission. The reason is that Finnish and Russian are substantially more morphologically rich languages than English; thus, the target words rarely appear in their dictionary forms in the usage examples. Moreover, in some cases, the orthography also differs between old and new periods.

To delimit context and gloss, Huang et al. (2019) use the special [SEP] token that is pre-trained into the BERT model via the next sentence prediction task. However, RoBERTa (Zhuang et al., 2021), and by extension XLM-RoBERTa, omitted the next sentence prediction task in the pre-training. As a result of that, the </s> token that is used by RoBERTa in place of [SEP] does not have the same classification-oriented meaning. For this reason, we employed the tabulation symbol as the delimiter instead.

For each language, we employed different variations of the base model and varying training setups. For Finnish, we used the large version of XLM-RoBERTa and trained for ten epochs in half-precision with a batch size of 128 and 3 steps of gradient accumulation. We observed that the training did not converge with a smaller effective batch size. For Russian, we trained the classifier adapter with the base version of XLM-RoBERTa for 50 epochs with a batch size of 144. We also experimented with the large version of the model for the Russian language; however, it showed no improvements compared to the base version. For German, we did not train the classifier from scratch. Instead, we continued training from the best checkpoint trained on the Finnish data. The motivation is that there is considerably more data in Finnish than in Russian in the shared task, so we assume the Finnish model to be stronger. We continued training the Finnish classifier for 20 epochs in half-precision with a batch size of 48 and 6 steps of gradient accumulation. All models were trained with a 5e-4 learning rate.

The threshold value for the classifier's probability to identify novel senses was selected as the highest scoring option in the first subtask using the evaluation script provided by the organizers. We tested a small number of values in the range of of 0.2 to 0.5 on Russian and determined the best value to be **0.35**. The same value was used for all languages without additional testing due to time limitations.

The models were trained on the University High-Performance Cluster (University of Tartu, 2018). We used a single Tesla V100 GPU for Russian and German, while for Finnish, we used a single A100 80GB GPU. The time elapsed on training is 9 hours for Finnish, 3 hours for Russian, and 9 minutes for German. We implemented our solution using the transformers[5] and the adapters[6] libraries. The source code and the data are available on GitHub[7] and HuggingFace Hub,[8] respectively.

[2] https://fi.wiktionary.org/

[3] https://ru.wiktionary.org/

[4] https://de.wiktionary.org/

[5] https://github.com/huggingface/transformers

[6] https://github.com/adapter-hub/adapters

[7] https://github.com/slowwavesleep/ancient-lang-adapters/tree/axolotl

[8] https://huggingface.co/datasets/adorkin/axolotl-wiktionary-definitions

Team	Fi-BLEU	Ru-BLEU	De-BLEU	Fi-BERTScore	Ru-BERTScore	De-BERTScore
TartuNLP (ours)	0.028	**0.587**	**0.01**	0.679	**0.869**	0.63
WooperNLP	0.023	0.027	**0.01**	0.675	0.656	**0.65**
ABDN-NLP	**0.107**	0.027	0.0	**0.706**	0.677	0.0
baseline	0.033	0.005	0.0	0.403	0.377	0.49

Table 3: Language specific results for the Subtask 2.

3 Results

The overall results of both subtasks are presented in Tables 1 and 2. For subtask 1, the metrics reported are the average macro-F1 score and the average Adjusted Rand Index (ARI) (Hubert and Arabie, 1985) across target words per language. The overall F1 and ARI scores are computed as the mean across all languages. For subtask 2, the evaluation metrics are the BERTScore (Zhang et al., 2020) and BLEU (Papineni et al., 2002) averaged across target words per language. BLEU and BERTScore values for the entire subtask are the respective averages across all languages. The overall score is the mean of BLEU and BERTScore.

Our submission attained the third place out of eight participants in the first subtask and the first place out of four participants in the second subtask (Table 2). This aligns with our expectations since we focused on the second subtask from the beginning and applied the system developed for the second subtask to the first subtask. When looking at the language-specific measures of subtask 2 (Table 3), one can see considerable differences between languages. Our system works the best in Russian while also performing well in German in terms of BERTScore (although the BLEU score is close to 0 for all systems). In Finnish, our system is competitive in terms of BERTScore but underperforms compared to the baseline in terms of BLEU.

4 Discussion

Our submission to the second subtask is well ahead of the other participants in the overall leaderboard (Table 2) despite the simplicity of our approach. However, the language-specific results show that it is not so clear-cut (Table 3). Some of the success can be attributed to accidentally matching the source of definitions for the Russian language, which is the Russian Wiktionary. We believe so because the value of the BLEU metric of our submission in the Russian language is higher than that of the other teams and in the other languages by an order of magnitude. However, we do not consider this a critical issue because the BERTScore metric is reasonably high and well above the baseline for all languages, suggesting that the matched definitions capture the expected senses well. However, the corresponding low BLEU scores highlight the inadequacy of the BLEU metric for this task.

Wiktionary language	Number of unique pages
Finnish	586,439
German	1,314,597
Russian	2,877,010

Table 4: The number of unique Wiktionary pages per language.

Secondly, our approach to the second subtask has limitations. More specifically, matching usage examples only against the definitions of the target word, while efficient, considerably limits the system's ability to describe completely new senses. Intuitively, a definition associated with a different word may be a more suitable description of a new sense. A more robust solution would involve matching usage examples against all available definitions. However, that would likely require using a bi-encoder architecture (as proposed by Blevins and Zettlemoyer (2020), for instance) instead of a cross-encoder due to the computational complexity of matching every example with every definition.

Accessing the definitions for all the words in a given language-specific Wiktionary is time-consuming because the layout, article structure, and templates used are completely different for each Wiktionary version. While there is a resource providing Wiktionary dumps in a much more convenient format,[9] it is mostly limited in its support to the English language, with the support for some languages, such as Russian and German, being work in progress, and for others, such as Finnish, completely missing at the time of writing. Moreover, the Finnish, German, and Russian Wiktionaries differ in size and the fullness of their coverage. A rough estimate can be made by accessing the **Special:Statistics** page of each Wiktionary and examining the total number of unique pages (Table 4).

[9] `https://kaikki.org/`

We note the correlation between the smaller sizes of the Finnish and German Wiktionaries and the lower performance of our system on these languages.

Lastly, although we did not focus on the first subtask, we believe the results of the sense prediction task obtained with our systems could also be improved. For instance, the choice of the threshold value for determining a new sense could be done in a more systematic manner or made learnable. Similarly, adjusting the training data or the hyperparameters might bring further improvements.

5 Conclusion

This paper described our solution to both subtasks of the AXOLOTL-24 shared task based on leveraging classifier probabilities for usage example/sense definition pairs. The developed system is conceptually simple, adopting a binary classification approach to predict the probability of a sense definition matching the usage example and employing the adapters framework to reduce computation resource requirements. Our submission attained the third place in the first subtask and the first place in the second subtask, showing the feasibility of our approach.

Acknowledgements

This research was supported by the Estonian Research Council Grant PSG721.

References

Terra Blevins and Luke Zettlemoyer. 2020. Moving Down the Long Tail of Word Sense Disambiguation with Gloss Informed Bi-encoders. In *Proceedings of the 58th Annual Meeting of the Association for Computational Linguistics*, pages 1006–1017, Online. Association for Computational Linguistics.

Alexis Conneau, Kartikay Khandelwal, Naman Goyal, Vishrav Chaudhary, Guillaume Wenzek, Francisco Guzmán, Edouard Grave, Myle Ott, Luke Zettlemoyer, and Veselin Stoyanov. 2020. Unsupervised Cross-lingual Representation Learning at Scale. In *Proceedings of the 58th Annual Meeting of the Association for Computational Linguistics*, pages 8440–8451, Online. Association for Computational Linguistics.

Jacob Devlin, Ming-Wei Chang, Kenton Lee, and Kristina Toutanova. 2019. BERT: Pre-training of Deep Bidirectional Transformers for Language Understanding. In *Proceedings of the 2019 Conference of the North American Chapter of the Association for Computational Linguistics: Human Language Technologies, Volume 1 (Long and Short Papers)*, pages 4171–4186, Minneapolis, Minnesota. Association for Computational Linguistics.

Mariia Fedorova, Timothee Mickus, Niko Tapio Partanen, Janine Siewert, Elena Spaziani, and Andrey Kutuzov. 2024. AXOLOTL'24 shared task on multilingual explainable semantic change modeling. In *Proceedings of the 5th Workshop on Computational Approaches to Historical Language Change*, Bangkok. Association for Computational Linguistics.

Neil Houlsby, Andrei Giurgiu, Stanislaw Jastrzebski, Bruna Morrone, Quentin De Laroussilhe, Andrea Gesmundo, Mona Attariyan, and Sylvain Gelly. 2019. Parameter-efficient Transfer Learning for NLP. In *International Conference on Machine Learning*, pages 2790–2799. PMLR.

Luyao Huang, Chi Sun, Xipeng Qiu, and Xuanjing Huang. 2019. GlossBERT: BERT for Word Sense Disambiguation with Gloss Knowledge. In *Proceedings of the 2019 Conference on Empirical Methods in Natural Language Processing and the 9th International Joint Conference on Natural Language Processing (EMNLP-IJCNLP)*, pages 3509–3514, Hong Kong, China. Association for Computational Linguistics.

Lawrence Hubert and Phipps Arabie. 1985. Comparing Partitions. *Journal of Classification*, 2:193–218.

Kishore Papineni, Salim Roukos, Todd Ward, and Wei-Jing Zhu. 2002. BLEU: a Method for Automatic Evaluation of Machine Translation. In *Proceedings of the 40th Annual Meeting of the Association for Computational Linguistics*, pages 311–318, Philadelphia, Pennsylvania, USA. Association for Computational Linguistics.

Dominik Schlechtweg. 2023. *Human and computational measurement of lexical semantic change*. Ph.D. thesis, Universität Stuttgart.

University of Tartu. 2018. UT Rocket.

Tianyi Zhang, Varsha Kishore, Felix Wu, Kilian Q. Weinberger, and Yoav Artzi. 2020. BERTScore: Evaluating Text Generation with Bert.

Liu Zhuang, Lin Wayne, Shi Ya, and Zhao Jun. 2021. A Robustly Optimized BERT Pre-training Approach with Post-training. In *Proceedings of the 20th Chinese National Conference on Computational Linguistics*, pages 1218–1227, Huhhot, China. Chinese Information Processing Society of China.

A Training Examples

Table 5 presents two training examples for the Russian word "Перо" (*Feather*). In the first row, we have a gloss and a matching usage example for the figurative meaning of the word (*a symbol of the writer's art*), which is denoted by the label **1**. Each usage example of the word in its other senses is paired with this gloss and used as a negative example labeled **0**. For instance, in the second row, the same gloss is paired with a mismatching usage example in the literal sense of the word. We omit the rest of the negative examples and the other senses for brevity.

Gloss	Usage example	Label
"Символ искусства писателя, писательского труда, его ремесла."	"У него бойкое, острое перо."	1
"Символ искусства писателя, писательского труда, его ремесла."	"Перья зверя."	0

Table 5: A subset of training examples for a single word.

EtymoLink: A Structured English Etymology Dataset

Yuan Gao[1, 2], Weiwei Sun[1],
[1]Department of Science and Technology, University of Cambridge, U.K.
[2]ALTA Institue, University of Cambridge, U.K.
{yg386,ws390}@cl.cam.ac.uk

Abstract

Etymology, and the field of lexicography, is often constrained by unstructured data formats buried in scholarly articles and dictionaries. This paper presents a methodology and an empirical study for creating a structured etymological dataset suitable for computational analysis. Using data from the Online Etymology Dictionary (Etymonline), we manually annotated a subset of entries to establish a high-quality ground-truth dataset and fine-tuned the FLAN-T5-base model to extract structured etymological relationships automatically. The resulting dataset contains over 103,000 relationships covering 63,603 English lexical terms. Our findings emphasise feasibility of using large language models for structuring lexicographical data, exploring the transferability of the model to other dictionary datasets with no additional manual annotation.

1 Introduction

Etymology, is the study of the origin and historical development of words. The etymological understanding of words not only reveals their origins, but also the cultural and historical contexts that have shaped their contemporary meanings. Figure 1 shows the etymology of the English word "research", meaning diligent and systematic inquiry. It is commonly understood that the word is made up of the prefix *"re-"*, meaning 'again', and the root *"search"*. The etymological trace leads further back to the reduplicated form of the Proto-Indo-European (PIE) root **sker-*, which means to cut or divide. The duplication of **sker* suggests a repetitive action, along with the prefix *"re-"* which adds another sense of intensity and repetitiveness. This understanding, traced all the way to Proto-Indo-European roots not only uncovers the origin, but also offers a deeper understanding of how the concepts of high scrutiny and repeated examination evolved into the modern concept of "research".

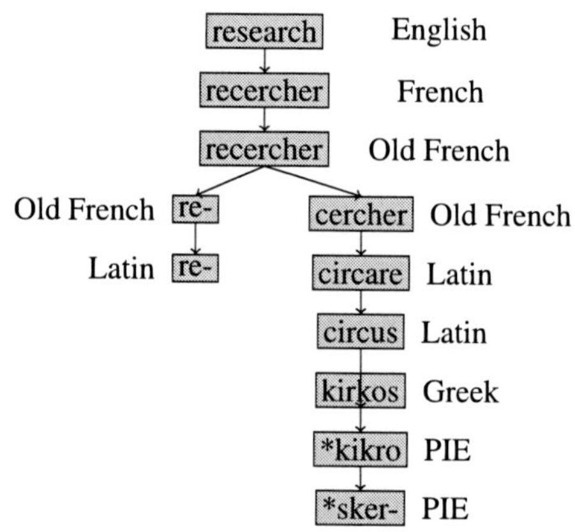

Figure 1: The etymology of the English word "research".

Traditional etymological studies have been limited to philosophical and comparative methods, relying heavily on linguistic expertise with a focus on specific languages and historical periods. This specialisation, while valuable, restricts the broader application etymology in large-scale comparative and computational linguistics. Most etymological data lives in scholarly articles, etymological dictionaries, or web resources. Such formats, although rich in detail, are inherently unstructured and not suited for computational approaches that require systematic data to process language on a large scale.

The field's reliance on verbose descriptions poses another challenge. These prose descriptions, typical of most etymological entries, make it difficult for computational tools to extract and analyze the relationships between words across languages and time periods. Consequently, the absence of structured, computation-suitable etymological databases has been a notable gap, leaving computational linguists without the resources necessary to quantitatively analyze historical linguistic

Proceedings of the 5th Workshop on Computational Approaches to Historical Language Change, pages 126–136
August 15, 2024

data effectively.

This paper introduces a new structured dataset specifically designed for computational etymology. We begin by crawling data from the Online Etymology Dictionary (or Etymonline)[1], an online dictionary compiled by historian Douglas Harper from various scholarly articles and books such as *The Dictionary of Etymology* (Barnhart and Steinmetz, 1988) and *A Comprehensive Etymological Dictionary of the English Language* (Ernest Klein, 1971). We manually annotated a subset of these entries to establish a high-quality baseline and ground-truth dataset. We then use the annotated dataset to fine-tune FLAN-T5 (Chung et al., 2022), an instruction fine-tuned encoder-decoder language model to extract etymological relations from the dictionary entries. This method allows us to explore Large Language Models (LLMs) and other automation techniques to systematically extract traditional prose-based etymological entries buried in scholar articles and dictionaries into a structured format. Ultimately, the structured dataset generated through this project will provide a valuable resource for computational linguists and other researchers, facilitating more large scale analysis of language evolution and enabling new insights into the interconnectedness of languages across time and space. Furthermore, this approach explores the feasibility of leveraging LLMs to curate structured data from traditional dictionary data.

The dataset comprises 63,603 entries crawled from Etymonline, with 5,361 entries manually annotated and 58,242 entries automatically annotated using the trained system. The final dataset includes 103,322 etymological relationships and 15,931 connected components, providing a comprehensive resource for examining language evolution and etymological connections. The dataset will be publicly accessible.

2 Linguistic Background

Diachronic change is an inherent aspect of linguistic evolution, driven by the need for effective communication within and between communities. Understanding the evolution of language requires examining various factors that contribute to linguistic change. Simplification of grammatical structures is a common trend in language evolution. For example, the transition from Old English and Modern English shows a significant reduction in verb conjugation complexity (Baugh and Cable, 1993). Technological advancement also impacts linguistic development. For example, the printing press contributed to the linguistic standardization and a more uniform spelling of the English language (Okrent and O'Neill, 2021).

2.1 Current Etymology Studies

Despite extensive research, many words still have unresolved origins.The Oxford English Dictionary, a prominent resource in this field, offers etymologies for over 600,000 words but lists a significant number as "origin unknown" or "of uncertain origin".

The absence of historical documentation is a significant barrier, especially for words from prehistoric times or non-literate cultures. For example, the etymology of the English word "dog" remains surprisingly unclear, as it appears in Middle English with no clear Old English predecessors (Gąsiorowski, 2006). Language contact adds another layer of complexity, particularly for borrowed words from extinct or significantly transformed languages. The semantic shift and phonetic changes over centuries obscure the word's origins.

Etymological research also faces methodological difficulties. Deciphering ancient languages requires specialized knowledge, and distinguishing borrowed words from native ones is challenging in linguistically diverse areas. Polysemy and homophony further complicate research, as words that sound similar may have different origins or meanings. For instance, "bank" can refer to a financial institution or a riverbank, each with separate etymological paths.

2.2 Computational Historical Linguistics

Computational etymology employs innovative approaches like automated etymology extraction, using natural language processing and machine learning to identify relevant relationships in large corpora. Cognate detection is an active area of research, with traditional methods measuring lexical similarity via string similarity (Ciobanu and Dinu, 2014; Gomes and Pereira Lopes, 2011; Simard et al., 1992). Recent trends involve machine learning to identify cross-lingual orthographic transformations (Bergsma and Kondrak, 2007; Mitkov et al., 2007), and neural networks are used to trace changes in word forms over time (Kanojia et al., 2019; Goswami et al., 2023; Bollmann, 2018).

The construction and analysis of linguistic

[1]https://www.etymonline.com/

databases are essential for large-scale computational linguistics. These databases store extensive data and support analytical queries revealing patterns in language evolution. CogNet (Batsuren et al., 2019) is a large-scale cognate database extracted based on WordNet. The Database of Cross-Linguistic Colexifications (CLICS^2) is a computer-friendly framework for analyzing cross-linguistic colexification patterns with the Cross-Linguistic Data Formats initiative (CLDF) (List et al., 2018).

3 Challenges in Modern Lexicography

Lexicography, the practice of compiling, writing, and editing dictionaries, has undergone significant changes in the digital age. Historically, dictionaries have served as authoritative references for language, offering definitions, etymologies, phonetic guides, and usage examples. However, traditional lexicographical methods are increasingly struggling to keep pace with computational approaches and the rapid evolution of language in the modern era.

Traditional lexicographic methods often lead to inconsistencies in dictionary data due to the subjective nature of language documentation and the variability in editorial practices. For instance, the noun "research" has four different definition in the Oxford English Dictionary (OED) but only three in Merriam-Webster. Another example is the etymology of "pumpkin". The word is traced to its French origin (*pompon* or *pompion*) in the OED, Merriam-Webster, and Etymonline, but each provides varying historical context. The OED links it to Classical Latin *pepōn-*, Merriam-Webster further identifies Greek *pépon*, and Etymonline traces it to the Proto-Indo-European root **pekw-*. These inconsistencies in the depth and nature of information reflect differing editorial standards and the lack of standardised lexicographical practices.

Digitizing traditional dictionaries presents another challenge due to their inherently non-structured, descriptive format, which is often incompatible with computational processing. Dictionary entries typically contain long, verbose paragraphs that are sometimes hard for humans to comprehend and even more challenging for computers to parse. This is further complicated by the lack of consistencies among dictionaries for data integration, such as differing abbreviations for parts of speech.

These challenges highlight the need for sophisticated computational approaches and collaboration between lexicographers and computational linguists. This project aims to explore using Information Extraction (IE) and NLP systems to automate structured data extraction from dictionaries, enabling systematic linguistic pattern analysis. Ultimately, the goal is to bridge the gap between traditional lexicography and modern computational linguistics, providing scalable and transferable solutions for mining valuable information.

4 Building an IE system for Lexicographical Mining

This paper presents the collection and annotation of etymological entries from Etymonline, using large language models to extend annotations. The aim is to convert unstructured dictionary data into a structured format suitable for linguistic analysis and computational processing.

4.1 Data Collection

For this study, Etymonline was selected as the primary source of data. The website aggregates etymological information from various scholarly sources, providing a detailed description of a word's origins, historical developments, and transformations within the English language. Below is an example entry of the word "research" whose structured etymology is given in Figure 1.

> **research** *(v.)*
> 1590s, "investigate or study (a matter) closely, search or examine with continued care," from French rercher, from Old French rercher "seek out, search closely," from re-, here perhaps an intensive prefix (see re-), + cercher "to seek for," from Latin circare "go about, wander, traverse," in Late Latin "to wander hither and thither," from circus "circle" (see circus).
>
> The intransitive meaning "make researches" is by 1781. Sometimes 17c. also "to seek (a woman) in love or marriage." Related: Researched; researching.

Etymonline is grounded in scholarly rigor, extensive coverage, and open accessibility. The dictionary is curated by Douglas Harper, who compiles information solely from scholarly sources, ensuring high accuracy and reliability. Harper's consistent approach to entry composition allows for systematic extraction and analysis of etymological data. This uniformity is crucial for applying computational techniques that require standardization data inputs.

A total of 63,603 entries were extracted from Etymonline.

4.2 Data Preprocessing

Simple data preprocess was conducted. For words with the same spelling but have different parts of speech, the POS tag remains part of the lexical term to differentiate between them, as illustrated in the "research (v.)" example. Homographs, such as "bank", are differentiated by an index, such as *bank (n.1)* and *bank (n.2)*. The typsetting information given by the original Etymonline entry was ignored, while hyperlinks were preserved to build a complete etymological network.

Since all entries used similar expository language to describe the etymological relations, regex, a pattern matching tool, was used to extract a collection of candidate lexical terms. The candidate terms extracted for the verb "research" are shown below.

> recercher, recercher, re-, re-, cercher, circare, circus, circus, Researched, researching

4.3 Manual Annotation

A main challenge of this paper is transforming the prose paragraph style of the Etymonline dictionary entries into structured formats. 5,361 entries were selected for manual annotation. A key criterion for selection was diversity in word initials to prevent overrepresentation of any particular prefix. In Etymonline, suffixes are represented by unique word initials, so varied initials also account for word endings.

In etymological studies, prefixes and suffixes are critical for tracing word origins as they often contain significant linguistic markers of historical and morphological transformations. Ensuring varied word initials prevents bias toward specific affix patterns, which is crucial to prevent machine learning models from skewing their learning toward particular initials. This approach enhances the generalizability and accuracy of the models.

The manual annotation of the dataset was executed by a single linguistics student, tasked with converting the text into edge list format. The target format of the entry "research" is an edge list shown below. In this study, the annotation task was designed to be straightforward and did not necessitate specialized expertise. Therefore, we opted to employ a single annotator for the task. While inter-annotator agreement is important for tasks requiring trained experts to ensure reliability and consistency, we deemed it unnecessary for this simple annotation task. The clarity and simplicity of the task ensured that the single annotator could perform it with sufficient accuracy and consistency.

> **research** *(v.)*
> research_E, recercher_F
> recercher_F, recercher_OF
> recercher_OF, re-_OF, cercher_OF
> cercher_OF, circare_L
> circare_L, circus_L

The edge list format used in this project is designed to represent the descendency relationships between words. Each line in the list represents a direct etymological link from one form to another. For example, the line "recercher_OF, re-_OF, cercher_OF" indicates that the Old French word *recercher* derives directly from the Old French prefix *re-* and the Old French word *cercher*. Further more, the suffixes attached to each word after the underscore, such as "_E", specify the language of the word form in question. Table 1 reports some language and their abbreviations. The complete list of languages and their abbreviation, refereed to as language labels from here on, used in this dataset can be found in appendix A.

Language Label	Language
PIE	Proto-Indo-European
F	French
ONF	Old North French
AF	Anglo-French
MF	Middle French
OF	Old French
...	...

Table 1: Language Labels and Corresponding Languages

One observation of the edge list is that it is not yet complete compared to the graph given in Figure 1. More specifically, it is still missing the etymological relationships from the Latin word *circus* to the Proto-Indo-European root **sker-*. These missing links are documented under the entry for the word "circus". Once the annotation process is completed for the entire dataset, these connections will be fully integrated, resulting in a complete representation of the word's etymological history.

4.4 Automatic Annotation

To fully annotate the entirety of the crawled entries from Etymonline, we employed the FLAN-T5-base model (Chung et al., 2022), a variant of the Transformer-based T5 model with 248 million parameters, which has been pre-trained on a diverse range of language understanding tasks. This section details the selection rationale, fine-tuning process, and the specific configurations used to adapt the model to the task of etymological annotation.

4.4.1 Model Selection

The open-source FLAN-T5-base model was chosen for its flexibility, strong performance in text generation tasks, and relatively small size compared to some state-of-the-art LLMs.The core architecture of FLAN-T5 is based on the Transformer model (Vaswani et al., 2017), utilizing self-attention mechanisms to process data sequences. These mechanisms, which compute the relevance of all other words in the sequence for each word in the input, are particularly beneficial as etymological relationships are buried within and across non-adjacent sentences. Unlike most current LLMs with a decoder-only structure, FLAN-T5 employs a dual structure with an encoder that processes input text and a decoder that generates output text. This setup is ideal for transforming verbose etymology descriptions into structured formats like edge lists. The encoder captures contextual relationships within the input, while the decoder uses this context to generate accurate, formatted output. Furthermore, FLAN-T5 has been fine-tuned to adapt to specific tasks with minimal task-specific data, crucial for high-quality annotation where such data is scarce. The model's robust pre-training enables it to generalize well across previously unseen tasks.

4.4.2 Fine-Tuning

The manually annotated subset of 5,361 entries from the initial data collection phase was split into a training dataset of 4,556 entries and a test dataset of 805. Each entry in the dataset was further processed and presented as a prompt to the model. As example of the input prompt to the model is given below.

> ###INSTRUCTION:extracting etymological relations from text and structuring this information into an edge adjacency list.
> ###WORD: research (v.)
> ###TEXT: 1590s, from Middle French recercher, from Old French recercher ""seek out, search closely,"" from re-, intensive prefix (see re-), + cercher ""to seek for,"" from Latin circare ""go about, wander, traverse,"" in Late Latin ""to wander hither and thither,"" from circus ""circle"" (see circus). Related: Researched; researching.
> ###CAND: recercher, recercher, re-, re-, cercher, circare, circus, circus, Researched, researching"

The target output is the edge list shown in section 4.3. The list is further processed into a string format as the model can only output sequence data. Each node in the edge is separated by a comma; each edge is encapsulated in parenthesis, and edges are separated by a semicolon. An example target output for the word "research" is shown below.

> (research_E, recercher_F);(recercher_F, recercher_OF);(recercher_OF, re-_OF, cercher_OF);(cercher_OF, circare_L);(circare_L, circus_L)

The model was trained for 2 epochs with a learning rate of 5.6×10^{-4} and a weight decay of 0.01. The fine-tuning of FLAN-T5-base was performed on three NVIDIA A100 Tensor Core GPU to facilitate computation.

4.5 Evaluation

Two types of evaluations were performed, string-based and edge-based metrics. String-based evaluation metrics are the current standard in Natural Language Generation (NLG) tasks, and what LLMs used in this project was originally evaluated on. Though they are useful for accessing the presence of important etymological elements by comparing the target and generated texts, is not sufficient on its own for tasks like etymological relationship annotation where structural accuracy is important. For this task, where the correct representation of relationships between words is essential, string-based metrics may overlook errors in the logical or hierarchical arrangement of data. Therefore, an edge-based assessment focusing on the structural and relational accuracy of the outputs is needed for a comprehensive evaluation approach.

4.5.1 String-based Evaluation

The string-based evaluation focuses on measuring the textual similarity between the model-generated output and the target (manually annotated) output. This involves the use of several well-established metrics in NLG tasks. Bilingual Evaluation Understudy (BLEU; Papineni et al., 2002) calculates the precision at word or phrase level between the model's output and the reference text. Recall-Oriented Understudy for Gisting Evaluation (ROUGE; Lin, 2004) emphasizes recall, ensuring all necessary etymological components are included. ChrF (Popović, 2015) evaluates the similarity at the character level, making it useful in this scenario where morphological differences between languages are significant. The results are reported in table 2. We observe a consistent and high accuracy among all three metrics.

String-based Evaluation	
BLEU	0.902
Rouge	0.920
ChrF	0.929

Table 2: String-based evaluation results

4.5.2 Edge-based Evaluation

The edge-based evaluation assesses the structural and relational accuracy of the outputs.

Edge-based Evaluation	
Edge Recall	0.905
Language Label Detection	0.990
Language Label Accuracy	0.909
Word Root Accuracy	0.905
Word Root Levenshtein Distance	0.321

Table 3: Edge-based evaluation metrics. Edge recall is the proportion of the etymological relationships (edges) in the data that the model identified, accurately or not. Language label detection reports the proportion of word roots that received a language label, accurately or not, while language label accuracy reports the proportion of word roots with the correct language label. Word root accuracy reports the proportion of the word roots correctly extracted and word root Levenshtein distance reports the average edit distance of predicted word roots from the actual roots.

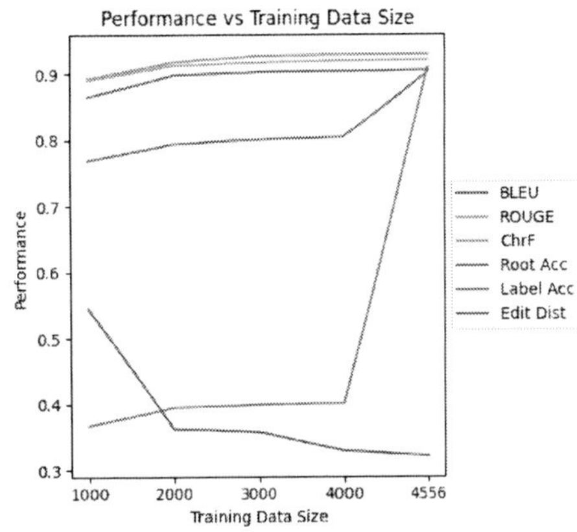

Figure 2: Performance on BLEU, ROUGE, ChrF, Root Accuracy, and Language Label Accuracy over different training data size.

Table 3 reports several relevant metrics. A relatively high edge recall indicates that the model is proficient at identifying the presence of etymological relationships. A high language label detection rate at 0.990 but a comparably lower language label accuracy at 0.909 means that the model is generally reliable in applying language labels to word roots, it struggles to extract and interpret the correct source of the words.

A relatively high word root accuracy shows the model's effectiveness in identifying and extracting the foundational elements of the words, though further improvement is needed. Lastly, an average Levenshtein distance of 0.370 indicates the wrongly identified words still remain similar to the actual words.

4.5.3 Effects of Training Data Size on Model Performance

One of the motivation of this project is to investigate the feasibility of leveraging LLMs to extract structured data from dictionaries. In this section, we wish to explore the effects of training data size on model performance, given most dictionary data has little to no structured annotation. The FLAN-T5-base model was trained with different subsets of the training corpus, including sizes of 1000, 2000, 3000, 4000, and the entire corpus of 4556. The hyperparameters were kept exactly the same as described in section 4.4.2. The results are reported in Figure 2.

As expected, performance generally improves with increasing training data size for all metrics, although the magnitude of improvement varies.

ROUGE, and ChrF scores both show a plateau effect, where performance gains diminish after reaching approximately 3000 training examples. Root accuracy also shows a similar trend, suggesting that the models no longer learns to extract the root words with more training samples. This might be attributed to the fact that these metrics are string-based, similar to what LLMs were pre-trained on, where they excel even with relatively small samples for fine-tuning. Hence, even limited data is sufficient to achieve strong results in these metrics.

Label Accuracy, measuring correctly predicted language labels, and BLEU show a significant surge from 4000 to 4556 samples, indicating that a larger dataset benefits these metrics. The sudden performance jump may reflect a threshold effect, where the additional 556 samples provide sufficient data to predict specific label patterns accurately. It remains unclear why this threshold occurs between 4000 and 4556 training samples. The BLEU score jump is likely due to improved Label Accuracy.

Edit Distance shows substantial improvement from 1000 to 2000 training samples, even with high root accuracy rates. This suggests that while root accuracy was high with 1000 samples, the model made significant mistakes on incorrect predictions. The extra 1000 samples helped the model better predict more challenging words.

Overall, these results emphasize the importance of training data size, particularly for non-string-based metrics like Label Accuracy. The plateau effect in ROUGE, ChrF, root accuracy, and Edit Distance suggests that LLMs can effectively structure lexicographical data with limited manual annotation. However, additional data significantly benefits more complex tasks like Language Label predictions.

5 Resulting Resource and Analysis

Out of the 63,603 entries crawled from Etymonline, 5,361 were manually annotated to fine-tune the system and the remaining 58,242 were automatically annotated with the trained system.

Using a regex-based method to pattern match the result, we found that the exact match rate for our model's output was 0.913, indicating that 53,148 out of the 58,242 output adhered to the expected format. Though the formatting of the dataset is relatively easy, LLMs, such as the one used in this study, often struggle with generating outputs that adhere to specialized formatting requirements, as they are predominantly trained to produce fluent, natural language text rather than structured or formatted data.

Upon further analysis, we discovered that a significant proportion of the mismatches were due to the absence of a language label for each node. This suggests that while the model was often successful in identifying etymological relationships (e.g., detecting the correct word roots and their connections), it frequently failed to append the appropriate language labels to these roots. To address this issue and better understand the model's capabilities in detecting relationships without the confounding factor of label generation, we modified our evaluation approach. We expanded the regular expression used in our assessment to no longer require a language label for each node, focusing instead solely on the detection of correct relationships between the word roots. This adjustment aimed to isolate the model's performance in understanding and reconstructing the etymological connections from the additional task of accurate language classification. After removing the language label constraint, 57,214 entries had the correct format, about 98.2% of the total entries, a significant improvement.

In total, 103,322 relationships were found, with 15931 connected components. The top 5 most connected lexical terms are given below in Table 4, all of which are affixes. This result is not surprising as affixes are one of the most productive morphological units in English.

Lexical Term	#Connections
'un-'	656
'-y'	552
'-ly'	388
'-al'	360
'-ism'	346

Table 4: Top 5 most connected lexical terms. The terms are all English, eliminated language labels for brevity.

More interestingly, Table 5 reports the top 3 most connected Proto-Indo-European roots. It is important to point out that the concept of most connected does not necessarily mean there are the most English words derived from it. It simply means the PIE root had evolved into the most distinct terms which then evolved into English terms.

We also analyzed the immediate word origins of the English words. Immediate word origins refer to the most recent source language from which

Term	Meaning	#Connections
'*kwo-'	stem of relative and interrogative pronouns	12
'*gno-'	to know	12
'*gene-'	give birth, beget	11

Table 5: Top 3 most connected PIE roots.

modern English words were borrowed or derived. We can better understand the linguistic influences that have shaped contemporary English Vocabulary. The top five immediate word origins, other than English itself, are

1. Latin
2. Old French
3. French
4. Old English
5. German

6 Related Work

6.1 Computational Resources in Lexicography

The Oxford English Dictionary was one of the earliest digital lexicographical projects, bringing traditional practices into the digital era by offering searchable and downloadable lexical data (Simpson and Weiner, 1989). Merriam-Webster's online dictionary similarly provides API access for integrating curated lexical information with computational systems. WordNet (Miller, 1995), a landmark in lexical resource development, is organized as a network of synonym sets (synsets) and provides rich semantic relationships between words. It has inspired projects like BabelNet (Navigli and Ponzetto, 2012), which integrates WordNet with multilingual resources. Wiktionary, a collaborative and open-source dictionary project, has grown into a significant resource for structural lexical information. However, due to its collaborative nature, quality and consistency issues arise, necessitating data refinement and filtering for computational applications (Meyer and Gurevych, 2012).

6.2 Computational Resources in Etymology

Etymological WordNet (de Melo, 2014) was one of the first significant attempts to create a structured multilingual etymological database. It aggregates etymology sections from Wiktionary and organizes them into a machine-readable network. Etymological WordNet contains over 500,000 lexical items from various languages and more than 2 million links, offering the first structured multilingual view of word origins and relationships across languages. Despite the significant contributions of Etymological WordNet, it relies entirely on data extracted from Wikitionary, which suffers from inconsistencies due to its collaborative natures and lacks granularity in tracking etymological relationships. Some entries on Wikitionary presents folk etymologies, such as the word "pumpkin". Out of the 2 million links within the network, a major portion of those emphasize cross-lingual cognates and derivational links, rather than genuine etymological relationships. Futhermore, de Melo (2014) uses custom pattern matching techniques to mine data, making it only applicable for Wikitionary, and thus not transferable to other dictionaries one wishes to structure.

7 Conclusion

In this paper, we presented a comprehensive methodology for building an information extraction system that transforms the unstructured textual data of the Online Etymology Dictionary (Etymonline) into a structured, computation-friendly format. Our system achieved 94.4% accuracy in correctly identifying relationships between word roots, demonstrating the feasibility and potential of leveraging large language models for structured data extraction from unstructured lexicographical sources.

Future work will focus on exploring is the transferability of the current model on different dictionary data, potentially eliminating the need for time-intensive manual annotation of other similar datasets.

Acknowledgments

We want to thank Li Liang for the data collection and annotation, and Junjie Cao for the initial implementation of a ranking system. We would like to also thank the anonymous reviewers for the insightful and valuable suggestions. This work is partly supported by Cambridge University Press & Assessment.

References

Robert K. Barnhart and Sol Steinmetz. 1988. *The Barnhart Dictionary of Etymology*. H.W. Wilson Company.

Khuyagbaatar Batsuren, Gabor Bella, and Fausto Giunchiglia. 2019. CogNet: A Large-Scale Cognate Database. In *Proceedings of the 57th Annual Meeting of the Association for Computational Linguistics*, pages 3136–3145, Florence, Italy. Association for Computational Linguistics.

Albert C. Baugh and Thomas Cable. 1993. *A History of the English Language*. Taylor & Francis.

Shane Bergsma and Grzegorz Kondrak. 2007. Alignment-Based Discriminative String Similarity. In *Proceedings of the 45th Annual Meeting of the Association of Computational Linguistics*, pages 656–663, Prague, Czech Republic. Association for Computational Linguistics.

Marcel Bollmann. 2018. Normalization of historical texts with neural network models.

Hyung Won Chung, Le Hou, Shayne Longpre, Barret Zoph, Yi Tay, William Fedus, Yunxuan Li, Xuezhi Wang, Mostafa Dehghani, Siddhartha Brahma, Albert Webson, Shixiang Shane Gu, Zhuyun Dai, Mirac Suzgun, Xinyun Chen, Aakanksha Chowdhery, Alex Castro-Ros, Marie Pellat, Kevin Robinson, Dasha Valter, Sharan Narang, Gaurav Mishra, Adams Yu, Vincent Zhao, Yanping Huang, Andrew Dai, Hongkun Yu, Slav Petrov, Ed H. Chi, Jeff Dean, Jacob Devlin, Adam Roberts, Denny Zhou, Quoc V. Le, and Jason Wei. 2022. Scaling Instruction-Finetuned Language Models. *Preprint*, arXiv:2210.11416.

Alina Maria Ciobanu and Liviu P. Dinu. 2014. Automatic Detection of Cognates Using Orthographic Alignment. In *Proceedings of the 52nd Annual Meeting of the Association for Computational Linguistics (Volume 2: Short Papers)*, pages 99–105, Baltimore, Maryland. Association for Computational Linguistics.

Gerard de Melo. 2014. Etymological Wordnet: Tracing The History of Words. In *Proceedings of the Ninth International Conference on Language Resources and Evaluation (LREC'14)*, pages 1148–1154, Reykjavik, Iceland. European Language Resources Association (ELRA).

Ernest Klein. 1971. *A Comprehensive Etymological Dictionary Of The English Language By Ernest Klein*.

Piotr Gąsiorowski. 2006. The etymology of Old English *docga. 111:275–284.

Luís Gomes and José Gabriel Pereira Lopes. 2011. Measuring Spelling Similarity for Cognate Identification. In *Progress in Artificial Intelligence*, pages 624–633, Berlin, Heidelberg. Springer.

Koustava Goswami, Priya Rani, Theodorus Fransen, and John McCrae. 2023. Weakly-supervised Deep Cognate Detection Framework for Low-Resourced Languages Using Morphological Knowledge of Closely-Related Languages. In *Findings of the Association for Computational Linguistics: EMNLP 2023*, pages 531–541, Singapore. Association for Computational Linguistics.

Diptesh Kanojia, Kevin Patel, Malhar Kulkarni, Pushpak Bhattacharyya, and Gholemreza Haffari. 2019. Utilizing Wordnets for Cognate Detection among Indian Languages. In *Proceedings of the 10th Global Wordnet Conference*, pages 404–412, Wroclaw, Poland. Global Wordnet Association.

Chin-Yew Lin. 2004. ROUGE: A Package for Automatic Evaluation of Summaries. In *Text Summarization Branches Out*, pages 74–81, Barcelona, Spain. Association for Computational Linguistics.

Johann-Mattis List, Simon J. Greenhill, Cormac Anderson, Thomas Mayer, Tiago Tresoldi, and Robert Forkel. 2018. CLICS2: An improved database of cross-linguistic colexifications assembling lexical data with the help of cross-linguistic data formats. *Linguistic Typology*, 22(2):277–306.

Christian M. Meyer and Iryna Gurevych. 2012. Wiktionary: A new rival for expert-built lexicons? Exploring the possibilities of collaborative lexicography. In *Electronic Lexicography*, pages 259–292. Oxford University Press.

George A. Miller. 1995. WordNet: A lexical database for English. *Communications of the ACM*, 38(11):39–41.

Ruslan Mitkov, Viktor Pekar, Dimitar Blagoev, and Andrea Mulloni. 2007. Methods for extracting and classifying pairs of cognates and false friends. *Machine Translation*, 21(1):29–53.

Roberto Navigli and Simone Paolo Ponzetto. 2012. BabelNet: The automatic construction, evaluation and application of a wide-coverage multilingual semantic network. *Artificial Intelligence*, 193:217–250.

Arika Okrent and Sean O'Neill. 2021. Blame the Printing Press. In Arika Okrent and Sean O'Neill, editors, *Highly Irregular: Why Tough, Through, and Dough Don't Rhyme—And Other Oddities of the English Language*, page 0. Oxford University Press.

Kishore Papineni, Salim Roukos, Todd Ward, and Wei-Jing Zhu. 2002. Bleu: A Method for Automatic Evaluation of Machine Translation. In *Proceedings of the 40th Annual Meeting of the Association for Computational Linguistics*, pages 311–318, Philadelphia, Pennsylvania, USA. Association for Computational Linguistics.

Maja Popović. 2015. chrF: Character n-gram F-score for automatic MT evaluation. In *Proceedings of the Tenth Workshop on Statistical Machine Translation*, pages 392–395, Lisbon, Portugal. Association for Computational Linguistics.

Michel Simard, George F. Foster, and Pierre Isabelle. 1992. Using cognates to align sentences in bilingual corpora. In *Proceedings of the Fourth Conference on Theoretical and Methodological Issues in Machine Translation of Natural Languages*, Montréal, Canada.

J. A. Simpson and E. S. C. Weiner. 1989. *The Oxford English Dictionary*. Clarendon Press.

Ashish Vaswani, Noam Shazeer, Niki Parmar, Jakob Uszkoreit, Llion Jones, Aidan N Gomez, Ł ukasz Kaiser, and Illia Polosukhin. 2017. Attention is All you Need. In *Advances in Neural Information Processing Systems*, volume 30. Curran Associates, Inc.

A Language Labels

Below is the complete list of languages and their labels (abbreviations) used to annotated the dataset.

Language Label	Language
PIE	Proto-Indo-European
F	French
ONF	Old North French
AF	Angolo-French
MF	Middle French
OF	Old French
L	Latin
MediL	Medieval Latin
ModL	Modern Latin
LateL	Late Latin
VL	Vulgar Latin
OE	Old English
PGer	Proto-Germanic
H	Hebrew
Avest	Avestan
IndoIr	Indo-Iranian
San	Sanskrit
G	Greek
GE	Greenland Eskimo
I	Italian
A	Arabic
Sy	Syriac
Per	Persian
Ira	Iranian
Por	portuguese
OHGer	Old High German
Adut	Afrikaans Dutch
Ger	German
AL	Anglo-Latin
Cel	Celtic
Tur	Turkish
ModG	Modern Greek
EG	Ecclesiastical Greek
OL	Old Latin
PI	Proto-Italic
Nor	Norse
ONor	Old Norse
Dan	Danish
FCan	French-Canadian
Fran	Frankish
Gae	Gaelic
Scot	Scottish
Hin	Hindi
Yid	Yiddish
Rus	Russian
Algo	Algonquian
preL	Pre-Latin
Serb	Serbian
Aben	Abenaki

ORus	Old Russian
OPro	Old Provencal
LGer	Low German
WGer	West Germanic
Ir	Irish
Nah	Nahuatl (Aztecan)
Mal	Malay
Ch	Chinese
Scan	Scandinavian
Wel	Welsh
Sem	Semitic
Norw	Norwegian
Swe	Swedish
Sla	Slavonic
Jap	Japanese
Ber	Berrichon
Afr	Africa
SerCro	Serbo-Croatian
Aram	Aramaic
Gas	Gascon
Egy	Egyptian
Tup	Tupi
Jav	Javanese
Ben	Bengali
Fin	Finnish
Kut	Kutchin
Guugu	Yimidhirr
Sio	Siouan
Nepa	Nepalese
Dra	Dravidian language
Pol	Polish
OFri	Old Frisian
Canto	Cantonese
Esto	Estonian
Lith	Lithuanian
GaRo	Gallo-Roman
CuSpan	Cuban Spanish
Araw	Arawakan
NEAL	Southern New England Algonquian
Nar	Narragansett
Flem	Flemish
Aztec	Aztec
ByG	Byzantine Greek
Que	Quechua
Afrika	Afrikaans
Ojib	Ojibwa
Hun	Hungarian
Lush	Lushootseed
Dako	Dakota
Cro	Croatian
EL	Extinct language

Complexity and Indecision: A Proof-of-Concept Exploration of Lexical Complexity and Lexical Semantic Change

David Alfter
Gothenburg Research Infrastructure in Digital Humanities (GRIDH)
Department of Literature, History of Ideas and Religion
University of Gothenburg, Sweden
david.alfter@gu.se

Abstract

This paper explores the intersection of lexical complexity prediction and lexical semantic change detection. We investigate the potential connection between changes in lexical complexity and lexical semantics, aiming to uncover how these two aspects of language evolution are intertwined. Our findings indicate that lexical complexity models human annotator uncertainty surprisingly well. Further, we find a moderate correlation between changes in lexical complexity and graded lexical semantic change. This highlights the potential for leveraging lexical complexity for lexical semantic change detection.

1 Introduction

Though seemingly distinct, the fields of lexical complexity prediction and lexical semantic change detection share surprising points of contact. One predicts the inherent difficulty of words (Lexical Complexity Prediction, LCP; North et al. 2023), while the other tracks shifts in meaning and usage (Lexical Semantic Change Detection, LSCD; Tahmasebi et al. 2021). Despite starting with words as their foundational unit, both have gravitated towards considering individual word *senses* thanks to advancements in transformer models (Vaswani et al. 2017) and contextualized word embeddings. While LSCD inherently deals with this concept, research in LCP suggests different senses within a word exhibit varying complexities (Crossley et al. 2010; Alfter 2021; Shardlow et al. 2022). It has also been noted that the manual annotation of both LSCD data (e.g., whether a word has the same, closely/distantly related, or unrelated sense in two given sentences) and LCP data (how complex a word is in a given sentence) is quite subjective (Shardlow et al., 2021; Schlechtweg et al., 2021). Given the shared focus on contextual meaning and the inherent subjectivity of the tasks, we postulate a potential link.

In this paper, we specifically explore whether lexical complexity can explain human uncertainty in annotation. Utilizing human judgments on semantic closeness of words in sentences, we analyze if lexical complexity differences between sentences correlate with annotator indecision. As a downstream task, we also look at whether lexical complexity can directly predict lexical semantic change.

The rest of the paper is structured as follows: in section 2 we contextualize our work and highlight the commonalities and gap in communication between these disciplines. In section 3, we detail the methodological framework, including the dataset and experimental design. In section 4 we present the key findings of our experiments. In section 5, we interpret our results in a broader context, discussing their implications and potential future directions.

2 Related Work

2.1 Lexical complexity prediction

Lexical complexity prediction tries to identify the *complexity* of words in a text, with downstream tasks such as text simplification of various genres (e.g., medical texts (Deléger and Zweigenbaum, 2009), legal texts (LoPucki, 2014)) for various groups (e.g., children (De Belder and Moens, 2010), language learners (Petersen and Ostendorf, 2007), people with disabilities (Devlin, 1998; Chung et al., 2013)). Lexical complexity prediction has been explored in several shared tasks and several languages: the Complex Word Identification 2016 shared task for English (Paetzold and Specia, 2016a), the Complex Word Identification 2018 shared task for English, Spanish, German and French(Yimam et al., 2018), the ALexS 2020 shared task for Spanish (Ortiz-Zambranoa and Montejo-Ráezb, 2020), and the Lexical Complexity Prediction 2021 shared task for English

Proceedings of the 5th Workshop on Computational Approaches to Historical Language Change, pages 137–143

(Shardlow et al., 2021).

Early tasks focused on binary complexity ("is the word complex or not?") while later tasks focus on graded complexity ("how complex is the word?"). While early system relied on feature engineering (e.g., Paetzold and Specia 2016b; Gooding and Kochmar 2018), later approaches use transformer-based models (e.g., Pan et al. 2021; Yaseen et al. 2021) or a combination of classical features and transformers (Paetzold, 2021). However, fully feature engineered systems still perform almost on-par with transformer-based systems; the best fully feature engineered system scored third place in the task (Shardlow et al., 2021; Agarwal and Chatterjee, 2021; Mosquera, 2021).

2.2 Lexical semantic change detection

Lexical semantic change detection tries to identify words that have undergone shifts in meaning over time, mainly as a task in itself, but also for downstream tasks such as OCR error correction (Morsy and Karypis, 2016) or document similarity computation (Chiron et al., 2017).

Lexical semantic change detection is an unsupervised tasks, and systems to detect this change generally use techniques such as word2vec (Mikolov and Dean, 2013) to represent words in a continuous vector space, allowing for the analysis of semantic similarities and changes over time (Tahmasebi et al., 2021). Other systems use co-occurrence information to build matrices and measure similarity between words based on their contexts (Sagi et al., 2009). Pointwise mutual information scores and cosine similarity are often employed to track changes in co-occurrence patterns over time to uncover how word meanings evolve and shift across different contexts (Teh et al., 2004; Gulordava and Baroni, 2011). Some methods use topic modeling to partition information based on word senses, allowing for the detection of sense changes over time (Lau et al., 2012). Topics are interpreted as senses, and new induction methods aim to infer sense and topic information jointly (Wang et al., 2015). Techniques such as word sense induction or discrimination aim to identify different senses of a word and track changes in these senses over time. Recent works use transformer-based models and average pairwise distance and prototype distance to detect change (Cassotti et al., 2023).

Lexical semantic change detection has been explored in several shared tasks for various languages: the SemEval 2020 task 1 on unsupervised lexical semantic change detection for English, German, Swedish and Latin (Schlechtweg et al., 2020), DIACR-Ita for Italian (Basile et al., 2020), RuShiftEval for Russian (Kutuzov and Pivovarova, 2021), and the SemEval 2022 task on semantic change discovery and detection in Spanish (Zamora-Reina et al., 2022).

The main common point between lexical complexity prediction and lexical semantic change lies in polysemy. Polysemy is a strong predictor of lexical complexity (Gala et al., 2013; Alfter and Volodina, 2018), as more polysemous words can occur in more varied contexts. As the context influences the specific meaning of the word, we expect the complexity to vary more strongly if the possible contexts are more numerous. In unsupervised lexical semantic change detection, the context is crucial in determining whether a word occurs in a given sense, and the degree of polysemy (and its change) is directly linked to lexical semantic change. To the best of our knowledge, there is no prior work investigating the role of lexical complexity in lexical semantic change.

3 Methodology

3.1 Data

For lexical semantic change detection, we use the English data from the Diachronic Word Usage Graph (DWUG) dataset (Schlechtweg et al., 2021) used in the SemEval 2020 shared task on unsupervised lexical semantic change detection (Schlechtweg et al., 2020). The shared task covered English, German, Swedish, and Latin, with labels for graded lexical semantic change as well as binary change. The English portion of the data set covers 46 target words, each with 200 sentences split across two time spans (100 per time span). The data was manually annotated using a Word-in-Context approach where annotators are asked to rate the semantic closeness of a word in two sentences on a scale from 1 (unrelated) to 4 (identical); as an additional annotation option, there is 0 which means 'cannot decide'. These judgments are then clustered to derive sense clusters, based on which a graded lexical semantic change score $\in [0 - 1]$ is computed (Schlechtweg et al., 2020).

For lexical complexity prediction, we use the data from the SemEval 2021 shared task on lexical complexity prediction (Shardlow et al., 2021). This data is only available for English. It contains about 9000 words from three genres (biblic, parliamentary, medical). The data was manually annotated using a five-point Likert scale from 1 (very easy) to 5 (very difficult). These judgments were aggregated and normalized into the range $[0-1]$.

3.2 Models

We first fine-tune a model for lexical complexity on the provided training data from the 2021 shared task, evaluating on the trial data and testing on the test data. We take inspiration from Pan et al. (2021), the top performing team at the shared task, and prepend the word to the sentence (see Figure 1), but we omit the genre information, since this information is not available for the semantic change detection data.

Pan et al.: [CLS] genre word [SEP] sentence
Our input: [CLS] word [SEP] sentence

Figure 1: Illustration of Pan et al. (2021)'s input format versus our input format

As a proof of concept experiment, we do not follow Pan et al. (2021) and other teams in creating an ensemble of transformers for prediction; instead, we use a single RoBERTa-base model.[1] We train the model for 20 epochs with the R^2 objective and early stopping.

We then apply the fine-tuned model to the lexical semantic change data set: for each target word, we predict the complexity for each context it occurs in. We then calculate the average complexity for time span 1 (C_{avg}^{t1}) and time span 2 (C_{avg}^{t2}). We then calculate the difference in complexity between these time spans (δ_C).

We explore whether lexical complexity can explain human uncertainty in annotation by retrieving the human judgments for each pair of sentences for each label for each word (29.000 judgments total), including the label 0 (cannot decide) and compare the complexity difference δ_C between the sentences. We rank the labels by absolute average difference $|\delta_C|$ from largest to smallest, with rank 1 being the label with the highest absolute difference in complexity.

For lexical semantic change detection, we calculate Spearman's rank correlation coefficient between the words' graded lexical change score and δ_C. As baseline, we use a vanilla RoBERTa-base model that was not fine-tuned.

[1]Preliminary experiments have shown a worse performance when using RoBERTa-large and XLM-RoBERTa.

4 Results and Discussion

Table 1 shows the results for the fine-tuned model on the task of lexical complexity prediction. For the limited scope of the study, our model shows acceptable performance. Mean Squared Error (MSE) measures the average deviance from the target, while $R2$ measures the proportion of the variance in the data the model explains. A lower MSE and a higher R^2 are generally better.

	MSE	R^2
Our model (val)	0.0070	0.687
Our model (test)	0.0078	0.524
Best model 2021	0.0061	0.621

Table 1: Results for lexical complexity prediction

Figure 2 shows the clustered column chart for the labels (on the x-axis) and rank counts (on the y-axis) for human uncertainty estimation. The figure clearly shows that the label 0 is ranked first in the majority of cases, indicating that a higher complexity difference coincides with human "cannot decide" judgments. Conversely, label 4 is systematically ranked last, indicating that sentence pairs with low complexity differences are annotated as having the same sense. We can also observe a systematic linear decrease in rank counts for labels 1 down to 3, suggesting that complexity difference inversely correlates with semantic relatedness: the higher the complexity difference, the less probable it is that the word senses in the two sentences are related.

	Spearman's ρ
Baseline	0.077
Our model C_{avg}^{t1}	0.014
Out model C_{avg}^{t2}	-0.089
Our model δ_C	0.444
Best model 2020	0.422
Cassotti et al. 2023	0.757

Table 2: Results for graded lexical semantic change detection

Table 2 shows the results for lexical semantic change detection. As can be gathered from the results, lexical complexity prediction in itself does not correlate with graded semantic change ('Our model' C_{avg}^{t1} and C_{avg}^{t2}), but the difference in lexical complexity ('Our model' δ_C) shows a moderate

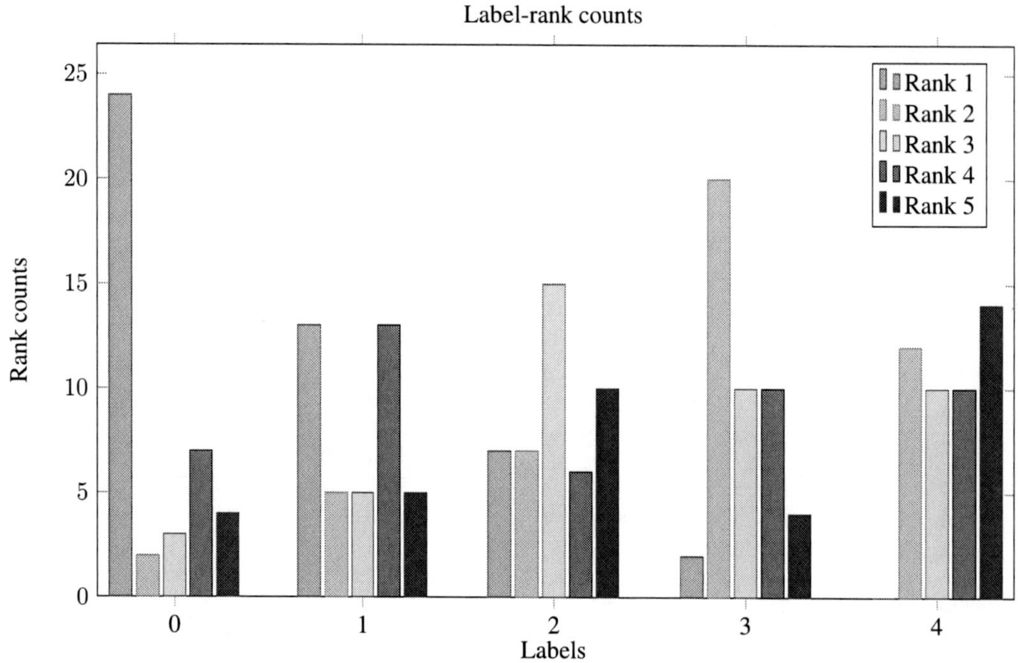

Figure 2: Label-rank counts showing the distribution of rank counts based on complexity difference between the sentence pairs to annotate. We calculate for each label of each word the average complexity difference and rank the labels according to the complexity difference, then aggregate the ranks over all words.

correlation with graded lexical semantic change as calculated by the SemEval 2020 shared task organizers. In fact, this model beats the best result of the shared task, although only by a small margin, and it is quite far behind the current state-of-the-art.

This finding suggests that variations in lexical complexity may be indicative of shifts in word meaning over time.

5 Implications and future work

The findings of this study underscore the interconnected nature of lexical change, highlighting the potential for leveraging lexical complexity prediction in detecting semantic shifts.

Leveraging state-of-the-art machine learning models, such as transformer architectures and contextual embeddings, can enhance the accuracy and scalability of lexical complexity prediction and semantic shift detection.

Our model exhibits surprising performance in graded lexical semantic change detection, outperforming the best result of the shared task by a small margin. While our model's performance would have been competitive, it falls short of the current state-of-the-art models in the field.

In the future, one should extend the analysis to (at least) the other languages covered by the lexical semantic change data (German, Swedish, Latin). However, there are no suitable lexical complexity data sets available for these languages. Hence, it would be necessary to first compile graded lexical resources including different word contexts.

Another promising avenue would be a hybridization of approaches that include lexical complexity prediction as a feature for lexical semantic change detection.

6 Conclusion

In conclusion, our proof-of-concept exploration has shed some light on the interplay between lexical complexity and semantic shift. In this paper, we have shown that pairs of sentences for which the absolute difference in lexical complexity is high tend to be annotated as "cannot decide" by human annotators; this finding suggests that high lexical complexity differences might create ambiguity for human judges, making it difficult for them to confidently discern the exact meaning of a word in the given sentences. We also uncovered a potential inverse correlation between lexical complexity and semantic relatedness. Finally, we have shown that lexical complexity prediction can be useful for lexical semantic change detection; differences in lexical complexity correlate with graded lexical semantic change to a moderate degree.

Limitations

The presented work focuses on English only due to the availability of resources. It would be beneficial to extend it to other languages. However, results may also be skewed due to the fact that the lexical complexity prediction data set only contains nouns, and the lexical semantic change data set mostly contains nouns. Results might thus not scale to other part-of-speech categories. Further studies with diverse data and evaluation settings are crucial to establish broader validity and generalizability.

Our method shows promising results, but we cannot be sure that it is indeed capturing differences in meaning as expressed through the different word contexts, or whether the model is relying on other (potentially confounding) information.

As a proof of concept study, we only fine-tuned a single model. Future work should explore a wider variety of models. However, fine-tuning models can be costly and may require the use of GPUs. We have only fine-tuned a single (smaller) model, as opposed to a larger or multiple models.

The current work utilizes a relatively limited data set. Therefore results should be interpreted with this limitation in mind.

Acknowledgements

This work has in part been funded by the research program Change is Key! supported by Riksbankens Jubileumsfond (under reference number M21-0021).

References

Raksha Agarwal and Niladri Chatterjee. 2021. Gradient Boosted Trees for Identification of Complex Words in Context. In *Proceedings of the First Workshop on Current Trends in Text Simplification*.

David Alfter. 2021. *Exploring natural language processing for single-word and multi-word lexical complexity from a second language learner perspective*. Ph.D. thesis, University of Gothenburg.

David Alfter and Elena Volodina. 2018. Towards Single Word Lexical Complexity Prediction. In *Proceedings of the 13th Workshop on Innovative Use of NLP for Building Educational Applications*, pages 79–88.

Pierpaolo Basile, Annalina Caputo, Tommaso Caselli, Pierluigi Cassotti, and Rossella Varvara. 2020. DIACR-Ita@ EVALITA2020: Overview of the evalita2020 diachronic lexical semantics (diacr-ita) task. *Evaluation Campaign of Natural Language Processing and Speech Tools for Italian*.

Pierluigi Cassotti, Lucia Siciliani, Marco DeGemmis, Giovanni Semeraro, and Pierpaolo Basile. 2023. XL-LEXEME: WiC Pretrained Model for Cross-Lingual LEXical sEMantic changE. In *Proceedings of the 61st Annual Meeting of the Association for Computational Linguistics (Volume 2: Short Papers)*, pages 1577–1585.

Guillaume Chiron, Antoine Doucet, Mickaël Coustaty, and Jean-Philippe Moreux. 2017. ICDAR2017 competition on post-OCR text correction. In *2017 14th IAPR International Conference on Document Analysis and Recognition (ICDAR)*, volume 1, pages 1423–1428. IEEE.

Jin-Woo Chung, Hye-Jin Min, Joonyeob Kim, and Jong C Park. 2013. Enhancing readability of web documents by text augmentation for deaf people. In *Proceedings of the 3rd International Conference on Web Intelligence, Mining and Semantics*, pages 1–10.

Scott Crossley, Tom Salsbury, and Danielle McNamara. 2010. The development of polysemy and frequency use in English second language speakers. *Language Learning*, 60(3):573–605.

Jan De Belder and Marie-Francine Moens. 2010. Text simplification for children. In *Proceedings of the SIGIR workshop on accessible search systems*, pages 19–26. ACM; New York.

Louise Deléger and Pierre Zweigenbaum. 2009. Extracting lay paraphrases of specialized expressions from monolingual comparable medical corpora. In *Proceedings of the 2nd Workshop on Building and Using Comparable Corpora: from Parallel to Non-parallel Corpora (BUCC)*, pages 2–10.

Siobhan Devlin. 1998. The use of a psycholinguistic database in the simplification of text for aphasic readers. *Linguistic databases*.

Núria Gala, Thomas François, and Cédrick Fairon. 2013. Towards a French lexicon with difficulty measures: NLP helping to bridge the gap between traditional dictionaries and specialized lexicons. *E-lexicography in the 21st century: thinking outside the paper., Tallin, Estonia*.

Sian Gooding and Ekaterina Kochmar. 2018. CAMB at CWI Shared Task 2018: Complex Word Identification with Ensemble-Based Voting. In *Proceedings of the Thirteenth Workshop on Innovative Use of NLP for Building Educational Applications*, pages 184–194.

Kristina Gulordava and Marco Baroni. 2011. A distributional similarity approach to the detection of semantic change in the Google Books ngram corpus. In *Proceedings of the GEMS 2011 Workshop on GEometrical Models of Natural Language Semantics*, pages 67–71, Edinburgh, UK. Association for Computational Linguistics.

Andrey Kutuzov and Lidia Pivovarova. 2021. RuShiftEval: a shared task on semantic shift detection for Russian. *Computational linguistics and intellectual technologies:.*

Jey Han Lau, Paul Cook, Diana McCarthy, David Newman, and Timothy Baldwin. 2012. Word sense induction for novel sense detection. In *Proceedings of the 13th Conference of the European Chapter of the Association for Computational Linguistics*, pages 591–601, Avignon, France. Association for Computational Linguistics.

Lynn M LoPucki. 2014. System and method for enhancing comprehension and readability of legal text. US Patent 8,794,972.

Tomas Mikolov and Jeff Dean. 2013. Distributed representations of words and phrases and their compositionality. *Advances in neural information processing systems.*

Sara Morsy and George Karypis. 2016. Accounting for language changes over time in document similarity search. *ACM Transactions on Information Systems (TOIS)*, 35(1):1–26.

Alejandro Mosquera. 2021. Alejandro Mosquera at SemEval-2021 Task 1: Exploring Sentence and Word Features for Lexical Complexity Prediction. In *Proceedings of the 15th International Workshop on Semantic Evaluation (SemEval-2021)*, pages 554–559.

Kai North, Marcos Zampieri, and Matthew Shardlow. 2023. Lexical complexity prediction: An overview. *ACM Computing Surveys*, 55(9):1–42.

Jenny A Ortiz-Zambranoa and Arturo Montejo-Ráezb. 2020. Overview of ALexS 2020: First Workshop on Lexical Analysis at SEPLN.

Gustavo Paetzold and Lucia Specia. 2016a. SemEval 2016 Task 11: Complex Word Identification. In *SemEval at NAACL-HLT*, pages 560–569.

Gustavo Paetzold and Lucia Specia. 2016b. Sv000gg at SemEval-2016 task 11: Heavy gauge complex word identification with system voting. In *Proceedings of the 10th International Workshop on Semantic Evaluation (SemEval-2016)*, pages 969–974.

Gustavo Henrique Paetzold. 2021. UTFPR at SemEval-2021 task 1: Complexity prediction by combining BERT vectors and classic features. In *Proceedings of the 15th International Workshop on Semantic Evaluation (SemEval-2021)*, pages 617–622, Online. Association for Computational Linguistics.

Chunguang Pan, Bingyan Song, Shengguang Wang, and Zhipeng Luo. 2021. DeepBlueAI at SemEval-2021 task 1: Lexical complexity prediction with a deep ensemble approach. In *Proceedings of the 15th International Workshop on Semantic Evaluation (SemEval-2021)*, pages 578–584.

Sarah E Petersen and Mari Ostendorf. 2007. Text simplification for language learners: a corpus analysis. In *Workshop on Speech and Language Technology in Education.*

Eyal Sagi, Stefan Kaufmann, and Brady Clark. 2009. Semantic density analysis: Comparing word meaning across time and phonetic space. In *Proceedings of the Workshop on Geometrical Models of Natural Language Semantics*, pages 104–111, Athens, Greece. Association for Computational Linguistics.

Dominik Schlechtweg, Barbara McGillivray, Simon Hengchen, Haim Dubossarsky, and Nina Tahmasebi. 2020. Semeval-2020 task 1: Unsupervised lexical semantic change detection. *arXiv preprint arXiv:2007.11464.*

Dominik Schlechtweg, Nina Tahmasebi, Simon Hengchen, Haim Dubossarsky, and Barbara McGillivray. 2021. DWUG: A large Resource of Diachronic Word Usage Graphs in Four Languages. In *Proceedings of the 2021 Conference on Empirical Methods in Natural Language Processing*, pages 7079–7091, Online and Punta Cana, Dominican Republic. Association for Computational Linguistics.

Matthew Shardlow, Richard Evans, Gustavo Paetzold, and Marcos Zampieri. 2021. Semeval-2021 task 1: Lexical complexity prediction. In *Proceedings of the 15th International Workshop on Semantic Evaluation (SemEval-2021)*, pages 1–16.

Matthew Shardlow, Richard Evans, and Marcos Zampieri. 2022. Predicting lexical complexity in English texts: the Complex 2.0 dataset. *Language Resources and Evaluation*, 56(4):1153–1194.

Nina Tahmasebi, Lars Borin, and Adam Jatowt. 2021. Survey of computational approaches to lexical semantic change detection. *Computational approaches to semantic change*, 6(1).

Yee Whye Teh, Michael I. Jordan, Matthew J. Beal, and David M. Blei. 2004. Sharing Clusters among Related Groups: Hierarchical Dirichlet Processes. In *Advances in Neural Information Processing Systems 17 [Neural Information Processing Systems, NIPS 2004, December 13-18, 2004, Vancouver, British Columbia, Canada]*, pages 1385–1392.

Ashish Vaswani, Noam Shazeer, Niki Parmar, Jakob Uszkoreit, Llion Jones, Aidan N Gomez, Łukasz Kaiser, and Illia Polosukhin. 2017. Attention is all you need. *Advances in neural information processing systems*, 30.

Jing Wang, Mohit Bansal, Kevin Gimpel, Brian D. Ziebart, and Clement T. Yu. 2015. A Sense-Topic

Model for Word Sense Induction with Unsupervised Data Enrichment. *Transactions of the Association for Computational Linguistics*, 3:59–71.

Tuqa Bani Yaseen, Qusai Ismail, Sarah Al-Omari, Eslam Al-Sobh, and Malak Abdullah. 2021. JUST-BLUE at SemEval-2021 Task 1: Predicting Lexical Complexity using BERT and RoBERTa Pretrained Language Models. In *Proceedings of the 15th International Workshop on Semantic Evaluation (SemEval-2021)*, pages 661–666.

Seid Muhie Yimam, Chris Biemann, Shervin Malmasi, Gustavo Paetzold, Lucia Specia, Sanja Štajner, Anaïs Tack, and Marcos Zampieri. 2018. A Report on the Complex Word Identification Shared Task 2018. In *Proceedings of the Thirteenth Workshop on Innovative Use of NLP for Building Educational Applications*, pages 66–78, New Orleans, United States. Association for Computational Linguistics.

Frank D Zamora-Reina, Felipe Bravo-Marquez, and Dominik Schlechtweg. 2022. LSCDiscovery: A shared task on semantic change discovery and detection in Spanish. *LChange 2022*, page 149.

Can political dogwhistles be predicted by distributional methods for analysis of lexical semantic change?

Max Boholm,[1] **Björn Rönnerstrand,**[2] **Ellen Breitholtz,**[3]
Robin Cooper[3] **Elina Lindgren,**[2] **Gregor Rettenegger,**[2] and **Asad Sayeed**[3]
[1]Gothenburg Research Institute (GRI),
[2]Journalism Media and Communication (JMG),
[3]Dept. of Philosophy, Linguistics and Theory of Science
University of Gothenburg
{max.boholm, asad.sayeed}@gu.se

Abstract

We show that meaning shifts in political dogwhistle expressions (DWEs) are explained by the expressions changing with regard to their "hidden" (in-group) and "public" (out-group) dimensions. We study the association between computational measures of Lexical Semantic Change (LSC) and the In-group/Out-group Ratio (IOR) of four Swedish DWEs. We use a combination of distributional modeling of DWEs in the online discussion forum *Flashback* and data collected from a lexical replacement survey of Swedish residents. We explore several vector-space meaning representation approaches and demonstrate that distributional methods can be used to identify semantic shifts relevant to dogwhistle development, particularly contextual representations from Swedish BERT, SBERT, and multilingual T5.

1 Introduction

Online media is important for political communication, but its fast pace makes it very susceptible to meaning manipulation and deceptive communication strategies. Analyzing communicative patterns in such large quantities of data requires computational methods (Theocharis and Jungherr, 2021). In the context of political discourse, this form of data analysis has been used to combat hate speech and related problems for online moderation.

A key challenge for automated analysis of text is identifying implicit meanings (Magu and Luo, 2018). In this work, we explore computational approaches for modeling the temporal dynamics of political dogwhistles. Following Lo Guercio and Caso (2022, p. 203), political dogwhistles can be defined as "speech acts that explicitly convey a certain content to an audience, while simultaneously sending a different, concealed message to a specific subset of that audience" (Saul, 2018; Howdle, 2023; Witten, 2023). Henceforth, we refer to the explicit meaning of dogwhistles as their *out-group meaning,* and the concealed meaning as their *in-group meaning*. We define a *dogwhistle expression* (DWE) as a linguistic form that encodes this dual function and carries both in-group and out-group meanings (Henderson and McCready, 2018).

Dogwhistles that secretly convey racist or otherwise derogatory attitudes are ethical problems for democratic society (Åkerlund, 2022; Lindgren et al., 2023; Bhat and Klein, 2020; Saul, 2018; Stanley, 2015; Haney-López, 2014). Independent of content, dogwhistles have been discussed as problems for democracy by obscuring political mandate and democratic legitimacy (Goodin and Saward, 2005; Howdle, 2023).

Previous work includes theoretical accounts of how dogwhistles work semantically (Breitholtz and Cooper, 2021; Henderson and McCready, 2018; Stanley, 2015; Khoo, 2017; Lo Guercio and Caso, 2022), experiments that test the consequence of dogwhistle communication for the acceptance of policies and attitudes (White, 2007; Wetts and Willer, 2019), and content analyses of how dogwhistles are used online (Bhat and Klein, 2020; Åkerlund, 2022). Less attention has been devoted to the distributional modeling of dogwhistle meaning (but see, e.g., Hertzberg et al., 2022; Mendelsohn et al., 2023; Boholm and Sayeed, 2023; Xu et al., 2021). In particular, while *semantic change* is essential to the concept of dogwhistle, it has only recently been systematically addressed (Boholm and Sayeed, 2023; Sayeed et al., 2024).

Our aim is to combine established methods of lexical semantic change (LSC) detection (Kutuzov et al., 2018; Tahmasebi and Dubossarsky, 2023; Tahmasebi et al., 2021; Tang, 2018) and survey data from linguistic replacement tests (Arefyev et al., 2022; Lindgren et al., 2023) to model the temporal dynamics of dogwhistle meaning over time. The research questions are **(1)** to what extent are computational measures of LSC associated with shifts in the in-group and out-group meanings of DWEs.

Proceedings of the 5th Workshop on Computational Approaches to Historical Language Change, pages 144–157
August 15, 2024

Moreover, we ask **(2)** how different approaches to modeling meaning compare with respect to the relationship between LSC and shifts in in-group and out-group meaning over time.

We analyse the relationship between rate of LSC and the in-group–out-group dynamics of dogwhistles through four ways of modeling meaning: (i) skip-gram with negative sampling (**SGNS**) (Mikolov et al., 2013), (ii) Bidirectional Encoder Representations from Transformer **BERT** (Devlin et al., 2019), (iii) Sentence-BERT (**SBERT**) (Reimers and Gurevych, 2019), and (iv) massively multilingual Text-to-Text Transfer Transformer (**mT5**) (Raffel et al., 2020; Xue et al., 2021). These methods *are* sensitive to the dynamic meaning changes of DWEs, suggesting that they can be developed for the detection and analysis of dogwhistle communication online. We also show that the pipelines with the large language models (LLMs) are better at predicting dogwhistle meaning shifts than the SGNS-based pipelines.

2 Related work

Methods of distributional semantics have recently been applied to the long-standing study of semantic change (Bréal, 1904). Advances include the development and validation of approaches for studying when, how, and how much words change. (Kutuzov et al., 2018; Tahmasebi and Dubossarsky, 2023; Tahmasebi et al., 2021; Tang, 2018). To study *how much* and *when* words change, the features of the vector representations can be compared. Formally, the semantic change of a word w in a transition from t_i to t_j can be defined as the distance of w's vector at t_i ($\overrightarrow{w}_{t_i}$) and its vector at t_j ($\overrightarrow{w}_{t_j}$):

$$\Delta_{t_i,t_j}(w) = distance(\overrightarrow{w}_{t_i}, \overrightarrow{w}_{t_j})$$

Diachronic word embeddings have been built as static word embeddings trained at time periods $t_1, \ldots t_n$ (Hamilton et al., 2016b; Kim et al., 2014), such as SGNS (Mikolov et al., 2013), PPMI (Levy et al., 2015) and GloVe (Pennington et al., 2014); by averaging over contextualized token embeddings at $t_1, \ldots t_n$ (Martinc et al., 2020a; Kutuzov and Giulianelli, 2020), using, for example, BERT (Devlin et al., 2019) and ELMo (Peters et al., 2018); and as probability distributions over clusters of contextualised token embeddings at $t_1, \ldots t_n$ (Giulianelli et al., 2020; Kutuzov and Giulianelli, 2020; Martinc et al., 2020b; Vani et al., 2020).

To investigate *how* words change, we can analyze how words' positions change in the vector space (Hamilton et al., 2016a,b). By measuring the distance between the vector of a word w and those of other words, the nearest neighbors of w at time t_i can be compared with its neighbors at t_j (Charlesworth et al., 2022; Vylomova and Haslam, 2021; Tripodi et al., 2019). With predefined concepts (or dimensions) of interest (Caliskan et al., 2017), w's distance to those "concepts" can be tracked over time (Mendelsohn et al., 2020). This latter approach enables exploration of conceptual shifts in large datasets, possibly over long time spans (Garg et al., 2018). For example, Mendelsohn et al. (2020) studied the dehumanization of LGBTQ people in US media by tracking over time the distance between the words for these groups and the vocabulary relevant for the analytical dimensions investigated (e.g., disgust and power). Other work has tested the theory of "concept creep" (Haslam, 2016) by analyzing the semantic shift of harm-related (Vylomova and Haslam, 2021) and health-related concepts (Baes et al., 2023).

The present work analyses dogwhistles and how their in-group and out-group dimensions of meaning change over time. Previously, philosophers of language and linguists have tried to explain the dual meanings of dogwhistles (Breitholtz and Cooper, 2021; Henderson and McCready, 2018). The role of convention versus pragmatic inference is one of the main theoretical issues addressed in this discussion (Breitholtz and Cooper, 2021; Henderson and McCready, 2018; Stanley, 2015; Khoo, 2017; Lo Guercio and Caso, 2022). Few attempts have been made to use distributional semantics to study dogwhistles, but notable exceptions exist. Hertzberg et al. (2022) partitioned in-group and out-group interpretations of DWEs in a word replacement experiment, using SBERT. Xu et al. (2021) built an annotated data set for Chinese dogwhistles. Similarly, Mendelsohn et al. (2023) presented an extensive database of dogwhistle definitions in a US context. In addition, they illustrated the ability of GPT-3 to identify dogwhistles, based on prompts with definitions from their database.

We expand on these efforts to study dogwhistles by combining LSC techniques and suvey data for modeling in-group–out-group dynamics of DWEs. Although time is essential for dogwhistles, since the in-group meaning evolves in parallel to an existing (out-group) meaning (Sayeed et al., 2024), only recently have the temporal aspects of dogwhistles been systematically studied. Boholm and Sayeed (2023) used computational methods of LSC analysis to model the rate of change of DWEs in different online discussion forums and found that the rate of semantic change of DWEs observed in the highly politically polarized online community diverged from the rate of semantic change of the same terms (at the same period of time) in the less polarized community, suggesting that dogwhistle evolution is community dependent (Quaranto, 2022; Clark, 1996). However, they did not systematically test whether the rate of change observed for the DWEs was explained by systematic variation in the in-group and out-group meaning of the expressions.

3 Data

3.1 Replacement survey

We use data from a word replacement test implemented via a survey of Swedish residents. The aim of this test was to quantify variability in how individuals understand the meaning of dogwhistles. In the first step, we collected potential dogwhistle words from political messaging in Swedish media. Twelve words were included in the replacement test (February and March 2021). The sample (*n*=1780) consisted of self-recruited panelists, pre-stratified to reflect the Swedish population in terms of age, gender and education.

Panelists were asked to read sentences and instructed to replace a potential DWE in each sentence with one or more words so that the meaning of the sentence remains largely the same. The replacement test was completed by 1,045 panelists, with a participation rate of 51%.

The test was followed by manual coding of responses. A coding manual was drafted and refined by the research group. Coders classified the replacement words into three categories: 1) the implicit dogwhistle meaning, 2) the explicit literal meaning, or 3) word(s) that could not be coded as 1 or 2. In this study, we take DWEs that had high inter-annotator agreement (Krippendorff's $\alpha > 0.6$) and acceptable corpus frequency (at least 10 instances per year when mentioned). We discuss these in the next section.

3.2 Four Swedish DWEs

The in-group meanings of the DWEs analyzed can be listed at a general level. With the out-group meaning of 'suburban gang', the in-group meaning of the dogwhistle ***förortsgäng*** is that of 'immigrant gang'. As such, this DWE works by a biased place-for-person metonymy, similar to *inner city* discussed in US context (Saul, 2018). The DWE ***återvandring*** ('re-migration') has in-group and out-group meanings based on the (in)voluntariness of the process, with a voluntary act as the out-group meaning, while 'deportation' is the in-group meaning. The DWE of ***berika*** ('enrich') is the result of malevolent irony, in response to positive opinions on multiculturalism, where the in-group meaning is the opposite of enrichment, namely criminal and destructive activities (by immigrants). In a Swedish context and elsewhere, ***globalist*** is used with several different in-group meanings, including an anti-Semitic reference to Jews, a nationalistic reference to anti-nationalists (i.e., opponents of nationalism), and a populist reference to elitism.

3.3 Corpus

Flashback is a discussion forum with over 1.5 million users and more than 80 million posts, as of 13 March, 2024 (according to the website's own claim). The topics of discussions are organized in "threads" under 15 general sections (e.g., drugs, economy, lifestyle and politics). With anonymous users, *Flashback* is known for discussion of controversial topics and the expression of controversial opinions, including discrimination and racism (Åkerlund, 2021; Blomberg and Stier, 2019; Malmqvist, 2015). Although hate speech and threats are not allowed by the rules, the website clearly contains offensive language. We here analyze *Flashback* data from 2000 to 2022, on the topic of politics. The corpus, which in total contains 49M sentences (posts) and 785M words, was collected from the Swedish national language data processing infrastructure Språkbanken Text.[1] On average, there are 2.1M sentences (*SD* = 1.4M) and 34.1M words (*SD* = 21.7M) per year.

There is considerable variation in frequency of the four DWEs analyzed in the corpus (Table 1). In particular, *förortsgäng* is much less frequent than the other terms. Moreover, term frequencies are very different in different years, which is reflected in the high values of the standard deviation.

The corpus has been preprocessed for all pipelines (SGNS, BERT, SBERT and mT5) by lower-casing and removing URLs and emojis. Corpus data for the SGNS approach have been further processed by removal of numbers and punctuation;

[1] https://spraakbanken.gu.se/en/resources/flashback-politik

DWE	Total	M	SD
berika	20936	27.92	12.18
förortsgäng	227	0.23	0.26
globalist	31156	32.07	39.62
återvandring	12999	13.19	22.20

Table 1: Total frequency and mean frequency per million per year

separation of compounds that contain the DWEs under analysis as their left-hand element, e.g., "globalistelit" is replaced by "globalist elit" (with space); and lemmatization of the DWEs analyzed, for example, "globalisten" (definite form of *globalist*) is replaced by "globalist" (lemma form). Regular expressions were used for lemmatization and splitting of compounds. For the other approaches, there was no additional step of preprocessing to the steps listed above, but some minor changes were made to facilitate mapping of input words and tokenisation for BERT and mT5.

4 Semantic modeling

Below we introduce four pipelines to test the relationship between the LSC and the in-group/out-group dynamics of DWEs. The piplelines have two basic steps: (a) modeling of the rate of semantic change of DWEs in the corpus; and (b) modeling of the degree of in-group vs. out-group meaning of the DWEs based on the replacements observed in the survey. The key difference between the four pipelines is the algorithm used for modeling meaning: SGNS, BERT, SBERT and mT5.[2]

4.1 LSC modeling

The semantic change of a word w in a transition from t_i to t_j, i.e., $\Delta_{t_i,t_j}(w)$, is defined as the angular distance of w's vector at t_i (i.e., $\vec{w}_{t_i}$) and its vector at t_j (i.e., $\vec{w}_{t_j}$) (Kim et al., 2014; Noble et al., 2021):

$$\Delta_{t_i,t_j}(w) = \frac{\arccos(cossim(\overrightarrow{w_{t_i}}, \overrightarrow{w_{t_j}}))}{\pi}$$

We apply four approaches to build time-indexed word vectors in the diachronic corpus C, which is a collection of sentences from the consecutive set of time periods, $T = \langle 2000, \ldots, 2022 \rangle$. Thus, $C = \langle c_{2000}, \ldots, c_{2022} \rangle$. Vectors are trained only for words at t with a minimum frequency of 10.

[2]Code for running experiments can be found at `https://github.com/mboholm/dogwhistle-lsc-predicition`.

4.1.1 The SGNS approach

A SGNS model is trained for each sub-corpus in C, in the sorted order of T, from first to last. The weights of the model are randomly initialized for the first time period, M_{2000}, but for every other model, M_{t_i}, where $t_i > 2000$, the weights of M_{t_i} are initialized with the trained weights of $M_{t_{i-1}}$. For every consecutive pair in T, i.e. the set of transitions $R = \langle\langle t_1, t_2\rangle, \ldots \langle t_{n-1}, t_n\rangle\rangle = \langle\langle 2000, 2001\rangle, \ldots \langle 2021, 2022\rangle\rangle$, and for every word w existing in both models M_{t_i} and $M_{t_{i+1}}$, the vectors $\overrightarrow{w_{t_i}}$ and $\vec{w}_{t_{i+1}}$ are compared for $\Delta_{t_i,t_j}(w)$. We train six SGNS variants for 100 and 200 dimensions and window sizes of 5, 10, and 15.

4.1.2 The BERT approach

The diachronic corpus B is a subset of C, such that it covers the same consecutive time periods in T, but where every sub-corpus $b_t = \{\text{sentence } s\text{: } s \text{ is in } c_t \wedge$ at least one the analyzed DWEs is in $s\}$. Sentences in B are encoded by Swedish BERT (Malmsten et al., 2020).[3] A word vectors of a DWE w at t is built in two steps: first, contextualised token embeddings of w in sentences from b_t, are built by averaging over the token embeddings of the last hidden layer of BERT that correspond to w in the input. Next, the mean vector of the contextualized token embeddings for w in t constitutes $\vec{w}_{t_i}$.[4]

4.1.3 The mT5 approach

The third approach uses the mT5 model (Xue et al., 2021), a multilingual variant of T5 (Raffel et al., 2020) trained on the multilingual extension of the Colossal Clean Crawled Corpus (C4), mC4, which in total contains 6.3T tokens. Swedish is among the 101 languages in mC4. With T5, every NLP task is generalized as text-to-text problem. The model is similar to the original transformer model in Vaswani et al. (2017), with some alternations of, for example, normalization of layers and position embeddings (Raffel et al., 2020; Xue et al., 2021). T5 was originally developed to test, in a unified and controlled way, the effectiveness of transfer learning on a variety of NLP tasks (Raffel et al., 2020). However, our implementation does not fine-tune the pre-trained model. Rather, our main motive for

[3]`https://huggingface.co/KB/bert-base-swedish-cased`

[4]For some compound words, the tokenization for BERT or mT5 does not perfectly match the DWE part of the compound. We then use the embeddings of tokens that maximize the similarity of the two strings by the Ratcliff et al. (1988) algorithm implemented as `SequenceMatcher` in Python.

using mT5 is to test a recent large-scale transformer. Here we use the 3.7 billion parameter version of the model, named XL.[5]

We build word vectors at *t* as in the BERT approach: contextualized token embeddings are built by averaging token embeddings of the last hidden layer, corresponding to *w* in the input sentence; $\overrightarrow{w}_{t_i}$ is the mean vector of the contextualised token embeddings at *t*.

4.1.4 The SBERT approach

The fourth and final approach uses Swedish SBERT (Rekathati, 2021).[6] SBERT (Reimers and Gurevych, 2019) is BERT (Devlin et al., 2019) fine-tuned for predicting the semantic similarity of two sentences. SBERT has a bi-encoder architecture to reduce the computational cost of sentence pair-regression in original BERT. Reimers and Gurevych (2019) show that a bi-encoder with fine-tuning reaches state-of-the-art performance on sentence similarity. Swedish SBERT is trained with transfer learning in Reimers and Gurevych (2020), where the objective is to make a student model[7] (of an under-resources language, here: Swedish) match the sentence embeddings of a high-performing teacher model[8] (developed for a well-resourced language, here: English) in a parallel corpus.

The implementation of the SBERT approach is in most respects similar to the implementation of the other transformer models, but does not require mapping between token embeddings and the DWE of the input, nor selection of layer, since SBERT output 1 × 768-dimensional vectors that serve as the contextualized token embedding. The mean vector of the contextualized embeddings for *w* at *t* constitutes $\overrightarrow{w}_t$.

4.2 In-group and out-group modeling

We modeled the semantic dimensions of in-group and out-group meaning of a DWE *w* at time *t* by measuring the similarity between (a) the embedding for *w* at *t* trained on online community data (as defined above, sect. 4.1) and (b) the (averaged) embedding for text replacements $R^w = \{r_1^w, ..., r_n^w\}$ for *w* in the replacement survey, annotated as "in-group" (I^w) or "out-group" (O^w). Details on how the in-group and out-group embeddings, $\overrightarrow{I^w}$ and $\overrightarrow{O^w}$, are built from I^w and O^w are presented in the following (sect. 4.2.1 - 4.2.2); each approach parallels those defined above for the analysis of LSC.

Once in-group and out-group embeddings for DWE *w* are derived, we use cosine similarity to calculate an in-group score (*IS*) and an out-group score (*OS*) at each time *t*:

$$IS_t(w) = cossim(\overrightarrow{w_t}, \overrightarrow{I^w})$$

$$OS_t(w) = cossim(\overrightarrow{w_t}, \overrightarrow{O_w})$$

Next, we define the In-group/Out-group Ratio (*IOR*) of DWE *w*, reflecting a normalized measure of *w*'s in-group meaning relative to its out-group meaning (Kapron-King and Xu, 2021):

$$IOR_t(w) = \frac{IS_t(w)}{IS_t(w) + OS_t(w)}$$

To measure the change in *IOR* for *w* over time, we define the absolute difference in *IOR* as:

$$\Delta_{t_i,t_j}^{IOR}(w) = abs(IOR_{t_j}(w) - IOR_{t_i}(w))$$

This study uses linear regression to test whether the difference in IOR (i.e., $\Delta_{t_i,t_j}^{IOR}(w)$) is a predictor of the LSC of DWEs (i.e., $\Delta_{t_i,t_j}(w)$). Regression models are described in more detail below (sect. 5.1), but first vectorization of in-group and out-group dimensions is addressed.

4.2.1 SGNS

For the SGNS approach, vectorization of in-group and out-group dimensions is based on the word embeddings trained for the diachronic corpus data (sect. 4.1.1). A bag-of-words (BOW) approach was implemented to build in-group and out-group embeddings from the SGNS models.[9]

The steps for building in-group and out-group embeddings from the BOW-sets are as follows:[10] first, stopwords were removed. Second, the top 3 words of each BOW set were selected based on

[5]https://huggingface.co/google/mt5-xl

[6]https://huggingface.co/KBLab/sentence-bert-swedish-cased

[7]https://huggingface.co/KB/bert-base-swedish-cased

[8]https://huggingface.co/sentence-transformers/paraphrase-mpnet-base-v2

[9]An alternative approach could have been to build token vectors of multi-word inputs (replacements) by pooling SGNS word vectors of the input and then averaging over those token vectors (similar to the approaches described below). The BOW approach implemented here has lower computational cost than a pooling of multi-word inputs would have had.

[10]We have tested different strategies for selection. Other examples of strategies include selecting the top 3 most frequent words in I^w and O^w without overlap.

their keyness (Gabrielatos, 2018), using the odds ratio, which is an asymmetric measure of the probability of a word in a target corpus relative to a reference corpus (e.g., the probability of finding a word x in the in-group replacements relative to the out-group replacements). Third, we generalize from the selected words, by *adding* related word forms of the same lexeme, using existing resources for Swedish morphology (Borin and Forsberg, 2009). For example, in the replacement survey participants were asked to replace the plural form of the DWE *globalist*, i.e., "globalist*er*" (plural). Consequently, the replacements for *globalist* are dominated by plural forms of nouns, e.g., "elitist*er*" (plural). However, embeddings for other wordforms than the exact ones used in the replacement survey might be relevant for modeling the in-group and out-group dimension. Once the word forms of each lexeme were identified, to minimize the influence of infrequent words, word forms that were not frequent enough to account for at least 20% of the frequency of the lexeme were removed. Finally, after selection and expansion, for each word in a remaining set, its SGNS embedding was collected. The in-group and out-group embeddings are defined as the average vector of the collected embeddings for each set (see Appendix A for examples of words).

4.2.2 BERT, mT5, and SBERT

For BERT and mT5, we represent each replacement r by the average embedding of the last hidden layer (Ni et al., 2021).[11] Since SBERT is designed to represent sentences, there is no need for (additional) pooling of token embeddings. Replacements are represented by sentence embeddings. We define the in-group ($\overrightarrow{I_w}$) and out-group embeddings ($\overrightarrow{O_w}$) as the mean vectors of the contextualized token embeddings for the replacements in I^w and O^w.

For examples of sentences from the *Flashback* training data, with high and low scores of IOR, see Appendix B.

5 Analysis

5.1 Regression models

The relationship between IOR and LSC is modeled by linear regressions (OLS), implemented in Python through `statsmodels` package. We try to predict the rate of semantic change of DWEs ($\Delta_{t_i,t_j}(w)$) from their change in IOR ($\Delta^{IOR}_{t_i,t_j}(w)$). If the coefficient for the (independent) variable is significant, the semantic change observed for the DWEs is explained by their shifting meaning with regard to in-group and out-group meanings. In addition to the significance of the coefficent for Δ^{IOR}, the pipelines defined above can be compared with respect to the total variance explained (R^2). In total, there are 64 DWE-time pairs in the data.

Previous research has shown that semantic change is strongly correlated with term frequency (Dubossarsky et al., 2017; Hamilton et al., 2016b). To avoid having term frequency as a confounding factor between $\Delta_{t_i,t_j}(w)$ and $\Delta^{IOR}_{t_i,t_j}(w)$, we control for the effect of term frequency by having term frequency per million (FPM) (at t_i, log_2-transformed) and proportional change in FPM from t_i to t_j as predictors (control variables).

Thus, we model the following relationship:

$$\Delta_{t_i,t_j}(w) = \beta_0 + \beta_1 \times \Delta^{IOR}_{t_i,t_j}(w) + \\ \beta_2 \times log_2(FPM_{t_i}(w)) + \beta_3 \times \Delta^{FPM}_{t_i,t_j}(w)$$

For comparability, the model variables are normalized by *z*-scores. We assess there being no problem with multicollinearity, since the variance inflation factor (VIF) for independent variables is close to 1 (below 2) in all models. For all regression models, except the ones based on the pipeline for 200-dimensional SGNS models, the residuals are not normally distributed, as measured by the Jarque-Bera test. Under the assumption of the central limit theorem, we proceed with the regression model proposed above, despite nonnormal residuals, relying on our sample size being sufficiently large (*N* = 64, with three predictors) (Weisberg, 2013; Schmidt and Finan, 2018). However, we did test transformations of variables to meet the assumption of normal residuals, see Appendix C. The overall patterns are the same.

5.2 Results

For most models, shifts in IOR ($\Delta^{IOR}_{t_i,t_j}(w)$) is a significant predictor of rate of semantic change ($\Delta_{t_i,t_j}(w)$). That is, the rate of change observed for DWEs using common methods for LSC-modeling is related to shifts in in-group and out-group meaning. Overall, these findings suggest that the established computational methods of LSC detection are, in fact, sensitive to the emergence and decline

[11] For BERT we also tested the embedding of the `CLS` token, which resulted in slightly higher R^2 scores. Here we focus on the mean pooling approach for comparability with the pipeline for mT5-XL, which lacks a `CLS` token (Ni et al., 2021).

	Dependent variable: Δ_{t_i,t_j}								
	SBERT	BERT	mT5-XL	SGNS-*w*5-*d*100	SGNS-*w*10-*d*100	SGNS-*w*15-*d*100	SGNS-*w*5-*d*200	SGNS-*w*10-*d*200	SGNS-*w*15-*d*200
$\Delta^{IOR}_{t_i,t_j}$	0.794***	0.546***	0.555***	0.250*	0.129	0.246*	0.273*	0.184	0.361**
	(0.059)	(0.103)	(0.102)	(0.121)	(0.130)	(0.122)	(0.112)	(0.123)	(0.114)
$\Delta^{FPM}_{t_i,t_j}$	-0.022	-0.078	-0.220*	0.256*	0.236	0.198	0.265*	0.202	0.206
	(0.057)	(0.099)	(0.103)	(0.122)	(0.126)	(0.123)	(0.113)	(0.120)	(0.114)
FPM (log)	-0.265***	-0.236*	-0.451***	0.049	-0.032	-0.078	0.347**	0.258*	0.223
	(0.059)	(0.103)	(0.099)	(0.122)	(0.130)	(0.123)	(0.113)	(0.125)	(0.115)
Const.	-0.000	-0.000	-0.000	-0.000	-0.000	-0.000	-0.000	-0.000	-0.000
	(0.057)	(0.098)	(0.097)	(0.120)	(0.125)	(0.122)	(0.112)	(0.119)	(0.113)
R^2	0.807	0.426	0.430	0.129	0.067	0.113	0.248	0.149	0.240
Adj. R^2	0.798	0.398	0.401	0.086	0.021	0.069	0.210	0.106	0.202
Resid. Std. Error	0.453 (df=60)	0.782 (df=60)	0.780 (df=60)	0.964 (df=60)	0.997 (df=60)	0.973 (df=60)	0.896 (df=60)	0.953 (df=60)	0.901 (df=60)
F Stat.	83.866***	14.862***	15.079***	2.971*	1.447	2.545	6.589***	3.495*	6.302***
	(df=3; 60)	(df=3; 60)	(df=3; 60)	(df=3; 60)	(df=3; 60)	(df=3; 60)	(df=3; 60)	(df=3; 60)	(df=3; 60)

Note: $N = 64$; *p<0.05; **p<0.01; ***p<0.001

Table 2: Explaining semantic change of DWEs (standardized coefficients)

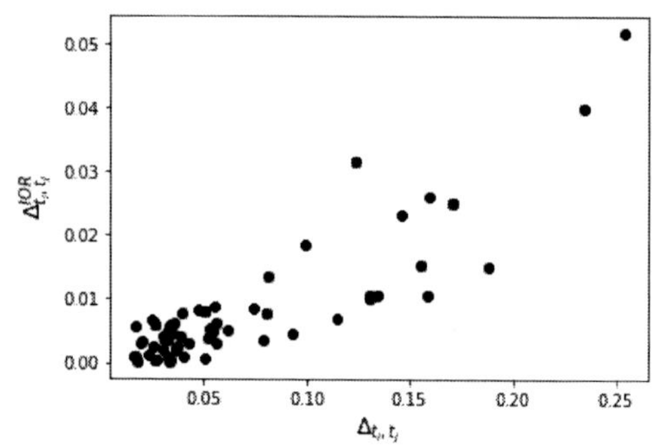

Figure 1: Relationship between LSC and IOR in SBERT pipeline

of dogwhistles. Exceptions to this general observation are found among variants of the SGNS models, where the coefficient for $\Delta^{IOR}_{t_i,t_j}(w)$ is not significant (at $\alpha = 0.05$); namely those with window size = 10. We return to this pattern below.

Out of the pipelines, the LLM-based pipelines explain more variability of the data and have larger coefficients for $\Delta^{IOR}_{t_i,t_j}$, than the SGNS-based models. Thus, in predicting semantic change, these models rely more on the semantic variability related to the IOR, than the SGNS models do. When comparing LLM-based pipelines, the SBERT-based approach shows higher R^2 and a stronger effect of Δ^{IOR} than the BERT and mT5 approaches. For SBERT, the strong correlation between LSC and IOR is illustrated in Figure 1. These observations suggest that sentence embeddings are beneficial for explaining the semantic change of dogwhistles (SBERT), compared with averaging over the embeddings of input tokens mapping to the DWE (BERT, mT5). Note that these findings derive from *pipelines* that contain both the rate of change *and* the IOR. Thus, the different observed can be a consequence of how replacements are represented, how LSC is modeled, or both.

An explanation for why SBERT explains more variability in the data might be that SBERT is fine-tuned for a task that has a similar structure as the one implemented in our pipeline for modeling in-group and out-group scores, namely to predict the similarity of embeddings (Reimers and Gurevych, 2019). It might also be the case that in-group and out-group meanings of DWEs are best captured holistically by sentence representations that give more prominence to the full context of DWEs.

The pipelines with BERT and mT5 are very similar in terms of R^2 and effect of Δ^{IOR}. On the one hand, the large computational overhead of mT5-XL compared to BERT does not result in stronger predictions, as modeled in the present context. On the other hand, the multilingual transformer performs on par with the language-specific one.

For the SGNS models, both the window size and the number of dimensions of the vectors matter. With higher dimensionality of the vectors, more variation in $\Delta_{t_i,t_j}(w)$ is explained. When different window sizes are compared, a U-shaped pattern emerges. For both 100- and 200-dimensional models, the strongest effect of Δ^{IOR} and the highest values of R^2 are observed for window size = 5. However, almost as strong effects are found for window size = 15, but smaller effect sizes for window size = 10. These observations indicate that words used both in close proximity and far away from the DWE are relevant to communicate in-group messages. This U-shaped pattern may be related to the fact that we model different DWEs. That is, for some DWEs, words in close context may be central to the in-group meaning, but for other DWEs, a wider context is important.

As in previous studies, term frequency (at t_i) explains the rate of semantic change (Hamilton et al., 2016b; Dubossarsky et al., 2017). For LLMs, the relationship is negative: the more frequent a word is, the less it changes, which is in line with "law of conformity" (Hamilton et al., 2016b). However, for the SGNS models, the relation between term frequency and semantic change is in most cases not significant; and when significant, the relationship is, unlike for the LLM pipelines, positive.The *change* in frequency from t_i to t_j have no effect on $\Delta_{t_i,t_j}(w)$, besides the case of SGNS, where window size = 5 and d = 100.[12] In both models for the BERT-pipelines, $\Delta^{IOR}_{t_i,t_j}(w)$ has a stronger effect on Δ_{t_i,t_j} than term frequency, while for mT5 pipeline, the effect of IOR and term frequency are in the same magnitude (though the latter is negative).

6 Discussion

We find that the observed meaning shifts for DWEs using distributional methods are explained by their in-group and out-group dimensions. That is, the methods for detecting LSC *are* sensitive to the dynamic meaning of DWE, suggesting that the measures of LSC could be used to detect dogwhistles online. However, it *could* have been the case that LSC measures did pick up on contextual drifts of DWEs, which were *not* directly related to their function as dogwhistles. After all, as an implementation of the distributional hypothesis, meaning is in LSC detection modeled as statistical correlation over context words.

But context can vary for various reasons, not all of which are straightforward cases of change in meaning (Bender and Koller, 2020). Words can be used in the *same* sense in relation to different topics of discussion at different times, which poses challenges for modeling meaning change (Hengchen et al., 2021; Tang, 2018). For example, previous work has showed that distributional methods for LSC sometimes overgeneralizes due to "referential effects", i.e., the observed change of word usage is explained by reference to different persons or events at different times (Del Tredici et al., 2018). In such cases, "the meaning of the word stays the same, despite the change in context" (Del Tredici et al., 2018, 2073). These types of "semantic" (or contextual) shifts are not clear examples of meaning change or differentiation of senses that have been mainly discussed in theoretical linguistics (Traugott and Dasher, 2002). But from the point of view of distributional semantics, it is difficult to distinguish these different aspects of variable usage (Geeraerts et al., 2024). Given a strict interpretation of the distributional thesis, a change in context *is* a change of meaning.

In the context of these potential challenges that have been raised for the interpretation of distributional LSC detection results, our results are notably interpretable. The rate of change of the DWEs is, in fact, related to changes in the in-group vs. out-group "senses" of these words. From the geometric viewpoint that defines distributional modeling of meaning, the shifting positions of DWEs in semantic space over time (as identified by LSC) are repositioning along the in-group vs. out-group axes (as identified by Δ^{IOR}). Given the high values of R^2, for many of the pipelines tested here, the IOR of the DWEs is a key factor in explaining their semantic variability over time.

The above findings suggest that the pipelines with LLMs are better than the SGNS models at the relevant meaning variation of DWEs. This finding is in line with the general trend, with transformer models having substantially improved the state-of-the-art for NLU tasks. The nuanced semantic representation enabled by these models seems to be important also for the related challenge of modeling dogwhistle meaning.

Future research should attempt to scale up the present approach for the analysis of a wider range of DWEs. A key challenge in doing so is inferring and representing the in-group and out-group dimensions of the DWEs. This study used a survey methodology to develop an independent basis for defining the in-group and out-group dimensions of DWEs, but such an approach is costly, especially at a large scale. Another possibility for future research is using definitions of dogwhistles in existing online databases to represent in-group and out-group embeddings (Mendelsohn et al., 2023).

[12] Other operationalisation of change in term frequency (than percental difference) were tested: (non-proportional) raw change in frequency and absolute difference of frequency, but the overall pattern persists: no effect for predicting $\Delta_{t_i,t_j}(w)$.

Limitations

This work applies to the political media context of Sweden. Although we believe that the general methodologies developed should also apply to other national, linguistic, and political contexts, this must be tested in other work.

Since DWEs emerge and disappear on the basis of politically relevant current affairs, it is not possible to develop a sample of relevant DWEs that allows analysis of DWEs themselves as a general category. As a result, our work shows our hypothesis for an admittedly limited set of dogwhistles from which we cannot make global generalizations. However, the fact that the effects are strong is a contribution that calls for future testing of the methodology at a larger scale, with additional terms, and in other national contexts.

Ethics Statement

When creating a system that detects potentially negative social phenomena, there is always a risk of malicious use of the system. In principle, the developed technology can be used for evaluating, for example, attempts to manipulate political discourse. However, we believe that actors motivated to do so can do so anyway and that public research should not avoid the analysis of harmful communication for this reason. Rather, tools should be developed to detect and combat these harmful phenomena. In addition, this work is part of the foundational work that contributes to understanding dogwhistle communication; it does not enable full detection on its own.

The corpus data used in this project were obtained from a national repository given responsibility for archiving Swedish documents of political and cultural significance. The replacement test survey was approved by the Swedish Ethical Review Authority.

Acknowledgements

Funding for this work was provided by the Gothenburg Research Initiative for Politically Emergent Systems (GRIPES) supported by the Marianne and Marcus Wallenberg Foundation grant 2019.0214 as well as a Swedish Research Council (VR) grant (2014-39) for the Centre for Linguistic Theory and Studies in Probability (CLASP). We wish to thank the anonymous reviewers for their constructive comments.

References

Mathilda Åkerlund. 2021. Influence Without Metrics: Analyzing the Impact of Far-Right Users in an Online Discussion Forum. *Social Media + Society*, 7(2):20563051211008831.

Mathilda Åkerlund. 2022. Dog whistling far-right code words: The case of 'culture enricher'on the Swedish web. *Information, Communication & Society*, 25(12):1808–1825.

Nikolay Arefyev, Boris Sheludko, Alexander Podolskiy, and Alexander Panchenko. 2022. Always keep your target in mind: Studying semantics and improving performance of neural lexical substitution. *arXiv preprint arXiv:2206.11815*.

Naomi Baes, Nick Haslam, and Ekaterina Vylomova. 2023. Semantic shifts in mental health-related concepts. In *Proceedings of the 4th Workshop on Computational Approaches to Historical Language Change*, pages 119–128.

Emily M. Bender and Alexander Koller. 2020. Climbing towards NLU: On meaning, form, and understanding in the age of data. In *Proceedings of the 58th Annual Meeting of the Association for Computational Linguistics*, pages 5185–5198, Online. Association for Computational Linguistics.

Prashanth Bhat and Ofra Klein. 2020. Covert hate speech: White nationalists and dog whistle communication on twitter. *Twitter, the public sphere, and the chaos of online deliberation*, pages 151–172.

Helena Blomberg and Jonas Stier. 2019. Flashback as a rhetorical online battleground: Debating the (dis) guise of the Nordic Resistance Movement. *Social Media+ Society*, 5(1):2056305118823336.

Max Boholm and Asad Sayeed. 2023. Political dogwhistles and community divergence in semantic change. In *Proceedings of the 4th Workshop on Computational Approaches to Historical Language Change*, pages 53–65.

Lars Borin and Markus Forsberg. 2009. All in the family: A comparison of saldo and wordnet. In *Proceedings of the Nodalida 2009 Workshop on WordNets and other Lexical Semantic Resources - between Lexical Semantics, Lexicography, Terminology and Formal Ontologies. NEALT Proceedings Series*, volume 7.

Michel Bréal. 1904. *Essai de sémantique (science des significations)*. Hachette.

Ellen Breitholtz and Robin Cooper. 2021. Dogwhistles as inferences in interaction. In *Proceedings of the Reasoning and Interaction Conference (ReInAct 2021)*, pages 40–46.

Aylin Caliskan, Joanna J Bryson, and Arvind Narayanan. 2017. Semantics derived automatically from language corpora contain human-like biases. *Science*, 356(6334):183–186.

Tessa E. S. Charlesworth, Aylin Caliskan, and Mahzarin R. Banaji. 2022. Historical representations of social groups across 200 years of word embeddings from Google Books. *Proceedings of the National Academy of Sciences*, 119(28):e2121798119.

Herbert H. Clark. 1996. *Using Language*. Cambridge university press.

Marco Del Tredici, Raquel Fernández, and Gemma Boleda. 2018. Short-term meaning shift: A distributional exploration. *arXiv preprint arXiv:1809.03169*.

Jacob Devlin, Ming-Wei Chang, Kenton Lee, and Kristina Toutanova. 2019. BERT: Pre-training of Deep Bidirectional Transformers for Language Understanding. In *Proceedings of the 2019 Conference of the North American Chapter of the Association for Computational Linguistics: Human Language Technologies, Volume 1 (Long and Short Papers)*, pages 4171–4186, Minneapolis, Minnesota. Association for Computational Linguistics.

Haim Dubossarsky, Daphna Weinshall, and Eitan Grossman. 2017. Outta control: Laws of semantic change and inherent biases in word representation models. In *Proceedings of the 2017 Conference on Empirical Methods in Natural Language Processing*, pages 1136–1145.

Costas Gabrielatos. 2018. Keyness analysis. In Charlotte Taylor and Anna Marchi, editors, *Corpus Approaches to Discourse: A Critical Review*, pages 225–258. Routledge, London.

Nikhil Garg, Londa Schiebinger, Dan Jurafsky, and James Zou. 2018. Word embeddings quantify 100 years of gender and ethnic stereotypes. *Proceedings of the National Academy of Sciences*, 115(16):E3635–E3644.

Dirk Geeraerts, Dirk Speelman, Kris Heylen, Mariana Montes, Stefano De Pascale, Karlien Franco, and Michael Lang. 2024. *Lexical variation and change: A distributional semantic approach*. Oxford University Press.

Mario Giulianelli, Marco Del Tredici, and Raquel Fernández. 2020. Analysing Lexical Semantic Change with Contextualised Word Representations. In *Proceedings of the 58th Annual Meeting of the Association for Computational Linguistics*, pages 3960–3973, Online. Association for Computational Linguistics.

Robert E Goodin and Michael Saward. 2005. Dog whistles and democratic mandates. *The Political Quarterly*, 76(4):471–476.

William L Hamilton, Jure Leskovec, and Dan Jurafsky. 2016a. Cultural shift or linguistic drift? comparing two computational measures of semantic change. In *Proceedings of the conference on empirical methods in natural language processing. Conference on empirical methods in natural language processing*, volume 2016, page 2116. NIH Public Access.

William L. Hamilton, Jure Leskovec, and Dan Jurafsky. 2016b. Diachronic Word Embeddings Reveal Statistical Laws of Semantic Change. In *Proceedings of the 54th Annual Meeting of the Association for Computational Linguistics (Volume 1: Long Papers)*, pages 1489–1501, Berlin, Germany. Association for Computational Linguistics.

Ian Haney-López. 2014. *Dog Whistle Politics: How Coded Racial Appeals Have Reinvented Racism and Wrecked the Middle Class*. Oxford University Press.

Nick Haslam. 2016. Concept creep: Psychology's expanding concepts of harm and pathology. *Psychological inquiry*, 27(1):1–17.

Robert Henderson and Elin McCready. 2018. How dogwhistles work. In *New Frontiers in Artificial Intelligence: JSAI-isAI Workshops, JURISIN, SKL, AI-Biz, LENLS, AAA, SCIDOCA, kNeXI, Tsukuba, Tokyo, November 13-15, 2017, Revised Selected Papers 9*, pages 231–240. Springer.

Simon Hengchen, Nina Tahmasebi, Dominik Schlechtweg, and Haim Dubossarsky. 2021. Challenges for computational lexical semantic change. *Computational approaches to semantic change*, 6:341.

Niclas Hertzberg, Robin Cooper, Elina Lindgren, Björn Rönnerstrand, Gregor Rettenegger, Ellen Breitholtz, and Asad Sayeed. 2022. Distributional properties of political dogwhistle representations in Swedish BERT. In *Proceedings of the Sixth Workshop on Online Abuse and Harms (WOAH)*, pages 170–175.

Giles Howdle. 2023. Microtargeting, dogwhistles, and deliberative democracy. *Topoi*, 42(2):445–458.

Anna Kapron-King and Yang Xu. 2021. A diachronic evaluation of gender asymmetry in euphemism. In *Proceedings of the 2nd International Workshop on Computational Approaches to Historical Language Change 2021*, pages 28–38, Online. Association for Computational Linguistics.

Justin Khoo. 2017. Code words in political discourse. *Philosophical Topics*, 45(2):33–64.

Yoon Kim, Yi-I Chiu, Kentaro Hanaki, Darshan Hegde, and Slav Petrov. 2014. Temporal analysis of language through neural language models. *arXiv preprint arXiv:1405.3515*.

Andrey Kutuzov and Mario Giulianelli. 2020. UiO-UvA at SemEval-2020 task 1: Contextualised embeddings for lexical semantic change detection. *arXiv preprint arXiv:2005.00050*.

Andrey Kutuzov, Lilja Øvrelid, Terrence Szymanski, and Erik Velldal. 2018. Diachronic word embeddings and semantic shifts: A survey. In *Proceedings of the 27th International Conference on Computational Linguistics*, pages 1384–1397, Santa Fe, New Mexico, USA. Association for Computational Linguistics.

Omer Levy, Yoav Goldberg, and Ido Dagan. 2015. Improving distributional similarity with lessons learned from word embeddings. *Transactions of the association for computational linguistics*, 3:211–225.

Elina Lindgren, Björn Rönnerstrand, Ellen Breitholtz, Robin Cooper, Gregor Rettenegger, and Asad Sayeed. 2023. Can Politicians Broaden Their Support by Using Dog Whistle Communication? In *119th APSA Annual Meeting & Exhibition, August 31 – September 3, 2023, Held in Los Angeles, California*, Los Angeles, California.

Nicolás Lo Guercio and Ramiro Caso. 2022. An account of overt intentional dogwhistling. *Synthese*, 200(3):203.

Rijul Magu and Jiebo Luo. 2018. Determining code words in euphemistic hate speech using word embedding networks. In *Proceedings of the 2nd workshop on abusive language online (ALW2)*, pages 93–100.

Karl Malmqvist. 2015. Satire, racist humour and the power of (un) laughter: On the restrained nature of Swedish online racist discourse targeting EU-migrants begging for money. *Discourse & Society*, 26(6):733–753.

Martin Malmsten, Love Börjeson, and Chris Haffenden. 2020. Playing with Words at the National Library of Sweden–Making a Swedish BERT. *arXiv preprint arXiv:2007.01658*.

Matej Martinc, Petra Kralj Novak, and Senja Pollak. 2020a. Leveraging contextual embeddings for detecting diachronic semantic shift. In *Proceedings of the Twelfth Language Resources and Evaluation Conference*, pages 4811–4819, Marseille, France. European Language Resources Association.

Matej Martinc, Syrielle Montariol, Elaine Zosa, and Lidia Pivovarova. 2020b. Discovery Team at SemEval-2020 Task 1: Context-sensitive Embeddings Not Always Better than Static for Semantic Change Detection. In *Proceedings of the Fourteenth Workshop on Semantic Evaluation*, pages 67–73, Barcelona (online). International Committee for Computational Linguistics.

Julia Mendelsohn, Ronan Le Bras, Yejin Choi, and Maarten Sap. 2023. From dogwhistles to bullhorns: Unveiling coded rhetoric with language models. *Preprint*, arXiv:2305.17174.

Julia Mendelsohn, Yulia Tsvetkov, and Dan Jurafsky. 2020. A Framework for the Computational Linguistic Analysis of Dehumanization. *Frontiers in Artificial Intelligence*, 3.

Tomáš Mikolov, Wen-tau Yih, and Geoffrey Zweig. 2013. Linguistic regularities in continuous space word representations. In *Proceedings of the 2013 Conference of the North American Chapter of the Association for Computational Linguistics: Human Language Technologies*, pages 746–751.

Jianmo Ni, Gustavo Hernández Ábrego, Noah Constant, Ji Ma, Keith B. Hall, Daniel Cer, and Yinfei Yang. 2021. Sentence-t5: Scalable sentence encoders from pre-trained text-to-text models. *Preprint*, arXiv:2108.08877.

Bill Noble, Asad Sayeed, Raquel Fernández, and Staffan Larsson. 2021. Semantic shift in social networks. In *Proceedings Of* SEM 2021: The Tenth Joint Conference on Lexical and Computational Semantics*, pages 26–37.

Jeffrey Pennington, Richard Socher, and Christopher D Manning. 2014. Glove: Global vectors for word representation. In *Proceedings of the 2014 Conference on Empirical Methods in Natural Language Processing (EMNLP)*, pages 1532–1543.

Matthew E. Peters, Mark Neumann, Mohit Iyyer, Matt Gardner, Christopher Clark, Kenton Lee, and Luke Zettlemoyer. 2018. Deep Contextualized Word Representations. In *Proceedings of the 2018 Conference of the North American Chapter of the Association for Computational Linguistics: Human Language Technologies, Volume 1 (Long Papers)*, pages 2227–2237, New Orleans, Louisiana. Association for Computational Linguistics.

Anne Quaranto. 2022. Dog whistles, covertly coded speech, and the practices that enable them. *Synthese*, 200(4):330.

Colin Raffel, Noam Shazeer, Adam Roberts, Katherine Lee, Sharan Narang, Michael Matena, Yanqi Zhou, Wei Li, and Peter J Liu. 2020. Exploring the limits of transfer learning with a unified text-to-text transformer. *Journal of machine learning research*, 21(140):1–67.

John W Ratcliff, David E Metzener, et al. 1988. Pattern matching: The gestalt approach. *Dr. Dobb's Journal*, 13(7):46.

Nils Reimers and Iryna Gurevych. 2019. Sentence-bert: Sentence embeddings using siamese bert-networks. *arXiv preprint arXiv:1908.10084*.

Nils Reimers and Iryna Gurevych. 2020. Making monolingual sentence embeddings multilingual using knowledge distillation. *arXiv preprint arXiv:2004.09813*.

Faton Rekathati. 2021. The KBLab Blog: Introducing a Swedish Sentence Transformer.

Jennifer Saul. 2018. Dogwhistles, political manipulation, and philosophy of language. In Daniel Fogal, Daniel Harris, and Matt Moss, editors, *New Work on Speech Acts*, pages 360–383. Oxford University Press, Oxford.

Asad Sayeed, Ellen Breitholtz, Robin Cooper, Elina Lindgren, Gregor Rettenegger, and Björn Rönnerstrand. 2024. The utility of (political) dogwhistles–a life cycle perspective. *Journal of Language and Politics*.

Amand F Schmidt and Chris Finan. 2018. Linear regression and the normality assumption. *Journal of clinical epidemiology*, 98:146–151.

Jason Stanley. 2015. *How Propaganda Works*. Princeton University Press.

Nina Tahmasebi, Lars Borin, and Adam Jatowt. 2021. Survey of computational approaches to lexical semantic change detection. Language Science Press Berlin.

Nina Tahmasebi and Haim Dubossarsky. 2023. Computational modeling of semantic change. In Claire Bowern and Bethwyn Evans, editors, *Routledge Handbook of Historical Linguistics*, 2nd edition. Routledge.

Xuri Tang. 2018. A state-of-the-art of semantic change computation. *Natural Language Engineering*, 24(5):649–676.

Yannis Theocharis and Andreas Jungherr. 2021. Computational social science and the study of political communication. *Political Communication*, 38(1-2):1–22.

"Elizabeth Closs Traugott and Richard B." Dasher. 2002. *Regularity in semantic change*. Cambridge University Press.

Rocco Tripodi, Massimo Warglien, Simon Levis Sullam, and Deborah Paci. 2019. Tracing antisemitic language through diachronic embedding projections: France 1789-1914. *arXiv preprint arXiv:1906.01440*.

K. Vani, Sandra Mitrovic, Alessandro Antonucci, and Fabio Rinaldi. 2020. SST-BERT at SemEval-2020 Task 1: Semantic Shift Tracing by Clustering in BERT-based Embedding Spaces. *ArXiv*, abs/2010.00857.

Ashish Vaswani, Noam Shazeer, Niki Parmar, Jakob Uszkoreit, Llion Jones, Aidan N Gomez, \Lukasz Kaiser, and Illia Polosukhin. 2017. Attention is all you need. *Advances in neural information processing systems*, 30.

Ekaterina Vylomova and Nick Haslam. 2021. Semantic changes in harm-related concepts in english. *Computational approaches to semantic change*, 6:93.

Sanford Weisberg. 2013. *Applied linear regression*, fourth edition, volume 528. John Wiley & Sons.

Rachel Wetts and Robb Willer. 2019. Who is called by the dog whistle? Experimental evidence that racial resentment and political ideology condition responses to racially encoded messages. *Socius*, 5:2378023119866268.

Ismail K White. 2007. When race matters and when it doesn't: Racial group differences in response to racial cues. *American Political Science Review*, 101(2):339–354.

Kimberly Witten. 2023. The definition and typological model of a dogwhistle. *Manuscrito*, 46:e–2023.

Canwen Xu, Wangchunshu Zhou, Tao Ge, Ke Xu, Julian McAuley, and Furu Wei. 2021. Blow the dog whistle: A Chinese dataset for cant understanding with common sense and world knowledge. *arXiv preprint arXiv:2104.02704*.

Linting Xue, Noah Constant, Adam Roberts, Mihir Kale, Rami Al-Rfou, Aditya Siddhant, Aditya Barua, and Colin Raffel. 2021. mt5: A massively multilingual pre-trained text-to-text transformer. *Preprint*, arXiv:2010.11934.

A In-group and out-group vocabulary for SGNS approach

Table 3 exemplifies the words whose embeddings are used to model the in-group and out-group embeddings of the four DWEs in the SGNS approach.

B Example sentences

Warning: the following examples may be upsetting or offensive to some readers.

Examples are selected from the training corpus (*Flashback*) to illustrate high and low IOR values from years with high and low general IOR values, as measured by BERT. To identify examples, IOR values for individual sentences were computed. That is, we compute $IOR_t(w)$, as defined above, but where $\overrightarrow{w}$ is not the diachronic embedding of *t*, but the embedding of a word instance from the time bin *t*. We show examples from the top ("high IOR") and bottom ("high IOR") five of the sentences of a year, measured by their individual IOR value.

B.1 *berika*

1. (low IOR, 2007) *den typen av invandring är bra och berikande och bör uppmuntras*
   (that kind of immigration is good and enriching and should be encouraged)

2. (high IOR, 2010) *kålsvart hår och mörkt hudpigment, troligen hemmavarande i Iran eller Irak, varför måste vi skandinaver berikas med detta drägg?*
   (coal black hair and dark skin pigment, probably native to Iran or Iraq, why do we Scandinavians have to be enriched with this dreg?)

B.2 *globalist*

3. (low IOR, 2006) *jag är alltså globalist, frihandelsförespråkare, demokrat och kapitalist för att detta är det bästa sättet att göra fattiga*

DWE	In-group	Out-group
berika	förstöra (destroy, inf.), förstör (destroy, pres.), utnyttjar (exploit, pres.), utnyttja (exploit, inf.), negativ (negative), negativa (negative, pl.), negativt (negative, neut.)	positiv (positive), positiva (positive, pl.), positivt (positive, neut.), ger (give, pres.), ge (give, inf.), gynna (benefit, inf.), gynnar (benefit, pres.)
globalist	judar (jews), eliten (elite, def.), elit (elite, indef.)	världsmedborgare (world citizen), internationellt (international, neut.), internationell (international), internationella (international, pl.)
återvandring	utvisning, skickar (send, pres.), skicka (send, inf.)	flytta (move, inf.), återvänder (return, pres.), återvända (return, inf.), hemland (home country, indef.), hemlandet (home country, def.)
förortsgäng	invandrargäng (immigrant gang, indef.), invandrare (immigrant, indef.), invandrarungdomar (immigrant youths)	utsatt (exposed), utsatta (exposed, neut./pl.), förorten (suburb, def.), förorter (suburbs, indef.), förorterna (suburbs, def.), ungdomsgäng (youth gangs, indef.)

Note: def. = definite; indef. = indefinite; inf. = infinitive; neut = neuter; pres. = present; pl. = plural

Table 3: Vocabulary for in-group and out-group

människor rikare och utvecklar alla länder som ingår i handelsutbytet
(so I am a globalist, free trade advocate, democrat and capitalist because this is the best way to make poor people richer and develop all countries that are part of the trade exchange)

4. (high IOR, 2008) *globalist-maffian med judarna i spetsen har ju mer eller mindre full kontroll över Amerika, och därmed har dom tillgång till världens starkaste armé*
(the globalist mafia with the Jews at the head has more or less full control over America, and thus they have access to the world's strongest army)

B.3 *återvandring*

5. (low IOR, 2011) *de flesta invandrar p.g.a studier, arbete, återvandring eller för att de har anhöriga i Sverige*
(most people immigrate due to studies, work, re-migration or because they have relatives in Sweden)

6. (high IOR, 2018) *återvandring och utvisning nu, det är enda lösningen*
(re-migration and deportation now, that is the only solution)

B.4 *förortsgäng*

7. (low IOR, 2014) *kan tillägga att vi var ett helsvenskt förortsgäng med 50 % skinnskallar och 50 % fotbollshuliganer*
(can add that we were an all-Swedish suburban gang with 50 % skinheads and 50 % football hooligans)

8. (high IOR, 2015) *ett passivt / slappt invandrarflöde orsakar sånt, och man måste aktivt minska folkvandringen som bosätter sig i förorterna om man vill bli av med förortsgäng*
(a passive / slack immigrant flow causes that, and you have to actively reduce the migration of people settling in the suburbs if you want to get rid of suburban gangs)

C Transformations

To maximize the number of models having normal distribution of residuals, we tested combinations of log transformation of variables. The log transformation of the dependent variable and of the $\Delta^{IOR}_{t_i,t_j}$ resulted in normally distributed residuals for all models but BERT and mT5-XL. No combination of transformed variables was found that makes the error term normally distributed for all models. The regression models for the transformed data are shown in Table 4.

	Dependent variable: $log_2(\Delta_{t_i,t_j})$								
	SBERT	BERT	mT5-XL	SGNS-*w*5-*d*100	SGNS-*w*10-*d*100	SGNS-*w*15-*d*100	SGNS-*w*5-*d*200	SGNS-*w*10-*d*200	SGNS-*w*15-*d*200
Δ^{IOR}	0.640***	0.424***	0.464***	0.286*	0.190	0.272*	0.285*	0.209	0.351**
	(0.066)	(0.092)	(0.091)	(0.119)	(0.128)	(0.121)	(0.109)	(0.120)	(0.113)
Δ^{FPM}	-0.006	-0.043	-0.159	0.259*	0.249	0.205	0.257*	0.207	0.205
	(0.065)	(0.088)	(0.092)	(0.120)	(0.125)	(0.122)	(0.110)	(0.117)	(0.113)
FPM (log)	-0.451***	-0.493***	-0.647***	0.097	-0.033	-0.071	0.400***	0.300*	0.268*
	(0.067)	(0.092)	(0.088)	(0.120)	(0.129)	(0.122)	(0.110)	(0.122)	(0.114)
const	0.000	0.000	0.000	0.000	0.000	0.000	-0.000	0.000	0.000
	(0.064)	(0.087)	(0.087)	(0.119)	(0.123)	(0.120)	(0.109)	(0.116)	(0.111)
R^2	0.757	0.541	0.549	0.156	0.089	0.129	0.289	0.189	0.256
Adj. R^2	0.745	0.518	0.527	0.114	0.043	0.085	0.253	0.148	0.219
Resid. Std. Error	0.509 (df=60)	0.699 (df=60)	0.693 (df=60)	0.949 (df=60)	0.986 (df=60)	0.964 (df=60)	0.871 (df=60)	0.930 (df=60)	0.891 (df=60)
F Stat.	62.391***	23.607***	24.378***	3.709*	1.949	2.958*	8.128***	4.659**	6.889***
	(df=3; 60)	(df=3; 60)	(df=3; 60)	(df=3; 60)	(df=3; 60)	(df=3; 60)	(df=3; 60)	(df=3; 60)	(df=3; 60)

Notes: $N = 64$; *p<0.05; **p<0.01; ***p<0.001
Relationship estimated: $log_2(\Delta_{t_i,t_j}(w)) = \beta_0 + \beta_1 \times \Delta^{IOR}_{t_i,t_j}(w) + \beta_2 \times log_2(FPM_{t_i}(w)) + \beta_3 \times \Delta^{FPM}_{t_i,t_j}(w)$

Table 4: Explaining semantic change of DWEs (standardized coefficients), log-transformed data

Towards an Onomasiological Study of Lexical Semantic Change through the Induction of Concepts

Bastien Liétard and **Mikaela Keller** and **Pascal Denis**
Univ. Lille, Inria, CNRS, Centrale Lille, UMR 9189 - CRIStAL, F-59000 Lille, France
first_name.last_name@inria.fr

Abstract

Lexical Semantic Change, the temporal evolution of the mapping between word forms and concepts, can be studied under two complementary perspectives: semasiology studies how given words change in meaning over time, while onomasiology focuses on how some concepts change in how they are lexically realized. For the most part, existing NLP studies have taken the semasiological (i.e. word-to-concept) view. In this paper, we describe a novel computational methodology that takes an onomasiological (i.e., concept-to-word) view of semantic change by directly inducing concepts from word occurrences at the different time stamps. We apply our methodology to a French diachronic corpus. We examine the quality of obtained concepts and showcase how the results of our methodology can <be used for the study of Lexical Semantic Change. We discuss its advantages and its early limitations.

1 Introduction

Lexical Semantic Change (LSC) is usually defined as the evolution of the meaning of words over time. In the last years, there has been an increasing number of computational approaches proposed to predict LSC between two periods (Schlechtweg et al., 2020; Zamora-Reina et al., 2022) or more (Kulkarni et al., 2015; Alsulaimani and Moreau, 2023). The most recent studies use contextualized word representations and compare how the representations from a later time period differ from those of an earlier period. While some of these approaches use aggregation of pairwise distances between representations of the two periods (Kutuzov and Giulianelli, 2020; Kutuzov et al., 2022), another range of work uses a clustering of a word's contextualized representations to distinguish its different senses, and compare sense inventories over time (Montariol et al., 2021; Laicher et al., 2021). However, this view of LSC is only focused on specific target words and their meanings: it considers change under an *semasiological* perspective. Another side of this two-faced problem is the *onomasiological* perspective, focused on changes in the way a given concept is expressed (Geeraerts et al., 2023).

While the semasiological perspective has been prevalent in recent NLP work on LSC, the onomasiological perspective is widespread in historical linguistics. And one can argue that this perspective has additional explanatory potential for uncovering and characterizing patterns of semantic change, as it takes a more systematic view of the lexicon. For instance, Traugott (1985) argues that the way we express abstract concepts usually borrows words from more concrete concepts; Georgakopoulos and Polis (2021) studied the mixed evolution of the naming of celestial objects and the naming of time-related concepts; Lehrer (1985) showed that animal metaphors of human traits (e.g. *snake* for *treacherous person*) often affect the whole naming of the animal over time. To the best of our knowledge, the only NLP work taking an onomasiological perspective is Franco et al. (2022), but it is limited in scope since they study the evolution of the lexical realizations of the concept DESTROY in Dutch.

One obvious obstacle for any large-scale onomasiological study of LSC is that it requires a concept inventory. In this paper, we propose a novel clustering-based approach that automatically induces concepts from the word occurrences in a diachronic corpus. In line with an onomasiological view, we propose to describe a concept as a set of lemmas that are used to express this concept in a corpus. Specifically, we use contextualized word vectors extracted from XLM-R to represent word occurrences. We rely on a two-step hierarchical clustering to learn the *concepts* from word occurrences at the different time periods. We obtain clusters of words that are supposed to represent concepts as well as a set of concepts that each lemma can refer to. We apply this methodology to a French corpus (the Presto Corpus, Blumenthal et al.

Proceedings of the 5th Workshop on Computational Approaches to Historical Language Change, pages 158–167
August 15, 2024 ©2024 Association for Computational Linguistics

2017), and discuss the quality of obtained clusters and the evolution of clusters and lemmas. Code for this study can be found at `https://github.com/blietard/towards-onomasio-semchange`.

2 Diachronic Concept Induction

We call *concept* the intended meaning behind the usage of a word, the mental representation associated with a word in a given context and abstracting over its denotation. In "*a bunch of people*" and "*a group of tourists*", "bunch" and "group" are synonymous and both denote the same concept. We call *naming* of a concept the set of lemmas used to refer to this concept. In this paper, we use the term "word" as a synonym of "lemma" to avoid repetitions.

Let W be a set of target lemmas. Let C be a corpus of texts spanning from time τ_{start} to time τ_{end}. The time span $[\tau_{start}, \tau_{end}]$ is divided into a set of M periods $T = \{t_1, \dots, t_M\}$. We call $o^w_{t,i}$ the i-th occurrence of the word $w \in W$ in the corpus in period t. We denote O^w_t the set of all $o^w_{t,i}$ for a given word w and given time period t.

2.1 Inducing concepts at a single period

Let us first consider a single time period t and only the corresponding occurrences. The goal is to automatically learn a clustering function that maps each word occurrence $o^w_{t,i}$ to a cluster c that represents a concept. Contrarily to Word Sense Induction that only regroups occurrences around the same word *sense*, our clustering aims to account for concepts shared across lemmas: all occurrences instantiating the same concept, whether they are of the same word or not, should be mapped to the same concept-cluster c. We propose to perform this concept clustering in two steps, a *lemma-centric* clustering and a *cross-lexicon* clustering.

In the first, lemma-centric clustering, an algorithm A_1 partitions each lemma w's occurrences to obtain a set of n_w clusters, as in Martinc et al. (2020), which we simply call *sense clusters*. The j-th sense of lemma w at time t group is represented with $s^w_{t,j}$. For each word w at time t we obtain the set $S^w_t = \{s^w_{t,1}, \dots, s^w_{t,n_w}\}$.

The second, cross-lexicon clustering aims at merging sense clusters containing occurrences with the same concept, and keep distinct sense clusters of occurrences with different meanings. In the representational space of all sense clusters of all lemmas ($\bigcup_{w \in W} S^w_t$), we apply another cluster algorithm A_2, obtaining clusters of sense clusters. The final obtained clusters are our *concept clusters*.

The mapping from occurrences to concepts is done by transitivity: if $s^w_{t,j}$ is clustered in a concept c, any occurrence $o^w_{t,i}$ clustered in the group represented by $s^w_{t,j}$ can be directly assigned to concept c. By extension, we say a concept cluster c contains a lemma w if one of the occurrences of w is assigned to c. Sense clusters of the same lemma w are said to be merged because their occurrences will appear in the same concept cluster in the end. Thus, when in our analysis we refer to the *senses* of a lemma and its degree of polysemy, we are only interested in the *concept-derived senses*, i.e. the set of the concept clusters that occurrences of a word are assigned to and not the intermediate sense clusters. A polysemous word is expected to be assigned to multiple clusters, while synonymous words are expected to be assigned to at least one common cluster.

2.2 Inducing concepts over time

For diachronic purposes, we need not only to consider concepts induced at one time t, but also to align concept clusters of different periods. Following existing work such as Kanjirangat et al. (2020), we propose to learn the clusterings merging all time periods, using all occurrences from C as a whole instead of learning clusterings for each time independently. Doing so, we can track the *evolution of a concept cluster* simply by looking at the occurrences from the different times that are assigned to this cluster. We can also track the *evolution of a lemma* by looking at the different clusters to which its occurrences are mapped over time. Not only does this allow to detect a semantic change, but it is also *characterizes* the type of change (revealing if the lemma gained and/or lost senses).

3 Experiments

We apply the proposed methodology (section 3.2) to an historical corpus. We discuss the quality of clusters in section 3.3, and conduct both semasiological and onomasiological studies in sections 3.4 and 3.5.

3.1 Diachronic Data

The Presto Corpus[1] is a French historical corpus of texts from 1500 to 1950 (Blumenthal et al., 2017).

[1]`http://presto.ens-lyon.fr/?page_id=584`

Most word occurrences are annotated with a Part-Of-Speech tag and the modern form of lemmas, allowing us to mostly ignore orthographic variations over time.[2] We use the freely available "Noyau" part which contains 53 documents. We focused this initial study study on Nouns. For statistical significance and because of the rather small size of the corpus, we selected the 623 most frequent noun lemmas across the overall time span to be our target words, tallying a total of 314k occurrences. In our analyses, we define 3 periods such that they all contain balanced portions of the data (33% of the target lemmas' occurrences): 1500-1699, 1700-1799 and 1800-1949. The 3 intervals share 498 out of the 623 selected lemmas. Unless stated otherwise (as in Section 3.4), our analyses are conducted using the full set of 623 lemmas. A discussion of our selection process and choice of periods can be found in Appendix A.3.

To decrease the impact of orthographic differences in old periods, we partially lemmatize sentences by replacing all nouns, verbs, adjectives and adverbs with their modern-form lemmas. While we acknowledge that these morphological replacements may bring a slight semantic deviation (e.g. singular instead of plural), we consider that overcoming orthographic discontinuities is a higher priority for the clustering to be as little as possible influenced by tokenization-based differences when using Contextualized Language Models to represent occurrences in a vector space.

French-English translations of examples used in this paper can be found in Appendix A.1.

3.2 Models and Algorithms

We use the XLM-R model (Conneau et al., 2020) (large) to get contextualized vector representations of occurrences of the 623 lemmas. For each lemma, we use Agglomerative Clustering with minimum linkage in place of algorithm A_1 to create (lemma-centric) clusters of occurrences, the sense clusters. As explained in Section 2.2, the clustering algorithm is applied on the *whole* set of occurrences for each lemma, regardless of time periods. Word embeddings contained in each cluster are averaged to obtain a single vector representation per sense cluster. The cross-lexicon clustering algorithm A_2 is applied to the set of sense cluster representatives of all words. In our experiments, A_2 is chosen to be Agglomerative Clustering with average linkage. In the end, occurrences are labeled with a concept cluster resulting from A_2 by transitivity from A_1, as described in 2.1.

We choose XLM-R because of its zero-shot cross-lingual transferability to French due to its multilingual training data. We extracted vectors from layers 14 to 17 (incl.), averaging over these layers to get the embeddings of the target word. Vectors of subwords were averaged if necessary to get a single vector. This choice of using intermediate/high layers of the model is motivated by the work of (Chronis and Erk, 2020) who found that lexical similarity (a core aspect of synonymy) was best represented in these layers. We also find these layers to produce qualitatively better clusters than last layers of the model (21 to 24).

In this diachronic data, there is no sense annotation to guide us in chosing the algorithm and hyperparameters. Therefore we relied on our expertise of French for accessing the quality of the obtained cluster in the most recent time period (1800-1949), similarly to analysis presented in Section 5. For a given combination of A_1 and A_2, we kept the set of hyperparameters that provides the highest number of concept clusters containing at least 2 but no more than 5 lemmas in the last time period. This upper limit of 5 was decided from preliminary observations that clusters containing more that 5 different lemmas almost always gathered lemmas that did not share a common concept but were linked by other non-semantic factors (for instance, words that shared a common subword token). In the absence of sense annotations to better evaluate the clusterings, this rule helps ensuring the recall of a maximum number of concept clusters, while avoiding clusters that are too large. For A_1, we tried K-means, Affinity Propagation and Agglomerative Clustering. For algorithm A_2, we tried Affinity Propagation and Agglomerative Clustering. To decide which algorithms to use, we kept the combination that produced the most plausible clusters of size 2 to 5 in this period, i.e. clusters containing actual (near-)synonyms. This process resulted in our preference for Agglomerative Clustering. More details on tried hyperparameter values in Appendix A.2.

Our double-clustering methodology using Agglomerative Clustering was benchmarked among other systems in a parallel study conducted in Liétard et al. (2024) on SemCor, a synchronic English corpus annotated with concepts from the original

[2]For the method to be applied on unannotated data, one could use a syntactic parser/lemmatizer with special rules for orthographic changes (e.g. VARD2, Baron and Rayson 2008).

Category	Total	Cluster size 2	3	4
Nb. of clusters	101	62	29	10
Synonyms	27%	32%	24%	0%
Near-synonyms	20%	15%	28%	30%
Lexical / topical	40%	42%	38%	40%
Invalid cluster	13%	11%	10%	30%

Table 1: Categorization of small induced concept-clusters in 1800-1949. Invalid clusters are those showing no semantic relation. Raw counts in Appendix A.6.

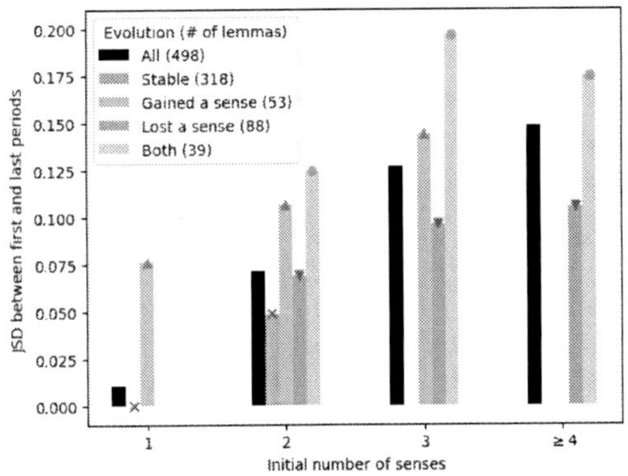

Figure 1: JSD and detected type of evolution of lemmas with respect to their initial number of senses. Missing points (no bar and no marker) indicate that no lemma in this category of evolution had this initial number of senses. Stable lemmas with 1 sense have a JSD of 0.

Princeton WordNet. It achieved the best results reaching a F_1 score of 0.60 and a precision of 0.80.

Improvement of the model selection criterion used in this initial study is left for future work.

3.3 Analysis of Induced Concepts

With the chosen clustering algorithms and corresponding hyperparameters, we obtain a total of 867 concept-clusters. In each period, 40% of the 867 clusters are not represented and another 40% are expressed with only a single lemma. In the 265 (31%) that are instantiated in *all* three periods, 54% of them also only contain a single lemma. This particular observation is in line with Clark (1993)'s principle of Conventionality : *"For certain meanings, there is a form that speakers expect to be used in the language community"*. These distribution details can be found in Appendix A.5. We also found that while only 16% of concept clusters contain multiple lemmas, 46% of words have at least two senses:[3] *polysemy* is a more frequent phenomenon that *synonymy*. We also noticed that a small fraction of clusters (less than 7) are very large and gather lemmas not based on semantic similarity (e.g. based on a common subwords after being processed by the tokenizer (e.g. "autor**ité**", "post**érité**")).

Clusters of smaller sizes are more reliable. Out of the 867 clusters, we manually evaluated the 101 concept-clusters of 2 to 4 lemmas in the last time interval, and the distribution of our annotations is displayed in Table 5. We focused only on the last time period because it is the closest to the current state of French. Only 10% of these small clusters are to be considered invalid. Around 30% are actual (cognitive) synonyms, and 20% are near-synonyms,[4] i.e. words that are not absolute synonyms but overlapping in meaning (e.g. "bourse", "fortune", "richesse", "trésor" denote an individual's wealth at different scales). The remainder exhibits a lexical (like hyper/hyponyms, antonyms, etc.) or another topical relation between words (e.g. "journée", "nuit", "soir"). This kind of clusters can be seen as partial semantic fields. Although they are not synonyms, we argue that they are still interesting for the study of LSC. For instance, the disappearance of a lemma from such a cluster could indicate a transfer of its unique semantic load to another word.

Concept Evolution	#Concepts
Expanded naming	27 (10%)
Shrinked naming	5 (2%)
Both	6 (2%)
Identical naming	227 (86%)

Table 2: Evolution of concept-clusters over time.

3.4 Evolution of Target Lemmas

In this section, we discuss the semantic evolution of target lemmas, i.e. a semasiological view. Here we only focus on the 498 (out of 623) lemmas that appear in every period and look at their concept-derived senses. We use these sense inventories to distinguish 4 categories of evolution a lemma can undergo. A lemma *gained a sense* if one of its senses in the last period is new compared to the first period. In the reverse scenario, we say the

[3]average polysemy: 2.28 senses per word ; average synonymy: 1.15 word per concepts

[4]using definitions of scales of synonymy provided by Stanojevic (2009).

lemma *lost a sense*. A lemma can also *both* gain and loose a sense between the first and the last time periods. A lemma is said to be *stable* if none of these cases apply.

Prior works like Giulianelli (2019) have proposed continuous measures of semantic change based on distribution in sense inventories. For each target word, we compute the Jensen Shannon Divergence (JSD) between the distribution of concept to which its occurrences are assigned in the first period and those of the last period. Both the categorical and the continuous approaches reflect LSC, the former allowing to charaterize the type of change and the latter accounting for the relative frequency of each sense.

Let us now consider the relation between LSC and polysemy. In Figure 1, we show these two measures of semantic change (evolution category and averaged JSD) with respect to the number of senses. 318 target lemmas out of 498 are *stable* in meaning and have lower JSD. Note that these stable lemmas have a very low number of senses (1 or 2). Conversely, lemmas with stronger semantic change are those with many senses. They are more prone to loose and/or gain a sense over time. We also find a significant (p-value < 0.01) positive correlation between the initial number of senses and JSD. This holds even if we only consider those with at east 2 initial senses. This observation echoes the Law of Innovation proposed by Hamilton et al. (2016) and studied by Luo and Xu (2018), stating that polysemy is positively correlated with semantic change.

3.5 Evolution of Induced Concepts

In this section, we adopt an onomasiological point-of-view. Let us focus on the 265 concepts that are instantiated at all time intervals. We are interested in the evolution of the naming of a given concept over time, i.e. changes in the set of lemmas appearing in the corresponding cluster between the first time interval (1500-1699) and the last one (1800-1949). Such a naming may have *expanded* (gained lemmas), *shrinked* (lost lemmas) or both, or neither and remained *identical*. The distribution of these cases is presented in Table 2

86% of induced clusters kept an identical naming, which we expected because we had no difficulty to understand the meaning of texts from 1550 in modern spelling.

In expanded-naming clusters, we find that it results in most cases from new lemmas *appearing* later in the corpus. We search their history in the TLFi, a reference dictionary for French[5], and find the introduction of the word in the corpus often coincides with a new meaning that is more general (less specific) than existing ones, and the cluster to which the new word is assigned indeed corresponds to this emerging sense. For instance, the word "tribu" appeared in the 1700-1799 interval in the corpus and is clustered with "peuple." The TLFi indicates that it was in 1734 that "tribu" acquired its new meaning of "*social group based on ethnic kinship*". Yet, we cannot verify that the introduction is caused by the new meaning. In other cases, the introduced word does not have existing senses and is newly created at the time of its appearence in the corpus (e.g. "incendie" (clustered with "feu"), only attested past 1600 in the TLFi).

In the case of shrinked-naming concepts, we can distinguish clusters in which a lemma disappeared from the corpus (e.g. "parquoi", old alternative to "pourquoi" with which it was clustered at the begining) and clusters in which a lemma was removed from the cluster while still existing (e.g. "amitié", no longer clustered with "amour", as its use for romantic feelings became old-fashioned.)

4 Conclusion

In this paper, we proposed a new methodology for inducing concepts from word occurrences. We mapped each word to a set of concepts and each concept to a set of words at different time period. Using historical data in French, we made of proof-of-concept of this methodology and showed in an initial study that this approach allows to characterize the evolution of a word's sense inventory, as well as those of a concept's naming. This offers a promising direction and can lead to a better understanding of Lexical Semantic Change and its *systemic* aspects, enabling the investigation of both the semasiological and the onomasiological aspect of Lexical Semantic Change.

5 Limitations

Without access to sense-annotated diachronic data, we cannot evaluate with certainty the quality of induced concept-clusters. Therefore, while we conducted a qualitative evaluation on a portion of the clusters at the lemma level, we cannot evaluate the precision of the clustering at the occurrence level, neither whether we retrieved all actual concepts.

[5]http://atilf.atilf.fr/

To select the best set of hyperparameters, we choose to maximize the number of obtained clusters containing between 2 and 5 lemmas. We discarded the conventional use of statistical criterion such as Silhouette score because (i) this score puts an assumption on the shape/density of clusters and we don't believe it applies ; (ii) Martinc et al. (2020) already showed that Silhouette score was not satisfying when inducing senses for Lexical Semantic Change. Our criterion is inspired by the objective to retrieve a maximum number of concept and complete naming, and the observation that clusters of more than 5 lemmas are usually noisy and invalid. Without annotated data, we cannot ascertain how good this heuristic is. A future study could attempt to compare different heuristics to determine the most relevant to induce concepts.

Prior studies of LSC with word-sense clustering (Martinc et al., 2020; Kutuzov et al., 2022) found that clustering in raw vector spaces from Language Models sometimes find clusters of word *usages* instead of actual word *meanings*, which may happen in our lemma-centric clustering. We think the impact of this in the onomasiological setting is limited; this may explain the number of clusters actually corresponding to lexical/topical relations instead of actual (near-)synonymy. Improving the lemma-centric clustering to avoid this could increase the precision of obtained clusters in future studies.

The small size and the sparse nature of the corpus prevents detailed analysis and fine-grained results. Taking smaller time periods lead to very unbalanced number of lemmas/occurrences, and the 18th century is prominent compared to other.

The fact that a lemma is missing at a given period does not necessarily mean that it was not used at all at the time; it could be just an artefact of the small size of the corpus.

Our clustering approach appears to group together word tokenized in multiple subwords, without actual semantic relation between them. Further research could be made about these invalid clusters and how to parse them into plausible clusters.

Acknowledgments

We gratefully thank the anynymous reviewers for their insightful comments. This research was funded by Inria Exploratory Action COMANCHE.

References

Ashjan Alsulaimani and Erwan Moreau. 2023. Improving diachronic word sense induction with a nonparametric Bayesian method. In *Findings of the Association for Computational Linguistics: ACL 2023*, pages 8908–8925, Toronto, Canada. Association for Computational Linguistics.

Alistair Baron and Paul Rayson. 2008. VARD2 : a tool for dealing with spelling variation in historical corpora. In *Proceedings of the Postgraduate Conference in Corpus Linguistics*. Aston University, Birmingham, UK.

Peter Blumenthal, Sascha Diwersy, Achille Falaise, Marie-Hélène Lay, Gilles Sourvay, and Denis Vigier. 2017. Presto, un corpus diachronique pour le français des xvie-xxe siècles. In *Actes de la 24eme conférence sur le Traitement Automatique des Langues Naturelles-TALN*, volume 17.

Gabriella Chronis and Katrin Erk. 2020. When is a bishop not like a rook? when it's like a rabbi! multi-prototype BERT embeddings for estimating semantic relationships. In *Proceedings of the 24th Conference on Computational Natural Language Learning*, pages 227–244, Online. Association for Computational Linguistics.

Eve V. Clark. 1993. Conventionality and contrast. In *The Lexicon in Acquisition*, Cambridge Studies in Linguistics, page 67–83. Cambridge University Press.

Alexis Conneau, Kartikay Khandelwal, Naman Goyal, Vishrav Chaudhary, Guillaume Wenzek, Francisco Guzmán, Edouard Grave, Myle Ott, Luke Zettlemoyer, and Veselin Stoyanov. 2020. Unsupervised cross-lingual representation learning at scale. In *Proceedings of the 58th Annual Meeting of the Association for Computational Linguistics*, pages 8440–8451, Online. Association for Computational Linguistics.

Karlien Franco, Mariana Montes, and Kris Heylen. 2022. Deconstructing destruction: A cognitive linguistics perspective on a computational analysis of diachronic change. In *Proceedings of the 3rd Workshop on Computational Approaches to Historical Language Change*, pages 23–32, Dublin, Ireland. Association for Computational Linguistics.

Dirk Geeraerts, Dirk Speelman, Kris Heylen, Mariana Montes, Stefano De Pascale, Karlien Franco, and Michael Lang. 2023. *Lexical variation and change*. Oxford University Press, London, England.

Thanasis Georgakopoulos and Stéphane Polis. 2021. Lexical diachronic semantic maps: Mapping the evolution of time-related lexemes. *Journal of Historical Linguistics*, 11(3):367–420. ISBN: 2210-2116 Publisher: John Benjamins Type: https://doi.org/10.1075/jhl.19018.geo.

Mario Giulianelli. 2019. *Lexical Semantic Change Analysis with Contextualised Word Representations*. University of Amsterdam - Institute for logic, Language and computation.

William L. Hamilton, Jure Leskovec, and Dan Jurafsky. 2016. Diachronic word embeddings reveal statistical laws of semantic change. In *Proceedings of the 54th Annual Meeting of the Association for Computational Linguistics (Volume 1: Long Papers)*, pages 1489–1501, Berlin, Germany. Association for Computational Linguistics.

Vani Kanjirangat, Sandra Mitrovic, Alessandro Antonucci, and Fabio Rinaldi. 2020. SST-BERT at SemEval-2020 task 1: Semantic shift tracing by clustering in BERT-based embedding spaces. In *Proceedings of the Fourteenth Workshop on Semantic Evaluation*, pages 214–221, Barcelona (online). International Committee for Computational Linguistics.

Vivek Kulkarni, Rami Al-Rfou, Bryan Perozzi, and Steven Skiena. 2015. Statistically significant detection of linguistic change. In *Proceedings of the 24th International Conference on World Wide Web*, WWW '15, page 625–635, Republic and Canton of Geneva, CHE. International World Wide Web Conferences Steering Committee.

Andrey Kutuzov and Mario Giulianelli. 2020. UiO-UvA at SemEval-2020 task 1: Contextualised embeddings for lexical semantic change detection. In *Proceedings of the Fourteenth Workshop on Semantic Evaluation*, pages 126–134, Barcelona (online). International Committee for Computational Linguistics.

Andrey Kutuzov, Erik Velldal, and Lilja Øvrelid. 2022. Contextualized embeddings for semantic change detection: Lessons learned. In *Northern European Journal of Language Technology, Volume 8*, Copenhagen, Denmark. Northern European Association of Language Technology.

Severin Laicher, Sinan Kurtyigit, Dominik Schlechtweg, Jonas Kuhn, and Sabine Schulte im Walde. 2021. Explaining and improving BERT performance on lexical semantic change detection. In *Proceedings of the 16th Conference of the European Chapter of the Association for Computational Linguistics: Student Research Workshop*, pages 192–202, Online. Association for Computational Linguistics.

Adrienne Lehrer. 1985. *The influence of semantic fields on semantic change*, pages 283–296. De Gruyter Mouton, Berlin, New York.

Bastien Liétard, Pascal Denis, and Mikaella Keller. 2024. To word senses and beyond: Inducing concepts with contextualized language models. *Preprint*, arXiv:2406.20054.

Yiwei Luo and Yang Xu. 2018. Stability in the temporal dynamics of word meanings. In *CogSci*.

Matej Martinc, Syrielle Montariol, Elaine Zosa, and Lidia Pivovarova. 2020. Capturing evolution in word usage: Just add more clusters? In *Companion Proceedings of the Web Conference 2020*, WWW '20, page 343–349, New York, NY, USA. Association for Computing Machinery.

Syrielle Montariol, Matej Martinc, and Lidia Pivovarova. 2021. Scalable and interpretable semantic change detection. In *Proceedings of the 2021 Conference of the North American Chapter of the Association for Computational Linguistics: Human Language Technologies*, pages 4642–4652, Online. Association for Computational Linguistics.

Dominik Schlechtweg, Barbara McGillivray, Simon Hengchen, Haim Dubossarsky, and Nina Tahmasebi. 2020. SemEval-2020 task 1: Unsupervised lexical semantic change detection. In *Proceedings of the Fourteenth Workshop on Semantic Evaluation*, pages 1–23, Barcelona (online). International Committee for Computational Linguistics.

Maja Stanojevic. 2009. Cognitive synonymy: A general overview. *Facta Universitatis, Series: Linguistics and Literature*, 7(2):193–200.

Elizabeth Closs Traugott. 1985. On regularity in semantic change. *Journal of Literary Semantics*, 14(3):155–173.

Frank D. Zamora-Reina, Felipe Bravo-Marquez, and Dominik Schlechtweg. 2022. LSCDiscovery: A shared task on semantic change discovery and detection in Spanish. In *Proceedings of the 3rd Workshop on Computational Approaches to Historical Language Change*, pages 149–164, Dublin, Ireland. Association for Computational Linguistics.

A Appendix

A.1 French-English translations

In this paper, we used a number of exemples in French, as our experimental data were in French. Translations can be found in Table 3.

A.2 Representations, Algorihtms, Hyperparameters

For k-means as A_1, we tried values of k between 2 and 10. For both A_1 and A_2, when using Agglomerative Clustering, we tried average, minimum and maximum linkage. We set a linkage threshold below which clusters are merged iteratively. Calling μ the average distance between occurrences of a considered set of occurrences, and σ the standard deviation, we set the value of this threshold to $\mu + n \times \sigma$, with n an hyperparameter. When using Agglomerative Clustering for A_1 on each set of occurrences of a lemma, n is shared across all lemmas but the linkage threshold is computed using each set of occurrences. As a result, we obtain a dynamic number of clusters that is more suited to

French	English
amitié	friendship, affection
amour	love
autorité	authority
bourse	purse
ennui	boredom
envie	envy
feu	fire
fortune	fortune, wealth
groupe	group
incendie	fire (vast and uncontrolled)
jour	day
journée	day, daytime
parquoi	old alternative for *pourquoi*
peuple	people
postérité	posterity
pourquoi	the *why*, an explaination
réseau	network
richesse	wealth
soir	evening
système	system
trésor	treasure
tribu	tribe

Table 3: French-English translations

each lemma. We tried value of n between -2 and +2.

A.3 Selection criterion

We find that the data are noisy, and a number of lemmas do not appear often. Indeed, the number of documents in the corpus is relatively small, leaving room for sparsity and discontinuity in the representations of lemmas. Therefore, we had to select a subset of them.

To this extent, we partition it into 50 years time spans. Doing so, we ensured that the number of documents was balanced between spans, and that we can control that selected lemmas are represented *frequently enough* and not sparsely across too large spans.

In order to mitigate the noise resulting from the sparse nature of the data, we apply the following selection criteria. We keep only lemmas :

- appearing in at least 3 consecutive spans,
- occurring at least 10 times in the overall corpus,
- at least 3 times in each spans where they are present,
- composed of a single word and of 3 characters at least.
- appearing in the first or the last span or both.

Doing so, we mitigate the risk for selected lemmas to be subject to unexplained discontinuity over time. The last criterion is applied because our analyses are conducted mainly by comparing early and late time periods.

After selection however, these 50 years long spans are not balanced enough in the corpus for fair analyses. See Appendix A.4.

A.4 Corpus description and choice of periods

Time span	#Doc.	$\|W\|$	#Occ.	Ratio
1500	6	484	12 014	24.8
1550	5	523	30 206	57.8
1600	6	537	35 202	65.6
1650	6	541	34 177	63.2
1700	4	547	10 729	19.6
1750	8	608	89 179	146.7
1800	6	614	46 778	76.2
1850	6	611	33 823	55.4
1900	6	599	22 146	37.0
Total	53	623	314 254	504.4

Table 4: Number of documents, of target words, of occurrences and ratio between occurrences and target words at the different spans (half centuries).

The number of documents, of selected target words and of their occurrences can be found in Table 4. Note that the number of occurrences is not uniform across the spans.

We remark here that the 18th century is an outlier. Its first half contains the lowest number of occurrences, but its second half is very big compared to any other span, containing around 28% of occurrences on its own.

Figure 2 shows that the number of target lemmas is not equally distributed over 50-years time spans, and that only a subset of them (425 out of 623) is actually appearing in all spans. The induction of concepts suffers a similar imbalance.

We posit three possible reasons for a lemma to be missing in a time span : (i) the lemma was not used in the language at the time, whether is appears later

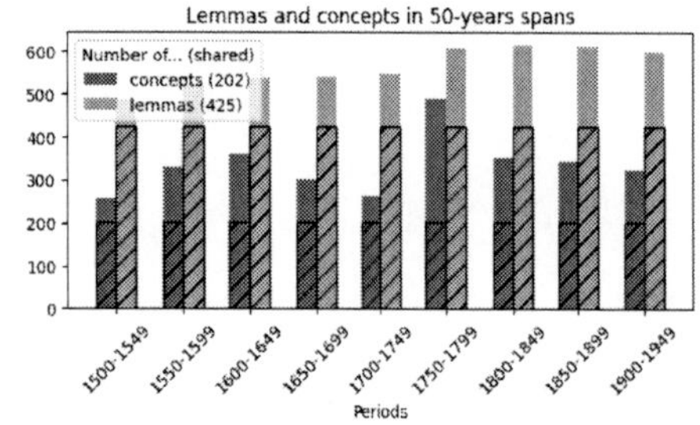

Figure 2: Number of lemmas and concepts in the different periods (half centuries). Hatched areas represent the 425 lemmas and 202 concepts appearing in all periods.

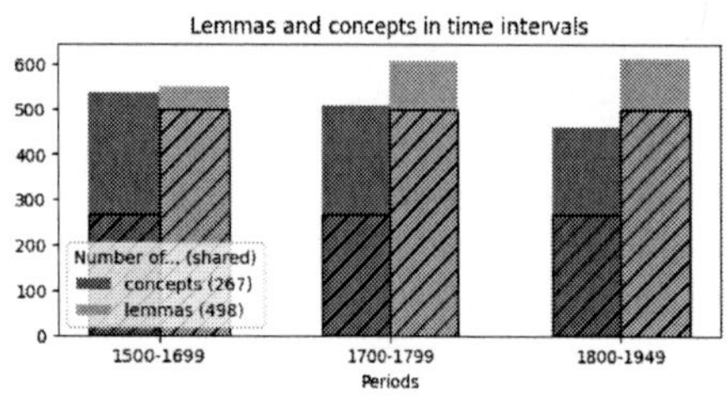

Figure 3: Number of lemmas and concepts in the different time intervals. Hatched areas represent the 498 lemmas and 265 concepts appearing in all periods.

or had already disappeared ; (ii) the lemma was used but is not represented in this span of corpus ; (iii) the lemma was used but rare, and as such does not appear in the corpus for this time span.

Similarly, we posit three possible reasons for concepts not to be instantiated: (i) some concepts may not exists in the language at some time spans (e.g. the concept of COMPUTER) ; (ii) this may be because the span is relatively short and the corpus is not uniformly distributed; (iii) our cluster induction may have failed to identify occurrences instantiating this concept. There is however no way for us to know which of these cases apply.

This leads us to consider larger time periods for our analyses : 1500-1699, 1700-1799 and 1800-1949. Such large periods would not be suitable for target words selection, as we need to ensure a word is *regularly* instantiated over time. At analysis time however, while large periods will prevent us to notice subtle or short-lived semantic changes, this balances the number of occurrences, of lemmas and of retrieved concepts (see Figure 3).

The length of considered periods for analysis has no influence on the actual clustering, as we apply the clustering algorithms on data from all periods.

Category	Total	Cluster size 2	3	4
Synonyms	27	20	7	0
Near-synonyms	20	9	8	3
Lexical/topical relation	41	26	11	4
Invalid cluster	13	7	3	3
Total	101	62	29	10

Table 5: Categorization of small induced concept-clusters in 1800-1949. Invalid clusters are those showing no semantic relation.

A.5 Distribution of concepts size over time

Figure 4 shows the distribution of concept sizes over time. At a given time, the concept size is the number of lemmas for which at least one occurrences is assigned to the concept.

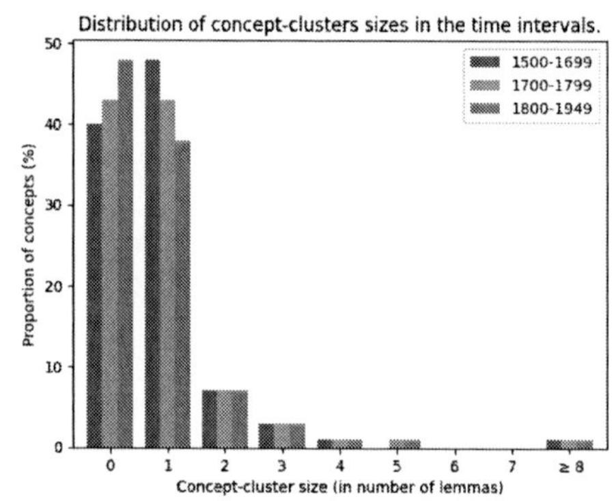

Figure 4: Distribution of the size of the 867 concept-clusters in the different time intervals. Size of 0 means that these concepts are not instantiated.

A.6 Qualitative analysis: raw counts

A.7 Evolution of the number of senses over time

Table 6 shows how the number of senses of lemma changes. Stable lemmas are those with a very low number of senses, while lemma that change have higher number of senses.

Evolution of lemmas	# Lemmas	Average number of senses 1500-1699	1700-1799	1800-1949
Lost a sense	88	2.84 ± 2.02	1.94 ± 1.44	1.32 ± 1.01
Gained a sense	53	1.15 ± 0.50	1.77 ± 1.12	2.30 ± 0.80
Both	39	4.95 ± 3.09	4.10 ± 2.60	4.18 ± 2.52
Stable	318	1.07 ± 0.25	1.18 ± 0.44	1.07 ± 0.25

Table 6: Evolution of the number of senses of target lemmas over time.

Deep-change at AXOLOTL-24: Orchestrating WSD and WSI Models for Semantic Change Modeling

Denis Kokosinskii[1,2], Mikhail Kuklin[1,3], and Nikolay Arefyev[4]

[1]Moscow State University, Russia
[2]SaluteDevices, Russia
[3]Yandex, Russia
[4]University of Oslo, Norway
kokosinskiidv@my.msu.ru, kuklin.mike@yandex.ru, nikolare@uio.no

Abstract

This paper describes our solution of the first subtask from the AXOLOTL-24 shared task on Semantic Change Modeling. The goal of this subtask is to distribute a given set of usages of a polysemous word from a newer time period between senses of this word from an older time period and clusters representing gained senses of this word. We propose and experiment with three new methods solving this task. Our methods achieve SOTA results according to both official metrics of the first substask. Additionally, we develop a model that can tell if a given word usage is not described by any of the provided sense definitions. This model serves as a component in one of our methods, but can potentially be useful on its own.

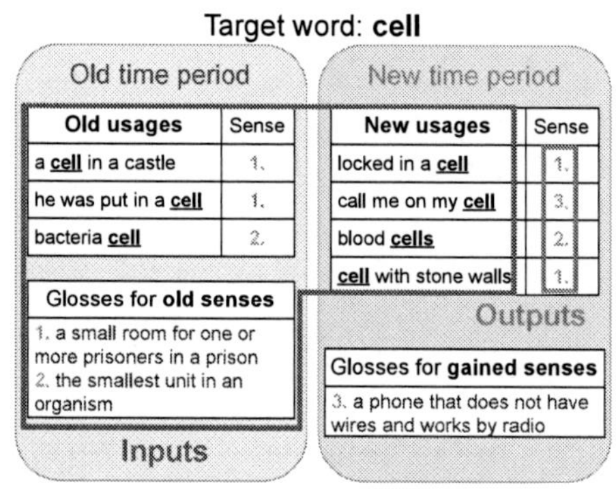

Figure 1: An example of data for the first subtask of AXOLOTL-24.

1 Introduction

The shared task on explainable Semantic Change Modeling (SCM) AXOLOTL-24 (Fedorova et al., 2024) is related to automation of Lexical Semantic Change (LSC) studies, i.e. linguistic studies on how word meanings change over time. It consists of two subtasks, however, we focus on the first one and skip the definition generation subtask. Unlike other shared tasks LSC held before, the first subtask of AXOLOTL-24 requires automatic annotation of individual usages of target words instead of target words as a whole. An example of the provided data and required outputs is shown on Figure 1. Namely, for each target word, two sets of usages from an older and a newer period are given (we will call them *old* and *new* usages). Additionally, a set of glosses describing word senses in the older time period (*old senses*) are provided, and the old usages are annotated with these sense glosses. Senses occurring among the new usages (*new senses*) should be discovered automatically. To be precise, the goal is to annotate each new usage with one of the given old sense glosses, or a unique sense identifier if none of them is applicable. We will refer to those senses that occur only among old and only among new usages as *lost* and *gained* senses, and all other senses as *stable* senses.

To solve the task, we experiment with three types of models. Word Sense Disambiguation (WSD) models for a given word usage select among given glosses the most suitable one. Word Sense Induction (WSI) models group word usages into clusters corresponding to word senses, they are applicable even when sense descriptions are not available. Finally, Novel Sense Detection (NSD) models find usages corresponding to unknown word senses, the ones that are not covered by the provided definitions. We propose three methods that solve the task. Our best solution denoted as Outlier2Cluster combines all three types of models in a novel way, essentially using an NSD model for each usage to decide whether to return a definition selected by a WSD model, or an identifier of a cluster this usage was put into by a WSI model. On average across languages, this solution achieves SOTA results among all participants of the first substask of AXOLOTL-24 according to both official metrics.

An important additional contribution is the pro-

Proceedings of the 5th Workshop on Computational Approaches to Historical Language Change, pages 168–179
August 15, 2024 ©2024 Association for Computational Linguistics

posed NSD model and the related experiments. We study the importance of different features of the NSD model and its effect on SCM quality. Our experiments suggest that improving NSD quality is the most promising direction for the future.

2 Related work

LSCD methods. Several shared tasks related to LSCD were organized in the past, including Schlechtweg et al. (2020); Kutuzov and Pivovarova (2021); Zamora-Reina et al. (2022). Unlike AXOLOTL-24 (Fedorova et al., 2024), they required word-level predictions from their participants, either in the form of word ranking or binary word classification. This type of task setup is generally mentioned under the name Lexical Semantic Change Detection / Discovery (LSCD). In the earlier shared tasks the best results were achieved by solutions that employed non-contextualized word-level embeddings such as word2vec (Mikolov et al., 2013) and vector alignment methods such as Canonical Correlation Analysis and Orthogonal Procrustes Alignment (Pömsl and Lyapin, 2020; Pražák et al., 2020). However, recently token-level methods (Laicher et al., 2021; Rachinskiy and Arefyev, 2021a, 2022) have surpassed them. These methods rely on masked language models fine-tuned on existing datasets for various tasks of lexical semantics. For instance, solutions relying on the contextualized embeddings from GlossReader, which is a WSD system, have shown SOTA results in the shared tasks on LSCD in Russian and Spanish (Rachinskiy and Arefyev, 2021a, 2022). Methods proposed in this work exploit GlossReader too, both as a WSD model and as a source of contextualized embeddings well-suited for LSC-related tasks.

GlossReader is a multilingual gloss-based WSD model originally developed to solve the Word-in-Context task (Rachinskiy and Arefyev, 2021b). It modifies the English WSD model BEM (Blevins and Zettlemoyer, 2020) replacing the backbone with the multilingual XLM-R language model (Conneau et al., 2020). The model consists of a gloss encoder and a context encoder, both initialized with the XLM-R weights and fine-tuned jointly learning to select among all glosses of a target word the one describing its sense in a given context. Specifically, the dot product between the context embedding and the correct gloss embedding is maximized.

NSD methods. Several methods were proposed to solve the NSD task. Some of them perform WSI internally. For instance, Lau et al. (2012); Cook et al. (2014) employ a topic modelling approach to jointly cluster old and new usages using the Hierarchical Dirichlet Process. Clusters are ranked based on the novelty score (the difference between estimated probabilities of a cluster appearing in the new and the old corpus). While the method was originally designed for LSCD, the novelty ranking of senses can be combined with a static threshold to identify novel senses.

Alternatively, Mitra et al. (2015) performs WSI separately for an old and a new corpus on graphs, where an edge weight between two words is proportional to the number of words appearing in bigrams with both of them. A cluster in the new corpus is labeled as a novel sense if words in this cluster have weak links with the target word in the graph for the old corpus. A recent method by Ma et al. (2024) uses BERT (Devlin et al., 2019) to build contextualized representations. It employs agglomerative clustering to perform WSI and then matches old and new clusters based on their centroids. The new clusters that are not matched are considered novel senses. Similarly to this method we use agglomerative clustering for WSI, but employing GlossReader to obtain contextualized embeddings.

In Erk (2006) several NSD methods were proposed to detect word senses that are not described in FrameNet (Baker et al., 1998). Instead of relying on WSI, similarly to our NSD method their best method formulates the task as an outlier detection problem. They employ distances between old and new usages requiring a significant number of old usages for each sense, which are not always available in AXOLOTL-24. Thus, we rely on distances between new usages and old glosses instead. Another similar method is introduced in Lautenschlager et al. (2024). They use the XL-LEXEME model (Cassotti et al., 2023) to build representations for usages and senses. Sense representations are built from glosses or example usages of senses taken from dictionaries. They do not always contain the target word, which makes application of XL-LEXEME non-trivial. Authors attempt to solve this problem by modifying glosses and example usages to include the target word. For each usage its nearest sense is found based on the cosine similarity or the Spearman's correlation between their embeddings. If the similarity is above a threshold, the usage is considered to belong to some non-described sense. Our methods also rely on usage and sense representations, but we use GlossReader which has a separate gloss encoder and does not require any preprocessing for glosses. We experiment with many measures of similarity between a sense and a usage embedding, and found the manhattan distance between l1-normalized embeddings to outperform other measures and a classifier on a combination of measures to perform best. However, we did not experiment with example usages from sense inventories. When such usages are available, being combined with glosses they may potentially improve sense representations.

3 Methods

3.1 Target word positions

All our methods assume that a usage is represented as a string and two character-level indices pointing to a target word occurrence inside this string. However, for the Russian subsets these indices were absent. To find them, we first generated all grammatical forms for each target lemma using Pymorphy2 (Korobov, 2015). Then retrieved all occurrences of these forms as separate tokens in the provided usages employing regular expressions.[1] For usages with several occurrences of the target word we selected one of them that has both left and right context of reasonable length.[2] We inspected new usages from the development and the test sets that did not contain any of the automatically generated word forms and added absent forms manually, then reran retrieval.[3]

3.2 WSD methods

The first group of methods in our experiments include pure WSD methods, which select one of the provided definitions of old senses for each new usage, and thus, cannot discover gained senses.

[1]E.g. `'\b(cat|cats)\b'`, where `\b` denotes a word boundary. Matching is case-insensitive.

[2]This idea is based on our observations that a word occurrence is encoded sub-optimally when it is either the first or the last token, which is probably related to confusion of Transformer heads that have learnt to attend to the adjacent tokens (Voita et al., 2019). The heuristic implemented takes the second to last occurrence if there are more than two of them. For two occurrences it takes $argmax_{u\in\{u1,u2\}} min(l_u, r_u)$, where l_u, r_u are the lengths of the left and the right contexts.

[3]Repeating this manual procedure for all Russian data requires significantly more efforts and would have few benefits for our methods. Thus, all old usages having this issue were left without indices and new usages from the training set we dropped.

GlossReader. We employ the original GlossReader model (Rachinskiy and Arefyev, 2021b) as the baseline. For a given **new** usage u of a target word w its usage representation r_u is built with the context encoder. Then gloss representations r_g are built for each gloss g of the target word w using the gloss encoder. Finally, the gloss with the highest dot product similarity to the usage is selected.

To improve the results, we further fine-tune the GlossReader model on the data of AXOLOTL-24.

GlossReader FiEnRu is fine-tuned following the original GlossReader training procedure on three datasets: the train sets of the shared task in Finnish and Russian, and the English WSD dataset SemCor (Miller et al., 1994) which GlossReader was originally trained on. We employ all old and new usages from the Russian and Finnish datasets along with their sense definitions. We fined-tuned for 3 epochs using 90/10% train/validation split to select the best checkpoint.[4]

GlossReader Ru is fine-tuned exactly the same way, but only on the train set in Russian.

GlossReader Fi SG is fine-tuned on the Finnish train set only. Unlike two previous models, we made an attempt to teach this model how to discover novel senses. Specifically, we replaced all glosses of gained senses with a Special Gloss (SG) "the sense of the word is unknown" in Finnish[5] and fine-tuned the model as before. For inference we tried adding the special gloss to the provided old glosses, essentially extending the WSD model with NSD abilities. However, this resulted in a noticeable decrease of the metrics on the Finnish development set. Thus, we decided to use the special gloss for training only.[6]

3.3 WSI methods

Unlike WSD methods, WSI methods do not use definitions or any other descriptions of word senses. Instead they discover senses of a word from an unlabeled set of its usages by splitting this set into clusters hopefully corresponding to word senses. WSI methods cannot attribute usages to the provided old glosses, but can potentially group usages

[4]The last checkpoint was selected, though after $\approx$0.5 epochs metrics improve very slowly.

[5]"sanan merkitystä ei tunneta" as translated by Google Translate

[6]The majority of words in the Finnish dataset have one sense only, see Section 4.2. Pure WSD methods always return perfect predictions for such cases, thus, it is very hard to compete with them on this dataset. In the future we plan to experiment with this model on the Russian dataset having much smaller proportion of such words.

of the same sense, including gained senses, into a separate cluster.

Agglomerative is the only WSI method we propose and experiment with. For each new usage its representation r_u is built using the context encoder of the original GlossReader model. Then we perform agglomerative clustering of old usages using the cosine distance and average linkage on these representations. This clustering algorithm was successfully used to cluster vectors of lexical substitutes, another kind of word sense representations, in several substitution-based WSI methods (Amrami and Goldberg, 2018, 2019; Arefyev et al., 2020; Kokosinskii and Arefyev, 2024), as well as for LSCD (Laicher et al., 2021; Ma et al., 2024).

Agglomerative clustering starts with each usage in a separate cluster, then iteratively merges two closest clusters. The distance between two clusters is the average pairwise cosine distance from the usages in the first cluster to the usages in the second one. Merging stops when the predefined number of clusters is reached. We range the number of clusters between 2 and 9 and select a clustering with the highest Calinski-Harabasz score (Caliński and Harabasz, 1974).[7]

3.4 SCM methods

WSD and WSI methods provide only partial solutions of the semantic change modeling task, the former cannot discover novel senses, and the latter cannot annotate usages with the old glosses provided. We propose three new methods developed to fully solve the task.

3.4.1 AggloM

Our first SCM method modifies the Agglomerative WSI method by incorporating old usages and senses into the clustering process. We perform agglomerative clustering of a set containing both old and new usages of a target word. Initially, each new usage is assigned to a separate cluster. The old usages are clustered according to the provided sense annotations. Then at each iteration we compute the distances from each cluster containing only new usages to all other clusters. The distance between two clusters is defined as the minimum cosine distance between the usage representations from the first and the second cluster.[8] We then merge two

[7]For one or two usages the Calinski-Harabasz score is not defined. We return a single cluster in such cases.

[8]This is known as single linkage.

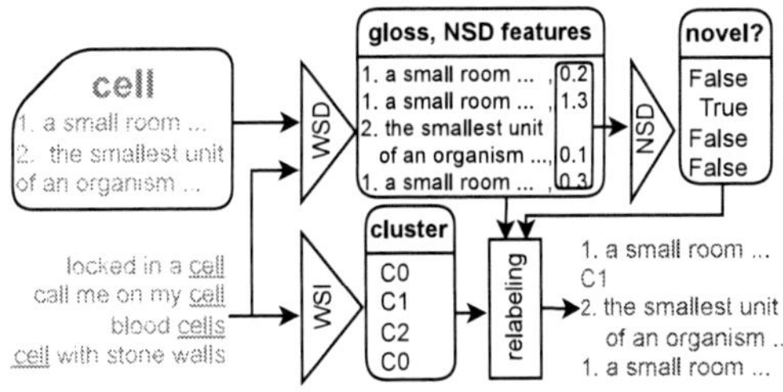

Figure 2: Outlier2Cluster pipeline. Inputs are in green and outputs are in blue. Triangles denote ML models.

nearest clusters, one of which contains new usages only. This iterative merging process stops when the number of clusters is larger than the number of old senses by $k \geq 0$. Therefore AggloM returns exactly k novel senses, where k is a hyperparameter.[9] We do not use this method on the Russian datasets because for most senses there are no old usages there.

AggloM FiEnRu is identical to AggloM but relies on the fine-tuned GlossReader FiEnRu.

3.4.2 Cluster2sense

In the second SCM method we first independently cluster new usages using the Agglomerative WSI method and annotate them with the old senses using GlossReader FiEnRu. We then keep the clustering obtained from WSI, but relabel those clusters that overlap heavily with one of the predicted senses. Specifically, we label a cluster c with a sense s if c has the highest Jaccard similarity to s among all the old senses of the target word, and at the same time s has the highest similarity to c among all the clusters built for new usages of this word. Notably, two clusters cannot be labeled with a single sense, thus the clustering of usages is identical to the one originally predicted by WSI. Some clusters will not be labeled with any sense, thus, Cluster2sense can discover gained senses. At the same time, some senses will not be assigned to any cluster, which means the potential to discover lost senses as well.

3.4.3 Outlier2Cluster

Unlike Cluster2Sense which relabels whole clusters, Outlier2Cluster relabels individual usages. Figure 2 shows the processing pipeline. First WSD and WSI predictions are independently made

[9]In the preliminary experiments on the Finnish development set we selected $k = 0$, which means that all new usages are eventually merged into clusters representing old senses. This is likely related to the low proportion of gained senses in this dataset and noisy usages which make them hard to discover.

by GlossReader FiEnRu and Agglomerative respectively. Then we discover usages of gained senses. For that we propose a Novel Sense Detection (NSD) model finding usages of those senses that we do not have definitions for.[10] Finally, we return WSI predictions for all these discovered usages, and WSD predictions for all other usages.

Novel sense detection. We treat the NSD task as an outlier detection problem, essentially finding those usages that are distant enough from all the provided definitions. Since GlossReader selects the most similar definition for a given usage, it is enough to check if this definition is distant enough to conclude that the usage is an outlier. To check this we employ a logistic regression classifier. Each input example corresponds to a single usage and a gloss selected for this usage by the WSD model. The output is 1 if this usage is an outlier, i.e. does not belong to the predicted sense, and 0 otherwise.

We use distances (computed with several distance functions) between GlossReader representations of the new usages and the glosses for old senses as features for logistic regression.

For the new usage u and the selected definition g we take the corresponding representations r_u and r_g from a gloss encoder and a context encoder respectively. We take these representations from two different GlossReader models, the original one and GlossReader FiEnRu, and calculate distances from r_u to r_g using different distance and normalization functions. This gives 10 different features presented in Table 1. We also include three extra features: the number of old usages, old senses, and new usages for the target word in the dataset. We employ the Standard Scaler to normalize features and train the logistic regression with L2 regularization of $C = 1$.

Thus, the trained logistic regression can be used for each usage to decide whether the WSD method has assigned a correct sense or should be replaced with some cluster corresponding to a gained sense. If the score is above a threshold of 0.65, which was selected on the development sets of the shared task, the usage is considered an outlier.

We train two NSD models on the Russian and the Finnish development sets separately and use the trained models for the corresponding test sets.

[10]In the context of the shared task these are gained senses. However, the approach is general enough to discover lost senses when a modern dictionary and old usages are given, or just senses from the same time period as the dictionary but not covered by it.

Distance Function		Cos.	Euclid.	Manh.
Encoders	**Normalized**			
GR FiEnRu	No	✓	✓	✓
GR FiEnRu	L1-norm			✓
GR FiEnRu	L2-norm		✓	
GR	No	✓	✓	✓
GR	L1-norm			✓
GR	L2-norm		✓	

Table 1: Ten distance-based features used in the NSD model. Distances are calculated between usage and gloss representations obtained from context and gloss encoders of the same GlossReader model. GR stand for GlossReader, Cos. is the cosine distance, Euclid. is the euclidean distance, Manh. is the manhattan distance.

For the surprise language, we do not have labeled data to select one of two models or train a separate model, thus, we simply report the results of both models.

Outlier relabeling. We experiment with two ways of assigning clusters to the detected outliers. Our first approach (**w/o WSI**) groups all outliers into a single new cluster. Alternatively, **w/ WSI** approach assigns the clusters predicted by the WSI method to outliers. We use the first option for the Finnish test set, as we observed that the words in the Finnish development set rarely have more than one gained sense. On the contrary, the words in the Russian development set have many gained senses, therefore, we employ w/ WSI for the Russian test set. For the surprise language Outlier2Cluster$_{fi}$ employs w/o WSI and Outlier2Cluster^{ru} employs w/ WSI.

All of the described methods are briefly summarized in Table 2.

4 Evaluation setup

The first AXOLOTL-24 subtask evaluates semantic change modeling systems in three diachronic datasets in Finnish, Russian, and German (Fedorova et al., 2024). Train and development sets are provided for the first two, but not for the last. We will now describe the datasets in more detail.

4.1 Data sources

The source for the Finnish dataset of the shared task is resource (1997). The usages are divided into two groups: before 1700 and after 1700. The usages in the dataset are not complete sentences but short phrases. Some parts of the phrase can be missing and replaced with double hyphens, presumably due to OCR errors. Furthermore, the usages from both the old and the new corpus exhibit no-

	Underlying embeddings	Requires usages of old senses	Requires old glosses	Requires a train set with gained senses*	Able to discover gained senses	Able to predict old senses
GR	GR	-	✓	-	-	✓
GR FiEnRu	GR FiEnRu	-	✓	-	-	✓
GR Ru	GR Ru	-	✓	-	-	✓
GR Fi SG	GR Fi SG	-	✓	✓	-	✓
Agglomerative	GR	-	-	-	✓	-
AggloM	GR	✓	-	-	if $k > 0$	✓
AggloM FiEnRu	GR FiEnRu	✓	-	-	if $k > 0$	✓
Cluster2Sense	GR, GR FiEnRu	-	✓	-	✓	✓
Outlier2Cluster	GR, GR FiEnRu	-	✓	✓	✓	✓

Table 2: A brief description of the proposed methods. GR stands for GlossReader model. *GR Fi SG is trained to predict the special gloss for usages of all gained senses. In Outlier2Cluster the NSD model is trained to detect usages of gained sense.

table differences from modern Finnish. They often feature characters (such as c, z, w, and x), that are not commonly found in contemporary Finnish. It is important to highlight that the glosses provided for word senses are in modern Finnish.

Two data sources used to create the Russian dataset are Dahl (1909) processed by Mikhaylov and Shershneva (2019) and Mickus et al. (2022). The first one was the source of old usages and glosses, and the latter provided new usages and glosses. However, the specific procedure used to map senses between these two sources was undisclosed at the time of the competition. Some old senses are not accompanied by old usages in the Russian datasets. Consequently, our methods for the Russian datasets do not rely on the old usages. Notably, the Russian datasets lack information regarding the position of a target word within a usage or the actual word form of the target word. As a result, we incorporate the identification of the target word's position within a usage as a preprocessing step in our solution.

The shared task also includes a test dataset in a surprise language revealed only at the test phase of competition with no development or train sets. The source of this dataset is a German diachronic corpus with sense annotations (Schlechtweg et al., 2020; Schlechtweg, 2023).

4.2 Data Statistics

To get insights into the data we categorize the target words within the train and the development sets based on several characteristics:

- Has lost senses: does the word have old senses for which there are no new usage?
- Number of gained senses: how many senses are there having new usages only?

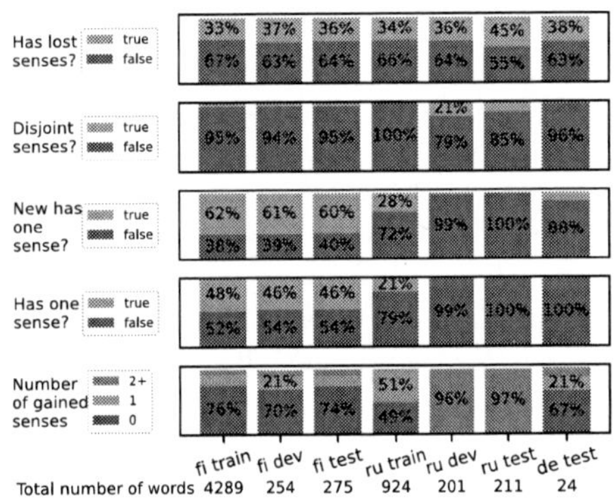

Figure 3: Proportions of target words falling into different categories in the shared task datasets.

- Disjoint senses: are the sets of senses for old and new examples disjoint?
- New has one sense: do all the new usages have the same meaning?
- Has one sense: do all the usages (both old and new) have the same meaning?

The number of target words in each category for all[11] the datasets of the shared task is presented on Figure 3.

In the Finnish datasets, almost half of target words have only one sense and approximately 70% of words have no gained senses. Therefore, the conservative methods that rarely discover gained senses are preferable for the Finnish datasets.

The main observation for the Russian datasets is the dramatic differences in proportions of almost all categories between the train and the development

[11]This information for the test sets was not available during the competition.

set. We can see that the statistics of the test set are similar to those of the development set. Contrary to the Finnish sets, almost all words in the Russian development set have gained senses. Therefore, methods which are prone to predict new senses rather than old ones are preferable for the Russian development set.

The German dataset is relatively small and contains 8 times fewer words than the other test sets. We can see that it is similar to the Finnish datasets in the proportion of gained and lost senses.

4.3 Metrics

The shared task employs two metrics to evaluate the systems, the Adjusted Rand Index (ARI) and the F1 score.

ARI (Hubert and Arabie, 1985) is a well-established clustering metric employed to evaluate how well new usages are clustered by a system. In the subtask, ARI is computed for all the new usages of a target word, the ground truth clusters correspond to senses. Notably, cluster labels are not taken into account by ARI. It means that old senses and gained senses are indistinguishable from each other in terms of ARI.

The F1 score is used in the first subtask to estimate how well a system can discriminate between old senses. It is computed only for the new usages of the old senses, and not for the usages of the gained senses. The F1 score for a target word is the average of the F1 scores for all old senses. If a target word does not have any new usages with the old senses, it is arbitrarily assigned the F1 score of 1 if old senses are not predicted for any of its usages and 0 otherwise. Thus, in this edge case a system is heavily penalized when even a single usage is misclassified as one of the old senses.

All new usages of the old senses which are (incorrectly) predicted as belonging to a gained sense are considered to belong to a single auxiliary "novel" class when calculating the F1 score. The F1 score for this class is zero as it has zero precision. For this reason, even a single usage misclassified as a gained sense can dramatically affect the overall score for a target word independently of the total number of its usages.[12]

5 Results

5.1 Our submissions

The number of submissions for the test sets per team was not limited in the competition. We evaluate ten models on the test sets: four WSD models (based on GlossReader, GlossReader FiEnRu, GlossReader Ru, and GlossReader Fi SG), one WSI model (Agglomerative with GlossReader representations), two AggloM models (based on GlossReader and GlossReader FiEnRu representations), Cluster2Sense, and Outlier2Cluster with different configurations for the German dataset: Outlier2Cluster^{ru} and Outlier2Cluster$_{fi}$. Table 3 demonstrates the evaluation results. We also include the best submissions from other teams for comparison.

WSD and WSI. The best results in terms of the F1 score are achieved by pure WSD methods. The F1 score is calculated only for the usages of old senses, this gives a huge advantage to WSD methods because incorrect prediction of old senses for usages of gained senses is not penalized, while the opposite reduces the F1 score severely as explained in Section 4.3.

WSD methods have notably higher ARI than Agglomerative and Cluster2Sense (both of them predict the same clusters but label them differently) for the Finnish and German datasets. On the contrary, Agglomerative and Cluster2Sense are the best-performing methods for the Russian dataset. Our explanation for this fact comes from the analysis in Section 4.2. The sets of senses of the new and the old usages in the Finnish and German datasets overlap heavily, which is beneficial for WSD methods. The overlap is much smaller for the Russian dataset, which hurts ARI of the WSD methods. Discovering gained senses is crucial for the Russian dev and test set.

AggloM. The AggloM method with the hyperparameter $k = 0$ (never predicts gained senses) does not fall far behind pure WSD methods. The main reasons for that probably are the usage of the same underlying context encoder and prediction of only old senses. Therefore, AggloM is a viable alternative to the GlossReader models when word senses are described with usage examples instead of sense definitions.

Outlier2Cluster. Outlier2Cluster achieves

[12]Assume the target word has k old senses. In case when only old senses are predicted: $F = \frac{F_1+\ldots+F_k}{k}$. If we replace one of the correct predictions of sense 1 with an incorrect prediction of a gained sense: $F' = \frac{F_1'+\ldots+F_k+\mathbf{0}}{\mathbf{k+1}} < \frac{F_1+\ldots+F_k+\mathbf{0}}{\mathbf{k+1}}$. The drop in this metric is $\frac{F}{F'} > \frac{k+1}{k}$ E.g. in the case $k = 1$, which is a frequent case in the Finnish AXOLOTL-24 dataset, an incorrect prediction of a gained sense for a single usage results in more than 2x decrease of the F1 score.

Method	ARI Fi	ARI Ru	ARI De	ARI FiRu	ARI AVG	F1 Fi	F1 Ru	F1 De	F1 FiRu	F1 AVG
WSD methods										
GR	0.581	0.041	0.386	0.311	0.336	0.690	◇0.721	0.694	0.706	0.702
GR FiEnRu	◇**0.649**	0.048	◇0.521	**0.348**	0.406	◇**0.756**	◇**0.750**	◇0.745	◇**0.753**	◇**0.750**
GR Ru	0.568	0.053	0.464	0.310	0.361	0.568	◇**0.750**	◇0.724	0.659	0.681
GR Fi SG	◇0.638	**0.059**	◇**0.543**	**0.348**	**0.413**	◇0.752	◇0.729	◇**0.758**	◇0.741	◇0.746
WSI methods										
Agglomerative	**0.209**	◇**0.259**	**0.316**	**0.234**	**0.261**	**0.055**	**0.152**	**0.042**	**0.104**	**0.083**
SCM methods										
AggloM	0.581	0	**0.492**	0.290	0.357	0.674	0	0.695	0.337	0.456
AggloM FiEnRu	◇0.631	0	0.485	0.315	0.372	◇0.731	0	0.639	0.366	0.457
Cluster2Sense	0.209	◇**0.259**	0.316	0.234	0.261	0.432	0.346	0.432	0.389	0.403
Outlier2Cluster $^{ru}_{fi}$	◇**0.649**	◇0.247	*0.322* *0.480*	◇**0.448**	*0.406* ◇***0.459***	◇**0.756**	**0.645**	*0.510* ◇***0.745***	**0.701**	*0.637* ◇***0.715***
Other teams										
Holotniekat	**0.596**	0.043	0.298	**0.319**	**0.312**	**0.655**	**0.661**	0.608	**0.658**	**0.641**
TartuNLP	0.437	0.098	**0.396**	0.267	0.310	0.550	0.640	0.580	0.595	0.590
IMS_Stuttgart	0.548	0	0.314	0.274	0.287	0.590	0.570	0.300	0.580	0.487
ABDN-NLP	0.553	0.009	0.102	0.281	0.221	**0.655**	0	**0.638**	0.328	0.431
WooperNLP	0.428	**0.132**	0	0.280	0.186	0.503	0.446	0	0.475	0.316
Baseline	0.023	0.079	0.022	0.051	0.041	0.230	0.260	0.130	0.245	0.207

Table 3: The results on the test tests. The best result for each metric is underlined, the best result in each group is in **bold font**. A diamond (◇) denotes those results that are worse than the best one, but the difference is practically insignificant (we consider relative differences smaller than 0.05 as practically insignificant). The official AXOLOTL-24 leaderboard is based on the average metrics across the languages having the training sets provided (the FiRu columns) and all languages (the AVG columns).

SOTA or near-SOTA ARI[13] for Russian and Finnish, but falls behind WSD methods for German, which has no labeled data to train a dedicated NSD model. However, Outlier2Cluster can discover gained senses unlike WSD methods. Thus, we consider Outlier2Cluster to be preferable for the SCM task and suggest training the NSD model for each language of interest.[14]

The important hyperparameter of the NSD model, and consequently the Outlier2Cluster model exploiting it as a component, is the threshold dividing usages into outliers and normal usages. Figure 4 shows the dependence of the metrics on the threshold value for the Finnish and Russian development sets. Both w/ WSI and w/o WSI versions of Outlier2cluster are included. We also compute the results of Outlier2Cluster with the WSI oracle which perfectly clusters the detected outliers according to their ground truth senses, and the NSD oracle which perfectly detects usages of gained senses. The methods we study in this Section are briefly summarized in Table 4.

We can see that the F1 score (computed only

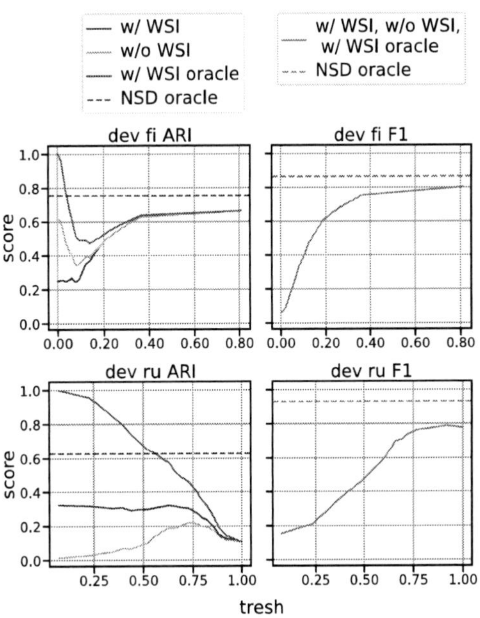

Figure 4: ARI and F1 on the development sets depending on the threshold of novel sense detector. Higher threshold means higher proportion of WSD predictions and less WSI predictions.

[13]We made Outlier2Cluster$_{fi}$ submissions in the competition separately for different datasets. For this reason, it was not selected as our best submission by the competition organizers.

[14]We used only small development sets with ≈ 200 target words to train novel sense detection models.

Method	WSD	WSI	NSD
w/ WSI	GR FiEnRu	Agglomer.	LogReg
w/o WSI	GR FiEnRu	One cluster	LogReg
w/ WSI oracle	GR FiEnRu	Oracle	LogReg
NSD oracle	GR FiEnRu	Agglomer.	Oracle

Table 4: A brief summary of methods for the NSD threshold study.

over new usages with old senses) monotonically increases with the increasing threshold, i.e. with fewer outliers detected. This again shows that trying to detect usages of gained senses and clean the old senses from them hurts the F1 score, supporting the criticism of this metric in Section 4.3.

ARI reaches a peak at the threshold of 0.65 for the Russian dataset with F1 being close to maximum as well. We therefore set the threshold at 0.65 for the Russian NSD model. This gives the SCM model that almost achieves the ARI of pure WSI predictions (threshold of 0) while having only a bit smaller F1 score compared to the best WSD model.

For the Finnish dataset, higher ARI monotonically increase with the threshold, i.e. with the proportion of predictions taken from the WSD model. This agrees with the observations from Table 3 that the pure WSD models give the best ARI for Finnish. We can also see that the threshold values in the middle, where neither WSI nor WSD predictions are dominant, result in a significant decrease in ARI. It means, that our NSD model cannot be used effectively to combine the predictions for Finnish. We select a high threshold of 0.65 for the Finnish dataset, resulting in a low number of outliers. Consequently, the novel sense detector predicts less than 1% of usages to be outliers in the Finnish test set, compared to 42% of usages predicted as outliers for the Russian test dataset.

We can observe that according to the F1 score, the NSD oracle performs better than the pure WSD method, especially on the Russian development set. The reason lies in the words with disjointed senses. Since there are no new usages of old senses for such words, the ordinary F1 score and it is arbitrarily defined as 1 if all usages are recognized as usages of gained senses, i.e. put into new clusters, and 0 otherwise. Thus, the ideal processing of these edge cases is crucial for the F1 score, but can hardly be achieved unless the NSD oracle is employed. For other words it does not help. Considering ARI, the NSD oracle performs much better than w/WSI on the Russian dataset. It means that better NSD models may help greatly improve clustering.

According to the results of w/ WSI oracle on the Finnish development set, it is impossible to increase ARI with better WSI method without a huge drop in the F1 score. For the Russian dataset situation is the opposite. The main reason is likely the average number of gained senses per word in these datasets as described in Section 4.2. Only 7% of words in the Finnish dataset have gained two or more senses, therefore the perfect clustering of the gained senses does not increase the results significantly compared to merging all gained senses into a single cluster. On the contrary, 97% of the word in the Russian have two or more gained senses, making WSI necessary.

6 Conclusion

We have proposed three new methods that solve the SCM task. Our solution achieves SOTA results among all participants of the first subtask of the AXOLOTL-24 shared task. Additional experiments propose directions of further improvement of the developed models, NSD being potentially the most promising one.

7 Limitations

While our methods can in theory be applied to any SCM dataset, we acknowledge that they may be overspecified for the first subtask of AXOLOTL-24. Notably, we extensively use the train sets provided for the competition in Finnish and Russian to train the embedding model and to optimize the hyperparameters. While we also evaluate on the German dataset in a zero-shot fashion, the results may be unreliable due to relatively small size of the dataset.

Semantic change modeling may be of particular interest in studies of older time periods, where the language is quite different from its modern state. The underlying model, GlossReader, is a finetuned version of XLM-R, which was not specifically designed to handle old languages. In this case dataset-specific finetuning of the base GlossReader may become even more relevant.

8 Acknowledgements

Nikolay Arefyev has received funding from the European Union's Horizon Europe research and innovation program under Grant agreement No 101070350 (HPLT).

References

Asaf Amrami and Yoav Goldberg. 2018. Word sense induction with neural bilm and symmetric patterns. *arXiv preprint arXiv:1808.08518*.

Asaf Amrami and Yoav Goldberg. 2019. Towards better substitution-based word sense induction. *arXiv preprint arXiv:1905.12598*.

Nikolay Arefyev, Boris Sheludko, Alexander Podolskiy, and Alexander Panchenko. 2020. Always keep your target in mind: Studying semantics and improving performance of neural lexical substitution. In *Proceedings of the 28th International Conference on Computational Linguistics*, pages 1242–1255.

Collin F. Baker, Charles J. Fillmore, and John B. Lowe. 1998. The Berkeley FrameNet project. In *36th Annual Meeting of the Association for Computational Linguistics and 17th International Conference on Computational Linguistics, Volume 1*, pages 86–90, Montreal, Quebec, Canada. Association for Computational Linguistics.

Terra Blevins and Luke Zettlemoyer. 2020. Moving down the long tail of word sense disambiguation with gloss informed bi-encoders. In *Proceedings of the 58th Annual Meeting of the Association for Computational Linguistics*, pages 1006–1017, Online. Association for Computational Linguistics.

T. Caliński and J Harabasz. 1974. A dendrite method for cluster analysis. *Communications in Statistics*, 3(1):1–27.

Pierluigi Cassotti, Lucia Siciliani, Marco DeGemmis, Giovanni Semeraro, and Pierpaolo Basile. 2023. XL-LEXEME: WiC pretrained model for cross-lingual LEXical sEMantic changE. In *Proceedings of the 61st Annual Meeting of the Association for Computational Linguistics (Volume 2: Short Papers)*, pages 1577–1585, Toronto, Canada. Association for Computational Linguistics.

Alexis Conneau, Kartikay Khandelwal, Naman Goyal, Vishrav Chaudhary, Guillaume Wenzek, Francisco Guzmán, Edouard Grave, Myle Ott, Luke Zettlemoyer, and Veselin Stoyanov. 2020. Unsupervised cross-lingual representation learning at scale. In *Proceedings of the 58th Annual Meeting of the Association for Computational Linguistics*, pages 8440–8451, Online. Association for Computational Linguistics.

Paul Cook, Jey Han Lau, Diana McCarthy, and Timothy Baldwin. 2014. Novel word-sense identification. In *Proceedings of COLING 2014, the 25th International Conference on Computational Linguistics: Technical Papers*, pages 1624–1635, Dublin, Ireland. Dublin City University and Association for Computational Linguistics.

V. Dahl. 1909. *Explanatory Dictionary of the Living Great Russian Language ed. by Boduen de Kurtene [Tolkovy slovar zhivogo velikorusskogo yazyka, pod red. I. A. Boduena de Kurtene]*. Helsinki: Kotimaisten kielten keskuksen verkkojulkaisuja 38.

Jacob Devlin, Ming-Wei Chang, Kenton Lee, and Kristina Toutanova. 2019. BERT: Pre-training of deep bidirectional transformers for language understanding. In *Proceedings of the 2019 Conference of the North American Chapter of the Association for Computational Linguistics: Human Language Technologies, Volume 1 (Long and Short Papers)*, pages 4171–4186, Minneapolis, Minnesota. Association for Computational Linguistics.

Katrin Erk. 2006. Unknown word sense detection as outlier detection. In *Proceedings of the Human Language Technology Conference of the NAACL, Main Conference*, pages 128–135, New York City, USA. Association for Computational Linguistics.

Mariia Fedorova, Timothee Mickus, Niko Tapio Partanen, Janine Siewert, Elena Spaziani, and Andrey Kutuzov. 2024. AXOLOTL'24 shared task on multilingual explainable semantic change modeling. In *Proceedings of the 5th Workshop on Computational Approaches to Historical Language Change*, Bangkok. Association for Computational Linguistics.

Lawrence J. Hubert and Phipps Arabie. 1985. Comparing partitions. *Journal of Classification*, 2:193–218.

Denis Kokosinskii and Nikolay Arefyev. 2024. Multilingual substitution-based word sense induction. In *Proceedings of the 2024 Joint International Conference on Computational Linguistics, Language Resources and Evaluation (LREC-COLING 2024)*, pages 11859–11872, Torino, Italy. ELRA and ICCL.

Mikhail Korobov. 2015. Morphological analyzer and generator for russian and ukrainian languages. In *Analysis of Images, Social Networks and Texts*, pages 320–332, Cham. Springer International Publishing.

Andrey Kutuzov and Lidia Pivovarova. 2021. Rushifteval: A shared task on semantic shift detection for russian. In *Computational linguistics and intellectual technologies*, 20, Russian Federation.

Severin Laicher, Sinan Kurtyigit, Dominik Schlechtweg, Jonas Kuhn, and Sabine Schulte im Walde. 2021. Explaining and improving BERT performance on lexical semantic change detection. In *Proceedings of the 16th Conference of the European Chapter of the Association for Computational Linguistics: Student Research Workshop*, pages 192–202, Online. Association for Computational Linguistics.

Jey Han Lau, Paul Cook, Diana McCarthy, David Newman, and Timothy Baldwin. 2012. Word sense induction for novel sense detection. In *Proceedings of the 13th Conference of the European Chapter of the Association for Computational Linguistics*, pages 591–601, Avignon, France. Association for Computational Linguistics.

Jonathan Lautenschlager, Emma Sköldberg, Simon Hengchen, and Dominik Schlechtweg. 2024. Detection of non-recorded word senses in english and swedish. *Preprint*, arXiv:2403.02285.

Xianghe Ma, Michael Strube, and Wei Zhao. 2024. Graph-based clustering for detecting semantic change across time and languages. In *Proceedings of the 18th Conference of the European Chapter of the Association for Computational Linguistics (Volume 1: Long Papers)*, pages 1542–1561, St. Julian's, Malta. Association for Computational Linguistics.

Timothee Mickus, Kees Van Deemter, Mathieu Constant, and Denis Paperno. 2022. Semeval-2022 task 1: CODWOE – comparing dictionaries and word embeddings. In *Proceedings of the 16th International Workshop on Semantic Evaluation (SemEval-2022)*, pages 1–14, Seattle, United States. Association for Computational Linguistics.

S. A. Mikhaylov and D. M. Shershneva. 2019. Dictionary aggregator vyshka.dictionaries. In *Proceedings of the International Conference on Computational Linguistics and Intellectual Technologies (Dialogue)*.

Tomas Mikolov, Ilya Sutskever, Kai Chen, Greg S Corrado, and Jeff Dean. 2013. Distributed representations of words and phrases and their compositionality. In *Advances in Neural Information Processing Systems*, volume 26. Curran Associates, Inc.

George A Miller, Martin Chodorow, Shari Landes, Claudia Leacock, and Robert G Thomas. 1994. Using a semantic concordance for sense identification. In *In Proceedings of the workshop on Human Language Technology*, pages 240–243. Association for Computational Linguistics.

Sunny Mitra, Ritwik Mitra, Suman Kalyan Maity, Martin Riedl, Chris Biemann, Pawan Goyal, and Animesh Mukherjee. 2015. An automatic approach to identify word sense changes in text media across timescales. *Natural Language Engineering*, 21(5):773–798.

Martin Pömsl and Roman Lyapin. 2020. CIRCE at SemEval-2020 task 1: Ensembling context-free and context-dependent word representations. In *Proceedings of the Fourteenth Workshop on Semantic Evaluation*, pages 180–186, Barcelona (online). International Committee for Computational Linguistics.

Ondřej Pražák, Pavel Přibáň, Stephen Taylor, and Jakub Sido. 2020. UWB at SemEval-2020 task 1: Lexical semantic change detection. In *Proceedings of the Fourteenth Workshop on Semantic Evaluation*, pages 246–254, Barcelona (online). International Committee for Computational Linguistics.

Maxim Rachinskiy and Nikolay Arefyev. 2021a. GlossReader at SemEval-2021 task 2: Reading definitions improves contextualized word embeddings. In *Proceedings of the 15th International Workshop on Semantic Evaluation (SemEval-2021)*, pages 756–762, Online. Association for Computational Linguistics.

Maxim Rachinskiy and Nikolay Arefyev. 2021b. GlossReader at SemEval-2021 task 2: Reading definitions improves contextualized word embeddings. In *Proceedings of the 15th International Workshop on Semantic Evaluation (SemEval-2021)*, pages 756–762, Online. Association for Computational Linguistics.

Maxim Rachinskiy and Nikolay Arefyev. 2022. GlossReader at LSCDiscovery: Train to select a proper gloss in English – discover lexical semantic change in Spanish. In *Proceedings of the 3rd Workshop on Computational Approaches to Historical Language Change*, pages 198–203, Dublin, Ireland. Association for Computational Linguistics.

Digital resource. 1997. *Vanhan kirjasuomen sanakirja [Dictionary of Old Literary Finnish*. Helsinki: Kotimaisten kielten keskuksen verkkojulkaisuja 38.

Dominik Schlechtweg. 2023. *Human and Computational Measurement of Lexical Semantic Change*. Ph.D. thesis, University of Stuttgart, Stuttgart, Germany.

Dominik Schlechtweg, Barbara McGillivray, Simon Hengchen, Haim Dubossarsky, and Nina Tahmasebi. 2020. SemEval-2020 Task 1: Unsupervised Lexical Semantic Change Detection. In *Proceedings of the 14th International Workshop on Semantic Evaluation*, Barcelona, Spain. Association for Computational Linguistics.

Elena Voita, David Talbot, Fedor Moiseev, Rico Sennrich, and Ivan Titov. 2019. Analyzing multi-head self-attention: Specialized heads do the heavy lifting, the rest can be pruned. In *Proceedings of the 57th Annual Meeting of the Association for Computational Linguistics*, pages 5797–5808, Florence, Italy. Association for Computational Linguistics.

Frank D. Zamora-Reina, Felipe Bravo-Marquez, and Dominik Schlechtweg. 2022. LSCDiscovery: A shared task on semantic change discovery and detection in Spanish. In *Proceedings of the 3rd International Workshop on Computational Approaches to Historical Language Change*, Dublin, Ireland. Association for Computational Linguistics.

A Ablation study of the NSD model

In this section we provide an ablation study of our NSD model. In order to get insights about the importance of the chosen features, we compare our trained classifiers and several pure similarity measures such as the predicted probability, the dot product and the distance from a usage to the gloss selected by GlossReader FiEnRu (Figure 5). It turns out that the probabilities and dot products are far behind the classifiers, and on the Finnish dev set they even perform no better than a random classifier. The manhattan distance with l1 normalization is a bit worse than the trained classifiers. The extra

Model	dev fi AP GR	dev fi AP GR FiEnRu	dev ru AP GR	dev ru AP GR FiEnRu
single features				
cosine	0.106	0.110	0.685	0.695
euclid.	0.106	0.110	0.684	0.694
l2/euclid.	0.106	0.110	0.685	0.695
manh.	0.106	0.113	0.685	0.690
l1/manh.	**0.154**	**0.242**	**0.816**	**0.822**
full classifiers				
classifier w/ extra	**0.378**		**0.840**	
classifier w/o extra	0.305		0.833	
best pairs of features w/o extra features				
l1/manh. + euclid.	0.194	**0.284**	0.818	**0.823**
l1/manh. + l2/euclid.	**0.195**	**0.284**	0.818	**0.823**
l1/manh. + manh.	0.192	0.277	**0.819**	**0.823**
best pairs of features w/ extra features				
l1/manh. + #old usages	0.190	**0.291**	0.820	0.827
l1/manh. + #new usages	0.153	0.249	**0.821**	**0.829**
#new usages + #old senses	**0.266**	0.266	0.643	0.643

Table 5: Average precision of novel sense detection models on the dev sets. Except for the block with full classifiers, models use distance-based features either from GlossReader or GlossReader FiEnRu. The best results in each group are in **bold font**. The overall best results are underlined.

features consistently help on the Finnish dev set, but are almost useless on the Russian dev set.

In Table 5 we compare different NSD models using the average precision on the dev sets. To understand which quality can be achieved using the minimal number of features, we evaluate all single distance-based features. Furthermore, we train classifiers on all possible pairs of features, where each pair contains distances only from the same GlossReader. Also we compare classifiers with or without extra features.

We observe that the manhattan distance with l1 normalization, which is the best single feature, works poorly on the Finnish dataset, especially for the embeddings from GlossReader that was not fine-tuned on the Finnish train set. However, on the Russian dev set it closely follows the best classifier. As for the classifiers, we found that including non-distance features is important for Finnish. What is more interesting, when using the original GlossReader model among all pairs of features the best one does not contain embedding-based features at all, only the number of old senses and the number of new usages. This signals that for the Finish dataset GlossReader provides poor embeddings without fine-tuning.

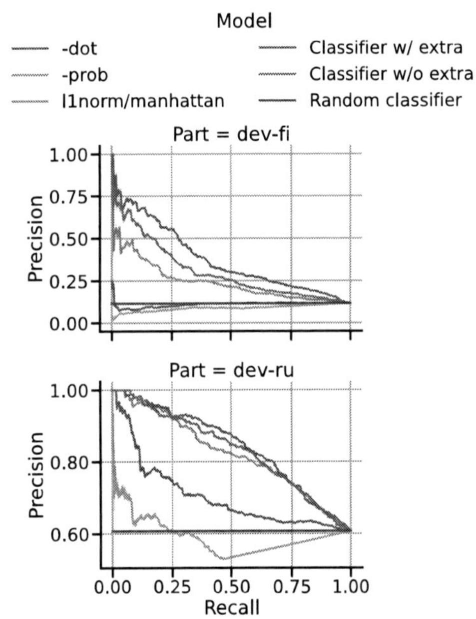

Figure 5: Precision-recall curves of novel sense detection models. Non classifier models are distances between usages and chosen glosses from GlossReader FiEnRu. Classifier w/ extra stands for classifier trained on distance-based and non distance-based features introduced in sub subsection 3.4.3. Classifier w/o extra stands for classifier trained only on distance-based features.

Exploring Sound Change Over Time: A Review of Computational and Human Perception

Siqi He
Shanghai Jiao Tong University
University of Heidelberg
hesiqiid@sjtu.edu.cn

Wei Zhao
University of Aberdeen
wei.zhao@abdn.ac.uk

Abstract

Computational and human perception are often considered separate approaches for studying sound changes over time; few works have touched on the intersection of both. To fill this research gap, we provide a pioneering review contrasting computational with human perception from the perspectives of methods and tasks. Overall, computational approaches rely on computer-driven models to perceive historical sound changes on etymological datasets, while human approaches use listener-driven models to perceive ongoing sound changes on recording corpora. Despite their differences, both approaches complement each other on phonetic and acoustic levels, showing the potential to achieve a more comprehensive perception of sound change. Moreover, we call for a comparative study on the datasets used by both approaches to investigate the influence of historical sound changes on ongoing changes. Lastly, we discuss the applications of sound change in computational linguistics, and point out that perceiving sound change alone is insufficient, as many processes of language change are complex, with entangled changes at syntactic, semantic, and phonetic levels.

1 Background

There has been ongoing scholarly interest in sound change over time for decades. A popular historical sound change is the Great Vowel Shift (Lass, 1992), where the long vowel [iː] in Middle English shifted to a diphthong /aɪ/ in Modern English for example. It took place over time from the 15th to 18th centuries, and greatly changed the English vowel system. Other examples include the loss of voiceless velars like [ç] in Modern English (Dobson, 1968), reduction of consonant clusters like [kn] $\rightarrow$ [n] (Turville-Petre and Burrow, 2020), and vowel reduction in unstressed syllables (Minkova, 2013). Many ongoing sound changes took place in the 20th century. For instance, in American regional dialects, a notable shift such as [ʌ] $\rightarrow$ [ɛ] in the vowel system occurred in the Northern Cities around the mid-20th century (Wolfram and Schilling, 2016).

While many works proposed computational approaches to perceive historical sound changes (Mielke, 2008; Dekker, 2018; Boldsen and Paggio, 2022) and others suggested using the listener-driven model to perceive ongoing sound changes (Janson, 1983; Sanker, 2018a; Quam and Creel, 2021), few works explored the intersection of both computational and human perception. The benefits of doing so can be substantial. Firstly, computational approaches perceive historical sound change by analyzing IPA transcriptions in etymological datasets, but these datasets lack acoustic features that human listeners/speakers can produce and perceive. Secondly, human perception observes ongoing changes through participation surveys over recording corpora, which lacks the considerations of acoustic and phonetic alignments between speakers that computational approaches can produce and perceive. Lastly, connections between etymological datasets and recording corpora are little explored; by combining both, one could conduct a comparative analysis of historical and ongoing sound changes, e.g., examining how historical changes impact ongoing changes. Thus, there is a need for a comparative review of computational and human perception.

In this work, we aim to fill the gap between two distant perception of sound change over time, with computational models on one hand and human observation on the other. To achieve this, we first review the tasks and methods from each perspective, and then present a unified view that combines both perception to explore sound change. Moreover, we discuss the connections of sound change to semantic and syntactic change, as well as the applications of sound change in computational linguistics.

Proceedings of the 5th Workshop on Computational Approaches to Historical Language Change, pages 180–186
August 15, 2024

2 Computational Perception

Sound change detection. Boldsen and Paggio (2022) connected semantic change detection with sound change detection and argued that diachronic distributional embeddings used for semantic change detection can track historical sound change. For lexical semantic change, diachronic word embeddings are guided by the distributional hypothesis suggesting that words that occur in similar contexts appear to have similar meanings. Interestingly, this idea also applies to phonology. Previous works showed that phonemes occurring in similar phonetic contexts likely belong to the same phonological class, demonstrating the applicability of the distributional hypothesis to phoneme embeddings (Mielke, 2008; Silfverberg et al., 2018).

Boldsen and Paggio (2022) proposed using phoneme embeddings trained on a historical Danish corpus to track sound changes over time. Their approach compared the embeddings of a phoneme pair across different periods to observe sound changes. For instance, [p] $\rightarrow$ [b] is observed when the distance between the phoneme embeddings of [p] and [b] becomes smaller over time. The results showed a decrease in distance between three phoneme embedding pairs: [p] and [b], [t] and [d], [k] and [g] over time, meaning that their approach recognized the phonetic changes from voiceless plosives to their voiced counterparts in Danish.

Phonetic alignment between cognate words. Phonetized cognate words consist of paired IPA transcriptions in two languages: either a proto-language and its descendant language or two descendant languages. Each transcription represents a sequence of phonemes. Translating a sequence of phonemes from one language to another can be framed as a machine translation task, as both execute a cross-lingual sequence-to-sequence task (Dekker, 2018; Fourrier and Sagot, 2020a).

For instance, Fourrier and Sagot (2020a) proposed using both statistical and neural machine translation models to perform phoneme-level translations between cognate words. The models investigated include Moses (Koehn et al., 2007) and MEDeA (Luong et al., 2015). The languages considered include Latin, Italian, and Spanish. For evaluation, the generated translations were compared to the ground-truths through BLEU (Papineni et al., 2002)—which calculates the overlap of n-grams phonemes between translations and the ground-truths. The results showed that the phonetic translations between cognate words from the proto-language to a descendant language (or from a descendant language to another) are much better than those from a descendant language to the proto-language. Moreover, the results demonstrated the superiority of the statistical model over the neural MT model on small datasets, whereas the neural model showed a greater ability to handle many-to-one mappings from various proto-forms to the same descendant form. It is important to note that the ground-truth translations were collected by automatically phonetizing cognate word pairs via Espeak (Duddington, 2007), and the automatic phonetization process is prone to errors, meaning that comparing generated translations with the ground truths may lead to inaccurate model assessment.

Markedness of phonemes. Markedness is a linguistic label separating common from less common phonemes in a phonological system. In English, the voiceless consonants [p], [t], and [k] are unmarked as they are more common compared to their voiced, marked counterparts [b], [d], and [g]. For vowels, peripheral high vowels such as [i] and [u] are marked while mid-central vowels like [ə] are unmarked (Jakobson, 1968; Haspelmath, 2006).

Ceolin and Sayeed (2019) proposed a probabilistic approach to model sound change by estimating the frequency of phonemes over time. Interestingly, they found that their approach could also recognize the markedness of a phoneme. Their approach was to estimate the frequency of each phoneme at a later time based on the frequencies of other phonemes observed at an earlier time through the split-merger process. The results showed that the unmarked phonemes at a later time appear to have higher frequencies compared to marked counterparts as postulated, meaning that their approach could separate unmarked from marked phonemes. We note that their approach considered neither phonetic nor acoustic features and was only evaluated on three phonemes in an artificial setup.

Sound convergence. Unlike historical sound change, which takes place gradually over centuries, sound convergence is a process of ongoing sound change through which speakers adjust their speech to align acoustically and phonetically with other speakers (Natale, 1975). Research showed that native speakers often phonetically converge to non-native speakers in interactive environments (Giles, 1973; Pardo, 2006; Babel, 2010; Yu et al., 2013). Recently, works by Lewandowski and Nygaard

(2018); Wagner et al. (2021) showed that sound convergence can also occur in non-interactive settings. For instance, Wagner et al. (2021) recruited 76 native Dutch speakers and a non-native speaker to read aloud a careful selection of words, and their speech was recorded. Importantly, although the native and non-native speakers have no interaction, the speech of non-native speakers was made available to the native speakers. This allows the native speakers to potentially adjust their speech. All the speech was transformed into acoustic features by using Praat (Boersma, 2011). Acoustic features (e.g., vowel and fricative duration) of the native speakers are compared to the non-native speaker by calculating the difference-in-distance score over these acoustic features. The positive score indicates convergence, otherwise divergence. The results showed that (a) the Dutch native speakers show sound convergence to the non-native speaker in the scenario where interaction is minimal and (b) the degree of sound convergence is affected by how much native speakers think the speech by the non-native speaker is native-like.

Despite being useful, relying on acoustic features to observe sound convergence has at least two limitations: Firstly, the convergence on the phonetic level is overlooked; for example, speakers who adjust their speech in terms of place and manner of articulation are not recognized as sound adaptation. Secondly, the outcome of sound convergence is affected by the quality of acoustic features—which relies on the recording quality and the efficacy of computer tools to extract these features from speech.

3 Human Perception

Perceptual similarity. The work by Goldinger (1998) introduced the perceptual similarity task that is concerned with how phonetic changes are received, processed and interpreted by listeners (Martin and Bunnell, 1981; Sanker, 2018b). This approach is known as the listener-driven model of sound change, where a group of listeners heard recordings of a speaker's initial speech and the later speech (after the speaker listened to a target speech by another speaker). The listeners were then asked to determine which of the two recordings sounded closer to the target speech the speaker was exposed to.

Sound convergence. Wagner et al. (2021) employed the perceptual similarity task to study sound convergence from native speech to non-native speech in Dutch. They recruited 16 listeners native in Dutch and asked them to perform the perceptual similarity task where the listeners heard participants' initial and later speech and had to choose which production sounded more similar to that of the model speaker non-native in Dutch. Moreover, the listeners were asked to rate the model speaker's speech in terms of how accented, comprehensible, and familiar it sounded. These ratings were included in the analyses to determine how they affected the degree of observed convergence. The results showed that the overall sound convergence score was slightly above the random chance, indicating a weakly perceived convergence in participants' speech after the target speech was exposed to them. Secondly, they found that several speech samples showed more sound convergence than others. Moreover, they noted that perceived convergence was affected by how strongly the model speaker's foreign accent was perceived.

Although human perception can observe ongoing sound changes, listeners may misperceive the acoustic and phonetic features of a speaker, resulting in incorrect judgments of sound changes (Babel and Johnson, 2010; Ohala, 2017; Sanker, 2018b).

4 A Unified Perspective

Computer-aided human perception. Using computational methods can partly automate and possibly refine the human perception process of sound changes. This is because doing so allows for observing subtle changes on phonetic and acoustic levels, such as vowel duration shift and nasal place assimilation that are sometimes not obvious to perceive by listeners. Additionally, combining computational and listener-driven methods would create a feedback loop where computational results could refine the human perception process and insights from listeners could be used to improve computational models.

Cross-studying etymological datasets and recording corpora. Etymological datasets contain phonetic transcriptions that reflect historical sound changes, which are commonly used for computational models to observe changes over centuries. In contrast, recording corpora are a database for listeners to perceive ongoing sound changes. Despite their different aims, it is intriguing to know the influence of historical sound changes on ongoing changes. A potential idea is to start with collecting shared words in etymological datasets and recording corpora, and then inspect their phonetic similarity and difference. Note that unlike recording corpora, phonetic transcriptions do not include acoustic features; therefore, a comparative study of historical and ongoing sound changes at the acoustic level is not possible.

5 Discussions

5.1 Connections to Other Changes

While there have been many works on computational modeling of semantic and syntactic change (Hamilton et al., 2016; Schlechtweg et al., 2020; Ma et al., 2024a,b; Merrill et al., 2019; Krielke et al., 2022; Chen et al., 2024), they often lack connections to sound change. Such connections are crucial because many changes simultaneously affect multiple linguistic levels. A notable case is homograph where two words share the same spelling but have different meanings and pronunciations. Examples include "present" ([ˈprɛzənt] vs. [prɪˈzɛnt]) and "bow" ([baʊ] vs. [boʊ]). Another case is grammaticalization—a process that incurs semantic, syntactic and phonetic changes. For example, "going to" grammaticalizes into "gonna", shifting from a verb to a future marker. This process changes the original meaning, impacts syntactic structure, and incurs phonetic reduction. To identify homographs and grammaticalization, it might be necessary to develop computational and human approaches to model/observe changes across multiple linguistic levels at once.

5.2 Applications in Computational Linguistics

Phylogenetic Inference. This task aims to reconstruct the evolutionary relationships among languages based on their shared linguistic features. For example, Proto-Indo-European, as the ancestral language, gives rise to many descendant languages within the Indo-European language groups such as Indo-Iranian, Germanic, and Celtic. Linguists construct a phylogenetic language tree by taking the ancestor language as the root and connecting it to descendant languages, based on the laws of sound changes over time (Hoenigswald, 1965). For instance, there exists a phoneme correspondence between High German [ts], Dutch [t], English [t], Swedish [t], and Icelandic [t], all of which are inherited from the proto-phoneme [*t] in their ancestry Proto-Germanic language group (where [*t] $\rightarrow$ [t] in High German). This phoneme correspondence is one of many reasons that these languages are the descendants of Proto-Germanic.

However, computer-based language phylogenies for major language groups like Dravidian (Kolipakam et al., 2018), Sino-Tibetan (Sagart et al., 2019), and Indo-European (Heggarty et al., 2023) often rely on cognate sets from semantically aligned word lists across languages. Campbell and Poser (2008) questioned the use of cognate sets for phylogenetic inference, as meanings in cognate words might undergo changes over time, resulting in the instability of a phylogenetic tree. Other works proposed reconstructing phylogenetic language trees using sound correspondences between cognate words instead of lexical cognates (Chacon and List, 2016; Cathcart, 2019; Chang et al., 2023; Häuser et al., 2024). For instance, Häuser et al. (2024) presented a framework that first identifies phonetic alignment between cognate words using LingPy and then uses BMrBayes (Ronquist and Huelsenbeck, 2003) and RAxML-NG (Kozlov et al., 2019) to reconstruct phylogenetic trees. For evaluation, the generated phylogenetic trees are compared to the ground-truth Glottolog tree (Hammarström et al., 2019) by computing their topological distance via generalized quartet distance (Pompei et al., 2011). The results showed that sound-based phylogenetic trees underperform cognate-based counterparts, i.e., that cognate-based trees are topologically closer to the gold Glottolog tree. This might be attributed to the lack of consideration for borrowing. For instance, two languages might not be related, although the phoneme sequences of their cognate words could be similar. Loanword is the example, where phonemes are borrowed from a third, unrelated language, rather than inherited from the proto-phoneme.

Quality assessment of etymological datasets. Etymological datasets are a crucial resource for phylogenetic inference, low-resource machine translation, and historical linguistic tasks. Many such datasets have been made available and are automatically generated from various data sources. For instance, EtymWordNet (De Melo, 2014) and CogNet (Batsuren et al., 2019) are derived from WordNet across hundreds of languages, while EtymDB 1.0 (Sagot, 2017) and 2.0 (Fourrier and Sagot, 2020b) are sourced from Wiktionary across over two thousand languages. However, the quality of these datasets remains unclear. Firstly, many datasets use a loose definition of cognacy to enlarge data coverage. Secondly, the automatic processes used to generate these datasets are prone to errors. Therefore, there is a need to estimate the quality of these etymological datasets.

Wettig et al. (2012) proposed using the degree of phonetic alignment between cognate words as a measure of the internal consistency of an etymological dataset. They postulated that the more phonetically similar cognates words are, the better quality a dataset would be. For instance, the English word 'house' and the German word 'Haus' are phonetically equivalent [haʊz], implying that this cognate word pair is likely correct. To achieve this idea, they use the Minimum Description Length, a dynamic programming algorithm, to calculate the cost of an optimal phoneme-level alignment between cognate word pairs for the Uralic language group. The alignment operates on phonetic features such as plosive/fricative and labial/dental. The challenge arises from the fact that phonemes inherited from the proto-phoneme may undergo sound changes over time, resulting in phonemes in one language potentially different from another. For evaluation, the generated alignments were not compared to the ground-truths due to the lack of gold phoneme-level alignments. Instead, their approach was evaluated in three scenarios: compression rates, rules of correspondence and imputation.

Note that phoneme-level alignments were not compared against the ground-truths. Thus, the efficacy of the measure based on these alignments in estimating the quality of etymological datasets remains unclear. Moreover, their approach only considers one-to-one phoneme-level alignment and ignores one-to-many. In doing so, their approach could wrongly penalize correct cognate word pairs with one-to-many alignments, such as [kæt] in 'cat' and [katsə] in the German word 'Katze'.

6 Conclusions

As two rarely connected disciplines, computational and human perception have their own interests, tasks and methods. However, we showed that these two perception benefit each other from the perspective of methods and datasets. Additionally, we showed that the applications of sound change are manifold in computational linguistics, including phylogenetic inference and quality assessment of datasets. Despite these positive aspects, we argue that a unified perception of multi-faceted change is crucial, as many changes are entangled across phonetics, syntax and semantics.

Acknowledgements

We thank the anonymous reviewers for their thoughtful feedback that greatly improved the texts.

References

Molly Babel. 2010. Dialect divergence and convergence in new zealand english. *Language in Society*, 39(4):437–456.

Molly Babel and Keith Johnson. 2010. Accessing psycho-acoustic perception and language-specific perception with speech sounds. *Laboratory phonology*, 1(1):179–205.

Khuyagbaatar Batsuren, Gábor Bella, Fausto Giunchiglia, et al. 2019. Cognet: A large-scale cognate database. In *ACL 2019 The 57th Annual Meeting of the Association for Computational Linguistics: Proceedings of the Conference*, pages 3136–3145. Association for Computational Linguistics.

Paul Boersma. 2011. Praat: doing phonetics by computer [computer program]. *http://www. praat. org/.*

Sidsel Boldsen and Patrizia Paggio. 2022. Letters from the past: Modeling historical sound change through diachronic character embeddings. In *Proceedings of the 60th Annual Meeting of the Association for Computational Linguistics (Volume 1: Long Papers)*, pages 6713–6722, Dublin, Ireland. Association for Computational Linguistics.

Lyle Campbell and William J Poser. 2008. Language classification. *(No Title)*.

Chundra Cathcart. 2019. Gaussian process models of sound change in Indo-Aryan dialectology. In *Proceedings of the 1st International Workshop on Computational Approaches to Historical Language Change*, pages 254–264, Florence, Italy. Association for Computational Linguistics.

Andrea Ceolin and Ollie Sayeed. 2019. Modeling markedness with a split-and-merger model of sound change. In *Proceedings of the 1st International Workshop on Computational Approaches to Historical Language Change*, pages 67–70.

Thiago Costa Chacon and Johann-Mattis List. 2016. Improved computational models of sound change shed light on the history of the tukanoan languages. *Journal of Language Relationship*, 13(3-4):177–204.

Kalvin Chang, Nathaniel Robinson, Anna Cai, Ting Chen, Annie Zhang, and David Mortensen. 2023. Automating sound change prediction for phylogenetic inference: A tukanoan case study. In *Proceedings of the 4th Workshop on Computational Approaches to Historical Language Change*, pages 129–142, Singapore. Association for Computational Linguistics.

Yanran Chen, Wei Zhao, Anne Breitbarth, Manuel Stoeckel, Alexander Mehler, and Steffen Eger. 2024. Syntactic language change in english and german: Metrics, parsers, and convergences. *arXiv preprint arXiv:2402.11549*.

Gerard De Melo. 2014. Etymological wordnet: Tracing the history of words. In *LREC*, pages 1148–1154.

Peter Dekker. 2018. Reconstructing language ancestry by performing word prediction with neural networks. *Master. Amsterdam: University of Amsterdam*.

Eric John Dobson. 1968. English pronunciation, 1500-1700. *(No Title)*.

Jonathan Duddington. 2007. 2015. espeak text to speech.

Clémentine Fourrier and Benoît Sagot. 2020a. Comparing statistical and neural models for learning sound correspondences. In *LT4HALA 2020-First Workshop on Language Technologies for Historical and Ancient Languages*.

Clémentine Fourrier and Benoît Sagot. 2020b. Methodological aspects of developing and managing an etymological lexical resource: Introducing etymdb 2.0. In *LREC 2020-12th Language Resources and Evaluation Conference*.

Howard Giles. 1973. Accent mobility: A model and some data. *Anthropological linguistics*, pages 87–105.

Stephen D Goldinger. 1998. Echoes of echoes? an episodic theory of lexical access. *Psychological review*, 105(2):251.

William L. Hamilton, Jure Leskovec, and Dan Jurafsky. 2016. Diachronic word embeddings reveal statistical laws of semantic change. In *Proceedings of the 54th Annual Meeting of the Association for Computational Linguistics (Volume 1: Long Papers)*, pages 1489–1501, Berlin, Germany. Association for Computational Linguistics.

Harald Hammarström, Martin Haspelmath, Robert Forkel, and Sebastiaon Bank. 2019. Glottolog. version 4.0. *Max Planck Institute for the Science of Human History, Jena*.

Martin Haspelmath. 2006. Against markedness (and what to replace it with). *Journal of linguistics*, 42(1):25–70.

Luise Häuser, Gerhard Jäger, Johann-Mattis List, Taraka Rama, and Alexandros Stamatakis. 2024. Are sounds sound for phylogenetic reconstruction? In *Proceedings of the 6th Workshop on Research in Computational Linguistic Typology and Multilingual NLP*, pages 78–87, St. Julian's, Malta. Association for Computational Linguistics.

Paul Heggarty, Cormac Anderson, Matthew Scarborough, Benedict King, Remco Bouckaert, Lechosław Jocz, Martin Joachim Kümmel, Thomas Jügel, Britta Irslinger, Roland Pooth, et al. 2023. Language trees with sampled ancestors support a hybrid model for the origin of indo-european languages. *Science*, 381(6656):eabg0818.

Henry M Hoenigswald. 1965. Language change and linguistic reconstruction.

Roman Jakobson. 1968. *Child language: aphasia and phonological universals*. 72. Walter de Gruyter.

Tore Janson. 1983. Sound change in perception and production. *Language*, 59:18.

Philipp Koehn, Hieu Hoang, Alexandra Birch, Chris Callison-Burch, Marcello Federico, Nicola Bertoldi, Brooke Cowan, Wade Shen, Christine Moran, Richard Zens, et al. 2007. Moses: Open source toolkit for statistical machine translation. In *Proceedings of the 45th annual meeting of the association for computational linguistics companion volume proceedings of the demo and poster sessions*, pages 177–180. Association for Computational Linguistics.

Vishnupriya Kolipakam, Fiona M Jordan, Michael Dunn, Simon J Greenhill, Remco Bouckaert, Russell D Gray, and Annemarie Verkerk. 2018. A bayesian phylogenetic study of the dravidian language family. *Royal Society open science*, 5(3):171504.

Alexey M Kozlov, Diego Darriba, Tomáš Flouri, Benoit Morel, and Alexandros Stamatakis. 2019. Raxml-ng: a fast, scalable and user-friendly tool for maximum likelihood phylogenetic inference. *Bioinformatics*, 35(21):4453–4455.

Marie-Pauline Krielke, Luigi Talamo, Mahmoud Fawzi, and Jörg Knappen. 2022. Tracing syntactic change in the scientific genre: Two Universal Dependency-parsed diachronic corpora of scientific English and German. In *Proceedings of the Thirteenth Language Resources and Evaluation Conference*, pages 4808–4816, Marseille, France. European Language Resources Association.

Roger Lass. 1992. Phonology and morphology. *The Cambridge history of the English language*, 2:1066–1476.

Eva M Lewandowski and Lynne C Nygaard. 2018. Vocal alignment to native and non-native speakers of english. *The Journal of the Acoustical Society of America*, 144(2):620–633.

Thang Luong, Hieu Pham, and Christopher D. Manning. 2015. Effective approaches to attention-based neural machine translation. In *Proceedings of the 2015 Conference on Empirical Methods in Natural Language Processing*, pages 1412–1421, Lisbon, Portugal. Association for Computational Linguistics.

Xianghe Ma, Dominik Schlechtweg, and Wei Zhao. 2024a. Presence or absence: Are unknown word usages in dictionaries? In *Proceedings of the 5th Workshop on Computational Approaches to Historical Language Change*, Bangkok. Association for Computational Linguistics.

Xianghe Ma, Michael Strube, and Wei Zhao. 2024b. Graph-based clustering for detecting semantic change across time and languages. In *Proceedings of the 18th Conference of the European Chapter of the Association for Computational Linguistics (Volume 1: Long Papers)*, pages 1542–1561, St. Julian's, Malta. Association for Computational Linguistics.

James G Martin and H Timothy Bunnell. 1981. Perception of anticipatory coarticulation effects. *The Journal of the Acoustical Society of America*, 69(2):559–567.

William Merrill, Gigi Stark, and Robert Frank. 2019. Detecting syntactic change using a neural part-of-speech tagger. In *Proceedings of the 1st International Workshop on Computational Approaches to Historical Language Change*, pages 167–174, Florence, Italy. Association for Computational Linguistics.

Jeff Mielke. 2008. *The emergence of distinctive features*. Oxford University Press.

Donka Minkova. 2013. *Historical phonology of English*. Edinburgh University Press.

Michael Natale. 1975. Social desirability as related to convergence of temporal speech patterns. *Perceptual and Motor Skills*, 40(3):827–830.

John J Ohala. 2017. Phonetics and historical phonology. *The handbook of historical linguistics*, pages 667–686.

Kishore Papineni, Salim Roukos, Todd Ward, and Wei-Jing Zhu. 2002. Bleu: a method for automatic evaluation of machine translation. In *Proceedings of the 40th Annual Meeting of the Association for Computational Linguistics*, pages 311–318, Philadelphia, Pennsylvania, USA. Association for Computational Linguistics.

Jennifer S Pardo. 2006. On phonetic convergence during conversational interaction. *The Journal of the Acoustical Society of America*, 119(4):2382–2393.

Simone Pompei, Vittorio Loreto, and Francesca Tria. 2011. On the accuracy of language trees. *PloS one*, 6(6):e20109.

Carolyn Quam and Sarah C. Creel. 2021. Impacts of acoustic-phonetic variability on perceptual development for spoken language: A review. *Wiley interdisciplinary reviews. Cognitive science*, page e1558.

Fredrik Ronquist and John P Huelsenbeck. 2003. Mrbayes 3: Bayesian phylogenetic inference under mixed models. *Bioinformatics*, 19(12):1572–1574.

Laurent Sagart, Guillaume Jacques, Yunfan Lai, Robin J Ryder, Valentin Thouzeau, Simon J Greenhill, and Johann-Mattis List. 2019. Dated language phylogenies shed light on the ancestry of sino-tibetan. *Proceedings of the National Academy of Sciences*, 116(21):10317–10322.

Benoît Sagot. 2017. Extracting an etymological database from wiktionary. In *Electronic Lexicography in the 21st century (eLex 2017)*, pages 716–728.

Chelsea Sanker. 2018a. A survey of experimental evidence for diachronic change. *Linguistics Vanguard*, 4.

Chelsea Sanker. 2018b. A survey of experimental evidence for diachronic change. *Linguistics Vanguard*, 4(1):20170039.

Dominik Schlechtweg, Barbara McGillivray, Simon Hengchen, Haim Dubossarsky, and Nina Tahmasebi. 2020. SemEval-2020 task 1: Unsupervised lexical semantic change detection. In *Proceedings of the Fourteenth Workshop on Semantic Evaluation*, pages 1–23, Barcelona (online). International Committee for Computational Linguistics.

Miikka P Silfverberg, Lingshuang Mao, and Mans Hulden. 2018. Sound analogies with phoneme embeddings. *Society for Computation in Linguistics*, 1(1).

Thorlac Turville-Petre and John Anthony Burrow. 2020. *A book of Middle English*. John Wiley & Sons.

Mónica A Wagner, Mirjam Broersma, James M McQueen, Sara Dhaene, and Kristin Lemhöfer. 2021. Phonetic convergence to non-native speech: Acoustic and perceptual evidence. *Journal of Phonetics*, 88:101076.

Hannes Wettig, Kirill Reshetnikov, and Roman Yangarber. 2012. Using context and phonetic features in models of etymological sound change. In *Proceedings of the EACL 2012 Joint Workshop of LINGVIS & UNCLH*, pages 108–116.

Walt Wolfram and Natalie Schilling. 2016. *American English: Dialects and variation*, 3 edition. Number 25 in Language in Society. Wiley Blackwell, Chichester, UK.

Alan CL Yu, Carissa Abrego-Collier, and Morgan Sonderegger. 2013. Phonetic imitation from an individual-difference perspective: Subjective attitude, personality and "autistic" traits. *PloS one*, 8(9):e74746.

A Few-shot Learning Approach for Lexical Semantic Change Detection Using GPT-4

Zhengfei Ren, Annalina Caputo, Gareth J. F. Jones,

ADAPT Centre, School of Computing, Dublin City University, Dublin 9, Ireland
zhengfei.ren3@mail.dcu.ie, annalina.caputo@dcu.ie, gareth.jones@dcu.ie

Abstract

Lexical Semantic Change Detection (LSCD) aims to detect language change from a diachronic corpus over time. We can see that over the last two decades there has been a surge in research dealing with the LSC Detection. Recently, a series of methods especially contextualized word embeddings have been widely established to address this task. While several studies have investigated LSCD using large language models (LLMs), an evaluation of prompt engineering techniques, such as few-shot learning with different in-context examples for improving the LSCD performance is required. In this study, we examine the few-shot learning ability of GPT-4 to detect semantic changes in the Chinese language change evaluation dataset ChiWUG. We show that our LLM-based solution improves the GCD evaluation metric on the ChiWUG benchmark compared to the previously top-performing pre-trained system. The result suggests that using GPT-4 with three-shot learning with hand-picked demonstrations achieves the best performance among our different prompts.

1 Introduction

Lexical semantic change detection (LSCD) aims to address the problem of automatically identifying meaning change in target words between the current period and earlier time periods (Kim et al., 2014), (Kulkarni et al., 2015), (Giulianelli et al., 2020) (Schlechtweg et al., 2020). The majority of current work on LSCD uses deep contextualized models, such as BERT (Devlin et al., 2018) or EMLO (Peters et al., 2018), to model the semantics of target words from different time-sliced corpus (Periti and Tahmasebi, 2024) (Kutuzov and Giulianelli, 2020) (Hamilton et al., 2016), (Giulianelli et al., 2020). Semantic change can then be detected by vector similarities between word embeddings using these models.

Recently, Large Language Models (LLMs) have showcased remarkable capabilities in solving natural language processing tasks based on zero-shot predictions (Karjus, 2023), (Karanikolas et al., 2023). Recent work has shown that LLMs can even excel in an wider range of applications with appropriate prompt instructions (Hou et al., 2024), (Marvin et al., 2023), (Chen et al., 2023a). However, current work on the LSCD using LLMs lacks a proper method that uses prompt engineering to build LSCD model, such as using example retrieval algorithm to find the most similar language change context pairs compared to input pairs.

In this paper, we apply prompt engineering on an LSCD task, where few-shot learning using GPT-4 is applied with in-context demonstrations of prompts based on manual selection or machine retrieval algorithms. Our proposed method is systematically tested on a Chinese evaluation dataset ChiWUG (Chen et al., 2023b) following the Diachronic Word Usage Graph (DWUG) annotation and evaluation framework. Our methods serve as an exploratory examination of LLM performance for LSCD with various prompting strategies. This may be applied to other LSCD tasks in different language which also follow the DWUG framework, such as English (EN), German (DE), Swedish (SW) and Latin (LA) (Schlechtweg et al., 2020) and Norwegian(NO) (Kutuzov et al., 2022).

2 Related Work

Lexical semantic change has been evaluated by both static models, such as skip-gram (Kim et al., 2014), (Kulkarni et al., 2015) or contextualized embedding methods, such as BERT (Kutuzov and Giulianelli, 2020), (Giulianelli et al., 2020). To quantitatively evaluate lexical semantic change, Semeval 2020 task 1 defined an evaluation framework for measuring lexical semantic change (Schlechtweg et al., 2020). Two tasks including binary change

Proceedings of the 5th Workshop on Computational Approaches to Historical Language Change, pages 187–192
August 15, 2024 ©2024 Association for Computational Linguistics

classification and graded change detection (GCD) were developed for evaluating systems seeking to address LSCD. Binary classification simply measures whether the meaning changes or not, while GCD aims to measure the correlation between true scores and change degrees for all the target words. Recent work has shown that LLM models have impressive reasoning and prediction ability on many natural language processing (NLP) including language change detection (Karjus, 2023), (Ziems et al., 2024), (Laskar et al., 2023). Moreover, some evaluations of ChatGPT have been built on a series of NLP tasks including Word Sense Induction (WSI) and Word Sense Disambiguation (WSD) (Laskar et al., 2023).

Meanwhile, one work compared the performances of LLM and pre-trained language models on the shot-term language change dataset TempoWIC and showed that zero-shot GPT-4 achieved superior results (Wang and Choi, 2023). More recently, ChatGPT web interface and the official OpenAI APIs have been evaluated on WSI and LSCD with GCD scores, results show that ChatGPT achieves slightly lower performance than BERT in detecting both long-term and shot-term changes on the HistoWIC dataset and TempoWIC dataset respectively (Periti et al., 2024).

To the best of our knowledge, only one study has employed a series of contextualized models to implement language change detection on all LSCD datasets including the ChiWUG task (Periti and Tahmasebi, 2024). The XL-LEXEME (Cassotti et al., 2023) with the average pairwise distance (APD) performs best among their models. The performance of GPT-4 was comparable to XL-LEXEME on three tasks relevant to LSCD: Word-in-Context (WIC), WSI and GCD task. GPT-4 and XL-LEXEME achieve close to human-level while other contextualized embeddings perform in a low-moderate level, the performance of GPT-4 was only slightly lower than the BERT model. However, their GPT-4 model was only evaluated on an English dataset, and not for any other language dataset for the LSCD task. In our study, we compare our approach to this system using GCD scores on the ChiWUG evaluation dataset.

3 LSCD using LLM

To implement LSCD using LLM, we use the official GPT-4 API to conduct our experiments, other versions of GPT-4 can be found in the OpenAI documentation [1]. Our basic prompt is to predict whether the meaning of a target word changes or not given two context sentences. The task instruction leverages a similar prompt template proposed in (Karjus, 2023). We show a prompt example of a one-shot learning method with this template in Appendix B. In this paper, we propose to use few-shot learning using GPT-4 with different methods to select the demonstration examples for further improvements in performance of LSCD prediction.

下海 *xiahai*
原本在大学担任生物学教授的他, 决定下海创办了一家生物科技公司. A professor of biology in a university decided to set up a biotechnology company
她曾是一名成功的时尚设计师, 后来选择下海,开设了自己的时装品牌 She was as a successful fashion designer before she chose to go to business and start her own fashion brand

Table 1: Our hand-picked context example in one-shot learning with label *Related*.

3.1 Prompt Engineering

To increase the prediction ability, we use the few-shot learning approach to enrich the LLM's representation ability for semantic change. Meanwhile, we set the temperature of the GPT-4 model to zero and to reduce the randomness of the generated language change results to improve the performance.

To construct the in-context example, we first develop our hand-picked examples and then design a method to select an example from the training corpora for providing similar semantic knowledge directly from the ChiWUG dataset and inject it into a prompt. In following subsection, we provide details of the selections of demonstration learning examples using both methods.

3.2 Manual Selection

Our manually selected examples are developed from searching online linguistic resources from the internet containing two context sentences of a target word. We show one of these examples in Table 1. This manually selected example contains a Chinese target word 下海, which means 'go into the sea' or 'to venture'.

[1]https://platform.openai.com/docs

This sample is labeled by the change type *Related*, in which the meanings between the two text inputs are basically similar, but with different background contexts. We suppose such information could improve representation of GPT-4 model for inferring related semantic change types.

3.3 Example with Retrieval

As well as manual selection, we explore selection of demonstration examples by retrieval from a corpus with similar semantic representation with input queries. The retrieval process relies on the Chinese Bert model from the Huggingface [2].

Specifically, the last four hidden state embeddings of the Chinese BERT base model for the target word in two input sentences from two time periods are extracted for constructing the word embedding. For computing the similarity, two context sentences are concatenated to form a single vector representation, then cosine similarity is calculated between the representations for the input context pairs and the sample context pairs from the dataset. Two contexts in the dataset with the highest similarity are used as the retrieved examples to construct the prompt demonstrations. The retrieval corpus was generated from the first 40 sentences among the whole dataset for each word. An example of retrieved and original context pairs is shown in Appendix B with input and retrieved sentence pairs.

Our idea of example retrieval is that the greater the similarity between the input context and the demonstration example, the higher probability that the model will improve the performance, such in-context information could provide LLMs with better representation ability for detecting similar semantic changes.

4 Experiments

In this section, we introduce the dataset used for our experiments, give details of our experiments with results and analyze our findings.

4.1 Dataset

The dataset used for our investigation is ChiWug (Chen et al., 2023b). This consists of 6,100 human semantic relatedness judgments for 40 target words. The ChiWUG dataset follows the DWUG framework for LSCD tasks (Schlechtweg et al., 2021). Moreover, the context pairs are annotated with the relatedness between them with a four-scale degree

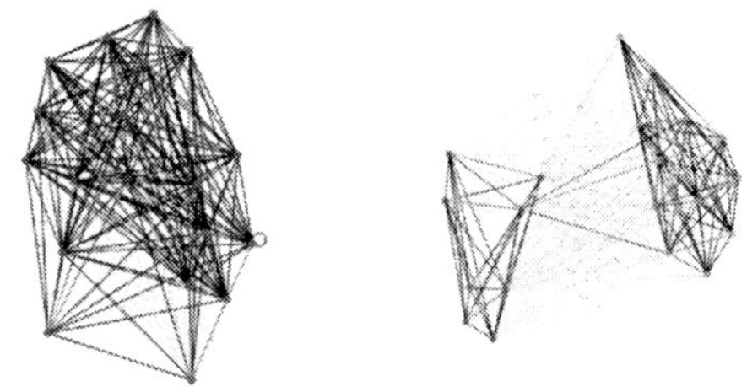

Figure 1: Word Usage Graph for word '下海' (xiahai). Nodes represents the word usages, the edges represent the usage relatedness between word usages (Chen et al., 2023b).

with 1 to 4 referring to semantic proximity from unrelated to the identical usages. The examples are represented in a DWUG with related semantic relations between target words, figure 1 shows one such word example for a target word 'xiahai'.

In ChiWUG, the corpora are divided into two sub-corpora, the EARLIER is from 1953 to 1978 and the LATTER is from 1979 to 2003. Three metrics are set within the dataset (Chen et al., 2023b): binary change, Jensen-Shannon Distance (JSD) and COMPARE. Binary change is the same as that used in the Semeval 2020 subtask1 and JSD can be regarded as the graded change scores.

4.2 Evaluations

In our system, we use two metrics to evaluate our method: binary change and the GCD score. To detect the binary change, we label target changed that contain more than 4 labels *unrelated* following similar criteria in (Karjus, 2023).

Moreover, we compute the GCD scores by calculating the Spearman correlation between the sum of all the change scores from 1 to 4 for a target word to ground truth scores. We evaluate these two metrics based on a sample of ChiWUG with solely 40 sentences pairs among 1,560 for each target word, which was shown to be a sufficient number of samples to predict correct change scores.

4.3 Zero-shot vs One-shot vs Few-shot

Zero-shot can be built directly with an initial prompt, where the instruction leveraged prompts used in (Karjus, 2023), a one-shot learning example with the same task introduction of the language change task is shown in the Appendix A.

As shown in Table 2, the three-shot model with hand picked examples shows the best re-

[2]https://huggingface.co/google-bert/bert-base-uncased

Approaches	Binary Change	GCD
XL-LEXEME	/	0.73
Zero-shot	0.65	0.65
Two-shot	**0.83**	0.73
Three-shot	0.70	**0.79**
One-shot Retrieval	0.70	0.72

Table 2: GCD predictions with different zero-shot or few-shot settings of GPT-4 models, XL-LEXEME is the previous best-performing model evaluated on ChiWUG (Periti and Tahmasebi, 2024), (Cassotti et al., 2023).

sults for both GCD scores and binary classification among these methods, which also outperforms the current best GCD prediction scores by XL-LEXEME model on ChiWUG benchmark dataset with smaller corpus for change prediction. Results for one-shot and three-shot models demonstrate improvement compared to zero-shot learning and two-shot-learning models. However, we do not see any improvements from two-shot learning compared to the one-shot learning method, the performance of one-shot learning model, with or without the machine selected demonstration example, is shown in the Table 2. Results show that they achieve the same scores, we leave the detailed discussion of this to the next section.

4.4 Discussion

Overall, we can see an upward trend of performance as the number of in-context demonstration examples increases. The three-shot method is better than all other established methods including zero-shot, one-shot and two-shot models. We can also see that few-shot method can benefit from our meticulously selected examples. Moreover, as shown in Table 2, our three-shot learning model outperforms the previously best contextualized word embeddings and achieves a new state-of-art performance on ChiWIG evaluation dataset, two-shot learning model with manually selected examples also shows superior change detection predictions over a pre-trained language model. We infer that few-shot learning with typical semantic change examples can improve LLMs in-context ability for language change detection.

Nevertheless, we get relatively similar results with one-shot learning using a manually selected demonstration example and automatically selected example, although the retrieved example is sharing similar semantic change context with input pairs, this method does not provide any improvements as we expected. We show one such example retrieved from the sample dataset in the Appendixm B to illusrate retrieved contexts and original inputs. Though they are most similar context pairs among our sample dataset according to BERT retrieval, the in-context learning may not improve from this directly. Our manually selected example in one-shot learning may be representative enough to provide semantic changes knowledge for GPT-4. Moreover, results show that two-shot learning with hand-picked examples may not provide further improvements in predicting language change results. This may also be because the quality of the added demonstration examples in two-shot learning may be poorer than other examples.

In the next stage of our work, we will examine different combinations of examples manually selected and retrieved for any improvements in performance. We leave the detailed reasons for the relation between the detection performance and the example similarity with the original query to the future work.

5 Conclusions

Overall, we have demonstrated higher performance of the proposed GPT-4's few-shot learning model on the LSCD task following the Semeval 2020 task 1 evaluation, compared to the previous contextualized embedding model. We tested the effectiveness of few-shot learning with hand-picked examples and the most similar samples from corpora with our retrieval method utlizing BERT. Our model, utilizing three-shot leaning featuring manually selected demonstration examples for semantic change detection, achieves the current highest GCD scores on the ChiWUG evaluation dataset. We show that few-shot learning with representative examples in prompts has the potential to increase the semantic representation ability of the LLM for this task. However, there is no evidence that one-shot learning with example retrieval increases GPT-4's prediction performance on the LSCD task. We leave developing explanations for the effect of retrieval on LSCD performance to future work.

Acknowledgments

This work was conducted with the financial support of the Science Foundation Ireland Centre for Research Training in Artificial Intelligence under Grant No. 18/CRT/6223, and partially as part of the ADAPT Centre at DCU (Grant No.

13/RC/2106_P2) (www.adaptcentre.ie). For the purpose of Open Access, the author has applied a CC BY public copyright license to any Author Accepted Manuscript version arising from this submission.

References

Pierluigi Cassotti, Lucia Siciliani, Marco DeGemmis, Giovanni Semeraro, and Pierpaolo Basile. 2023. XL-LEXEME: WiC pretrained model for cross-lingual LEXical sEMantic changE. In *Proceedings of the 61st Annual Meeting of the Association for Computational Linguistics (Volume 2: Short Papers)*, pages 1577–1585, Toronto, Canada. Association for Computational Linguistics.

Banghao Chen, Zhaofeng Zhang, Nicolas Langrené, and Shengxin Zhu. 2023a. Unleashing the potential of prompt engineering in large language models: a comprehensive review. *arXiv preprint arXiv:2310.14735*.

Jing Chen, Emmanuele Chersoni, Dominik Schlechtweg, Jelena Prokic, and Chu-Ren Huang. 2023b. ChiWUG: A graph-based evaluation dataset for Chinese lexical semantic change detection. In *Proceedings of the 4th Workshop on Computational Approaches to Historical Language Change*, pages 93–99, Singapore. Association for Computational Linguistics.

Jacob Devlin, Ming-Wei Chang, Kenton Lee, and Kristina Toutanova. 2018. Bert: Pre-training of deep bidirectional transformers for language understanding. *arXiv preprint arXiv:1810.04805*.

Mario Giulianelli, Marco Del Tredici, and Raquel Fernández. 2020. Analysing lexical semantic change with contextualised word representations. In *Proceedings of the 58th Annual Meeting of the Association for Computational Linguistics*, pages 3960–3973, Online. Association for Computational Linguistics.

William L Hamilton, Jure Leskovec, and Dan Jurafsky. 2016. Diachronic word embeddings reveal statistical laws of semantic change. *arXiv preprint arXiv:1605.09096*.

Yupeng Hou, Junjie Zhang, Zihan Lin, Hongyu Lu, Ruobing Xie, Julian McAuley, and Wayne Xin Zhao. 2024. Large language models are zero-shot rankers for recommender systems. In *European Conference on Information Retrieval*, pages 364–381. Springer.

Nikitas Karanikolas, Eirini Manga, Nikoletta Samaridi, Eleni Tousidou, and Michael Vassilakopoulos. 2023. Large language models versus natural language understanding and generation. In *Proceedings of the 27th Pan-Hellenic Conference on Progress in Computing and Informatics*, pages 278–290.

Andres Karjus. 2023. Machine-assisted mixed methods: augmenting humanities and social sciences with artificial intelligence. *arXiv preprint arXiv:2309.14379*.

Yoon Kim, Yi-I Chiu, Kentaro Hanaki, Darshan Hegde, and Slav Petrov. 2014. Temporal analysis of language through neural language models. In *Proceedings of the ACL 2014 Workshop on Language Technologies and Computational Social Science*, pages 61–65, Baltimore, MD, USA. Association for Computational Linguistics.

Vivek Kulkarni, Rami Al-Rfou, Bryan Perozzi, and Steven Skiena. 2015. Statistically significant detection of linguistic change. In *Proceedings of the 24th international conference on world wide web*, pages 625–635.

Andrey Kutuzov and Mario Giulianelli. 2020. UiO-UvA at SemEval-2020 task 1: Contextualised embeddings for lexical semantic change detection. In *Proceedings of the Fourteenth Workshop on Semantic Evaluation*, pages 126–134, Barcelona (online). International Committee for Computational Linguistics.

Andrey Kutuzov, Samia Touileb, Petter Mæhlum, Tita Ranveig Enstad, and Alexandra Wittemann. 2022. Nordiachange: Diachronic semantic change dataset for norwegian. *arXiv preprint arXiv:2201.05123*.

Md Tahmid Rahman Laskar, M Saiful Bari, Mizanur Rahman, Md Amran Hossen Bhuiyan, Shafiq Joty, and Jimmy Huang. 2023. A systematic study and comprehensive evaluation of ChatGPT on benchmark datasets. In *Findings of the Association for Computational Linguistics: ACL 2023*, pages 431–469, Toronto, Canada. Association for Computational Linguistics.

Ggaliwango Marvin, Nakayiza Hellen, Daudi Jjingo, and Joyce Nakatumba-Nabende. 2023. Prompt engineering in large language models. In *International conference on data intelligence and cognitive informatics*, pages 387–402. Springer.

Francesco Periti, Haim Dubossarsky, and Nina Tahmasebi. 2024. (chat)GPT v BERT dawn of justice for semantic change detection. In *Findings of the Association for Computational Linguistics: EACL 2024*, pages 420–436, St. Julian's, Malta. Association for Computational Linguistics.

Francesco Periti and Nina Tahmasebi. 2024. A systematic comparison of contextualized word embeddings for lexical semantic change. In *Proceedings of the 2024 Conference of the North American Chapter of the Association for Computational Linguistics: Human Language Technologies (Volume 1: Long Papers)*, pages 4262–4282, Mexico City, Mexico. Association for Computational Linguistics.

Matthew E. Peters, Mark Neumann, Mohit Iyyer, Matt Gardner, Christopher Clark, Kenton Lee, and Luke Zettlemoyer. 2018. Deep contextualized word representations. In *Proceedings of the 2018 Conference of* the North American Chapter of the Association for Computational Linguistics: Human Language Technologies, Volume 1 (Long Papers), pages 2227–2237, New Orleans, Louisiana. Association for Computational Linguistics.

Dominik Schlechtweg, Barbara McGillivray, Simon Hengchen, Haim Dubossarsky, and Nina Tahmasebi. 2020. SemEval-2020 task 1: Unsupervised lexical semantic change detection. In *Proceedings of the Fourteenth Workshop on Semantic Evaluation*, pages 1–23, Barcelona (online). International Committee for Computational Linguistics.

Dominik Schlechtweg, Nina Tahmasebi, Simon Hengchen, Haim Dubossarsky, and Barbara McGillivray. 2021. DWUG: A large resource of diachronic word usage graphs in four languages. In *Proceedings of the 2021 Conference on Empirical Methods in Natural Language Processing*, pages 7079–7091, Online and Punta Cana, Dominican Republic. Association for Computational Linguistics.

Ruiyu Wang and Matthew Choi. 2023. Large language models on lexical semantic change detection: An evaluation. *arXiv preprint arXiv:2312.06002*.

Caleb Ziems, William Held, Omar Shaikh, Jiaao Chen, Zhehao Zhang, and Diyi Yang. 2024. Can large language models transform computational social science? *Computational Linguistics*, pages 1–55.

A Prompts for One-shot Learning

Initial prompt for the the system introduction:

`You are a expert in multilingual language change detection, determine whether the target word has changed its semantic meaning between given sentences, answer with Same, Related, Linked or Distinct.`

Prompt for one-shot learning:

```
This is very important to my career. Consider the use of target word in two contexts of sentences, determine whether the target word has changed its semantic meaning between those sentences. Do the refer to the Same, different but Related, distant Linked or unrelated objects.

Determine the meaning change of target word target in following sentences:
1. [sentence1]
2. [sentence2]
Answer: choose from (Same, Related, Linked, Distinct).
Provide your answer without any illustration
```

B Retrieved Example

Target word, 下海 **xiahai,** `go to the sea or join a business`

Query input:

1. 辽西省在春汛下海时即已组成九十个渔业生产合作社，一百四十五个互助组。
When the spring floods hit the sea, Western Liaoning Province had already formed 90 fishery production cooperatives and 145 mutual aid groups.

2. 福建省沿海各地民兵积极配合人民解放军加强海防巡逻和解放台湾的斗争，并组织了武装护渔队、巡逻队，保卫渔民下海捕鱼。
He militias in various coastal areas of Fujian Province actively cooperated with the People's Liberation Army in strengthening coastal defense patrols and the struggle to liberate Taiwan, and organized armed fishing teams and patrols to protect fishermen fishing in the sea.

Retrieved sentence:

1 "他瞅了瞅他现在穿的新皮大氅，又说："过去我下海、在家，总是穿一件又腥又破的棉短袄；吃呢，一天挣来的钱连啃窝窝头吃都不够......有一次我们有四个人在葫芦岛下潮（出海），半路遇着大风，一个三丈多高的浪头，打翻了我们的小船，其中一个同伴被打下水以后没有踪影了，剩我们三个人在孤岛上冻饿了好几天，好容易才返回来。
He took a look at the new leather cloak he was wearing now, and said: "In the past, when I went to the sea and at home, I always wore a fishy and torn cotton jacket. When it came to eating, the money I earned in a day even cost me a lot of money. Not enough... One time, four of us went out to sea in Huludao. We encountered strong winds on the way, and a wave more than three feet high capsized our boat. One of our companions was knocked into the water and disappeared without a trace. The three of us froze and starved on the isolated island for several days, and finally returned with great difficulty

2. 他们说："只要能治好唐山亲人的伤病，别说上山捉毒蛇，就是下海擒蛟龙，俺们也在所不辞。
'They said: "As long as we can cure the injuries and illnesses of our relatives in Tangshan, we will do whatever we can to catch venomous snakes in the mountains or go to the sea to catch dragons."

Author Index